The Clinical Effectiveness of Neurolinguistic Programming

'For sceptics and advocates of NLP, this book makes essen ... an international collaboration of researchers and writers lead by Lisa Wake, a leader in the NLP research community. Over 12 chapters they systematically review existing research relating to the effectiveness of NLP regarding specific diagnoses and health conditions and they conclude that there is enough evidence of the efficacy of NLP to warrant further research. This book demonstrates how a growing number of NLP practitioners are thinking critically and engaging with various types of evidence in order to inform their practices and set standards in the NLP community.'
    Susie Linder-Pelz MPH, MPhil, PhD, behavioural scientist and author of over twenty refereed articles and five books.

Despite widespread use, Neurolinguistic Programming (NLP) is a topic of much debate, often receiving criticism from academic and professional sectors. In this book, international academics, researchers and therapists are brought together to examine the current evidence of the clinical efficacy of NLP techniques, considering how NLP can be effective in facilitating change, enrichment and symptom relief.

Lisa Wake and her colleagues provide a critical appraisal of evidence-based research in the area to indicate the benefits of the approach and identify the need for an increase in randomized well-controlled clinical trials. Contributors also explore how NLP has been used to treat various disorders including:

- post-traumatic stress disorder
- phobias
- addictions
- anxiety disorders
- mild depression.

Illustrated throughout with clinical examples and case studies, this book is key reading for practitioners and researchers interested in NLP, as well as postgraduate students.

Lisa Wake is a Neurolinguistic Psychotherapist, and an internationally recognized Master Trainer of NLP. She is Director of Awaken Consulting and Training Services Ltd, which offers corporate consultancy, training, coaching and psychotherapy services. She is also Director of Awaken School of Outcome Oriented Psychotherapies Ltd, which provides UKCP accredited psychotherapy trainings. Lisa has also served as Vice Chair and Chair of UKCP.

Richard M. Gray is Assistant Professor at the School of Criminal Justice, Fairleigh Dickinson University, and former substance abuse treatment coordinator in the United States Probation Department, Eastern District of New York, Brooklyn, New York.

Frank S. Bourke, PhD, is the Executive Director and founder of the Research and Recognition Project, a not-for-profit corporation committed to bringing NLP and related technology into evidentiary medicine. He completed his PhD research at the Institute of Psychiatry in London, has taught at Cornell University and worked in the mental health field as a clinician, trainer and administrator for over 40 years.

Advances in Mental Health Research series

Books in this series:

The Clinical Effectiveness of Neurolinguistic Programming
A critical appraisal
Edited by Lisa Wake, Richard M. Gray and Frank S. Bourke

The Clinical Effectiveness of Neurolinguistic Programming
A critical appraisal

Edited by Lisa Wake, Richard M. Gray and Frank S. Bourke

LONDON AND NEW YORK

First published 2013
by Routledge
2 Park Square, Milton Park, Abingdon, Oxfordshire OX14 4RN

Simultaneously published in the USA and Canada
by Routledge
711 Third Avenue, New York, NY 10017
First issued in paperback 2014

Routledge is an imprint of the Taylor & Francis Group, an informa business

© 2013 selection and editorial matter, Lisa Wake, Richard M. Gray and Frank S. Bourke; individual chapters, the contributors

The right of the editor to be identified as the author of the editorial material, and of the authors for their individual chapters, has been asserted in accordance with sections 77 and 78 of the Copyright, Designs and Patents Act 1988.

All rights reserved. No part of this book may be reprinted or reproduced or utilised in any form or by any electronic, mechanical, or other means, now known or hereafter invented, including photocopying and recording, or in any information storage or retrieval system, without permission in writing from the publishers.

Trademark notice: Product or corporate names may be trademarks or registered trademarks, and are used only for identification and explanation without intent to infringe.

British Library Cataloguing-in-Publication Data
A catalogue record for this book is available from the British Library

Library of Congress Cataloging-in-Publication Data
The clinical effectiveness of neurolinguistic programming : a critical appraisal / edited by Lisa Wake, Richard M. Gray & Frank S. Bourke.
p. cm.
Includes bibliographical references and index.
ISBN 978-0-415-63515-8 (hbk)
1. Neurolinguistic programming. I. Wake, Lisa, 1962- II. Gray, Richard M., 1943- III. Bourke, Frank S., 1943-
RC489.N47C55 2013
616.8'0419–dc23
2012015536

ISBN 978-0-415-63515-8 (hbk)
ISBN 978-1-138-80853-9 (pbk)
ISBN 978-0-203-08366-6 (ebk)

Typeset in Baskerville
by GreenGate Publishing Services, Tonbridge, Kent

Contents

List of figures and tables	vii
List of contributors	viii
Foreword	xii
Introduction LISA WAKE, FRANK S. BOURKE, RICHARD M. GRAY	1

PART I
Clinical and practitioner evidence   5

1   Phobias   7
RICHARD M. GRAY, RICHARD BOLSTAD

2   Post-traumatic stress disorder   32
RICHARD M. GRAY, RICHARD BOLSTAD

3   Other therapeutic applications   47
LISA WAKE, LUCAS DERKS, PRZEMYSŁAW Ł. TURKOWSKI

4   Anxiety disorders   69
BRUCE GRIMLEY

5   Addictions   95
RICHARD M. GRAY

6   Depression symptom clusters   126
LISA WAKE, KARL NIELSEN, NANDANA NIELSEN, CĂTĂLIN ZAHARIA

PART II
Neurolinguistic programming contemporary research 151

7 Indirect research into the applications of neurolinguistic programming 153
RICHARD M. GRAY, LISA WAKE, STEVE ANDREAS, RICHARD BOLSTAD

8 Research and the history of methodological flaws 194
RICHARD M. GRAY, RICHARD F. LIOTTA, LISA WAKE, JOE CHEAL

PART III
Towards the future 217

9 Certification and training 219
LISA WAKE, FRANK S. BOURKE, PETER SCHÜTZ, RICHARD M. GRAY

10 Future directions 234
FRANK S. BOURKE, RICHARD M. GRAY, LISA WAKE

References 241
Index 268

Figures and tables

Figures

4.1	The APET model	78
4.2	Systemic change	80
4.3	DAPS profile for John pre-treatment	82
4.4	DAPS profile for John post-treatment	85
4.5	Median anxiety scores before NLP and after NLP in patients who subsequently had a successful MR and those who failed	90
8.1	A proposed model for NLP clinical research	211

Tables

1.1	Phobia treatment studies	15
2.1	Treatment studies of the VK/D (rewind, RTM) protocol	39
3.1	Research studies	62
4.1	Descriptive statistics of outcome variables	88
4.2	Mean pre- and post-treatment scores	92
6.1	A comparison of linguistic patterns from CBT and NLP	138
7.1	A syntax for behavioral change in emotional memory	191
8.1	Study levels and types	210
8.2	Bateson's levels and their relationship to NLP theory and practice	216
9.1	Current standards of training	226

Contributors

Steve Andreas has been learning, training, researching and developing NLP models and protocols for 33 years (steveandreas.com). He is the author of *Six Blind Elephants, Transforming Your Self,* and *Virginia Satir: the patterns of her magic*. He is co-author, with his wife Connirae, of *Heart of the Mind,* and *Change Your Mind – and Keep the Change,* and they edited the four classic NLP books by Richard Bandler and John Grinder: *Frogs into Princes, Trance-formations, Reframing,* and *Using Your Brain – for a Change*. Steve has a BS in Chemistry from Caltech, and an MA in Psychology from Brandeis University.

Richard Bolstad is a registered nurse, a trained teacher and a member of the New Zealand Association of Psychotherapists. His doctorate is in Clinical Hypnotherapy. With his partner Julia Kurusheva, Richard teaches NLP in New Zealand, Asia, Europe and the Americas. He particularly teaches NLP techniques for use in areas of the world where there has been major trauma either from natural events (2011 tsunami in Japan; 2009 tsunami in Samoa; 2011 earthquake in Christchurch, New Zealand) or from war (Bosnia-Herzegovina in the 1990s; Caucasus region near Chechnya early this century).

Frank S. Bourke completed his PhD at the Institute of Psychiatry in London. He has worked mainly as a clinical psychologist and mental health administrator for 40 years. He studied NLP in the 1970s while lecturing in Psychology at Cornell University. Called to New York after the 9/11 attacks, he worked for a year with 800 building survivors. The year after 9/11, he was diagnosed with severe bladder cancer and underwent surgery for a neo-bladder using NLP techniques to manage the pain, chemotherapy and healing, with great success. He is committed to foster their scientific advancement and broad clinical dissemination.

Joe Cheal is an NLP Master Trainer and has been working with NLP since 1993. He holds an MSc in Organisational Development and Neurolinguistic Technologies, a degree in Philosophy and Psychology, and diplomas in Coaching and in Ericksonian Hypnotherapy, Psychotherapy and NLP. Joe is the author of *Solving Impossible Problems:*

Working Through Tensions and Paradox in Business, and editor of *Acuity: The ANLP Journal*. He is a co-founder of the Positive School of Intrinsic Neurolinguistic Psychology (www.psinlp.com) and a partner in the GWiz Learning Partnership (www.gwiztraining.com), working as a Management and Organisational Development Specialist.

Lucas Derks (Netherlands) has a Masters in Social Psychology from the University of Utrecht. During his studies (in 1977) he became attracted to the pragmatism and subjectivism in NLP. He worked for six years as a researcher in several Dutch museums doing visitor research at large exhibitions. He then became a full-time NLP trainer, therapist and developer. Together with the clinical psychologist Jaap Hollander, Lucas wrote *Essenties van NLP* ('The essence of NLP', 1996), which still functions as an NLP textbook in the Netherlands and Russia. His main contribution to the field of NLP is called 'The Social Panorama Model' (1994); a tool to help analyse and improve any type of social relationship. This found its way in the 2002 book *Social Panoramas*, of which Dutch, Polish, German and Portuguese translations exist.

Richard M. Gray, PhD, is Assistant Professor of Criminal Justice, Fairleigh Dickinson University. He is the creator of the Brooklyn Program, an NLP-based substance abuse programme which operated for seven years in the Federal Probation System. Dr Gray is the author of *Archetypal Explorations* (Routledge, 1996) *Transforming Futures: The Brooklyn Program Facilitators Manual* (Lulu, 2011) and *About Addictions: Notes from Psychology, Neuroscience and NLP* (Lulu, 2008). Dr Gray served for more than 20 years in the US Probation Department, Brooklyn, New York. He is a Certified Master Practitioner of NLP and a Certified Ericksonian Hypnotist.

Bruce Grimley is a UK Chartered Occupational Psychologist registered with the HPC. Bruce was a founding Council member for the Association for Coaching and currently works as an Assessor for them as well as for the British Psychological Society, believing coaching relationships within the workplace are the way forward. During Bruce's chartership journey he specialized in one-to-one work, and in his coaching practice works with clinical clients being registered as a psychotherapist with NLPtCA. Bruce provides accredited NLP certification and is currently undertaking a PhD, researching how best to create work environments where employees want to work.

Richard F. Liotta is a psychologist in private practice. Since 2008 he has worked closely with the NLP Research & Recognition Project in their efforts to facilitate NLP research. He co-authored a chapter about the project with Frank S. Bourke for the book *Innovations in NLP*, and a journal article in Traumatology with Richard M. Gray (*PTSD: Extinction, Reconsolidation and the Visual-Kinesthetic Dissociation Protocol*) for publication. He frames NLP as being within the context of a 'Full Spectrum

Cognitive Behavioral Therapy', noting that when people know how NLP fits into established science they can appreciate the unique contributions it offers.

Nandana Nielsen, President of the International Association of Coaching Institutes (ICI), and **Karl Nielsen**, President of the International Association of NLP Institutes (IN), were both born in Germany. From 1980 to 1990 they carried out research on effective factors for human communication and published the results in two books and many professional articles. Since 1997 they are CEOs of the NLP & Coaching Institute in Berlin. In 2008 they were appointed as Professors for distance learning studies in Psychology, with a major in Communication, NLP and Coaching. They are currently developing Neuro Linguistic Psychology as an Applied Psychology.

Peter Schütz MSc Vienna, Austria. Trained in psychodrama and groupdynamics 1974–88 (OEAGG trainer), NLP (Grinder, Dilts, Early) 1983–9 (trainer). Peter is a lecturer at Vienna University in medical psychology and communications, a government-accredited health psychologist, a teaching psychotherapist (ECP, DG, NLPt), and a coach, mediator and management consultant (CMC). He is President of three organizations (www.eucf.org, www.nlpzentrum.at, oebvnlp.org) and Secretary General for the European Association for Neurolinguistic Psychotherapy (www.eanlpt.org). Peter edited *Theorie & Praxis der Neurolinguistischen Psychotherapie* (2001) and co-authored several published studies on NLPt (www.nlpt.at/res1.pdf).

Przemysław Ł. Turkowski MSc, MA, graduated in Biology and Psychology from the College of Inter-Faculty Individual Studies in Mathematics and Natural Sciences at Warsaw University. He works as a psychotherapist and coach at the Polish Institute for Neurolinguistic Programming. He is interested in research on neurolinguistic psychotherapy, especially in the connections between mind and body. As a psychotherapist he works with clients with problems with relationships, depression, sexual abuse, bereavement, psychosomatics and the identity level (especially men). He is one of the founding members of the Polish Neurolinguistic Psychotherapy Association.

Lisa Wake, former nurse and NHS manager, is a Master Trainer of NLP, UKCP accredited psychotherapist and, at the time of writing, a PhD candidate at the University of Surrey. She has served as Chair of UKCP, and is a proponent of the effectiveness of brief therapy, actively campaigning for rigour of standards, ethics and research in psychotherapy. She has contributed to the neurolinguistic psychotherapy field with the publication of her groundbreaking book for the 'Advancing Theory in Therapy' series for Routledge, *Neurolinguistic Psychotherapy: A Postmodern Perspective*, followed by *The Role of Brief Therapy in Attachment Disorders* for Karnac.

Cătălin Zaharia, MD, MSc in bioengineering (biomedical informatics and health systems management). He is a licensed psychiatrist, neurolinguistic psychotherapist, trainer and supervisor. Cătălin is President of EANLPt (EANLPt.org) and is involved in academic research, as well as being a consultant and trainer for PEP Potential Evaluation Program (imde.net) and manager of mindmaster.ro. He supports high-quality training and research standards for NLPt and represents the method in the European bodies and within the EAP.

Foreword

Steve Andreas

Like any new development in therapy, Neurolinguistic Programming (NLP) arose out of the clinical perceptions of the successes and failures of practice with troubled clients. However, NLP arose out of a new paradigm, the study of the *processes* of behavioral change, rather than their content, which is the principle focus of most therapies. The originators of NLP, Richard Bandler and John Grinder, brought their expertise in the more rigorous fields of linguistics and mathematics to the study of three of the most effective therapists of the 1960s: Milton H. Erickson (1985), Virginia Satir, (1991), and Fritz Perls (1969). Although many would say that the work and style of these three therapists couldn't be more different, Bandler and Grinder discovered that many of the processes that they used with clients were very similar. These processes became an explicit and detailed foundation for this new field and its early publications (1975).

Like any emerging field, NLP has made progress by fits and starts. New techniques were developed and tested, and a new methodology was developed to understand the common principles underlying the different successful techniques. This new or revised methodology then pointed the way toward developing new specific techniques to be tested.

As in every developing field, NLP has had difficulties with many factors that are irrelevant to its intellectual integrity and validity. Personalities, turf wars, hangers-on, and marketing get-rich-quick artists have often distracted observers from thoughtfully examining its core principles and methods. (Think of all the questionable nutritional supplements that tarnish the quite respectable field of nutrition, or the wide variety of quack cancer cures that still dog the field of medicine.) As a result, many have dismissed the promise of NLP, throwing out the baby with the bathwater. (As any parent can attest, a new baby can produce a prodigious amount of very dirty bathwater.)

From the very beginning, the epistemology of NLP has been the radical empiricism featuring testing and falsification described by Karl Popper in *The Logic of Scientific Discovery* (1934) and *Conjectures and Refutations* (1963), the fundamental foundation of the scientific method. This could be summarized by, "Test it and find out if it works or not."

In most therapies, the test of a method is a global client report of satisfaction, long after a number of sessions, and often measured by a pencil-and-paper test. That kind of general outcome is not only very difficult to quantify, but even more difficult to attribute to one or more of the many different interventions that occurred in many different therapy sessions over a protracted period of time—or to the spontaneous or unrelated life events that occur outside of therapy.

By contrast, NLP has always been characterized by specific intervention protocols, and the test of effectiveness has been specific, operationally defined observable behavioral changes, such as the absence of a phobic response after a single session. This is something which is quite easy to verify objectively by an impartial observer; either a client flushes, tenses, and avoids a phobic stimulus, or they remain calm and unflappable in the presence of the same stimulus that had terrified them just prior to the intervention. A complete nine-minute video of such a session, including pre-test and post-test verification can be found at: http://www.youtube.com/watch?v=VtUatMghbHg. A video interview with the client 25 years later can be found at: http://www.youtube.com/watch?v=TjjCzhrYJDQ.

As this example demonstrates, it would be very easy to test the effectiveness using a rigorous double-blind protocol, and the same is true of many other specific NLP methods for specific presenting problems or outcomes.

Most of the research done on NLP in the early 1980s was hampered by several significant obstacles. One was the somewhat disorganized state of the field in its early stages of development, which is inevitable in any beginning field. Another was the failure of researchers to understand the principles that they sought to investigate. A third was that none of the research tested the actual treatment methods used with clients, but instead sought to test general principles. These factors caused insurmountable errors in protocol, experimental design, and controls, usually resulting in negative or ambiguous results.

There is already abundant rigorous research that verifies many aspects of NLP principles and methodology. A foremost example is Daniel Kahneman's *Thinking Fast and Slow* (2011). In this book he presents abundant research by himself and his colleagues into the dual system theory, showing the differences between what he calls "system 1," which corresponds to what has often been described as immediate unconscious responding, and "system 2," which corresponds to rigorously rational conscious thinking. Kahneman shows compellingly that system 2 takes considerable conscious training and effort, and that it usually defers to the much faster and more intuitive and error-prone system 1 processing. Baumeister's (2011) research applies this paradigm to the study of willpower, the ability to sustain system 2 in the face of the immediate sensory lures and demands of system 1.

Most of the problems that clients have are the result of errors in system 1 processing, and the inability or unwillingness of system 2 processing to overcome these errors. For instance, a client who is phobic of water may consciously know very well that a bathtub of water is not significantly dangerous, yet responds emotionally as if it were life threatening because of a vivid memory of a near drowning years earlier. A client who consciously knows perfectly well that eating junk food will result in obesity will often still eat that food because of system 1 urges that are out of their system 2 control. Most NLP interventions are directed at changing the sensory parameters of the images, sounds, and feelings (and occasionally smell and taste) that are the basis for system 1 processing.

The linguistic model that originally guided NLP explorations was Chomsky's Transformational Grammar (1972). While responsible for many useful developments in the field, NLP is now principally guided by more recent and rigorous work in Cognitive Linguistics, as described by George Lakoff in his book *Women, Fire, and Dangerous Things: What Categories Reveal About the Mind* (1990). The direct application of the principles of cognitive linguistics to understanding NLP processes for therapeutic change has been described in detail (Andreas, 2006b).

It is long past time to do rigorous controlled research on the specific protocols that NLP has developed for specific behavioral outcomes, which include the resolution of phobias, PTSD flashbacks, internal conflicts, anxiety, grief, and many other problems and outcomes. The primary goal of this book is to provide a detailed understanding of the methodology and technology of NLP, in order to guide and support research to test specific intervention protocols for specific problems. The final aim is to certify them as evidence-based client care. As adjuncts to that goal, this book also corrects many misunderstandings about NLP found in the professional journals, and overviews future needs for the field including effective clinical training, and certification programs to ensure quality control of therapist delivery of these methods.

Introduction

Lisa Wake, Frank S. Bourke, Richard M. Gray

The purpose of this book is to present sufficient evidence of the clinical efficacy of Neurolinguistic Programming (NLP) techniques to justify and motivate rigorous scientific research. The growing research movement within NLP circles believes that these techniques have significant contributions to make as part of evidence-based client care. This will only be fully realized by sound clinical research and the development of an international organizational structure that ensures operational integrity, through certified clinical training and clinical performance standards. As an inherently empirical discipline, all NLP processes include specific, testable behavioral outcomes. This book presents B-, C-, and some D-level studies of NLP techniques and practices (classifications from the Agency of Health Care Policy and Research) in phobias, PTSD, anxiety symptoms, indirect NLP research support, and other therapeutic applications including depressive symptoms and addiction.

- Level A evidence is based upon randomized well-controlled clinical trials for individuals.
- Level B evidence is based upon well-designed clinical studies, without randomization or placebo comparison for individuals.
- Level C evidence is based on service and naturalistic clinical studies combined with clinical observations that are sufficiently compelling to warrant use of the treatment technique or follow the specific recommendations.
- Level D evidence is based on long-standing and widespread clinical practice that has not been subjected to empirical tests.

There are no A studies yet completed for NLP techniques. However, the recently published *Effects of Neurolinguistic Psychotherapy on Psychological Difficulties and Quality of Life in Counseling and Psychotherapy Research* (Stipancic et al., 2010), demonstrates the serious efforts being put forth by Neurolinguistic Psychotherapy (NLPt) in Europe and the UK where NLP techniques have been developed into a recognized therapeutic approach within formal psychotherapy structures that have rigorous training and clinical practice standards. The B, C, and D studies included in Chapters 1 through 7 are an insufficient body of evidence to classify any of the specific techniques, such as the Phobia Protocol, as evidence-based medicine. We will demonstrate that these studies contain sufficiently promising clinical findings to warrant further research. NLP is a developing model that is following the natural progression for evidence-based practice from the initial development of ideas, to clinical case studies, to observational studies and controlled studies.

Given the development of NLP methodology outside academia, largely by individuals presenting learning seminars in the for-profit arena, the lack of research parallels many other clinical developments, e.g. Cognitive Behavioral Therapy and its forerunner, Rational Emotive Psychotherapy. As such, it now behooves us to move toward formal scientific validation of our experience in accordance with standard evidence-based procedure.

The first priority of the NLP research movement is to further research the efficacy of NLP methods and techniques. The authors' intent is to conduct a systematic review of the evidence base to date and subject it to critical appraisal, to provide a solid basis for moving forward with rigorous research. The chapters are arranged largely in the format of the DSM-IV-R diagnostic categories to facilitate reading and use by members of the mental health field, other professionals in primary care and those working with long-term conditions.

Part I Clinical and practitioner evidence

Chapter 1 Phobias

Specific phobias are defined and three recognized clinical treatments are overviewed before presenting the evidence and NLP techniques of the VK/D-RTM model, collapsing anchors and a modified systematic desensitization. Hypothetical neurological and behavioral models are proposed along with several testable hypotheses for further research.

Chapter 2 Post-traumatic stress disorder

An in-depth examination of an NLP intervention (VK/D) is presented for treating PTSD, including a number of studies supporting further research. A neurological mechanism, reconsolidation, that explains the observed results, is also examined. Directions for further research are outlined in detail.

Chapter 3 Other therapeutic applications

Research in this chapter is reviewed, including case studies that apply NLP techniques to DSM-IV-R diagnostic categories not discussed in other chapters. Recommendations for future studies are also made for a number of clinical areas, such as eating disorders, pain management, cardiac rehabilitation, claustrophobia, and asthma.

Chapter 4 Anxiety disorders

Three sub-categories of anxiety are reviewed: panic disorder, obsessive compulsive disorder (OCD), and generalized anxiety disorder (GAD). Models of the disorders and treatments from CBT are examined and contrasted with NLP-based approaches. NLP techniques for the treatment of anxiety disorders are discussed and a case study is presented that illustrates the application of NLP to GAD. An overview of published studies in which NLP is used to treat anxiety disorders is presented and suggestions for future research are made.

Chapter 5 Addictions

This chapter presents results from The Brooklyn Program, an NLP-based Addiction Treatment Program. It sets the stage for serious future NLP studies by redefining the addiction field based on neurological criteria.

Chapter 6 Depression symptom clusters

Depressive disorders are reviewed, with currently recognized treatments, followed by NLP as a model of therapy for depressive symptoms. The limited research evidence to date is then critically reviewed and future studies proposed.

Part II NLP Neurolinguistic programming contemporary research

Chapter 7 Indirect research into the applications of NLP

The editors of this chapter present sound academic research that indirectly supports NLP clinical processes and practices that have been well documented for over 20 years.

Chapter 8 Research and the history of methodological flaws

This chapter examines literature reviews in which the efficacy of NLP was discussed, providing explanations and rebuttals for many of the negative findings. It then overviews NLP as a field within the context of social science, offering suggestions for its future development.

Part III Towards the future

Chapter 9 Certification and training

This chapter critically reviews the training and certification procedures and organizations in the United States and abroad, recommending and defining future training standards, ethics and practices, which will only be fully realized by sound clinical research and the development of an international organizational structure that ensures operational integrity.

Chapter 10 Future directions

An overview of the previous chapters and suggestions for future directions for NLP is presented followed by specific recommendations for research, training/certification, and the academic and professional networking and integration that will be necessary if NLP is going to join the mainstream of evidence-based health care.

Summary

Organizationally, much more needs to be done before the clinical contributions NLP has to offer can be fully realized. First, NLP must be more fully and more formally researched. Second, professionally recognized, certified training procedures must be developed based upon the use of clinical protocols established and formalized by high-quality academic research. Lastly, a recognized, international certification organization needs to be developed that delivers effectively trained clinical practitioners who are competent at managing and treating clinical conditions. Additionally, NLP would benefit greatly by developing and publishing a clinical system that integrates its cognitive and behavioral tools into a clearer philosophy of both preventive and problem-oriented treatment, for the whole person (Gawler-Wright, 2004, 2006; Wake, 2008). There are important clinical tools arising from the field that have already been published. These include: alleviating the nightmares and flashbacks associated with PTSD (Gray and Liotta, 2012), identifying and replacing self-limiting beliefs (Dilts, 1990), and building strong, positive self-images (Andreas, 2002). These and many others provide well-defined, researchable, clinical protocols (Andreas and Andreas, 1987, 1989; Bolstad, 2002; Dilts et al., 1990; Gray and Liotta, 2012; Gray, 1997, 2001, 2001b, 2002, 2003, 2004, 2006, 2008a, 2008c, 2011; Kostere and Maletesta, 1990; Wake, 2008, 2010, Walker, 2004). Prospectively they offer the basis of a self-actualizing, client-centered, positive, approach to evidence-based clinical treatment.

Part I
Clinical and practitioner evidence

1 Phobias

Richard M. Gray, Richard Bolstad

Phobias and their treatment

Clinically, a phobia (from the Greek φόβος, or "fear") is a persistent fear of a situation or object, due to which the person invests disproportionate energy into avoiding or coping with that stimulus object or situation, compared to the minimal danger involved in it. The DSM-V (proposed), in its listing of anxiety disorders, refers to three very different types of situations using this same term: specific phobias, social phobias, and agoraphobias. Social phobia refers to fear of being with and being observed by others, and Agoraphobia involves a fear of leaving the person's familiar safe area, often with additional social phobia and fear of the possibility of panic attacks in unsafe places. These latter two diagnoses have a more complex structure than simple phobias, and treatment by all methods has yielded less convincing research results (Roth et al., 2005).

Specific phobias have seven diagnostic criteria (APA, 2010) which can be summarised as:

A   Fear cued by the presence or anticipation of the stimulus.
B   Exposure consistently provokes fear or anxiety.
C   The object or situation is actively avoided or its presence is endured with intense fear or anxiety.
D   The fear or anxiety is out of proportion to the actual threat posed.
E   Duration at least six months.
F   Avoidance interferes with functioning in major life contexts.
E   Not a result of another condition.

Phobias represent classically conditioned fear responses to objects or situations (Öhman and Mineka, 2001; Schweckendiek et al., 2011). They are disproportionate to the actual threat presented by the phobic stimulus, sometimes represent incidents of one trial conditioning (Öhman et al., 1975; Öhman and Mineka, 2001; Seligman, 1971), are often associated with what may be evolutionarily prepotent stimuli (Domjian, 2005; Gerdes et al., 2009; Öhman and Mineka, 2001; Öhman et al., 1975; Ohman et al., 1976) which are more resistant to extinction than truly neutral stimuli (Öhman and Mineka, 2001; Öhman et al., 1975; Ohman et al., 1976).

The United States' National Institute of Mental Health notes that phobias are the most common mental illness among women in all age groups and the second most common illness among men older than 25 (the first being depression, see Kessler et al., 2005a, b). Successful and efficient treatments for phobias are of considerable importance. There is good evidence that any short-term benefits of pharmacotherapy with anxiolytics is quickly lost and that their use may even increase later anxiety responses. Exposure to the phobic stimulus under certain conditions may reduce phobic response. Wilhelm and Roth (1997) randomised 28 clients with flight phobias to receive either the anxiolytic drug alprazolam or a placebo while undertaking a first flight. They found that in a second flight, those who had received the active medication had much higher levels of anxiety than those who received the placebo, indicating that those who had the placebo may have benefitted from the exposure in the first flight and reduced their fear. Thom et al. (2000) conducted a randomized study of clients with a phobia of dentistry, who received either benzodiazepines (anti-anxiety drugs), a stress-management package (relaxation training, exposure to the dentistry situation, and cognitive therapy), or no intervention. Both treated groups initially reported a reduction in anxiety, but only 20 percent of drug treatment clients actually completed their dentistry, as compared to 70 percent of those receiving the stress management package.

NLP has identified several procedures for the treatment of phobias. The best known and most well attested is the NLP Fast Phobia Cure, otherwise known as the Visual Kinesthetic Dissociation Protocol (V/KD). Two other techniques predate the V/KD protocol and are used less frequently. The first is a counter-conditioning protocol called collapsing anchors, and the second is the six-part reframe. The six-part reframe has, for many, fallen from use and will not be discussed here. The two NLP procedures reviewed here can be considered imaginal exposure techniques (Wolitzky-Taylor et al., 2008).

Classical models and approaches

Two specific types of intervention have been the focus of the most successful psychological research: systematic desensitization and exposure. Systematic desensitization generally involves a prolonged, gradual introduction of the feared stimulus, done over a large number of sessions and using a base of training in relaxation. Therapist-controlled exposure has proven more successful, and clinically significant improvement in one or a few intensive sessions tends to be as good as improvement over a prolonged series of short sessions, and to average 70–85 percent reductions in symptoms. Exposure results in what researchers have called extinction of the fear response. There is evidence to suggest that, although *in-vivo* experience provides immediate improvements relative to imaginal exposure, follow-up studies have shown that initial differences disappear over time (Wolitzky-Taylor et al., 2008).

Extinction is one of the basic phenomena in classical conditioning. It describes the case in which, after multiple unreinforced exposures, the previously conditioned response attenuates or disappears. Extinction, however, is not permanent but is subject to various kinds of response recovery (Bouton, 1994; Bouton and Moody, 2004; Pavlov, 1927; Rescorla, 1988).

When the memory linkage between a conditioned stimulus (CS) and a fear evoking event (UCS) is extinguished, a new memory is created that communicates the absence of the feared object and blocks access to the original memory that signaled the onset of the feared event. These new memories tend to be context sensitive and somewhat more fragile than the original memories. Extinction, therefore, in the classical learning paradigm, refers to the learning of new information about the changed learning context as it is now provided by the CS. It does not refer to the elimination, forgetting, or modification of the memory. Extinction is characterized by four specific effects through which the behavior may be re-established or through which relapse occurs. As they appear in the post-treatment or relapse behavior of phobic patients, they may be viewed as a clear indication of the fact that extinction is the specific mechanism underlying the treatment. These effects are spontaneous recovery, contextual renewal, reinstatement, and rapid reacquisition (Bouton, 2004; Bouton and Moody, 2004; Dillon and Pizzagalli, 2007; Hartley and Phelps, 2009; Massad and Hulsey, 2006; Quirk and Mueller, 2007; Rescorla, 1988; Vervliet, 2008).

Spontaneous recovery refers to the re-occurrence of the extinguished or unreinforced fear response after the passage of time. It was first observed by Pavlov (1927) and is one of the first evidences that extinction does not remove the memory. As noted, extinction involves the creation of a new contextual association signifying that in this context, the CS does not predict the UCS and, therefore, the fearful response is irrelevant. That new memory of the new contingencies, if unreinforced, is subject to a time-based delay. It is forgotten over time and the fear re-emerges (Bouton, 2004; Bouton and Moody, 2004; Dillon and Pizzagalli, 2007; Massad and Hulsey, 2006; Rescorla, 1988; Vervliet, 2008).

Contextual renewal refers to the re-emergence of the conditioned response in a new circumstance where the extinction memory was not created. If the patient is subjected to unreinforced (extinction) trials in one context, so that the CS fails to evoke the feared response in that context, a subsequent test of that same CS in another context may show little or no reduction in expression. Even though the original fear response may generalize to multiple contexts, extinction phenomena are much more context dependent. Contextual renewal is contextually bound; the response is only renewed in the contexts where the UCS has again appeared (Bouton, 2004; Bouton and Moody, 2004; Dillon and Pizzagalli, 2007; Massad and Hulsey, 2006; Rescorla, 1988; Vervliet, 2008).

Reinstatement occurs when the fearful stimulus, the UCS, is presented without the CS. In that context where the original UCS is presented, despite the fact that the fearful response had been fully extinguished, the CS will be restored. It will not, however, reappear in other contexts where the UCS has not been presented (Bouton, 2004; Bouton and Moody, 2004; Dillon and Pizzagalli, 2007; Massad and Hulsey, 2006; Rescorla, 1988; Vervliet, 2008).

Rapid reacquisition, as the name suggests, describes the reacquisition of the fear memory after it has been successfully extinguished. In this case there is a net savings in the number of trials needed to reacquire the memory. If, for example, the original fear association took ten trials to install, during post-extinction training, it may take only three (Bouton, 2004; Bouton and Moody, 2004; Dillon and Pizzagalli, 2007; Massad and Hulsey, 2006; Rescorla, 1988; Vervliet, 2008).

Extinction, as exposure to the fear-evoking stimulus, has traditionally been held to be one of the tools of choice for the treatment of phobias and post-traumatic stress disorder (PTSD). Foa and her colleagues have indicated that in its various forms, from desensitization through imaginal and *in-vivo* exposure, inter alia, it is the most well-researched and most highly regarded of treatments and represents the scientific treatment of choice (Foa et al., 2000; Foa and Meadows, 1997; Rothbaum and Davis, 2003; Wessa and Flor, 2007; Wolitzky-Taylor et al., 2008).

The other most commonly encountered tool for dealing with phobias is systematic desensitization, itself a variant of an exposure/extinction paradigm.

Systematic desensitization was the theoretical brainchild of Wolpe (1958). Basing his ideas on the work of Pavlov, Watson, and their followers, Wolpe held that if an anxiety-reducing stimulus were presented in the presence of an anxiety-evoking stimulus so that the anxiety was either reduced or eliminated, the conditioned association between the anxiety-producing stimulus and the anxiety would be weakened. This was based on the principle that two competing or antagonistic responses (sympathetic and parasympathetic) could not exist simultaneously in an individual's neurology and that one could be manipulated to overpower the other (Rachman, 1967; Schaeffer and Martin, 1969; Wolpe, 1958).

Using conditioned place learning, Wolpe began by training cats to become neurotically anxious in a specific experimental circumstance. After installing the neuroses, he began feeding the cats in neutral contexts that bore no resemblance to the original neurosis evoking context. Gradually, in measured increments, he began to introduce more and more elements from the original context into the feeding context. At last, the cats were able to feed in the context where the anxious response had been learned without any sign of the previous anxiety (Rachman, 1967).

In transferring the pattern to humans, Wolpe understood that feeding was not an optimal counter-conditioning stimulus and decided to use Jacobson's progressive muscle relaxation as the positive stimulus. Wolpe believed that this procedure could be used with human subjects to successfully compete with anxiety. Originally beginning with physical objects and photographs of the aversive stimulus, he soon switched to imaginal presentations of the problem stimuli (Rachman, 1967; Schaeffer and Martin, 1969; Wolpe, 1958).

The pre-treatment procedure consisted of the creation of a ranked list of progressively more powerful anxiety-producing stimuli and the training of the subject in Jacobson's technique. Treatment proceeds through several sessions in which the patient, beginning with the least anxiety-producing stimulus, is instructed to relax and, while relaxing, imagine the stimulus. While still remembering the stimulus he is to reinstate the relaxed state. From within the relaxed state he is then instructed to relax further. Finally, in the absence of the anxiety-producing stimulus, the patient is instructed to relax again. This procedure continues over multiple sessions with successively more intense stimuli from the previously created hierarchy until the patient experiences no anxiety—even in the presence of what had been the most potent of the anxiety-producing stimuli. An abbreviated version of the technique often limits the procedure to the least significantly disturbing versions of the phobic stimulus and is executed in the course of one session (Rachman, 1967; Richardson and Suinn, 1974; Schaeffer and Martin, 1969; Wolitzky-Taylor et al., 2008; Wolpe, 1958).

In an early study of the effectiveness of desensitization in the treatment of snake phobias reported by Rachman (1967), 24 college students with demonstrated snake phobias were subjected to 11 sessions of systematic desensitization preceded by five training sessions. Lang and Lazovik (1963) reported that experimental subjects showed a marked reduction in symptoms and that the symptom reduction was tied to the level of the subjects' progress through the hierarchy. However, it is noted that several of the subjects did not complete the entire hierarchy. This suggests that the complete absence of the phobic response is not always the criterion of success.

In his extensive review of the experimental data to date, Rachman (1967) reported that the standard result for systematic desensitization is a significant reduction in the anxiety, not elimination of the response. He also indicated that he and other researchers had reported a consistent relapse rate of 50 percent. More recent studies place the effectiveness of desensitization at about 80 percent reduction in symptoms.

Visual Kinesthetic Dissociation or the NLP Fast Phobia Treatment

Procedure

The V/KD procedure first appeared in Bandler's *Use Your Brain for a Change* (1985). An expanded version of the procedure, and its first application to post-traumatic stress disorder (PTSD), appeared in the Andreas' *Heart of the Mind* (Andreas and Andreas, 1989). Dilts and DeLozier (2000) provide a slightly different version of the protocol in their *Encyclopedia of Systematic NLP and New Coding*. The technique has also been popularized in the UK as the *rewind* technique (Guy and Guy, 2003; Muss, 1991, 2002; Utuza et al., 2012). More recently, the NLP Research and Recognition team has formalized the procedure and renamed it The Reconsolidation of Traumatic Memories Protocol (RTM) (Gray and Liotta, 2012).

Bandler explains the origin of the NLP treatment for phobias and traumas, in his book *Time for a Change*. "I went out and found two people who had a phobia and who got over it. Then I found out what they did" (Bandler, 1993, p. 7). The solution he found was that people who had ongoing phobic responses remembered the traumatic events (or imagined traumatic events) as if seeing them through their own eyes (associated), while the two people who had recovered remembered the events as they would look seen from a distance (dissociated). He designed the NLP Phobia process to "install" the more useful dissociated recall of the experience. The V/KD procedure is described in detail in Chapter 2.

Published reports of the V/KD Protocol and phobias

Phobias and PTSD

From an NLP perspective, the cognitive structure of a simple phobia and the cognitive structure of a PTSD response are often considered to have enough similarity to indicate the use of the same restructuring techniques. The V/KD protocol in its application to PTSD is extensively reviewed elsewhere in this volume and the reader is referred there for a complete discussion.

Early research into the process used with phobias, by Einspruch and Forman (1988) found the NLP 15-minute phobia process behaviorally as successful as the much longer systematic desensitization process. In 1988 the University of Miami Phobia and Anxiety Disorders Clinic confirmed the value of the fully developed technique (used in combination with Ericksonian hypnotherapy). Thirty-one clients with specific phobias, social phobias, or agoraphobias were studied. All of them completed the Beck Depression Inventory and the Mark Phobia Questionnaire before and after treatments averaging two to three sessions. Clients showed marked improvement on inventories for both phobia and depression symptoms (Einspruch and Forman, 1988).

Allen (1982) studied 36 undergraduate students with snake phobias who were assigned to an NLP treatment group, a Massed Systematic Desensitization procedure, or a wait-group control. Secondary reports of their research suggest it is an implementation of the V/KD procedure. Upon examination of the original document, however, the technique appears to be neither the V/KD nor the standard collapsing anchors protocol but an ad hoc assemblage of NLP techniques. Beyond this, it relies on anchoring as a one-shot learning procedure which the authors hold to be largely an invalid definition for therapeutic uses. While it is correctly reported that neither the NLP process nor the desensitization protocol was any better than a wait-group control, the results are irrelevant to any evaluation of NLP protocols. In reviewing this study Mahishika (2010) suggests that, because the study did not rely on standard measures but tested the willingness of subjects to actually handle a snake, the measure may have mooted any measurable outcomes. We disagree. The poor results were the result of an ad hoc technique based broadly on NLP techniques and a false, if commonly promulgated, understanding of the anchoring procedure. From this examination, it would appear that neither the critics nor the defenders of NLP have read the original paper.

Liberman (1984), after relating her experiences of success with multiple phobia clients using NLP techniques, describes her experiment with 12 subjects who met the DSM-III criteria for simple phobia. Liberman, lacking access to a standardized model of the V/KD protocol, assembled her own procedure. This procedure included anchors for the phobic and resource states with the number of CS/UCS pairings appropriately guided by calibration. The positive anchor was used to reinforce positive dissociation during the procedure (much like Andreas' dissociative anchor) while the negative anchor was used to associate the observed phobic event with affectively related events. In the remainder of the session, the client is led through what seems to be a quadruple dissociation (watching herself in the projection booth, watching herself in the theatre, watching the movie of the trauma). In the second session, she repeats the dissociative procedure and then applies a modified collapse anchors protocol (see below), applying the positive anchor to a series of situations that client identifies as potentially problematic. While this protocol is not a true test of the V/KD-RTM treatment, it validly incorporates appropriate NLP techniques that would provide a reasonable test of the efficacy of NLP treatments.

Treatment was evaluated using a pre-test–post-test control-group design, in which the experimental (NLP) group was led through the procedure described while the control group imagined pleasant scenes. Subjects met with the therapists twice for treatment and once for follow-up after three weeks. Treatment sessions for both groups lasted less than one hour. All subjects were evaluated at pre-test, post-test, and at the three-week follow-up on multiple measures of phobic response. They also completed a two-month follow-up questionnaire. The NLP treatment effectively reduced phobic behavior and subjective distress. The NLP phobia treatment was superior to the control condition; it improved approach behavior, reduced fear, discomfort, and the overall intensity of symptoms. The differences between pre-treatment and post-treatment approach scores were significant at the .05 level (Liberman, 1984).

Subjects in the NLP treated group showed reduction in global fears (FSS-II) and specific fear responses, as well as reducing a wide range of problem symptoms. A test of hypnotic susceptibility (SHSS) showed that this success was unrelated to hypnotic ability.

University Microfilms, in a search for "NLP and Phobia" lists Hale's (1986) study of NLP with regard to speech anxiety and incompetence. A review of the research found a small sample group (eight) and no test of a specific technique—therapists were free to use the Primary Representational System (PRS), mirroring and pacing, anchoring, reframing, new-part creation, six-step reframe, and parts negotiation. After a review of the file the study was rejected from further consideration.

Goodrich (1994) reports an unpublished 1992 study of the NLP V/KD model using a population of "simple" phobics who were divided into three groups. Two experimental groups were treated with either the NLP process or an accelerated progressive-desensitization treatment. A third group was a wait-group control. All three groups were interviewed weekly about their symptoms for the following five weeks. The subjects were re-evaluated at six months, one year, and five years, and grouped by the level of returning symptoms: none, few, many, or all. At the end of the five-year follow-up, more than 90 percent of the NLP group reported no return of symptoms ("none"). Thirty-five percent of the desensitization group reported no symptom return ("none"), 33 percent reported "few" returning symptoms, and the remainder report that "many" or "all" of the symptoms had returned. Ninety percent or more of the control group reported the return of "all" symptoms.

Table 1.1 summarizes this data.

Proposed mechanism

We propose that this intervention takes advantage of the same reconsolidation mechanism described in Chapter 2 on PTSD. In short, whenever a memory is recalled, the same processes of protein synthesis that allowed its consolidation as a late-phase, or long-term, memory are reawakened. This makes the memory subject to modification. If the expression of the problem memory is terminated after a brief evocation, the protein synthesis continues and other experiences may be incorporated into the memory structure. If the memory is allowed to continue to be expressed beyond the brief evocation, the result is not memory modification, but either extinction or retraumatization with resultant reinforcement of the original experience (Alberini, 2005; Hupbach et al., 2008; Labar, 2007; Lee, 2009; Loftus and Yuille, 1984; Tronel et al., 2005).

There is growing evidence that a reminder of an older learned association (e.g. a traumatic event or a phobic conditioning event), presented briefly before the acquisition of new information (e.g., the V/KD protocol) leads to the incorporation of the new information into the older memory (Forcato et al., 2007, 2009; Hupbach et al., 2007, 2008, 2009; Kindt and Soeter, 2009). Recent research with human subjects indicates that the reconsolidation window begins about ten minutes after presentation of the reminder stimulus, and closes within six hours (Schiller et al., 2010; Schiller and Phelps, 2011).

Table 1.1 Phobia treatment studies

Study	Treatments	N	Number/duration of treatments	Outcome measures	Effect sizes	Comments
Einspruch and Forman (1988)	V/KD, SD	31	2–3	BDI, MPQ	N/A	Marked improvement (abstract only).
Allen (1982)	Ad Lib NLP Technique	36		BSS-II, BAT, FT	N/A	Wait-group control. No difference in treatment groups; both superior to control. NLP group more convinced of success.
Liberman (1984)	V/KD	12	2hrs + follow-up	FSS-II, SCL-9DR, FT, SHSS	N/A	Visualization control, pre–post design; reduction personal distress and symptoms; improved approach behavior, reduced fear, discomfort, and the overall intensity of symptoms.
Goodrich (1994)*	V/KD, ASD			Interview		Wait-group control. Five-year follow-up: NLP, 95% symptom-free; ASD, 35% none, 33% few, 38% all; Control, 90+% all symptoms returned.
Bigley et al. (2010)**	CA	58	1hr	Behavioral test		No control. Pre–post design. 38 of 50 treated patients (68%) successfully completed MRI.

Treatments: V/KD, Visual Kinaesthetic Dissociation Protocol; SD, Systematic Desensitization; CA Collapse Anchor; MSD, Massed Systematic Desensitization; ASD, Accelerated Systematic Desensitization.
Measures: BAT, Behavioral Avoidance Test; BDI, Beck Depression Inventory; BSS II, Beck Scale for Suicidal Ideation; FSS-II, Fear Survey Schedule II; FT, Fear Thermometer; MPQ, Multidimensional Personality Questionnaire; SCL-90R, Symptom Checklist-90-Revised; SHSS, Stanford Hypnotic Susceptibility Scale.

* Unpublished. ** Reported below

This mechanism implies a specific syntax. The reconsolidation mechanism only applies to long-term memories, while simple extinction is sufficient for a newly formed—or forming—memory. After consolidation of the original fear memory, a brief exposure to the CS, sufficient to evoke the fear response, is used to elicit the phobic response. The response must be allowed to continue sufficiently to produce measurable or observable signs of anxiety, but not so far that the response becomes overwhelming. After termination of the phobic response, the amnestic or interfering stimulus is introduced. This might be a conflicting CS, an alternate imagined scenario, or as in the V/KD protocol as a series of dissociated images. It appears that the strength and novelty of the new stimulus are important. In the V/KD protocol, the novelty and complexity of the task contribute to the reconfiguration of the memory.

This syntactic requirement suggests an alternate desensitization protocol in which a brief exposure to the phobic stimulus is followed by the evocation of a previously anchored and enhanced experience of an empowering resource state. This alternative is discussed in more detail below.

Case study

In the following case study, Steve Andreas, one of the original creators of the technique, used the V/KD-RTM protocol with a long-standing (20-year) phobia of bees. This session, from January 1984, took less than seven minutes. Lori's non-verbal response to bees in her imagination was clearly very different at the end of the session than it had been at the beginning. Several times during the next summer Steve contacted her and asked if she had seen any bees, because he wanted to know what her "real world" response had been. Each time she said she hadn't seen any bees. Finally, in December 1984, he took a jar containing about a dozen honeybees to her house. In a video-recorded follow-up interview she comfortably held the jar of bees and examined them closely. When he let several of them out of the jar, she watched them crawling on her living room window without any reaction. More than five years after the session, Lori reported that she still hadn't noticed any bees, though she admitted, "There must have been some around me." Her responses were equally positive 20 years later.

Here follows a transcript of the treatment session with the steps of the process interspersed in bold characters. A slightly more extensive transcript is provided by Andreas and Andreas (1989). Please note that steps four and five are reversed but this does not materially affect the outcome.

TRANSCRIPT OF STEVE ANDREAS AND LORI: BEE PHOBIA

Steve: Lori, I haven't spoken to you at all.
Lori: No.
Steve: You talked with Michael, I guess.
Lori: Umhmm.
Steve: I don't know what kind of outrageous promises he's made. [smiling]
Lori: [laughing] I won't tell you. I won't tell you what he promised.

1 Ensure that the client has a phobic type response to the stimulus.

Steve: Anyway, you have a phobia, which we won't tell them [the group] about, OK?
Lori: All right.
Steve: And, it's a very specific thing, right?
Lori: Umhmm.
Steve: Is it just one thing, or is it kind of a class of things?
Lori: It's one thing.

2 Evoke the phobic response, with or without description (most NLP interventions can be completed content-free).

Steve: Just one. OK. And what I'd like you to do first—well, think of it right now. If one of these were flying around right now.
Lori: Ohhh! [she rolls her head around in a counter-clockwise circle, laughing tensely]

3 Interrupt the re-emergence of the response as soon as the client begins to show physiological signs of its onset. Changes in breathing, skin color, posture, pupil dilation, and eye fixation are typical signs of memory access. As they appear, the state is to be broken by reorienting the client to the present, by changing the subject, redirecting their attention into a different sensory system, or firing off a pre-existing anchor. However it is accomplished, it is important to stop the development of the symptoms before they take control of the client's consciousness.

Steve: This is what we call a "pre-test". That's fine; come back. [Lori is still laughing nervously] Look at the people here. Look at me. Hold my hand.
Lori: Thank you ... OK.
Steve: We're not going to do stuff like that, right? OK.
Lori: OK. Whew!
Steve: Now look out at the folks here. How is it just being in front of these folks? [Lori looks out at the group] Is that a little nervous-making too?
Lori: [breathes out strongly] Not bad.
Steve: Is that OK?
Lori: Yeah, that's fine.

Steve: OK. You've got a friend over there, right?
Lori: Yeah.
Steve: He's got a nice smile.
Lori: He sure does. He's a great friend.

5 Instruct the client to imagine that they are sitting in a movie theatre and that they are watching a safe scene on the screen.

Steve: Yeah, good. OK. Now what I'd like you to do first, before we do anything—the whole procedure by the way is very simple, and you won't have to feel bad and stuff like that. But we need to make a few preparations. What I'd like you to do first, is imagine being in a movie theatre.
Lori: OK.
Steve: And this might be easier with your eyes closed.
Lori: Alright. [She closes her eyes]

4 After a few minutes away from the phobic response, ask the client to think of a time before the trauma when they were doing something pleasant in a safe, neutral context.

Steve: And I want you to see a picture up on the screen, of yourself—a black and white snapshot. And it could be of the way you're sitting right now, or something you do at home or at work ... Can you see a picture of yourself?
Lori: [nods] Umhmm.
Steve: Is that pretty easy for you?
Lori: Uhhuh.

6 Have the client imagine that they can float out of that body (in the theatre) and into the projection booth, perhaps behind a thick window, where they can watch themselves, seated in the theatre, watching the safe, neutral picture.

Steve: Good. Now I want you to leave that black-and-white picture on the screen, and I want you to float out of your body that's sitting here in the chair, up to the projection booth of the movie theatre. Can you do that? Take a little while ...
Lori: OK.
Steve: OK, so from now on I want you to stay up in that projection booth. Can you see yourself down in the audience, there?
Lori: [smiles slightly] Umhmm.
Steve: And you can also see the black-and-white picture up on the screen?
Lori: Yeah.
Steve: OK. Of yourself?
Lori: Yeah.
Steve: Pretty interesting.
Lori: [laughs] It's good.

Phobias   19

Steve: Do you know you could go to a workshop on "Astral Travel" and pay $250 to learn how to do this?
Lori: [laughs]
Steve: OK, now I want you to stay up in that projection booth, and see yourself down in the audience, and see that black-and-white picture on the screen of yourself.
Lori: Umhmmm.
Steve: Got that?
Lori: Umhmm.
Steve: OK, I want you to stay up in that projection booth, until I tell you to do something else.
Lori: OK.

7 Ask the client to imagine that the movie on the screen, watched by their dissociated body seated in the theatre, becomes a black and white movie of the trauma that runs from the safe place before the trauma to a safe place after the trauma.

8 From the perspective of the safe projection booth, have the client focus on the responses of the dissociated watcher in the theatre as THEY watch the movie.

Steve: So you can kind of see through the glass, and there are holes in the glass so you can hear the movie, because we're going to show a movie pretty soon. What I want you to do is run a movie of yourself in one of those bad times when you used to respond to that particular thing. And run it from beginning to end, and you stay back in that projection booth. You might even put your fingers on the glass and feel the glass. Just run a whole movie, clear to the end. See yourself freaking out over there, in response to one of those situations. That's right. Take all the time you need, and just let me know when you get to the end.
Lori: It's hard to get to the end.
Steve: OK. What makes it difficult?
Lori: It just seems to stop. The thing seems to go over and over. [gesturing with her right hand in a circle] The particular incident goes over and over and over and doesn't seem to have an end, although I know it ended.
Steve: OK. So it tends to go over and over and over.
Lori: Umhmm.
Steve: OK. Let's speed up the movie. How many times does it have to go over and over before you can get to the end ...?
Lori: Um, half a dozen.
Steve: OK. So let it flip through half a dozen, so it'll let you get to the end ... And when I say "end," I mean after the whole thing happened and you're back normal again.
Lori: OK.
Steve: OK. Got to the end?
Lori: Umhmm.

9 Repeat the black-and-white movie process until the client can do it with no discomfort.

Steve: Was that fairly comfortable for you, watching that?
Lori: A little uncomfortable, but not bad.
Steve: A little uncomfortable, but not bad. Not like the real thing.
Lori: No.

10 After completing the dissociated movies, have the client imagine floating down from the projection booth and stepping into their own body that is seated in the theatre. Having reassociated into that body, let them imagine getting out of the seat, walking to the movie screen and stepping into the black-and-white image of the safe, neutral activity with which they ended the black and white rehearsal.

Steve: OK. Now in a minute I'm going to ask you to do something, and I don't want you to do it until I tell you to go ahead. What I want you to do is to get out of the projection booth, and out of that chair in the audience, and go into the movie at the very end, when everything's OK and comfortable. And then I want you to run the whole movie backwards, including those six times around. Have you ever seen a movie backwards, in high school or something?
Lori: Yeah.
Steve: OK. I'm going to have you run it backwards in *color*, and I want you to be *inside it*, so it's just like you took a real experience, only you ran it backwards in time, and I want you to do it in about a second and a half. So it will go "Bezzzoooouuuuuurrrrrpppp," about like that.
Lori: OK.

11 As the client steps into the movie screen, have them turn on the sound, color, motion, smells, and tastes of the safe neutral representation on the screen. Then, instruct them to experience a movie of the trauma in full sensory detail, BACKWARDS and very quickly (two to three seconds). Let them end the movie with a still color picture of themselves in the safe, neutral place from before the problem ever started.

Steve: OK. Go ahead. Do that ...
Lori: [takes a deep breath, shudders] Whooof!
Steve: OK. Did you come out on the other side all right?
Lori: Yeah. [laughing]
Steve: A little weird in the middle there, eh?
Lori: [shaking her head and continuing to laugh] Ooooh.

12 Repeat the reversed representation enough times so that it can be done easily and quickly, and the client has a sense of being comfortable. When the client can repeat the process easily with no experience of discomfort the process is finished.

Steve: OK. Now I'd like you to do that a couple more times, and do it *faster*. So go into the end, right at the end, jump into it, and then go "Bezourp," real fast, through the whole thing ... Now do it a third time, real fast ...

Lori: OK.
Steve: OK. Was it easier the third time?
Lori: Umhmm.
Steve: OK. Now, that's all there is to it.
Lori: [opens her eyes, looking *very* sceptical, grabs the chair with both hands, shakes her head, and then starts laughing loudly] I'm glad I didn't pay for this one!

13 Attempt to reactivate the phobic response. Ask the client to go back to it, to think of things that normally brought the problem to life. Test for the response in as many ways as can be found.

Steve: Fine. It's all right. We love to joke. Joking is one of the nicest ways to dissociate. Think about it. When you're joking, when you're having a humorous response to something, there's really no way to do it other than popping out for a while, looking at yourself, and sort of putting a different frame around what's happening, such that it's funny. It's a really valuable way of dissociating. We believe that dissociation is the essence of a lot of humour—not all; there are different kinds of humour, and so on. But we definitely recommend it ... Now, Lori, would you imagine now that one of these little critters—came. [Gesturing with one finger, like the flight of a bee, toward Lori]
Lori: OK.
Steve: What's it like?
Lori: Um hay de hay. [at a loss for words, and begins laughing] Um ...
Steve: Do you still have it [the phobia]?
Lori: [looking down, surprised] No! [she laughs and puts her hand on her chest]

14 If the client still has an experience of distress repeat the reversed movie several more times.

15 When the phobic response cannot be evoked, the procedure is over.

Steve: This is a nice response because it looks like, "What?" Consciously she's expecting to have this [old] response. She's had it for—how long have you had this?
Lori: Twenty years.
Steve: She's had the response very, very dependably for twenty years. It's been a very unpleasant and overwhelming response. There's a very strong conscious expectation. And what you saw there was this conscious expectation, "Ooooh! It's going to be terrible" ... What?
Lori: [laughing] It's true.
Steve: Now let's make it a real bad one, you know. Have one come in and land on your hand or something. [Lori looks down at her hand] Can you imagine that?

Lori: Umhmm. [she shakes her head in disbelief] Whew!
Steve: What's it like?
Lori: Ummmm ... (neutrally, shrugging her shoulders) It's like having one sitting on my hand.
Steve: That's a typical answer—is what's so funny "It's like being in an elevator, you know." Isn't that a mind-boggler?
Lori: Yeah, it is! Because I had that happen within the first year after the first incident, I had one land on me, woof!
Steve: And it was different, right?
Lori: Yeah! (looking down at her hand again)

A video of the treatment session can be found at: http://www.youtube.com/watch?v=VtUatMghbHg. The follow-up video can be found at: http://www.youtube.com/watch?v=TjjCzhrYJDQandfeature=related.

Collapsing anchors

Collapsing anchors is one of the original techniques created by NLP founders Bandler and Grinder. Versions of it appear in *Frogs into Princes* (1979), *Patterns in the Hypnotic Techniques of Milton Erickson, MD, Volume II* (1975), *Roots of NLP* (1983), *NLP Volume One* and other foundational texts. Dilts and DeLozier (2000) report a slight modification of the technique in their Encyclopedia. In general, the technique is recommended for specific phobias, that is phobias to specific objects or rooted in one specific event (APA, 1994). It is not recommended for agoraphobia or General Anxiety Disorders.

The technique is recommended for cases where the triggering stimulus can be imaginally evoked without the onset of severe traumatization. If the phobia cannot be accessed without a severe onset of panic, a modification of the technique or a different technique may be indicated.

The basic technique consists of creating an anchor (see below) for the feelings associated with the phobic response or the original traumatizing event. In common use, the anchors here are kinaesthetic, touch-based anchors, although in principle any kind of anchor that can be fired off simultaneously may be used. After breaking state, a separate anchor is created for a resource state. A resource state can be the memory of any experience that would be sufficient in quality or intensity that had it been present during the traumatizing event, the problem response would not have been learned or it may be a more general, powerful positive experience. After both experiences are anchored so that they can be reliably evoked by the gesture, movement word or other conditioned stimulus, both anchors are evoked simultaneously. This usually results in a state of physiological confusion in which elements of the two states arise simultaneously in facial and bodily reactions. It may provoke laughter or expressions of surprise. When those responses have quieted, the subject is asked to re-access the problem state. If she cannot, the procedure ends. If she can, the presupposition is that the positive anchor was either inappropriately contextually bound, not sufficiently strong, or not appropriate to the problem state. The procedure is repeated until after integration, the problem cannot be accessed.

Anchoring

Anchors can range from immediate, one-shot learnings evoked by a single word or touch (like phobias), to classically conditioned, stimulus-response connections that are built up over several trials. When one-trial conditioning or anchoring occurs, it usually occurs in response to a powerfully emotional stimulus, an extraordinarily novel experience or something that is life threatening. Examples here are phobias, PTSD and flashbulb memories—the vivid recollections of a traumatic or extremely novel experience. In other cases, it may occur when a new experience matches a pre-existing set of beliefs or behaviours so that it becomes a natural part of a pre-existing schema or pattern (Bouton, 1994; Bouton and Moody, 2004; Diamond et al., 2007; Morris, 2006). Moreover, one-shot learnings may depend upon the distinctive nature of the conditioned stimulus (Bouton and Moody, 2004; Rescorla, 1988).

It is important to note that, although NLP has often promoted anchoring as a one-shot learning of two associated stimuli, like a touch or a word combined with an emotion or mood; for therapeutic purposes, this is not always a reliable means of establishing the anchor. In most cases, the anchor stimulus must be paired multiple times (five to seven) with the desired response until that response arises reliably and automatically. Done this way, anchoring is a dependable and automatic expression of Pavlovian delayed conditioning (Dilts and DeLozier 2000; Gray, 2008a, 2008b; Bandler and Grinder, 1979; Klein, 2008; Linden and Perutz, 1998; O'Connor and Seymour, 1999; Pavlov, 1927; Rescorla, 1988). A review of the process as described by Dilts (1983) and Dilts et al. (1980) confirms the classical pattern, despite protestations otherwise.

Delayed conditioning specifies a paradigm where the conditioned stimulus (originally neutral) is presented after the onset of the unconditioned stimulus and terminates while the unconditioned response is still present. For example, your client begins to talk about a pleasant experience and you observe a change in their physiology that reflects their enjoyment (the UCR). While that state is still increasing, you repeatedly anchor the experience by tapping your finger on the table (the CS). This is delayed conditioning (Klein, 2008).

A considerable body of research suggests that, not only are certain stimuli more easily conditioned in a relevant context (Domjian, 2005; Rescorla, 1988), but that others are more likely to be conditioned in certain subjective contexts. Significant examples of stimuli that appear to be predisposed to links with fear include spiders, snakes, and objects that resemble them as well as water and enclosed spaces. Such objects are much more readily associated with fearful or anxiety producing stimuli, but are also much more difficult to extinguish. On the other hand, relatively meaningless stimuli—those unrelated to the learning context—may be easily conditioned but are also easily extinguished (Domjian, 2005; Gerdes et al., 2009; Mineka and Oehlberg, 2008; Öhman et al., 1975; Ohman et al., 1976; Öhman and Mineka, 2001).

Published report

Bigley et al. (2010) used a version of the NLP technique collapsing anchors to determine if it was possible to reduce levels of claustrophobia in patients that required an MRI. In general, extremely anxious patients undergo the MRIs under general anaesthesia at a substantial increase in costs. If the number of patients needing anaesthesia were to be reduced, it would result in a significant savings to the medical service.

The study group consisted of individuals who had previously failed an MRI scan because of a claustrophobic reaction. A total of 50 patients were recruited and their anxiety states pre- and post-treatment were measured using the Spielberger's State Anxiety Inventory. The technique used for the intervention was Clare's Fast Phobia Cure (Rushworth, 1994), a variant of the collapsing anchors technique.

According to the authors, the technique varies from the standard anchor-based protocol in that the negative and positive stimuli (problem and resource anchors) are anchored in different sensory systems. In this case, the anxiety evoking stimulus was anchored visually—presumably by attending to a certain object—and the positive anchor was a stacked kinaesthetic anchor. That is, the positive stimulus consisted of multiple positive resource states, chosen for their relevance to the problem state, stacked together into a single kinaesthetic (touch) anchor stimulus. After the two anchors had been established, the patient was instructed to look at the anchor for the negative stimulus while the facilitator simultaneously fired off the anchor for the stacked positive stimulus. After a moment of integration, the client was asked about their current feelings toward the negative visual stimulus.

After treatment, a total of 38 of the original 50 subjects (76 percent) were able to complete the MRI scan. These 38 had significant decreases in anxiety scores ($p<.05$). The 12 patients who did not complete the scan had reduced anxiety scores in post-tests, but their reductions did not reach the levels achieved by the scan-completers. They also had statistically higher anxiety scores before NLP than the remaining patients. There was a statistically significant reduction in the median anxiety score for all patients, and a cost savings of 65 percent (£31,900) was realized by using NLP rather than completing the MRI scan under general anaesthetic.

Procedure

Begin by identifying the problem state and one or more stimuli that evoke it. Before proceeding, also identify a resource state, a memory of a specific time and place where the subject had an experience that was strong enough so that if they had been able to access the resource at the time, the problem response would not have been created.

1 Ensure that the client has a phobic type response to the stimulus.
2 Evoke the phobic response, with or without description (most NLP interventions can be completed content free).
3 Interrupt the re-emergence of the response as soon as the client begins to show physiological signs of its onset. Changes in breathing, skin color, posture, pupil dilation, and eye fixation are typical signs of memory access. As they appear, the state is to be broken by reorienting the client to the present, by changing the subject, redirecting their attention into a different sensory system, or firing off a pre-existing neutral anchor. However it is accomplished, it is important to stop the development of the symptoms before they take control of the client's consciousness.
4 Permissions and anchor choice. The technique is typically executed by means of kinesthetic anchors that are used here. Obtain permission from the client to touch them on the hand or some other mutually agreeable, non-suggestive place. It is usually best to choose places marked by a crease, tattoo, mole, joint, scar, or freckle to ensure that the touch stimulus can be replicated. Ensure that both sites can be easily accessed by the practitioner at the same time.
5 Anchor the response. Begin by evoking the problem state. Ask the client to think about the precipitating event or stimulus, as soon as the client begins to show physiological signs of its onset—changes in breathing, skin color, posture, pupil dilation, and eye fixation are typical signs of memory access—touch the anchor spot in a manner that can be replicated in terms of placement and pressure. Hold the anchor for a second or two and release the anchor.
6 Interrupt the re-emergence of the response as soon as you have released the anchor stimulus. The state is to be broken by reorienting the client to the present, by changing the subject, redirecting their attention into a different sensory system, or firing off a pre-existing neutral anchor. However it is accomplished, it is important to stop the development of the symptoms before they take control of the client's consciousness.
7 After the client has returned to a more normal physiology, repeat the process. Evoke the state, apply the anchor, break the state. Repeat until the anchor stimulus increases the intensity of the problem state as indicated by increased and more immediate changes in observable physiology.

8 Test the state. After returning the client to a centered, non-traumatized state in the present, that is, when their pulse and breathing have slowed, their color has returned to normal, extended veins, sweat and other signs of fear have dissipated, fire off the anchor stimulus. If the physiology of the phobic response returns, break the state and continue with the next step. If it does not, repeat the anchoring procedure until the touch stimulus reliably reproduces the state. Interrupt the re-emergence of the response as soon as you have released the anchor stimulus.
9 Evoke the resource state, with or without description.
10 After the state has emerged, allow the client to enjoy it briefly then interrupt the response. Changes in breathing, skin color, posture, pupil dilation, and eye fixation are typical signs of memory access. Break the state by reorienting the client to the present, by changing the subject, redirecting their attention into a different sensory system, or firing off a pre-existing neutral anchor.
11 Permissions and anchor choice.
12 Anchor the response. Begin by evoking the resource state. Invite the client to recall the event from within their own body, seeing what they saw, hearing what they heard and feeling what they felt. Instruct them to make their representation bigger, brighter, and closer. Suggest that they turn on the sound and turn up the volume to a point where the state is strongly enhanced. Let them notice where in their body the feeling is centered and whether and how it moves. Changes in breathing, skin color, posture, pupil dilation, and eye fixation are typical signs of memory access. Touch the anchor spot in a manner that can be replicated in terms of placement and pressure. Hold the anchor for five seconds and release the anchor. After the state has emerged, allow the client to enjoy it briefly then interrupt the re-emergence of the response.
13 After the client has returned to a more normal physiology, repeat the process. Evoke the state, apply the anchor, break the state. Repeat until the anchor stimulus increases the intensity of the resource state as indicated by increased and more immediate changes in observable physiology.
14 Test the state. After returning the client to a centered, non-extraordinary state in the present, that is, when their pulse and breathing have slowed, their color has returned to normal, and other signs of altered state have dissipated, fire off the anchor stimulus. If the physiology of the resource state returns, break the state and continue with the next step. If it does not, repeat the anchoring procedure until the touch-stimulus reliably evokes the state.
15 Collapse anchors. After the client has returned to normal consciousness, fire, and hold both anchors simultaneously. Hold them until the client's physiology begins to change. Release the negative anchor

first, hold the positive for at least a further five seconds, then release the positive and observe the client until their physiology settles into a steady state.
16 Test. Ask the client to access the problem state or the triggering stimulus. If the intervention has been successful they will be able to access the trigger or the memory of the precipitating event without evoking the phobic response. If this test is successful, fire off the anchor associated with the problem or phobic state. If the intervention has been successful, the anchor should elicit none of the physiological indicia of the phobic response.

Alternate models

Desensitization protocol

Another approach to using anchors for the treatment of phobias calls for the creation of a resourceful anchor and using it in an imaginal desensitization regimen. This approach is similar to timeline approaches (Andreas and Andreas, 1989; James and Woodsmall, 1988). Gray (personal communication, 2011) reports the treatment of a fear of flying. The subject reported that the entire process of preparing to travel and traveling by air was emotionally paralyzing. More specifically, her loss of control over the entire situation grew to intolerable levels as she imagined anything related to air travel. She was then facing a 17-hour flight to Japan for business. After a discussion of how she would need to feel in order for flying to be possible, an appropriate resource state was found in which she was confident, fearless, and fully in control. After a self-anchor had been established (the anchor stimulus was a gesture that she could make at any time), she was asked to imagine the steps of her journey from packing her bags, to calling the cab, to boarding the airplane, and taking off. At each stage of the imagined process, whenever she noticed that she was becoming anxious, she was instructed to fire off the anchor repeatedly while continuing to imagine the current journey context, until all of the discomfort had dissipated and she was feeling confident and in control. She then continued with the imaginal journey from a point just before she had begun to notice the onset of anxiety in the previous sequence. Her journey continued until she began to experience anxiety again. In that imaginal context, she was again to fire off the anchor until the positive state was asserted in the new imaginal context. The process continued in the same stepwise fashion until she was able to imagine herself flying with no discomfort.

Ten years after the original visit the subject was contacted for an update. She reported that the initial treatment had worked well and that she had been able to make the 17-hour trip to Japan with no problem. She reports that over the years she has added to the original intervention and continues to fly with minimal discomfort.

While it would be difficult to claim that this one intervention completely resolved her flying phobia, we can confidently say that it broke the ice and allowed her to make a grueling journey where previously any flight had been impossible. With this background, she has been able to fly as needed whenever business required.

While this technique is very similar to Wolpe's (1958) systematic desensitization, it differs significantly in that: 1) the limited experience of the phobic response precedes the positive resource; 2) the positive resource is immediate in application, does not require conscious effort (after the anchor has been established); and 3) the resource has been chosen specifically to counter the phobic response. The importance of these distinctions will be made clear below.

Proposed mechanism

As noted above, and unlike the classical treatments which are extinction based, we propose that this intervention takes advantage of the reconsolidation mechanism described briefly above and more fully in Chapter 2 on post-traumatic stress disorder. In short, memory recall activates the same processes of protein synthesis that resulted in the consolidation of the memory as a late-phase, or long-term memory. This labilizes the memory which makes it subject to modification. If, after a brief evocation, the problem memory is terminated within the window of opportunity, the protein synthesis continues and other experiences may be incorporated into the memory structure. If the memory is allowed to continue beyond the brief evocation, the result is not memory modification, but either extinction or retraumatization with resultant reinforcement of the original experience. In this case, the phobic memory is evoked first, leaving its structure subject to change. The newly conditioned resource combines with the phobic memory and transforms it (Alberini, 2005; Hupbach et al., 2008; Labar, 2007; Lee, 2009; Loftus and Yuille, 1984; Tronel et al., 2005).

Directions for future research

Because there exists the possibility of a strong selection-based predisposition to phobias related to spiders, snakes, water, and enclosed spaces (Domjian, 2005; Gerdes et al., 2009; Öhman et al., 1975, 1976; Öhman and Mineka, 2001), participants should meet DSM criteria for specific, patently irrational phobias evoked by otherwise affect-neutral stimuli. Insofar as we have suggested that there are two NLP-based interventions that should meet or exceed the standards of mainline treatments (reduction of symptoms in 50 percent of clients for systematic desensitization (Rachman, 1967), we would propose a test consisting of four experimental groups and one wait-condition control group. The experimental conditions would be assigned to V/KD treatment, collapse anchors treatment, exposure/extinction treatment, and accelerated systematic desensitization. Subjects would be provided with manualized treatments by trained providers of each protocol. Each subject would receive pre-tests on a standard instrument for the evaluation of phobic symptoms. In light of research suggesting the possibility of differences in behavioural and questionnaire-based assessments, we would suggest that both be employed (Wolitzky-Taylor et al., 2008). Post-treatment evaluations using the same instrument would be given to each subject immediately post treatment, with one-week, one-month, and six-month follow-ups using the same instrument.

Because of the regular misunderstanding of NLP anchoring as something other than an instance of a classical Pavlovian paradigm, the procedure for the collapse anchor protocol must be based upon multiple parings of the proposed anchors with the appropriate positive and negative stimuli. Any other interpretation of anchoring will render the results invalid.

We would set forth the following hypotheses:

> Within group (pre–post) comparisons will be superior for the two NLP groups as compared to the two standard treatments and the wait-group controls.
>
> If the NLP group responses, as measured by the designated instruments immediately post-treatment are equivalent to or better than the standard treatments, the adjustment revealed in the subsequent follow-up testing will show increasing levels of discomfort in 50 percent or more of the standard treatment groups, while results from the two NLP groups will remain stable or continue to improve over time.

Implications of the NLP perspective

One of the important prospects that emerges from this research is the identification of a behavioural syntax rooted in recent studies of reconsolidation and the fast acquisition of newly learned memories. Originally articulated by Gray and Liotta (2012) it has been further articulated by Gray (2011).

Briefly, when a memory is created, it passes through several stages, after varying time frames, including as little as 24 hours for emotional memories (in higher organisms), the "memory trace" becomes solidified as an assemblage of synaptic connections throughout the brain. This is basic memory consolidation (Amaral et al., 2008; Kandel, 2001; Schiller et al., 2010).

Each time the memory is activated after its consolidation as a long-term memory trace, the chemical processes that created the neural trace are reactivated. If the circumstances are similar to the original event, the synaptic connections are maintained or strengthened. If, however, the situation has significantly changed, the connections themselves can change. In the first case the memory is strengthened, in the second it may be modified or erased. The repeated strengthening or weakening of the memory connections through the reactivation of protein synthesis is called reconsolidation because it repeats the original process by which the trace was consolidated (Alberini, 2005; Hupbach et al., 2008; Labar, 2007; Lee, 2009; Loftus and Yuille, 1984; Tronel et al., 2005).

When the memory has been activated for a sufficiently short period and interrupted before its full expression, the reconsolidation phenomenon opens a temporal window during which new versions of the experience may be introduced, the emotional impact of the event can be changed or, (theoretically) the memory may be erased completely (Kindt et al., 2009; Schiller et al., 2010).

This mechanism gives rise to a pattern that consistently appears in NLP interventions from the basic pattern interrupt, to the simple protocol of collapsing anchors and the RTM procedure: evoke the problem state, interrupt it before it is fully expressed, introduce the amnestic or transformative stimulus (Gray, 2011c). We believe that this constitutes a well-formedness condition for memory-based interventions rooted in emotional experiences (Schiller et al., 2011).

This pattern appears to provide a behavioural parallel to a phenomenon described by Morris (2006) and Tse et al. (2008). These authors have shown that new memories evoked in the context of a late-term, "permanent" memory schema may be consolidated into that schema as part of the long term-structure. As opposed to the longer (ca. 30 days) hippocampal process of memory consolidation as originally suggested by Squire (Schiller and Phelps, 2011), this process of incorporation can be accomplished in as little as 24 hours. This suggests again that the memory that is to be changed, modified or (possibly) erased must precede the amnestic or modifying memory. In this, we may have discovered the reason why results with systematic desensitization are so unreliable: it violates the basic syntax of memory modification. If the sequence is reversed in desensitization, problem presentation followed by resource presentation, we propose that the results would improve. We would suggest that part of the reason for the now largely anecdotal efficacy of the NLP interventions, the V/KD protocol and collapsing anchors, is that they observe the syntactic constraints identified above and supported by the work of Morris and Tse et al. Given the understanding that memories can be permanently changed by observing these constraints, the reconsolidation paradigm provides a syntax for designing interventions with a firm neurological base.

Summary

This chapter has presented the evidence and techniques that surround the NLP approach to the treatment of specific phobias. These include the V/KD-RTM model, collapsing anchors, and a modified systematic desensitization model. A review of published research finds little in the way of published material, with several of the published studies being significantly misrepresented and perhaps not read by the commentators. Standardized versions of the techniques were presented and integrated with hypothetical neurological and behavioural models. The chapter ended with the proposal of several testable hypotheses for the root mechanism and a basic research outline for testing the techniques.

2 Post-traumatic stress disorder

Richard M. Gray, Richard Bolstad

Post-traumatic stress disorder (PTSD) presents a growing problem for therapists and caregivers. The incidence of unpredictable violence in the present age provides a continuing source of trauma as its promulgation by the media magnifies its effects. The increasing role of first responders also increases the trauma load of the many who aid and care for primary victims.

The prevalence of PTSD among veterans of the Gulf War, Operation Iraqi Freedom, and Operation Enduring Freedom has been estimated at nearly twice the rate of the non-combat population (six percent). The incidence among Gulf War veterans lies at 10–11 percent and for veterans of the wars in Iraq and Afghanistan at 13–17 percent (Gradus, 2010; Hogue et al. 2004). These returning servicemen present serious problems for treatment professionals on two fronts. First, they represent a significant influx of problem patients for whom there are few trained staff, and second, the currently approved and most thoroughly researched treatments for PTSD provide inconsistent results with varying levels of effectiveness and subsequent relapse. Central to the second problem is the observation that extinction-based treatments, which have enjoyed a favorable position among the existing treatment options, often require long-term commitment in spite of their inconsistent results (Foa and Meadows, 1997; Foa et al., 2000; McNally, 2007; Massad and Hulsey, 2006; Rothbaum et al., 2000; Rothbaum and Davis, 2003; Shalev et al., 1996; Wessa and Flor, 2007; Schiller et al., 2010; Ursano et al., 2004).

This chapter will focus on one of the primary NLP interventions used to treat PTSD symptoms, the Visual Kinesthetic Dissociation protocol (V/KD). It is supported by a neurological mechanism that explains its efficacy and provides directions for further research.

PTSD is defined by the DSM-IV in terms of four criteria. The first of the criteria is the traumatizing event. In order to qualify as a traumatizing event both of the following must appear:

1   The person experienced, witnessed, or was otherwise confronted with one or more events that actually involved or threatened death, serious

injury, or some other threat to the physical integrity of that individual or others.
2 The individual's response involved intense feelings of horror, fear, or helplessness.

The diagnostic criteria are divided into three symptom clusters, the re-experiencing cluster, the avoidance/numbing cluster, and the arousal cluster. According to Foa and Meadows (1997), the intrusion or re-experiencing symptoms include the hallmark signs of PTSD including nightmares, intrusive thoughts, and flashbacks. The avoidance group includes efforts to avoid memories of the traumatic experience and symptoms of emotional numbing. The third symptom cluster includes symptoms of hyper-arousal including sleeplessness, irritability, and hyper-vigilance (APA, 1994).

Diagnosis is made when symptoms (at least one from the re-experiencing cluster, three from the avoidance cluster and two from the hyper-arousal cluster) cause clinically significant distress or discomfort and have persisted for a minimum of one month (APA, 1994).

The V/KD protocol is an intervention designed in the early 1980s for use with phobias. The protocol is one of many practitioner-reported evidence-based interventions that emerges from the field of NLP.

The V/KD procedure first appeared in Bandler's *Using Your Brain for a Change* (1985) as the Fast Phobia Cure. An expanded version of the procedure, and its first application to PTSD, appeared in *Heart of the Mind* (Andreas and Andreas, 1989). Dilts and DeLozier (2000) provide a slightly different version of the protocol in their *Encyclopedia of Systematic NLP and New Coding*.

The V/KD procedure

The following description of the basic protocol depends upon extensive personal communications with Steve Andreas, Robert Dilts, and Tim Hallbom and continued reference to their descriptions of the protocol in several written sources (Andreas and Andreas, 1989; Bandler, 1985; Dilts and DeLozier, 2000; Figley, 2002). This protocol has been renamed several times. In the UK it has found wide acceptance as the Rewind Technique (Guy and Guy, 2003; Muss, 1991, 2002; Utuza et al., 2012) and the Fast Phobia Model. For research and replication purposes, a standardized version of the protocol, Reconsolidation of Traumatic Memories (RTM), has been developed by members of the NLP Research and Recognition Project, including Steve Andreas, Tim Hallbom, William McDowell, and Richard Gray. For clarity and to retain its historical identity, it will here be referred to as the V/KD procedure.

The procedure is relatively simple:

1 Ensure that the client has a phobic-type response to the stimulus or the trauma. That is, in the presence of reminders of the trauma, he

must experience the quick onset of fear, panic, flashbacks; his life may be characterized by hyper-vigilance, he may be nervous around others, he may need to be in control and unable to feel safe; and he may have nightmares in which the trauma reappears. The protocol is not recommended for PTSD sufferers for whom these are not the main symptoms or where there is an underlying psychopathology.

2 Evoke the trauma, with or without description (most NLP interventions can be completed content free).

3 Interrupt the re-emergence of the trauma as soon as the client begins to show physiological signs of its onset. Changes in breathing, skin color, posture, pupil dilation, and eye fixation are typical signs of memory access. As they appear, the state is to be broken by reorienting the client to the present, by changing the subject, redirecting their attention into a different sensory system, or firing off a pre-existing anchor (a conditioned stimulus that evokes a reorientation to the present circumstances). However it is accomplished, it is important to stop the development of the symptoms before they take control of the client's consciousness.

4 After a few minutes away from the trauma, ask the client to think of a time before the trauma when they were doing something pleasant in a safe, neutral context.

5 Instruct the client to imagine that they are sitting in a movie theatre and that they are watching that scene on the screen.

6 Have the client imagine that they can float out of that body (in the theatre) and into the projection booth, perhaps behind a thick window, where they can watch themselves, seated in the theatre, watching the safe, neutral picture.

7 Ask the client to imagine that the movie on the screen, watched by their dissociated body seated in the theatre, becomes a black-and-white movie of the trauma that runs from the safe place before the trauma to a safe place after the trauma.

8 From the perspective of the safe projection booth, have the client focus on the responses of the dissociated watcher in the theatre as **THEY** watch the movie.

9 Repeat the black-and-white movie process until the client can do it with no discomfort.

10 After completing the dissociated movies, have the client imagine floating down from the projection booth and stepping into their own body that is seated in the theatre. Having re-associated into that body, let them imagine getting out of the seat, walking to the movie screen and stepping into the black-and-white image of the safe, neutral activity with which they ended the black and white rehearsal.

11 As the client steps into the movie screen, have them turn on the sound, color, motion, smells, and tastes of the safe neutral representation on the screen. Then, instruct them to experience a movie of the trauma

in full sensory detail, BACKWARDS and very quickly (two to three seconds). Let them end the movie with a still color picture of themselves in the safe, neutral place from before the problem ever started.
12 Repeat the reversed representation enough times so that it can be done easily and quickly, and the client has a sense of being comfortable. When the client can repeat the process easily with no experience of discomfort the process is finished.
13 Attempt to re-activate the trauma. Ask the client to go back to it, to think of things that normally brought the problem to life. Test for the trauma in as many ways as can be found.
14 If the client still has an experience of distress, repeat the reversed movie several more times.
15 When the trauma cannot be evoked, the procedure is over.

Andreas (personal communication, 2008) recommends, as does Muss (2002), that some training in imagining a black-and-white movie and in imagining a reversed movie precede the actual clinical trial.

Unlike other treatments for phobias or PTSD, the V/KD either eliminates the memory completely, or leaves the memory intact but without traumatic affect so that the client can talk about it without distress.

Published reports

Reports of the efficacy of the V/KD cover nearly a quarter century. Among the anecdotal reports are those provided by Richard Bandler, Steve and Connierae Andreas, Robert Dilts, and William McDowell, who relate that, as a group, they have treated thousands of persons suffering from PTSD and phobic conditions with immediate, lasting results. In many cases they report complete symptom alleviation after long-term follow-up (Andreas and Andreas, 1989; Bandler, 1985; Dilts and DeLozier, 2000; McDowell and McDowell, nd).

Psychological investigations of the technique are limited to four scientific studies, two reviews, and several mentions in the literature. Each of the referenced studies recommends the technique as a valuable tool for treating PTSD and makes suggestions for further research (Carbonell and Figley, 1999; Dietrich, 2000; Dietrich et al., 2000; Figley, 2002; Hossack and Bentall, 1996; Koziey and McLeod, 1987; Muss, 1991, 2002; Utuza et al., 2012). There is also one non-peer reviewed study that is reported online (Guy and Guy, 2003). Frank Bourke of the NLP Research and Recognition Project (personal communication, November, 2011) indicates that, as of yet, unpublished pilot studies have been conducted at Marshall University and the Brain Resource Center in New York using the standardized version of V/KD named, Reconsolidation of Traumatic Memories (RTM). Bourke reports that, in those studies, the protocol has removed the PTSD symptoms of nightmares and flashbacks in less than half the time of current therapies, often in fewer than two or three sessions.

Koziey and McCleod (1987) reported their experiences of treating two rape victims with a mixed technique employing Bandler's three-place dissociation in combination with hypnotic trance. An initial pre-treatment session was used to review the technique and complete an assessment package. In a second session, the authors used hypnotic trance to provide a resource state to ensure that the traumatic memories would not become overwhelming. One week later, in a second treatment session, the patients completed another set of evaluations, were hypnotized, and then the hypnotized subjects were led through the three-part dissociation. Consistent with the standard procedure, they were led through an imagined, dissociated review of the trauma in which they watched themselves, watching themselves, watching a movie of the trauma. The movie began with a still image of the client in a safe time before the traumatic event, projected on an imaginary screen. The experience ended with a safe place after the trauma with each of the clients merging with their own dissociated identities and sharing the learnings from their experience. Unspecified measures of 28 dependent variables showed significant changes in pre–post comparisons with near-total abatement of symptoms in one of the subjects.

Muss (1991, 2002) reports having used the technique first with 19 police officers who met DSM-III diagnostic criteria for PTSD, and, later, with all manner of traumatized persons (Muss, 2002). In nearly all of the 19 police cases, he reports remission of symptoms. He provides no control conditions and few details of the study, however, in long-term follow-ups (three months to three years) in 15 of the 19 cases, he reports a complete absence of intrusive imagery. Crucially, as noted by Andreas, Muss indicates that the technique is appropriate to clients whose primary symptoms are experienced as intense, suddenly arising experiences of the trauma, usually experienced as flashbacks or panic reactions (Andreas, personal communication, 2008).

Hossack and Bentall (1996) treated five subjects with a combination of guided visualizations, Jacobsen's deep-muscle relaxation and two sessions of the VK/D protocol. Although one of the five subjects was unable to complete the visualizations associated with the VK/D procedure, three of the four completers reported significant reduction of intrusive images and were able to return to normal life activities. A fifth participant began with such low levels of symptoms that an effect could not be verified.

Guy and Guy report that the technique (the rewind technique) was applied to 30 people between 2000 and 2002. All were diagnosed with PTSD or partial PTSD. Participants were interviewed ten days post-treatment. Forty percent adjudged their improvement as extremely successful, 53 percent as successful and seven percent as acceptable. None rated the treatment either as poor or as a failure (Guy and Guy, 2003).

Utuza et al. (2012) applied the rewind technique to 23 survivors of the East Rwanda genocide. The subjects consisted of 11 males and 13 females who scored above 34 on the Impact of Event Scale (IES). The subjects were treated using Muss' modification of the V/KD protocol in a group setting. Instructions for the protocol were presented in English with simultaneous translation into Kinya-Rwandan. Of the 24 original participants, 21 completed the re-evaluation at two weeks post-treatment. Of those, 18 had decreased scores, one subject remained the same and two others experienced an increase in symptoms. The pre-test mean score on the IES was 38.5 and the mean post-test score for the 18 who improved was 15.14. Researchers concluded that the group implementation of the V/KD could be a useful tool for the treatment of PTSD where vast numbers of traumatized people are beyond the reach of treatment on a one-to-one basis.

While the anecdotal reports are abundant, well-controlled, and well-designed, studies are limited or lacking. Of the four studies discussed here, none is randomized, all lack control groups and two of the four rely on significant variants of the practice as described here. While it might be noted that these are typical of the shortcomings of reports of clinical interventions, they leave much to be desired in terms of studies that might validate the technique.

Koziey and McLeod (1987) use the central elements of the technique in the context of a hypnotic trance. They indicate that for one patient who began with 15 of 28 clinical measures elevated above normal, 18 of the 28 measures were reduced in a significant manner. Much of that change (11 measures) was reported after the hypnosis session, and the rest three weeks after the V/KD sessions. Substantially similar results were reported for the other patient. She began with elevated scores in 16 of the measures. Nine of those measures decreased significantly after the hypnosis session. After the V/KD session, nine scores were significantly affected.

Koziey and McLeod (p. 279) indicate that they used the following clinical measures:

> The assessment package consisted of the SCL-90-R (Derogatis, 1983), the Veronen-Kilpatrick Modified Fear Survey (MFS-II) (Veronen and Kilpatrick, 1983), the Profile of Moods States (POMS) (McNair et al., 1981), and the State-Trait Anxiety Inventory, Form Y: self-Evaluation questionnaire (STAI) (Spielberger, 1993).

Muss provides little in the way of detail. However, his rewind method corresponds well with the procedure outlined here. Although he describes the technique as subject to significant modifications, those modifications appear to be practice sessions in which the client is trained to do the basic procedures before dealing with the traumatic event and well-scripted variants of the technique for use with survivors and first responders (Muss, 1991).

While he reports that 15 of his 19 police subjects were symptom-free at follow-up, there is little in the way of evaluative criteria provided. He indicates in a later document (Muss, 2002) that he used the Impact of Events

Scale for assessing pre- and post-symptom intensity, but it appears that the initial study relied on evaluator assessments and patient reports.

Hossack and Bentall's (1996) report of five patients used a multiple-baseline (wait-condition) control, and provides data for well-established, valid measures of general psychological status, PTSD symptoms, and depression. The following measures were used to assess general psychopathology at intake: the General Health Questionnaire (GHQ-30) (Goldberg et al., 1978), and the Symptom Check List 90-Revised (SCL-90R) (Derogatis, 1977). The Impact of Event Scale (IES) (Horowitz et al., 1979) was administered at intake, immediately post-treatment, one month post-treatment, and three months after the last treatment contact. During each weekly therapy session subjects completed the Hospital Anxiety and Depression scale (HAD) (Zigmond and Snaith, 1983). Their implementation, however, like Koziey and McLeod's, departs significantly from the standard protocol described here in that it included two sessions of guided visualization and Jacobsen deep muscle relaxation before the V/KD protocol was implemented. These authors provide detailed measures showing symptom reduction on all measures for three of the five patients over time. One patient seems to have received no benefit from the treatment. They ascribe that patient's failure to an inability to complete the necessary imaginal tasks. In examining their results, however, Hossack and Bentall indicate that changes in symptomatology did not occur gradually but suddenly, immediately after the V/KD sessions. For this reason, they attributed the change to the V/KD protocol and not to the other elements of the treatment.

Utuza et al. (2012) report a clinical application without control executed in a group setting through the intermediary of a simultaneous translator. Unfortunately, their only measure was the IES but they did report significant pre–post differences in mean scores. They offer no explanation for the three subjects who either worsened or experienced no change.

Although all of the authors cited recommend the V/KD protocol as worthy of further consideration, the results in two cases are ambiguous as implementations of the protocol. By significantly deviating from the standard protocol, the studies of Koziey and McLeod and Hossack and Bentall make it difficult to determine the source of the observed change. Despite Hossack and Bentall's affirmation that the V/KD protocol was the effective agent, the use of guided visualization and relaxation techniques make it objectively difficult to identify the source of the change. Despite the paucity of information provided in his 1991 publication, Muss' later (2002) full description of his method suggests that his results arise unambiguously from the V/KD.

Table 2.1 summarizes the published research.

Table 2.1 Treatment studies of the VK/D (rewind, RTM) protocol

Study	Treatments	Sample	Number and length of treatments	Outcome measures	Effect sizes	Comments
Koziey and Macleod, 1997	Hypnosis + V/K D	2 rape victims	4 sessions 2 treatment sessions	SCL-90-R MFS-II POMS STAI	N/A	Clinical report. No control. Unspecified but significant improvement in multiple measures.
Muss, 1991	V/K D (Rewind technique)	19 police officers diagnosed with PTSD	3 sessions (avg)	Personal reports 2 years post Tx.	N/A	Clinical report. No Control. 15 of 19 return to work and report elimination of intrusive images and thoughts.
Hossack and Bentall, 1996	2× JDMR 2× V/KD	5 males diagnosed with PTSD	4 sessions	GHQ-30 SCL-90-R IES, HAD Diaries and personal interviews post Tx.	N/A	Wait-condition control. Two patients showed complete cessation of symptoms. One showed decreased IES scores but continuing intrusive thoughts. One could not imagine the procedure. One had weak symptoms from outset and showed little change.
Utuza et al., 2012	V/KD (Rewind technique)	11 males, 13 females IES scores >34	1 session	IES	N/A	Clinical report. No control. 21 subjects completed pre and post evaluations. Pretest IES, Mean = 38.5). 18/21 scored below cutoff at post-test (mean =15.14) $p<.001$

Notes:
Treatments: V/KD, Visual Kinesthetic Dissociation Protocol; JDMR, Jacobsen Deep Muscle Relaxation.
Measures: SCL-90-R, Symptom Checklist-90 Revised; MFS-II, Modified Fear Survey; POMS, Profile of Moods States; STAI, State-Trait Anxiety Inventory; IES, Impact of Events Scale; GHQ-30, General Health Questionnaire; HAD, Hospital Anxiety and Depression Scale.

Extinction has traditionally been held to be the tool of choice for the treatment of PTSD. Foa and her colleagues have indicated that in its various forms, from desensitization through imaginal and *in-vivo* modalities, exposure is the most well researched and most highly regarded of treatments for PTSD and, in combination with cognitive behavioral interventions or supplements, it represents the scientific treatment of choice (Foa et al., 2000; Foa and Meadows, 1997a,b; Rothbaum and Davis, 2003; Wessa and Flor, 2007).

Mechanisms

Bandler (1985) suggested that the mechanism underlying the change in behavior associated with the use of the V/KD protocol was related to the process of dissociation; that somehow the memories were rewritten in a dissociated rather than an associated form. He also suggested that other memory structures could be rewritten as in his change history technique. He was, however, unable to specify a more precise mechanism.

Foa and Kozack (1986), in their discussion of the treatment of PTSD and its relationship to memory structures, likewise suggest that, in an effective treatment for PTSD, the memory must be rewritten by adding information to the memory schema that effectively changes its meaning. Relying on exposure models, they point to extinction as a probable candidate for the mechanism. However, extinction does not rewrite the memory; it provides what is ultimately a temporary alternate association that blocks the original memory. Because extinction mechanisms are impermanent by their nature, the treatments are often subject to decay.

Extinction is a classical conditioning phenomenon in which a conditioned response, after multiple unreinforced trials, seems to disappear. Extinction does not affect the original memory structure, but creates a new memory that is associated with the same circumstance. Extinction memories have some ability to block the expression of the original memory but they do not change it. In extinction, the original memory is masked, not changed (Bouton, 2004; Bouton and Moody, 2004).

Extinction, especially as it is applied to traumatic memories is problematic in that extinction memories are subject to decay so that spontaneous recovery, the return of the original memory, is almost assured. Extinction also depends heavily upon context. The new memory that masks the original experience is often limited to the specific kinds of circumstances in which the new learning occurred; extinction memories do not generalize easily to other contexts. These problems have plagued PTSD treatments based on exposure and the extinction mechanism (Gray and Liotta, 2011; Schiller et al., 2010). Extinction patients typically have poor adjustment, recurrence of symptoms over time, and are generally in need of supplementary treatment. All of the hallmarks of extinction, spontaneous recovery, contextual renewal, reinstatement, and rapid re-acquisition characterize their post-treatment experience. The V/KD protocol provides symptom abatement that does not manifest the classical indicia of extinction-based behavioral interventions and that seem to strengthen over time (Bouton, 2004; Bouton and Moody, 2004; Dillon and Pizzagalli, 2007; Massad and Hulsey, 2006; Rescorla, 1988; Vervliet, 2008).

Gray and Liotta (2012) suggest a neural mechanism that appears to explain the results achieved with the V/KD protocol. They suggest that the protocol invokes a memory mechanism known as reconsolidation. Briefly, whenever a relatively permanent memory is evoked, the same processes of protein synthesis that encoded it in long-term memory are re-activated and render the memory subject to change. If the memory re-traumatizes the patient or the original event recurs, the memory is strengthened. When the experience of the memory is interrupted so that the client is not re-traumatized, or the original events do not reoccur, the continuing protein synthesis allows the memory network to incorporate new elements, effectively rewriting the memory. The memory rewrite happens on the level of systems or schemas so that the new information, in this case, dissociation, active participation, control of the original perception (change of colour, sequence, association/dissociation, and distance) is incorporated into the structure of the memory that evokes the traumatic experience. As a result, the memory is changed by the incorporation of new information; as predicted by Bandler and by Foa and Kozack.

Although much of the work on reconsolidation has been done on animal subjects, there is a growing body of data that confirms that memory in humans, even long-standing memories are rendered labile or malleable when re-activated and that during that malleable period, the memory can be significantly changed. There is growing evidence that a reminder of an older learned association (e.g. a traumatic event), presented briefly before the acquisition of new information (e.g. the V/KD protocol) leads to the incorporation of the new information into the older memory (Forcato et al., 2007, 2009; Hupbach et al., 2007, 2009, 2008; Kindt and Soeter, 2009). Recent research with human subjects indicates that the reconsolidation window begins about ten minutes after presentation of the reminder stimulus and closes within six hours (Schiller et al., 2010; Schiller and Phelps, 2011).

The mechanism applied to the process

As noted above, the technique begins with a short-term activation of the traumatic experience. The experience is monitored by the clinician to ensure that it is marked by significant changes in physiology. This calibration ensures that there is a full, but not overwhelming, activation of the event. Here, full activation does not imply flooding, only sufficient activation of the core memory to render it labile. Nevertheless, in order to prevent the loss of control that often accompanies PTSD symptoms, the client is quickly distracted from the trauma and his attention returned to the present context. This not only prevents re-traumatization but it limits the activation of the memory to a temporal window that is appropriate to reconsolidation (Akirav and Maroun, 2006; Alberini, 2005; Foa and Kozak, 1986; Hupbach et al., 2008; LeBar and Phelps, 1998; Riccio et al., 2006).

This foreshortening of exposure is crucial to the initiation of memory labilization that allows for reconsolidative memory modification. If the traumatic revivification lasts too long, the patient may be re-traumatized. According to Pedreira et al. (2004), reconsolidation is not possible without the termination of the conditioned stimulus—the fear-evoking stimulus. The fear-evoking context must be terminated before new learning can occur.

Having awakened the traumatic memory, it now becomes subject to reinforcement or modification, depending upon the immediate stimulus context. Remembering that the memory is still active in the background through its intentional revivification and its presence in the semantic context, the VK/D model now provides several experiences of dissociation: the dissociative anchor, the dissociated safe representation on the imagined movie screen, and the client's floating out of the body to view the viewer who is sitting in the theater watching the screen. Insofar as the memory is dissociated, and is not actively reinforcing the fear response, its novel stimulus properties may preferentially support memory updating through reconsolidation (Pedreira et al., 2004).

At this point, the first of several layers of active intervention in the structure of the traumatic memory begins. The dissociated black-and-white movie provides a multi-levelled opportunity for reshaping the memory. First, it is triply dissociated (Dietrich, 2000; Hossack and Bentall, 1996; Koziey and McLeod, 1987; Muss, 2002). Second, insofar as it is a voluntary re-experience of the trauma, the context is restructured as voluntary rather than involuntary. This is what various authors have described as prescribing the symptom. It is also a direct remedy for the loss of control described by Foa as a significant contributor to PTSD symptomatology (Bandler and Grinder, 1979; Erickson and Rossi, 1989; Foa and Meadows, 1997; Haley, 1973). In this context, the *novelty* of symptom prescription may enhance the reconsolidation response, as noted by Pedreira et al. (2004) and also by Lee (2009). These authors indicate that unexpected stimulus properties—novelty—support the reconsolidative updating of memory content. Third, because the movie is viewed in black and white, its emotional impact is further decreased (Bandler, 1985; Bandler and MacDonald, 1987; Kringelbach, 2005). In theory, all of these elements are incorporated into the structure of the original memory.

Once the client has successfully completed the dissociated review, another layer of new meanings is added to the memory through the reverse, associated rewind of the memory. At this point, attempts have been made to recall the affect associated with the traumatic event and, by now, it should already be difficult. This rewind phase constitutes a significant restructuring of the memory. The associated reversal of the experience leaves the client with a subjective memory of the problem, "undoing itself." This is performed quickly. The speed takes advantage of the narrow window of memory lability, and the heightened salience accorded to fast moving, multisensory stimuli (Bandler, 1985; Simons et al., 2000).

As with many of the elements of this intervention, novelty may be a significant element in its efficacy. It has already been noted how the unexpected features of the intervention may support the reconsolidation mechanism. The complexity of this part of the intervention may also support further modification of the experience through simple cognitive overload. Given the limited capacity of short-term memory, the simple fact of learning and executing the reverse rehearsal may not leave sufficient capacity in short-term memory to access the fear response. It might be considered that cognitive overload is layered into the memory and provides a neutral emotional overlay (Miller, 1956; Pedreira et al., 2004).

After completing the multisensory, high speed, reversed, imaginal exposure, the client is again debriefed and every effort is made to re-access the trauma response. If the intervention has been successful, the client may retain declarative access to the event, but without the strong negative affect that characterizes the symptoms of PTSD (Andreas and Andreas, 1989; Bandler, 1993; Dilts and DeLozier, 2000; Kindt et al., 2009; Muss, 1991).

In some cases, an imagined restructuring of the original event is added to the protocol. In such cases the effect may be as simple as layering-in another set of experiences that are incompatible with the trauma. Moreover, the addition of modified memories reflects one of the standard reappraisal methods of cognitive regulation strategies. Such interventions are known to increase activity in the ventro-medial prefrontal cortex, which exercises a modulatory influence on the amygdala. Insofar as the emotional impact of the traumatizing memory has already been significantly modified, the new version of the traumatic event may serve to provide a coherent narrative for the now, non-traumatizing memory (Diamond et al., 2007; Hartley and Phelps, 2009; Williams et al., 2006).

Because the experience, when originally evoked is marked by significant changes in physiology, it meets Foa and Kozak's suggestion that an appropriate intervention be rooted in a full activation of the event. Here, it must be again emphasized that full activation does not imply flooding, only sufficient activation of the core memory to activate the reconsolidation process and to render the original memory subject to change. Nevertheless, in order to prevent the impairment of cognitive capacities detailed by Diamond et al. (2007), the client's attention is returned to the present context, as quickly as possible. This prevents re-traumatization and limits the activation of the memory to a temporal window that is appropriate to reconsolidation, but too brief to support extinction (Akirav and Maroun, 2006; Alberini, 2005; Foa and Kozak, 1986; Hupbach et al., 2008; LeBar and Phelps, 1998; Riccio et al., 2006).

This foreshortening of exposure may be crucial to the initiation of memory labilization that allows for reconsolidative memory modification. According to Pedreira et al. (2004), neither reconsolidation nor extinction is possible without the termination of the conditioned stimulus. According to their research, a stimulus offset is required to effect significant change. Both processes require the termination of the fear context before new learning can occur.

On one more level, we note that in previous human studies of reconsolidation in the treatment of conditioned fear, a failure to appreciate the multi-systemic nature of memory may have allowed top-down episodic memories of fear to regenerate fear conditioning centred in the amygdala (Schiller and Phelps, 2011). Here, the multi-sensory, multi-systemic nature of the intervention provides a link, not to a simple conditioned stimulus (CS) fear-evoking event (UCS) association, but to the much broader experience of fear in a whole-life context.

Case study

A recent case study was provided by William A. McDowell, PhD, Professor Emeritus and Chair of Counselling, Marshall University, Huntington, WV (William, McDowall, personal communication, July 9, 2010). It involved a 30-year-old veteran of the Iraq war. The Veterans Administration had diagnosed him with PTSD and he reported to the NLP therapist after more than a year of standard treatment from the Veterans Administration including individual and group psychotherapy with no abatement of symptoms. At the time that he came to the NLP-trained therapist, he was reporting the following symptoms: flashbacks, nightmares, high-anxiety while driving (unable to let others drive him, panicked by large trucks near him, often forcing him to pull off the road). He also reported a fear of crowds and enclosed spaces (restaurants, classrooms) where he felt he had to be near an exit with a clear view of the entire space. He also reported some anger problems at home and an inability to have the doors unlocked. The patient minimized family problems but his wife reported that the family was experiencing severe difficulty.

The client was seen for three, one hour, video-recorded sessions with a three-day break between sessions. Pre- and post-tests using the PTSD Checklist (PCL) (Weathers et al., 1993, 1994) were completed before treatment, at the beginning of the second treatment session, after the third session and 30 days post-treatment. Pre-treatment scores on the PCL were in the 90 percent range. After the first treatment session, they were reduced to 30 percent. All symptoms disappeared after the third treatment. Thirty days post-treatment the symptom scores were still zero and no symptoms were reported by the client.

After the second session, the client reported no more nightmares and abatement of all symptoms by the end of treatment. In order to behaviorally evaluate the client's post-treatment improvement, after the last session *he was driven* to a crowded, noisy McDonald's restaurant and ate, sitting with his back to the door. He reported having no anxiety with someone else driving him and was able to eat without being concerned for the exits. A video record of the excursion validates his visible physiological responses and demeanour.

He and his wife were interviewed together at the last session and in a one-month follow-up, during which he reported being able to allow his wife to drive and experienced no anxiety while driving near large trucks. He also reported being anxiety-free while in crowded places.

For independent verification, the client's family was asked to substantiate his recovery. Three months after termination of treatment, his wife reported that her husband no longer checked the locks in the house more than once, was able to let her drive, and no longer demonstrated the high anxiety and anger at home that he had before treatment. In her words, "I feel like I have my husband like he was before he left for Iraq."

Research directions

This analysis leads to several falsifiable predictions and diagnostic indicators of the underlying mechanism in PTSD treatments. Because the mechanism outlined here depends upon the process of reconsolidation, interventions for PTSD may be behaviorally evaluated in terms of their results to determine whether extinction or reconsolidation is operative. Where extinction mechanisms have been invoked, spontaneous recovery, contextual renewal, reinstatement, and rapid reacquisition will characterize the post-treatment period and further treatment will be necessary in order to deal with the intrusive elements of the disorder (Bouton, 2004; Bouton and Moody, 2004; Dillon and Pizzagalli, 2007; Massad and Hulsey, 2006; Rescorla, 1988; Vervliet, 2008). Where reconsolidative mechanisms have been appropriately marshalled, as in the V/KD protocol, the memories will be transformed, rendered inaccessible, and, if accessible to declarative and episodic recall, they will have been rendered non-traumatizing. The resulting change in experience will not be subject to spontaneous recovery, contextual renewal, reinstatement, and rapid reacquisition (Cao et al., 2008; Duvarci and Nader, 2004; Forcato et al., 2007; Kindt et al., 2009; Lee et al., 2006).

These predictions can be tested behaviorally in terms of treatment outcomes in an experimental setting in which PTSD patients are randomly assigned to a VK/D treatment group, a standard extinction protocol group, and a wait-group control. They should be evaluated for the presence of PTSD using any of a number of highly reliable and well-validated instruments for the presence of PTSD as defined by the DSM criteria. Post-treatment testing, employing the same instrument(s) used at intake, should occur at termination, and at one and three months post-treatment.

In line with the exclusion criteria emphasized by both Muss (1991) and Andreas (personal communication, 2008), subjects who have developed significant symptoms beyond the root symptoms of PTSD, such as substance use disorders and severe interpersonal deficits, should be eliminated from the study. In light of the need to eliminate pre-existing conditions that could confound the results, all subjects should be subjected to psychiatric evaluations. Persons with pre-existing Axis One disorders and significant personality disorders should be excluded from the study.

It would be expected that the VK/D group would show significant symptom remission at one- and three-month follow-ups with continuing improvement over time. The extinction treatment group would be expected to show initial symptom improvement with some decline in adjustment over time as the concomitants of extinction: spontaneous recovery, contextual renewal, reinstatement, and rapid re-acquisition manifest themselves. After follow-up, in which they would be expected to perform least well, the wait-group controls would be offered treatment using the modality of their choice.

Future research into this technique should look toward large-scale trials of the protocol in the treatment of PTSD. These studies should follow the recommendations for well-controlled studies set forth by the International Society for Traumatic Stress Studies (Foa et al., 2000). The international troops returning from service in various theatres of war could provide a significant test population for this already established and relatively unknown treatment. There remain hundreds of thousands of war victims, refugees from earthquakes and tsunamis who would provide a significant pool of possible subjects.

Follow-up studies and surveys to take advantage of existing practitioner evidence compiled by NLP practitioners would also be instructive. Such follow-up studies could provide crucial long-term reports of the incidence of post-treatment relapse that would be capable of falsifying the proposal that the technique is rooted in reconsolidation rather than extinction.

Summary

This chapter has made an in-depth examination of an NLP intervention (VK/D) that many have found successful for treating PTSD. A neurological mechanism that explains the observed results and why they differ from standard extinction protocols was also examined. Most particularly, the discussion focused upon the process of reconsolidation, which may underlie the effectiveness of these interventions. Directions for further research have also been outlined in detail.

3 Other therapeutic applications

Lisa Wake, Lucas Derks, Przemysław Ł. Turkowski

There are many studies that consider other therapeutic applications of NLP. This chapter will only review published studies and will exclude studies included in other chapters. We also provide clinical case studies in some instances.

General psychotherapy

Early research into NLP as a psychotherapy was heralded by the publication of the Genser-Medlitsch and Schutz (1997, 2004) paper which reported a controlled trial with 55 NLPt clients with a range of DSM diagnoses. This study critically acclaimed for the study of NLP under the guidelines for evidence- based practice.

The study focused on the following areas:

- Is NLPt immediately effective?
- Are there significant interactions between group membership and non-specific time trends?
- Are positive changes still present at six-month follow-up?
- How do the three variables: duration, gender and age interact with the major dependent and independent variables?

Not only has the study's design been critically acclaimed, but it presents extensive data analysis and discussion of the observed results. Measurements were taken at pre, post and six months after the intervention. Measurement tools included the Individual Discomfort List, the IPC questionnaire on locus of control, the Self-Report Symptom Inventory and the Stress Management Questionnaire. Socio-demographic data was also collected. The authors discuss each of the relevant variables and observe that the control group generally reported lower levels of symptoms at recruitment. The positive effect of NLPt was enhanced when gender and length of therapy were taken into consideration with more positive effect (60 per cent) in more of the clinical subscales demonstrated where clients had longer time in therapy. Men showed more positive treatment effects in 40 per cent of the scales compared to women, and 63.15 per cent of younger clients in the 19–35 age range experienced greater effect than the older age group. Comparisons between effects observed in treatment and control groups were significant ($p < .05$). The authors provide a descriptive and non-interpretative summary of these findings. The authors measured effect longitudinally, at six months post-treatment and found that 88 per cent (22 scales) had remained stable over this period of time. While most scales remained stable at follow-up, further reductions in social insecurity and an increase in aggression were observed. The authors do not comment on the change in aggression scores.

A range of interventions were utilised within the therapy, all of which are standard NLP techniques. The authors indicate that the therapists were either trained NLPt therapists in private practice or students who had nearly completed their training. Protocols consisted of standard NLP interventions and were used in accordance with the therapists' best judgement. The treatments were not manualised. Techniques used are listed in percentage-used order with reframing (60 per cent), outcome frame (56 per cent) and parts work (34 per cent) being the most commonly used tools. As research in the field has developed, it is of interest to note that in this study, sub-modalities (10 per cent), trauma (six per cent) and phobia work (six per cent) are some of the least used tools.

The authors conclude that 76 per cent of clients experienced positive changes in 25 of 33 dimensions including self-perception, reduction in drug use, and reduction in anxiety, paranoid thoughts, social insecurity, compulsive behaviours and depression.

A more recent case control study was conducted by Stipancic *et al.* (2010) into the effects of NLPt on psychological difficulties and quality of life. The study identified two specific outcomes, the short- and long-term effects of NLPt on clinical symptoms and the short- and long-term effects on quality of life. The study utilized a wait-list control group who were told that they would receive therapy after three months, when they would be measured again and then offered therapy. The study group were measured pre, post and at five months. The authors discuss the ethical and research bias implications of using a wait-list control group. The study included 106 clients who were recruited through word of mouth, attending lectures and via the internet. Clients were assigned alternately to each group, with 54 in the therapy group and 52 in the control group. Assessments were conducted using the Structured Clinical Interview for DSM-IV Personality Disorders (SCID II) for clinical symptoms and the Croatian Scale of Quality of Life (KVZ) for quality-of-life measures. There was a significant decrease in clinical symptoms and increase in quality of life for the study group, with effect sizes ($n=54$) of .65 SCID II, .65 KVZ predictor variable, .51 KVZ criterion variable when measured T1-T2, and, 1.09 SCID II, .69 KVZ predictor variable and .73 KVZ criterion variable at T1-T3 five-month follow-up. The authors propose that these findings are equivalent to the effects of Cognitive Behavioural Therapy

(CBT). The authors do not comment on the therapeutic methodology used specifically other than 'the use of standardised, goal oriented questions, different intervention methods were used depending on the clients' symptoms, which followed a well-defined theoretical system as it is taught in NLPt courses using the programme of the Austrian Training Center' (2010, p. 42).

There are some studies that provide case examples of therapeutic interventions using NLP. Field (1990) reports two cases using dissociative techniques including anchoring and three-part dissociation for one client with severe anxiety, and a client with anger and negativity. The author suggests that both techniques were effective in ending hyperactive episodes in the first client and integrating feelings and knowledge into personal consciousness with the second client.

Weaver (2009) reports on the use of the CORE Systems Research Tool to assess the effectiveness of neurolinguistic psychotherapy with clients seen in private practice. A total of 41 clients were assessed, with the author using data from 33 clients in the data analysis. This study can be considered practice-based evidence with an effective commentary given on some of the findings. The author uses no form of randomisation and does not report the intervention used. The author concludes that clients experience a reduction in problems after an average of seven weekly sessions of psychotherapy.

Wake (2009, 2010) conducts a grounded theory study of NLPt and makes connections to the relationship between how some NLPt processes are utilised by therapists and their similarity to object relations theory. Her later work (2010) brings NLPt therapy into line with other brief therapy approaches and considers how this can be used to work with attachment disorders.

There are a number of case-report-based studies that support the use of NLP in therapy specifically for those experiencing relationship challenges. Davis and Davis (1983) report on their utilisation of NLP therapy with married couples. They give an overview of the techniques used which include dissociated state rehearsal for future oriented behaviours. Baddeley (1992) also discusses the use of a combination of Ericksonian hypnosis, analytical hypnotherapy and NLP as an intervention in marital and relationship counselling. He argues through three case reports that these processes are more potent than traditional counselling. A case report is also given by Zika (1985) where he identifies a model referred to as transformational hypnotherapy, combining NLP and analytic therapy models within a holistic framework. He proposes that this offers a positive therapeutic model for maladaptive behaviour. Bertoli (2002) provides a new model of divorce therapy in a project for those in trauma and crisis. The therapeutic model is based on a combination of NLP and emotionally focused therapy with the aim of replacing attachment to the ex-spouse and re-engaging in order to develop new interactional patterns as co-parents.

Vianna et al. (2006) conducted a phenomenological study with five groups of women who were receiving support as part of a domestic violence project.

All of the women had been raped. The purpose of the workshops was to foster self-esteem. The author used a combination of psychodrama and NLP techniques, although the study does not report on the specific interventions offered within the workshop. Thematic analysis was utilised for the evaluation, which demonstrated that attendees were able to reflect on and develop a change in attitude and perceive new roads ahead. The author reports that three of the women went on to attend a university and were motivated to take the self-esteem workshops into their local communities.

NLPt has also been used in family therapy, utilising NLP as an outcome-oriented approach. A case study is presented by Shelden and Shelden (1989) demonstrating their work with an adult male patient who had been sexually abused by his mother as a child. They discuss the utilisation of NLP and biofeedback to alter identified unuseful patterns of behaviour and to focus on a future desired state.

Juhnke *et al.* (2008) provide a clinical case experience summary of their work using an adapted form of the NLP swish pattern to support couple survivors of suicide and parasuicide. A comprehensive description of the technique is given, along with a transcript of a therapy session. The authors conclude that the pattern is useful when supporting couples who have survived a child's suicide or parasuicide. They also make recommendations that the pattern should not be used when the client has severe psychopathology. The authors conclude that the pattern provides clients with an opportunity to reconnect with memories of their loved one in a more positive way.

Brandis' (1986) experimental intervention utilised the Parental Provocation Inventory and the Parents' Report to measure changes in parental anger responses following NLP. Brandis describes a specific intervention that utilises anchoring. Anchoring is an NLP technique that is grounded in classical conditioning theory. It creates stimulus-response (SR) linkages to access specific internal states. The process also enables the collapsing of current SR linkages to create a different neurological response, leading to a change in state. Brandis reports that resource anchoring, where the parent was taught to self-apply the anchor and collapse anchors, were both used in this study. Results of Kruskal-Wallis' One-way Analysis of Variance (ANOVA) and Eta (η) coefficients showed no significance, and post-hoc analysis demonstrated a strong experimental effect in half of the experimental group. Upon further investigation this result was attributed to the utilisation of the resource anchor.

There are some studies that have implications for neurolinguistic psychotherapy where indications are given for the use of the technology in improving quality of life and self-actualisation. Duncan *et al.* (1990) utilised the Personal Orientation Inventory to measure development towards self-actualisation in a group of NLP trainees following a 21-day residential NLP training programme. Self-actualising individuals were identified as those who became more present-oriented, more inner-directed, more flexible, self-aware and responsive to others. Significant positive changes were observed in nine of 12 scales for 18 trainees, and 10 of 12 scales for 36 trainees at the end of the training.

Morin's (2011, 2007, 2005, 2004, 1990) writings on the role of inner speech, self-awareness of internal state and internal processes, and the notion of self-modelling provides encouraging insight into the effectiveness of some of the NLP methodology, particularly those areas that encourage self-reflection and awareness of internal processes and states and external behaviour.

Unobtrusive measures; a case of NLP

Since the middle of the 1980s only a few universities invested in the testing of NLP's validity. However, among NLP users there seems to be little doubt about the effectiveness of their work. They tend to argue that NLP practice shows its effectiveness by the briefness of the therapy, through many client referrals, the low costs of the treatment, the wide range of NLP applications, the worldwide spread, the great number of trained practitioners and NLP institutes, the clear influence of NLP on other brands of therapy and the growing demand for training. Little quantitative data exists to support this argument. Convinced practitioners do not feel any pressure to prove NLP's value to an academic audience. This results in NLP being rather popular, while at the same time maintaining a low (academic) status (Hollander, 1999).

Undertaking serious studies for testing NLP's effectiveness is complicated by the fact that NLP is a package of hundreds of techniques and methods. This makes the standardization of an experimental treatment protocol that matches NLP's reality rather difficult. By contrast, EMDR could be tested relatively easily since this consists of just one single procedure.

In the following case report one of NLP's techniques for dealing with post-traumatic stress disorder is provided and could be evaluated under circumstances that would convince most therapists. Yet it is cases like these that reduce the urgency to invest in a more formal evaluation. However, a sample of similar cases could provide valuable evidence based upon their unobtrusive measures (Webb *et al.*, 2000).

War veteran, by Lucas Derks

> In 1998 I worked with a client called Rob on issues about his career. He mentioned that he was raised in a family strongly influenced by his father's war experiences. This upbringing had interfered with his self-esteem at work.
>
> Two years later I was phoned by Jan, who introduced himself as Rob's father. He mentioned that Rob had done well after the session with me. Now he was looking for assistance himself. Although Jan lived 100 miles away, we made an appointment.

Jan appeared to be a gentle grandfather of 72. He explained that he was aged 18 in 1945, when the Second World War came to its conclusion. In the next year, a war of independence broke out in the Dutch East Indies (now Indonesia). He volunteered and was confronted with guerrilla warfare.

Two years later Jan returned utterly unharmed to Holland, at a moment when the country had already given up on its colony. His situation was similar to that of many Vietnam veterans at the end of that war. These veterans received little respect and their stories were avoided. Jan found a job and a wife and together they raised a family.

It was only 50 years later (in 2000) that he started to suffer from sleepless nights, in which he was tormented by the flashbacks of two specific wartime events:

1 He had been raped by a superior while he was standing on guard one night.
2 He had taken an active part in the killing (murdering) of an unarmed Indonesian.

I did not mention to Jan that sexual abuse among men had proven to be a difficult type of trauma, since it tends to undermine self-worth and comes with shame and guilt. Just as being a murderer is very hard to bear. Instead I created an atmosphere of acceptance and I suggested that many people overcame such experiences.

Jan did not give many details, nor did I ask for them. As an experienced NLP therapist I do not expect any change from the detailed exploration and emotional expression of traumatic memories. However, I had already verified the idea that it is the application of latent resources to these issues that is helpful in overcoming them. The whole of the NLP trauma approach is aimed at having the client find the coping skills that he failed to have during the historic traumatic event, then let him imagine using these skills in the traumatic situation, and link this *made-up history* to the present and the future.

I instructed Jan to envision the trauma 1) as seen from a distance. Next, we explored the coping skills he was lacking at the time, and also the resources that the perpetrator failed to have; these shortcomings led him to misbehave in order to satisfy his needs. Jan had no difficulty with exploring all of that and could stay out of the emotions at the same time.

It was immediately clear to Jan that his inability to stand his ground within a hierarchical relationship had been his major obstacle in keeping himself from becoming a victim. The difference in age and formal rank, within the insecure context of war, made that difficult as did the serious threats made against him if he refused or talked about it. These warnings were realistic in an atmosphere where soldiers died on a daily basis. All of that had made resisting his superior close to impossible for him. On the other hand, the perpetrator lacked respect for the integrity of others and failed to have a way to deal with his sexuality in an acceptable manner within the armed forces. The army as an institution also needed some additional skills to deal with sexual variations among its ranks.

Technically speaking, Jan was sitting while visualising his timeline. From this position he observed his younger self during the traumatic episode from a distance, just detailed enough to know what capacities were missing.

All these failing capabilities were named and listed. When Jan was asked to search for moments in his life where he did possess these skills (one by one), it proved relatively easy for him to find clear examples of these. In fact, life's experience had already changed him into a far more assertive person. Next, he stepped into concrete examples of using these resources as he had experienced them in unrelated instances in his recent life. When fully reconnected with these, mostly strong positive memories, he projected them into the visualization of the trauma. Transferring these various capabilities in his imagination to his younger self was easy for Jan. In addition to that he was helped to imagine supporting his younger self as a victim (just after it happened). He was also able to encourage his earlier self to be self-accepting and to remain proud of himself, even though he had gone through this situation. He also imagined transferring capabilities to the army at large (in a fantasy about a pre-war epoch) and sending resources to his superior at the time he was a baby – aiming at providing him with a higher standard of ethics. We also dealt with some of Jan's limiting beliefs.

All that work was accomplished relatively quickly. It was all founded upon Jan's creation of a very clear image of how he would have coped with this situation if all involved had possessed the appropriate resources. The main NLP technique was the Visual Kineasthetic Dissociation Protocol (V/KD) (Bandler and Grinder, 1979) and re-imprint (Dilts *et al.*, 1990).

We only moved on when Jan was sure that his imagined solutions were sufficient to deal with the situation. Then I asked him to imagine, to go through the situation anew, as if everyone was more resourceful. The critical thing in this stage is to keep the client away from historic memories and the connected emotions. When this was successfully accomplished we took a short break.

We used a quite similar approach for the second trauma. A little less than two hours had passed before Jan signalled that he was certain that he could deal with the second memory now. We concluded the session with some chatting. Just as in many similar cases this appeared to be the last I would see of him.

However, one and a half years later he phoned me again. When he arrived at my office he told a fascinating story. The Dutch government had responded to criticism on how they had treated their veterans in the 1950s. A significant sum was designated to give them extra help. Jan had been called by a social worker who was involved in this nationwide project and she asked him, 'Do you or did you have any psychological problems related to your war experience?' Jan said that he had indeed suffered from such difficulties, and that he had seen a therapist a year ago (me) for that. The social worker asks to visit him at his home some weeks later, when she asked, 'What is the worst thing you remember about your experience in Indonesia?' Jan did not mention the two incidents that we had been working on the year before, but he remembered another event. The social worker helped Jan to remember the details and reconnect himself to the feelings. In an empathic way she encouraged him to go through it in specific detail. He expressed the emotions of fear, shame, guilt, anger and helplessness. He said that he really appreciated the attention and the care of the social worker. He also appreciated the whole gesture of a nation that finally showed gratitude for its fighting boys. However, after this meeting his sleep was disturbed by flashbacks and nightmares.

It was nice to hear from Jan that our one session the year before had worked fine and that he had been without complaints until recently. This promoted my self-confidence as a therapist and I liked the implicit sense of competition. Jan hoped we could deal with this in a similar fashion as we did one and a half years before. Jan could be easily brought to see the difficult situations from a distance. But it was plain that the memory stressed him considerably. He explained the following: they had been under infrequent, light rifle fire from an invisible enemy for about five hours. All this time Jan had been laying in a ditch, several metres from a medic that was badly injured and losing lots of blood. Jan could not make any move to come to the medic's assistance. Not even to give him water.

Because of his experience with NLP trauma treatment we could start off immediately. We explored some beliefs about his responsibility first. Then we could find better fitting resources. Again, Jan was able to recreate the incident as if he had been more resourceful. At age 73 he was creative enough to imagine the previously missing resources.

This session took about as long as the first (two hours). We parted in the knowledge that we could not predict if we would ever meet again. Jan seemed confident that the job was done.

Two years later, Jan's granddaughter phoned me with a phobic complaint. She said that when she had expressed her difficulties, her father and grandfather both had independently referred her to me. I have no memory or record of the work with the granddaughter, and this is not important for this case report.

Cases such as this are part of many therapists' practice. Not only the ones that work with NLP. To all they will be convinced of the effect of their approach.. Experimental psychologists (Bem, 1967) showed that, just like psychotherapy researchers (Hubble *et al.*, 1999), therapists, like people in general, select the evidence that supports their preferred beliefs. In an uncertain trade such as psychotherapy one needs to believe in one's method. Without the therapist believing in his work, the effect is reduced (Fuller, 1986). Thus, counter evidence is filtered out by forgetting or rationalization. When therapy works it is both the therapist and his methods that are to be congratulated. But when it fails it is the client and society that are to blame.

To me, the above means that I must have had many traumatised clients that I could not help with NLP. But since I did not keep precise records and systematic evaluations of my work, these non-successes are easily filtered out of my memories. While it is true that clinicians create favourable images of their results, we need experimental set-ups with matched control groups to judge the value of NLP. But since such testing is difficult with the full range of NLP practice, we must also include other sources of evidence.

In conclusion, the nature of NLP as a package of many techniques severely complicates designing a study that fulfils the criteria of contemporary social and medical science. The problem is mainly that the variation and sophistication in methods used in the real world of NLP practice are hard to incorporate in such a design. When the study is not realistic NLP-ers will argue it is not testing NLP.

This design difficulty does not hold for testing of the components of NLP. However when we found one NLP component to be effective, this does not allow us to draw conclusions about NLP as a whole.

A case like the one above is drawn from the memory of a therapist (me). To me it proves the value of NLP's approach for the treatment of traumas since it seems that, within four therapy hours, three difficult issues could be overcome by the client in a lasting manner. The third issue was ineffectively treated with another method, suggesting the superiority of NLP.

We need to realise ourselves that most NLP-ers convince themselves with similar anecdotal data. This does not mean that it is false, but it is not hard evidence.

In the case above I used no DSM diagnosis and no follow-up in the sense of a post-treatment inventory or a computerised client monitoring system. Nor did I make a video or audio record, so no outsiders could judge my work. Since the subjective evaluation of therapists of their own work is reputedly biased we may look for other spontaneous evidence.

In the case above one can find at least semi-unobtrusive measures that can be quantified over the three clients involved:

1 The reported absence of previously treated issues (Rob ×1, Jan ×2).
2 Clients return with yet untreated issues (Jan ×1).
3 Number of referrals (Jan ×1, granddaughter ×1).

4   The mean treatment duration per successfully treated issue (2 hours).
5   The number of appointments (Rob ×1, Jan ×2, granddaughter ×1).
6   The amount privately paid per successfully treated issue ($180).
7   The time before relapse (with Jan 1½ years, 0 for Rob and unknown for the granddaughter).

The collection of the above or similar data does not ask for a complex experimental design. It can be collected by a neutral examiner calling former clients once, two years after the last visit. This type of evidence offers alternative opportunities to test the effectiveness of a therapy. To test NLP in general, a matched (on DSM and client factors) or random sample (just a large number of cases) could be compared to a similar sample of cases treated with an already established system.

Directions for future research

There are some promising studies for the use of NLP as a psychotherapy. Weaver's study provides an effective starting point, particularly as the CORE methodology is utilised nationally across the UK and therapists are able to gain comparative data and benchmark services against the national picture. Genser-Medlitsch and Schutz' study could be repeated using measurements such as the PHQ-9 (Patient Health Questionnaire for Depression). Although NLPt as it is practised in the UK and Europe tends to be provided in a co-created relational therapeutic space, it is possible to design a research protocol to only use specific techniques within the therapy. As NLP has some similarities to CBT it is proposed that a randomised control trial is conducted to compare NLPt, CBT and a wait-group for depression. This would be a relatively easy process to design and measure, and longitudinal studies would provide evidence of the effectiveness of NLP by complete symptom resolution over time as suggested by Derks' intervention above.

From a wider psychotherapy perspective, Wake (2008) has presented a series of case studies using NLPt with a range of presenting symptoms. Additionally, Wake (2010) has proposed that NLPt meets many of the core requirements of Schore's (2003) principles of psychotherapeutic repair in clients with affect dysregulation. Wake (2011) has already commenced case studies into the effect of brief NLP interventions in adolescents with behaviours suggestive of affect dysregulation, and these studies could be extended to investigate if changes are occurring at a neurological level in the brain structures of the youngsters as a result of the intervention.

Adolescents

Wake (2011) reports on a project evaluation of a programme working with adolescents who are identified as at risk of offending behaviour. The programme consists of a two-hour workshop that utilises a number of

NLP techniques within a workbook and structured interventions. A total of 53 young people were selected and attended the programme through convenience sampling. The principle tools used were identifying values, developing internal dialogue awareness, state management and goal setting. The programme has been developed using neuroscience theory to harness the optimum conditions that present themselves at puberty to work with brain plasticity in facilitating a change in attachment relationships and develop a more coherent sense of self. The programme combines learning, emotional processing and rationalisation of emotional state, cortisol flow and right-brain to right-brain communication to create the potential for repair and growth (Chugani, 1996, Greenough and Black, 1992). The author provides a comprehensive summary of each of the tools used and how these are utilised within a neurological framework that informs the understanding of reward, punishment, awareness of behaviours, motivation and goal attainment.

The project is independently evaluated (Tope et al., 2010). A total of 26 of the 29 people who responded to the evaluation reported that they enjoyed the workshop. The authors report on a number of benefits from the workshop: improved behaviour, thinking of the future, positive outlook and changes in social activities. The authors validate the reported outcomes with a list of changes that are measurable as a result of attending the programme. Validity and reliability is discussed (Wake, 2011), especially with reference to the high ratio of youth workers to young people and use of the workshop material in an unstructured format. In conclusion, this programme provides practice-based evidence of the effectiveness of NLP interventions with this client group and is thought to 'crucially divert these kids away from the criminal justice system' (Tope et al., 2010 p. 26).

Directions for future research

As already discussed, this study could be expanded to investigate evidence of changes in brain structures using neuroimaging studies. It is also important to investigate the longitudinal effect of this intervention and whether this process reduces recidivism in this group of young people.

Asthma and allergic responses

A number of meta-analytic studies suggest that there is a correlation between psychological stress and immunological responses (Segerstrom and Miller, 2004), where specific interventions are utilised to influence coping strategies (Denson et al., 2009). The most consistent evidence offered for immune modulation appears in studies that utilise components of hypnosis and conditioning responses (Miller and Sheldon, 2001).

Witt (2003, 2008) has conducted two studies that utilise an adapted version of NLPt to test its effect on allergic responses. In his 2008 randomised study he used a NLPt treatment of Birch Pollen allergy with skin-prick stimuli of saline solution and histamine provocation as placebo and positive controls. Clear exclusion criteria were used. Psychological tests utilised were Krampen-AT-Symptom scale and Rehabilitations-Psychologische-Diagnosesystem. Interval-scale data was normally distributed using the Kolmogorov-Smirnov-Test and variance homogeneity using the Bartlett-Test allowed variance analysis. Both groups were tested at the beginning using ANOVA and a multiple t-test, and no significant differences were found.

Medicine consumption and ailments were recorded in daily diary entries. Ailments were counted ANOVA to determine if the group's ranking was normally populated and effects were measured using Mann–Whitney U and Wilcoxon Rank Sum tests. Medication consumption was counted as binary data using Chi-squared.

Results demonstrated an interesting observation in the skin-prick test. The control group were noted to have a highly significant increased difference in histamine wheal area. The author notes that these indicate that skin reactions are influenced by psychological intervention. Psychological test results demonstrated that well-being increased significantly in the study group between $t0$ and $t1$ and remained stable between $t1$ and $t2$. There was no significant increase in the control group. The analysis of variance over time showed a highly significant effect in the NLPt group. Mood of well-being showed a highly significant increase in the NLPt group $t0-t1$ and remained stable $t1-t2$. The control group remained stable $t0-t2$. The state of illness decreased significantly in the NLPt group between $t0-t1$ and again remained stable $t1-t2$. There was a decrease in the placebo group $t1-t2$ that is unexplained, although the author does discuss that some members of the placebo group were unable to cope without medication and took this in the latter days of the study period, which may have had an effect on the results. When measuring ailments, the study group showed significantly fewer symptoms. Medication use was significantly less in the study group and Chi-squared test was used to confirm that this result was not coincidental.

In the discussion, the author proposes that psychological NLPt intervention has an effect on allergy sensitivity with the author referencing psychoneuro-endocrinological research that suggests a dialogue between the immune system and the nervous system. The author concludes that 'NLPt methods seem to provide the interface between the environment and the organism and between medicine and behaviour'.

Directions for future research

Witt (2003, 2008) has laid out a comprehensive randomised study that could easily lend itself to a randomised control trial. We propose therefore that this research is conducted within a controlled environment and that it should also make the cost–benefit analysis of treating allergic conditions in this way.

Eating disorders

Eating disorders are defined as abnormal eating behaviours, usually with onset in the late teens and more common in females. There is currently no evidence for the effectiveness of NLPt with anorexia nervosa. There is one study that demonstrates its effectiveness in the management of bulimia. Bulimia is not thought to involve distorted body image and is frequently associated with mood disturbance and poor self-esteem around body shape and weight. The DSM-IV criteria note that a client with bulimia will eat in binges and will consume more food than most people would under similar circumstances and over similar time, and, the client feels that their eating is out of control. The client utilises various means to control their weight including fasting, self-induced vomiting, excessive exercise, use of laxatives, diuretics and other drugs with the aim of controlling their weight. The behaviour occurs at least twice a month and over at least three months.

Scott (1987) used the NLP technique of reframing to facilitate change in a group of clients with bulimia. Reframing is based on the work of Bateson *et al.* (1956) and Watzlawick (1978) who adapted Frankl's therapeutic approach to assist clients find meaning in their lives. Reframing provides a means to change the way we perceive a situation that then alters the meaning of the situation. All reframing involves separating intent from behaviour, e.g. a client that has binged because their mother has forgotten to send them a birthday card. This might be reframed by saying, 'Isn't it good that you recognise how important your mother is to you?' Reframing works by enabling the client to dissociate from the current emotional state and problem situation and access higher levels of non-emotional thinking.

In this study by Scott, a number of self-report variables were used to measure effectiveness of treatment. These included the number of binges and purges per week, average daily calorific intake, duration of binges and binge obsession intensity. Additional assessment tools of the Eating Disorder Inventory and the Tennessee Self-Concept Scale were also used, with clients completing self-report journals. Five clients participated in the research and all met the DSM-III criteria for bulimia. Results demonstrated complete remission of symptoms in three clients, near remission in one client and limited improvement in one client. Scott recommends further standardisation of instruments that would include the affective facets of bulimia.

Pain management

There are some studies that look at the effectiveness of NLP as one of a range of holistic approaches in the management of pain. Bowers (1996), in a control study compares the use of NLP as an adjunctive therapy versus regular chiropractic care with 48 patients with acute pain. The measurement tool utilised was the Visual Analogue Scale with the author comparing pain reduction between the two groups. The author reports on an average reduction of 6.2 over 2.1 NLP sessions compared to the non-treatment group experiencing a reduction of 1.7 over the same period of time. Limitations of the study are reported including group size, lack of control on degree of patient participation and therapeutic judgement.

Directions for future research

There is substantial anecdotal evidence from practitioners of the effectiveness of NLP in enabling the management of pain. Some holistic therapy services allied to cancer care centres across the UK are using visualisation processes for the management of pain. As these services are already in existence, it would be relatively easy to conduct a randomised control trial that compares the effects of pain management with NLP visualisation and sub-modality processes compared with more traditional pain management techniques such as a TENS (transcutaneous electrical nerve stimulation) and patients using pharmacological management. This type of study would raise ethical issues and it should also be recognised that pain is a subjective process for many.

Cardiovascular

There is evidence of one study that utilised an NLP intervention with clients in post-cardiac rehabilitation (Sumin *et al.*, 2000). A total of 103 clients were recruited to the control study and 47 clients were offered five group psychotherapy sessions alongside a standard cardiac rehabilitation programme. The group psychotherapy included NLP, progressive muscular relaxation, Ericksonian hypnosis and metaphors. Findings demonstrated a decrease in heart rate, decrease in ventricular extrasystole, and stimulated tonicity of the parasympathetic nervous system. The test group had higher exercise tolerance and lower reactivity of central haemodynamics in all exercise tests.

Claustrophobia

In 2010 Bigley *et al.* utilised NLP to determine if it was possible to reduce levels of claustrophobia in patients that required an MRI scan. The study group consisted of individuals who had previously failed to complete an MRI scan because of a claustrophobic reaction. A total of 50 patients were recruited and their pre- and post-anxiety state was measured using the Spielberger's State Anxiety Inventory. The technique used for the intervention was Clare's Fast Phobia Cure. A total of 38 of the original 50 study subjects were able to complete the MRI scan. The 12 patients who did not complete the scan had statistically higher anxiety scores before NLP than the remaining patients. There was a statistically significant reduction in the median anxiety score, and a predicted 65 per cent cost saving if NLP were used compared to an MRI scan under general anaesthetic.

Cancer

Bokuro-Shafé *et al.* (2011) report on the use of NLP in the holistic treatment of cancer. At the time of writing the authors have trained over 300 medical professionals across Japan in the use of anchoring, sub-modality mapping across, reframing and using neurological levels with patients. Bokuro-Shafé *et al.* report that 96 per cent of patients experience an improvement in their symptoms following NLP, with over 60 per cent experiencing significant improvement after only one or two sessions. They provide examples of a simple three-step protocol for the holistic treatment of cancer:

- Step 1: Take time with the patient to create a shared map.
- Step 2: Visualise cancer cells being controlled by immune cells.
- Step 3: Check beliefs and change them if necessary.

A case example is given of a 76-year-old male patient with stage 3b inoperable lung cancer. The blood CEA (carcinoembryonic antigen) level at step 1 is shown at 65, post-chemotherapy there is a typically a drop in the CEA which is only temporary before it returns to its previous elevated level. In this patient report, an NLP-trained nurse provided support to the patient using the three steps outlined above and the patients CEA level remained at a low score over for 11 months. The patient remained well and healthy four years later.

Directions for future research

The authors propose that medical NLP applications of NLP are researched, and we would also suggest research of:

- clear and simple protocols stated in specific scripts or step-by-step formats
- environmental flexibility by utilising natural conversation patterns and pre-filled questionnaires.

We would also advocate a combined approach to bringing NLP into the medical world for cancer care, combining accepted medical model interventions alongside a holistic model for cancer care as outlined by the authors.

Summary

The authors recognise that substantial effort has been made by clinicians to empirically test and evidence their work. This has resulted in a number of level B, C and D studies, summarised in Table 3.1. It is proposed that future studies are developed from the findings and recommendations of the studies included in this chapter.

Table 3.1 Research studies

Authors	Publication	Study title	Study level	Measurement tools	Comments
Witt, K. (2008)	*International Journal of Psychotherapy* 12(1): 50–60	Neurolinguistic psychotherapy (NLPt) treatment can modulate the reaction in pollen allergic humans and their state of health.	B	Psychological tests – Krampen-AT-Symptomscale and Rehabilitations-Psychologische-Diagnosesystem. Interval-scale data was normally distributed using the Kolmogorov-Smirnov-Test Variance homogeneity using the Bartlett-Test allowed variance analysis. Pre-testing using ANOVA and Multiple t-test. Medicine consumption and ailments recorded in daily diary entries. Ailments were counted using ANOVA to determine if groups ranking was normally populated and effects were measured using Mann–Whitney U and Wilcoxon Rank Sum tests. Medication consumption was counted as binary data using Chi-squared.	Psychological test results demonstrated that well-being increased significantly in the study group between $t0$ and $t1$ and remained stable between $t1$ and $t2$. No significant increase in control group. Analysis of variance over time showed a highly significant effect in the NLPt group. Mood of well-being showed a highly significant increase in the NLPt group $t0–t1$ and remained stable $t1–t2$. The state of illness decreased significantly in the NLPt group between $t0–t1$ and stable $t1–t2$. Unexplained decrease in the placebo group $t1–t2$. Study group showed significantly fewer symptoms. Medication use was significantly less in the study group. Psychological NLPt intervention has an effect on allergy sensitivity

Authors	Publication	Study title	Study level	Measurement tools	Comments
Witt, K. (2003)	Psychosomatics, 4: 33–7	Psychological treatment can modulate the skin reaction to histamine in pollen allergic humans.	B	Skin-prick test of saline solution and a histamine provocation as a positive control.	Control group were noted to have a highly significant increased difference in histamine wheal area.
Bigley, J., Griffiths, P.D., Prydderch, A., Romanowski, C.A.J., Miles, L., Lidiard, H., Hoggard, N. (2010)	The British Journal of Radiology, 83: 113–17	Neurolinguistic programming used to reduce the need for anaesthesia in claustrophobic patients undergoing MRI.	B	Spielberger's State Anxiety Inventory.	38 of the original 50 patients were able to complete the MRI scan. 12 patients who did not complete the scan had statistically higher anxiety scores before NLP than the remaining patients. There was a statistically significant reduction in the median anxiety score, and a predicted 65 per cent cost saving if NLP were used compared to an MRI scan under general anaesthetic.
Bowers, L.A. (1996)	Thesis (PhD), Graduate School of the Union Institute, Cincinnati, OH.	An exploration of holistic and non-traditional healing methods including researching the use of neuro-linguistic programming in the adjunctive treatment of acute pain.	B	Visual Analogue Scale.	Average reduction of 6.2 over 2.1 NLP sessions compared to the non-treatment group experiencing a reduction of 1.7 over the same period of time.

Continued

Table 3.1 Continued

Authors	Publication	Study title	Study level	Measurement tools	Comments
Genser-Medlitsch, M. and Schütz, P. (2004)	Self-Published, Austria, 1997. *Nowiny Psychologiczne* (Psychological News), issue 1.	Does neurolinguistic psychotherapy have effect? New results shown in the extramural section.	B	Individual Discomfort List, IPC questionnaire on locus of control. Self-Report Symptom Inventory. Stress Management Questionnaire, Sociodemographic data.	76% of clients experienced positive changes in 25 of 33 dimensions. Six months post-treatment 88 per cent (22 scales) were stable.
Stipancic, M., Renner, W., Schütz, P. and Dond, R. (2010)	*Counselling and Psychotherapy Research*, 10(1): 39–49.	Effects of neurolinguistic Psychotherapy on psychological difficulties and perceived quality of life.	B	Structured Clinical Interview for DSM-IV Personality Disorders (SCID II) for clinical symptoms. Croatian Scale of Quality of Life (KVZ) for quality of life measures.	Significant decrease in clinical symptoms and increase in quality of life for the study group, with effect sizes ($n=54$) of 0.65 SCID II, 0.65 KVZ Predictor variable, 0.51 KVZ Criterion variable when measured $t1-t2$, and, 1.09 SCID II, 0.69 KVZ Predictor variable and 0.73 KVZ Criterion variable at $t1-t3$ five month follow up.
Brandis, A.D. (1986)	*Dissertation Abstracts International*, 47(11), 4642-B, California School of Professional Psychology.	A neurolinguistic treatment for reducing parental anger responses and creating more resourceful behavioural options.	C	Parental Provocation Inventory. Parents' Report used for comparison.	ANOVA and Eta coefficients showed no significance. Post-hoc analysis demonstrated strong experimental effect in half of the experimental group, when investigated attributed result to utilisation of resource anchor.

Authors	Publication	Study title	Study level	Measurement tools	Comments
Duncan, R.C., Konefal, J. and Spechler, M.M. (1990)	*Psychological Reports*, June, 66(3 Pt 2):1323–30.	Effect of neurolinguistic programming training on self-actualization as measured by the Personal Orientation Inventory.	C	Personal Orientation Inventory.	Significant positive changes were observed in nine of twelve scales for 18 trainees, and 10 of 12 scales for 36 trainees at the end of the training.
Field, E.S. (1990)	*American Journal of Clinical Hypnosis*, January, 32(3): 174–82.	Neurolinguistic programming as an adjunct to other psychotherapeutic/ hypnotherapeutic interventions.	C		Both techniques effective in ending hyperactive episodes in the first client and integrating feelings and knowledge into personal consciousness with the second client.
Sumin, A.N., Khairedinova, O.P., Sumina, L., Variushkina, E.V., Doronin, D.V. and Galimzianov, D. (2000)	*Klin Med (Mosk)*, 78(6): 16–20.	Psychotherapy impact on effectiveness of in-hospital physical rehabilitation in patients with acute coronary syndrome.	C	Exercise tolerance tests. Central haemodynamic measures.	NLP, progressive muscular relaxation, Ericksonian hypnosis and metaphors. The test group had higher exercise tolerance and lower reactivity of central haemodynamics in all exercise tests.

Continued

Table 3.1 Continued

Authors	Publication	Study title	Study level	Measurement tools	Comments
Wake, L. (2011)	Current Research in NLP. ANLP, pp.43–53.	Waking up and moving on – a programme evaluation of an intervention with adolescents identified as at risk of offending behaviour.	C	Independent Service Evaluation Report (Tope, Thomas and Jones 2010).	The authors report on number of benefits from workshop: improved behaviour; thinking of the future; positive outlook; changes in social activities. Reported outcomes are validated.
Weaver, M. (2009)	Current Research in NLP: Proceedings of 2008 NLP Conference, 1, pp.67–83.	An exploration of a research-based approach to the evaluation of clients' experience of neurolinguistic psychotherapy within a private practice making use of the CORE model.	C	CORE Systems Research Tool.	33 clients. Clients experience a reduction in problems after an average of 7 weekly sessions of psychotherapy.
Baddeley M. (1992)	Australian Journal of Clinical Hypnotherapy and Hypnosis, 13(2): 87–92.	The use of hypnosis in marriage and relationship counselling.	D	3 case reports.	Combination of Ericksonian hypnosis, analytical hypnotherapy and NLP. These processes are more potent than traditional counselling

Authors	Publication	Study title	Study level	Measurement tools	Comments
Bertoli, J.M. (2002)	C.R. Figley. Westport, CT US, Greenwood Press/ Greenwood Publishing Group: 207–25.	The use of neurolinguistic programming and emotionally focused therapy with divorcing couples in crisis. Brief treatments for the traumatised: a project of the Green Cross Foundation.	D	Project report.	Combination of NLP and Emotionally Focused Therapy with the aim of replacing attachment to the ex-spouse and to reengage with the aim of developing new interactional patterns as co-parents.
Davis, S.L. and Davis, D.I. (1983)	Journal of Marital and Family Therapy, 9(3), July: 283–91.	Neurolinguistic Programming and family therapy.	D	Case report.	Overview of techniques used which include dissociated state rehearsal for future oriented behaviours.
Juhnke, G.A., Coll, K.M., Sunich, M.F. and Kent, R.R. (2008)	The Family Journal, 16: 391, originally published online 11 August.	Using a Modified neurolinguistic programming swish pattern with couple parasuicide and suicide survivors.	D	Clinical case example.	Adapted form of the NLP swish pattern to support couple survivors of suicide and parasuicide. Authors conclude that pattern provides clients with an opportunity to reconnect with memories of their loved one in a more positive way.
Scott, E.K. (1987)	Dissertation Abstracts International, 48(7), 1713-A 1714-A, Northern Arizona University.	The effects of the neurolinguistic programming model of reframing as therapy for bulimia.	D	Group case study.	NLP technique of reframing to facilitate change.

Continued

Table 3.1 Continued

Authors	Publication	Study title	Study level	Measurement tools	Comments
Shelden, V.E. and Shelden, R.G. (1989)	Family Therapy, 16(3), 249–58.	Sexual abuse of males by females: the problem, treatment modality, and case example.	D	Single case study.	Utilisation of NLP and biofeedback to alter identified ur useful patterns of behaviour and to focus on a future desired state.
Vianna, L.A.C., Bomfim, G.F.T. and Chicone, G. (2006)	Revista Latino-Americana de Enfermagem, 14(5), Sept–Oct: 695–701.	Self-esteem of raped women.	D	Phenomenological study with 5 groups of women.	Combination of psychodrama and NLP techniques. Thematic analysis demonstrated that attendees were able to reflect on and develop a change in attitude and perceive new roads ahead.
Wake, L. (2009)	Current Research in NLP. 1: 50–66.	A study of the relationship between the core belief structures of neurolinguistic psychotherapy and object relations theory.	D	Grounded theory qualitative study.	Relationship between some NLPt processes and their similarity to object relations theory.
Zika. B. (1985)	Australian Journal of Clinical Hypnotherapy and Hypnosis, 6(2), Sept: 57–66	Transformational hypnotherapy: historical antecedents and a case example.	D	1 case report.	Combination of NLP and analytic therapy models. A positive therapeutic model for maladaptive behaviour.

4 Anxiety disorders

Bruce Grimley

This chapter examines anxiety disorders that have not already been covered in other chapters. Using the Diagnostic and Statistical Manual of Mental Disorders (DSM-IV-TR, 2000) as the criterion, this leaves panic disorder, obsessive compulsive disorder (OCD), acute stress disorder, generalized anxiety disorder (GAD), anxiety disorder due to a general medical condition, substance-induced anxiety disorder, and finally anxiety disorder not otherwise specified.

This chapter will review the specifics of each disorder and the current treatments. As there is an element of co-morbidity within these anxiety disorders, the chapter will focus on three: panic disorder, OCD and GAD. The second part of the chapter will explain how NLP works within the current theoretical perspectives on anxiety but from a patient centered perspective rather than the theoretical perspective which informs treatment. The second part of the chapter also relates a case history to provide the reader with a flavour of NLP therapy in action, a review of the research to date and an explanation of the basics of NLP therapy.

The difference between anxiety and depression

Generally, anxiety is differentiated from depression in that depression, according to the cognitive content specificity hypothesis, is related to loss or deprivation, whereas anxiety involves physical or psychosocial threat together with the client's underestimate of their own coping and rescue factors. Beck's distinction (1988) between depression and anxiety seems to have wide psychometric support (Clark *et al.*, 1990; Beck and Clark 1988; Clark *et al.*, 1994; Lamberton and Oei, 2008).

The unitary perspective has support in the emergence of what appears to be a single primary factor with significant loadings from both anxiety and depression measures and a high co-morbidity rate for major depression and anxiety states, such as panic disorder, agoraphobia and generalized anxiety. Clark and Beck, however, give sound reasons for their distinction. Many of the well-known self-report and clinician-based measures of anxiety and depression contain a mixture of depressive and anxious items. This overlap results in lower discriminant validity and thus a high correlation between measures. They propose that correlations between constructs are typically lower when researchers use factor validated measures or instruments that were developed for the express purpose of aiding in differential diagnosis (Clark *et al.*, 1990).

Clark and Watson (1991) further suggest a tripartite model to explain the high correlations that arise from the unitary perspective. They suggest that both measures of depression and anxiety have in common a third dimension: negative affect (NA). This is to be contrasted with positive affect (PA), and both, according to this model, can be regarded as stable traits. NA is characterized by tendencies to be distressed, worried, anxious, self-critical and to have a negative view of oneself. PA, by contrast, is characterized by pleasurable engagement with the environment and has components of well-being, energy, affiliation, social dominance and adventurousness.

If anxiety is considered a separate cluster of symptoms from depression, the societal cost is massive.

Research from the Netherlands puts the annual cost *per capita* for panic disorder only at *10,269 Euros*, using a population-based study (N=5504) (Batelann *et al.*, 2007). The research of Kessler *et al.* (2005a) suggests 2.7 per cent of the adult US population have a 12-month prevalence of panic disorder, while further research (Kessler *et al.* 2005b) suggests that 4.7 per cent of the US population have a lifetime prevalence of panic disorder. Even with the recognition that one cannot speculate and generalize too much from nation to nation, one can safely assume the national health bill for panic disorder alone will run into the billions.

Panic disorder

Butler *et al.* (2008) state that, when Beck developed a treatment manual for anxiety in 1985, the main thrust was a trans-diagnostic approach. Since that time, however, careful clinical observation has resulted in the development of specific cognitive models for separate anxiety disorders. Butler *et al.* (2008) report that one of the earliest was Clark's cognitive model of panic (1986).

Clark's main theoretical assumption is that the normal body sensations someone experiences when they are anxious, such as palpitations, breathlessness and dizziness, are interpreted catastrophically by the sufferer. This increases the anxiety and panic ensues. Hibbert (1984) discusses how common cognitive themes in those who suffer from panic attack are death, disease, social rejection or failure. Beck *et al.* (1974), propose that stress activates schemas, which lead to patterns of cognitive activity with the following characteristics:

1   Systematic misconstruing of experiences leading to catastrophizing.
2   Specific thoughts or images which are often clearly related to past negative experiences.

3   Anxiety is commensurate with the degree of plausibility (to the patient) of the hypothetical danger; the patient's notion of the severity of harm, and his estimate of the likelihood of the dreaded event to occur.

Hibbert's research (1984) suggests that the DSM distinction between general anxiety disorder and panic disorder is warranted. He found that those who presented without panic attacks ($N=8$) collectively had fewer of the catastrophic misinterpretations compared with those who presented with panic attacks ($N=17$).

Specifically, thoughts of illness, death and loss of self-control, were found 38 times in those with panic attacks, compared to only four in those who did not have panic attacks. These were significant differences (Fisher Exact). Research also supports the sequence of events suggested by Clark's model. Sufferers will usually report that the first thing they notice during a panic attack is a physical feeling. (Hibbert, 1984; Ley, 1985). Hibbert (1984, p.622) concluded 'the ideational content of those experiencing panic attacks can be understood as a reaction to the somatic symptoms, a connection insisted upon by all but two of the patients'.

Barlow (1988) believes that certain individuals have a tendency to be 'neurobiologically overactive to stress'. They react to negative life events with a false alarm. Clark seems to think of this propensity to misinterpret bodily symptoms in a catastrophic way is a 'relatively enduring characteristic' (Clark, 1986, p.465) and he airs various explanations.

1   The reduced efficiency of central adrenergic α_2-autoreceptors, (Charney *et al.*, 1984). Noradrenergic neurons in the locus coerulus and other brain-stem areas play an important role in the control of the autonomic nervous system. The α_2-adrenergic autoreceptor has an inhibitory influence on presynaptic noradrenergic neurons. A deficiency in this autoreceptor would mean that release of noradrenaline would not be damped by presynaptic inhibition and individuals with such a deficiency would experience larger than normal surges in noradrenaline and sympathetic nervous system activation in response to a perceived threat.
2   The fact that more patients than controls will experience panic attacks when they are induced through infusions of sodium lactate suggests that misinterpreting bodily sensations as catastrophic is an enduring characteristic.
3   Expectancy due to a lack of standardization in research is also an element. Clark discusses the research of Appleby *et al.* (1981). Researchers suggested pre-infusion to patients they may experience *panic attacks*. However, to the controls they merely suggested they may experience symptoms analogous to those of *public speaking*. Results supported the conclusion that expectation influenced the interpretation of bodily sensations.

Treatments

The main thrust of treatment for panic disorder is to correct misinformation about panic and breathing and to institute re-training, cognitive restructuring and interoceptive exposure (Mattis and Ollendick, 2002). Interoceptive exposure has been tested with good results. Clark *et al.* (1985) asked participants to engage in voluntary hyperventilation. During this process participants were educated about the nature of panic and how their hyperventilation has been associated with maladaptive thoughts through conditioning which then reinforces the hyperventilation and other somatic symptoms associated with panic. After this, participants were trained how to breathe from the diaphragm in a slow and relaxed way during times of pressure. Then, based upon the discussion above, participants were engaged in developing more useful thoughts and beliefs for use as they experienced the pressure. Finally, after reviewing their own 'panic diaries', participants could more clearly identify previous triggers and introduce this protocol. So, after a bout of high caffeine intake, the participant could now reinterpret the associated arousal as the effects of the caffeine rather than something more sinister as was previously the case.

Obsessive compulsive disorder (OCD)

In this disorder, obsessive refers to the persistent ideas, thoughts, impulses or images which intrude into the patient's life and compulsive refers to the repetitive behaviours or mental acts which occur because the patient believes they will prevent or reduce the anxiety created by the intrusion. These intrusions are relevant to the disorder in that they cannot be interpreted just as excessive worries about real-life problems, but they are inappropriate and do cause marked anxiety and distress. Many people may joke about their little OCDs, for example 'you always have to go back to ensure the door is locked', or 'he cleans his car every Saturday at 10:00am'. These are just idiosyncratic behaviours which do not cause distress and help define a particular person. What is characteristic about OCD is that the patient knows, recognizes and will admit their thinking and consequent adjustment behaviours are excessive and unreasonable. This is one way in which OCD differs from OCPD (obsessive compulsive personality disorder). Individuals with OCPD are often characterized by a preoccupation with details, rules, lists, orderliness, perfection and mental and interpersonal control at the expense of flexibility and openness. However, for these people, this is just the way they operate. Such characteristics do not cause them distress and they often are not really aware of it unless co-workers or relatives point such characteristics out for them. The aetiology of OCD is neither based in a foreign substance (substance-induced anxiety) nor a general medical condition (anxiety disorder due to a general medical condition) but usually begins in childhood or adolescence. A genetic component is evidenced by a higher concordance for monozygotic twins than dizygotic twins (DSM-IV-TR, 2000). OCD is not that rare with the prevalence being 1 in 40 in the US, translating into 7.6 million people (Hyman and Pedrick, 2010). Previously, lower estimates are believed to be a function of the embarrassment and shame experienced by sufferers.

OCD creates a vicious cycle in which there is momentary relief for the sufferer after they get a 'feel' that their compulsive mental act or behaviour has done its job and they can then proceed with other activities. However, this relief is short lived and further intrusions trigger the compulsions soon after. There are many overt compulsions such as washing and cleaning, ordering and reordering, being overly scrupulous or hoarding, however there are covert behaviours as well, as in the case of Primarily Obsessional OCD. This implies the presence of obsessive thoughts without overtly performed compulsions. Research over the past 20 years has shown that such sufferers do perform compulsions but they are subtle and covert such as in the case of mental acts (Freeston and Ladouceur, 1997). Themes for Primarily Obsessional OCD are almost always of a violent or sexual nature. Often OCD sufferers will change their compulsion, so an individual may be a compulsive washer and after a year lose this compulsion and become a compulsive hoarder. There seems to be no pattern to this changing of compulsive behaviour but it does seem to be the norm.

Freud believed OCD was caused by internal conflict, however, some experts in the field categorically state that this is not the case and point to a pharmacological treatment which regulates the supply of serotonin as evidence of a biological basis (Hyman and Pedrick, 2010). Until 1960 psycho-analysis was routinely used to treat OCD, and it was not until 1966, when British psychologist Meyer began using exposure to feared objects while preventing the accustomed compulsive responses in accordance with the principles of behavioural psychology, that treatment protocols changed. This protocol seemed to work very well with marked reduction in symptoms being reported (Steketee, 1993).

In the 1980s, researchers Salkovskis and Emmelkamp applied the ideas of cognitive therapy as an adjunctive treatment alongside behavioural therapy and, for many, this alliance provides the best treatment for a disorder which, according to some authors, has no cure (Hyman and Pedrick, 2010).

The actual cause of OCD is not known. There are of course theories. The psychodynamic theories mentioned above still exist although they are no longer popular. The biological explanation seems to be the most popular. Childhood onset has been theoretically linked to the antibodies that fight beta-haemolytic streptococci which causes strep throat. These same antibodies go on to attack neurons in the basal ganglia area of the brain which is believed to be related to OCD.

Treatment

OCD is treated mainly by a behavioural therapy known as exposure and response prevention (ERP) and cognitive behavioural therapy (CBT). Behaviour therapy is particularly apt as, from a medical point of view, the structures affected in the biological explanation have to do with non-conscious functioning and thus will not respond well to reasoning, or talking out a response. In such instances, *in-vivo* (real-life) exposure to situations that provoke the anxiety and also compulsion prevention, preventing the client from acting out the compulsive behaviour, are used in conjunction. Sufferers construct a subjective unit of distress scale (SUDS), first used by Wolpe in the 1960s, and rate situations from 0 (no anxiety), 50 (moderate anxiety), to 100 (extreme anxiety). They then start with lower anxiety items and expose themselves to the situation while creating a different response from the one they are normally compelled to make. It is a bit like refusing to scratch an itch while using the sensation as a trigger to take the dog for a walk, or make a cup of tea. This new response eventually becomes a classically conditioned response triggered by the obsessive urge. As success occurs at lower levels of the SUDS scale, items at a higher level are gradually introduced.

Standard neurophysiological models of OCD relate to a circuit that joins the orbital gyrus, the cingulate, the thalamus, the caudate nucleus and the palidum in a circuit that regulates both normal and ritualized behaviour. Self-regulation appears to be centred in the head of the caudate and the anterior cingulate. Some hypothesize that over-stimulation of the dorsal striatum is responsible for ritualized repetitive behaviors (Guehl *et al.*, 2008; Roth *et al.*, 2006).

In accordance with the biological model of OCD, deep-brain stimulation (DBS) of the core of the nucleus accumbens, which is richly interconnected with the caudate nucleus, has been used with successful results with two patients who were resistant to pharmacological (SSRIs) and psychological treatments. However, the authors conclude that further investigations are required (Franzin *et al.*, 2010).

Generalized anxiety disorder (GAD)

GAD is different from the above in the sense it is not about panic, neither about the control of obsessive thinking through compulsion, but about worry. When individuals worry to such an extent that their lives become excessively disrupted, then GAD is normally at the root. The chronicity of GAD and its resistance to treatment have led some researchers to conceptualize GAD more in terms of a personality disorder (Blazer *et al.*, 1991). GAD is also characterized by being associated with many other co-occurring conditions. Some research studies have shown co-morbidity rates ranging from 45 per cent to 91 per cent (Brawman-Mintzer and Lydiard, 1996).

The largest study to report prevalence data (DSM-III-R criteria) indicates that rates of GAD are 1.6 per cent and 5.8 per cent for current and lifetime incidence respectively (Wittchen *et al.*, 1994). While evidence suggests a general heritability of such traits as anxiety and negative affect rather than GAD specifically, the stable traits of neuroticism and introversion have been found to indicate later vulnerability for anxiety and anxiety disorders (Gershuny and Sher, 1998). There are three aetiological models of GAD, which I will discuss next.

Wells' Metacognitive theory (1995) suggests there are two types of worrying. Type 1 worry refers to external events and somatic events – these can include phobias and panic disorder. Type 2 worry refers to worrying about one's own thinking, or worrying about one's worrying. This is called 'meta-worry'. Wells proposes that the key characteristic of GAD is meta-worry. He distinguishes three other important dimensions in his model, which are meta-beliefs, cognitive consciousness, and strategies. His recommendation for treatment is to challenge meta-worry and to develop more adaptive metacognitive strategies. When type 2 worry occurs, the patient is to use strategies to disengage and in that disengaged context create constructive meta-cognitions.

Ladouceur *et al.* (1998) have presented a model that identifies four main variables: intolerance of uncertainty, beliefs about worry, poor problem orientation and cognitive avoidance. Intolerance of uncertainty leads to the anticipation of threatening events and thus dysfunctional behaviour. Research (N=1,230) conducted exploratory factor analysis on the English version of the Intolerance of Uncertainty Scale and identified two factors: the beliefs that 'uncertainty has negative behavioral and self-referent implications', and that 'uncertainty is unfair and spoils everything'. Both factors had high correlations with pathological worry (Sexton and Dugas, 2009).

Individuals with GAD, according to Rygh and Sanderson (2004), tend to overestimate the advantages of worry and underestimate the disadvantages of worry. This means they are more likely to make use of worry as a strategy for adjustment. The third variable is poor problem orientation, which falls into the category of a meta-cognition in this model. Problem orientation is not a specific set of problem-solving skills, but rather a higher order cognition having to do with confidence and control over the ability to create problem solving strategies. Research by Ladouceur *et al.* (1998) examined whether problem-orientation and problem-solving skills differ according to GAD symptom level or clinical status, and whether intolerance *of* uncertainty and beliefs about worry vary according to GAD symptom level or clinical status (N=43). The results showed problem orientation, intolerance *of* uncertainty, and beliefs about worry were significantly related for those with GAD, but not for the group who did not meet GAD criteria. These results support three aspects of Ladouceur's four-element model. The final variable is cognitive avoidance based upon Borkovec *et al.*'s (2004) avoidance of threatening images. This theory suggests that strategies are used by sufferers of GAD to internally avoid having to process threatening images. Their recommendation for treatment is that it should focus on increasing tolerance for uncertainty, which is the variable with the highest loading. The therapist typically challenges the assumption that uncertainty can and should be avoided using CBT techniques.

Borkovec's Avoidance Theory (2004) suggests that the nature of worry is predominantly auditory rather than visual. This led to the belief that the motivation to focus primarily on auditory (thought) in worry was to avoid affectively charged visual representations. The idea was based upon Lang's (1985) theory that somatic activation of emotion occurs by way of imagery. From this perspective conceptual activity, which is predominantly auditory, acts as a buffer against anxiety because the intensity of emotion evoked by auditory imaginings is not so great as the heightened physiological response associated with internal images. Treatment from the avoidance theory perspective is similar to panic disorder and OCD treatments including response prevention, progressive muscular relaxation and cognitive restructuring.

Treatment

No doubt it will be appreciated that treatment for GAD will be textured according to the theoretical orientation of the therapist.

Techniques to deal with the meta-cognitive deficit, as suggested by Wells (1995), would include such techniques as 'vertical descent'. Rather like laddering in personal construct therapy, beliefs are de-layered until core beliefs, which have almost existential status, are uncovered and challenged. Vasey and Borkovec (1992) used this method to uncover core beliefs associated with worry. From a utilitarian point of view, rather than an existential point of view, the two themes often associated with worry are that worry helps to find solutions to problems, and that worry can prevent or minimize negative outcomes (Freeston *et al.*, 1994).

If, as Ladouceur *et al.* (1998) believe, the core variable in a client's construction of GAD is an inability to cope with uncertainty, then assisting the patient to accept uncertainty as a reasonable constant in modern life will underpin treatment. This is usually accomplished through cognitive restructuring. Once a patient can feel more comfortable in the presence of cognitive uncertainty they can then face the world with more effective problem orientations, including beliefs about worry and avoidance. It is interesting that Rygh and Sanderson (2004) point out that, from this perspective, the treatment of worry about improbable events in the future requires cognitive exposure to threatening images while using *covert* response prevention. One ethical theme that consistently plagues an NLP perspective is the use of 'manipulation' techniques in a *covert* way. It is very important within a therapeutic environment, when patients are usually more suggestible than the normal population that this whole area of covert operation is adequately and ethically dealt with.

Finally, Borkovec's avoidance theory, based upon Lang, would suggest treatment which makes more use of imagery and less use of intellectualizing or rationalizing, through such imagery techniques as creating an alternate set of historical records which are stored in memory through imagination (Rygh and Sanderson, 2004).

Neurolinguistic Programming theoretical orientation

NLP theoretically draws from many strands. The four key strands are: transformational grammar (Chomsky, 1957), systems theory/cybernetics, (Von Bertalanffy, 1968; Bandler *et al.*, 1976; Bateson, 1972), modelling (Bandura, 1977a, b, c, d) and general semantics (Korzybski, 1933).

NLP readily lends itself to counselling/psychotherapy as the first exemplars to be modelled were all therapists; Perls (Gestalt therapy), Satir (Family therapy) and Erickson (Clinical Hypnosis). As a result of these modelling projects in the 1970s, design variables, known as patterns in NLP, were explicated and these formed the basis of early NLP workshops. NLP does not advocate a technical approach but an attitudinal approach and it is modelling that is at the heart of this attitude. Rogers tells us

> no approach which relies upon knowledge, upon training, upon the acceptance of something that is taught, is of any use ... such methods are in my experience futile and inconsequential. The most they can accomplish is some temporary change, which soon disappears leaving the individual more than ever convinced of his inadequacy.
>
> (Rogers, 1967)

Similarly, the NLP approach to therapy can best be summarized within the attitudes that spring from the NLP presuppositions. Even though these presuppositions have not been formalized, the below list is taken from Tosey and Mathison (2009, p.98) and is a translation from the German (Walker 1996, p.111).

1 Every behaviour is potentially communication (Bateson, Perls, Satir, Erickson).
2 Mind and body are part of the same cybernetic system (Bateson, Perls, Satir, Erickson).
3 People have all the resources they need to make changes (Perls, Satir, Erickson).
4 People orientate themselves by their internal maps, their model of the world and not to the world itself (Korzybski).
5 The map is not the territory (Korzybski).
6 People make the best choices that present themselves to them (Satir),
7 Choice is better than no choice (Satir),
8 Every behaviour is generated by a positive intention (Satir).

9 The meaning of a communication is the response it elicits, not the intention of the communicator (Erickson).
10 Resistance is a message about the communicator (or therapist) (Erickson).
11 If what you are doing isn't working, do something different (Erickson).
12 There is no failure, only feedback (Erickson).
13 The most flexible variable controls the system (Ashby's law of requisite variety).
14 Everything that a human being can do can be modelled (Bandler and Grinder).

Adopting a counselling attitude which springs from these 'presuppositions', NLP makes use of many patterns to assist individuals with specific disorders regain an internal reference point which provides them with the tools to effectively manage their anxiety.

In modelling the psychiatrist Erickson, Gilligan, O'Hanlon and also Bandler and Grinder, noticed that Erickson always treated his patients as though they were totally different. Even though he unconsciously made use of the linguistic patterns formalized in 'patterns' (Bandler and Grinder, 1975b), he believed every patient was totally unique and needed a different model of therapy to assist them. More specifically, he aimed to help his patients obtain an internal reference point and communication with the unconscious mind so that they could make use of the natural tools of thinking and feeling in a constructive manner. Part of this strategy involved producing the appropriate language and behaviour to take each client to the outcomes they wished for.

A clinical model that resembles the NLP perspective in terms of information processing comes from Griffin and Tyrell (2000). They contrast the APET model with the ABC model of Albert Ellis (1962). This model agrees there is always an activating event or trigger (A), which sets off an anxiety response in the mind–body system of any patient. However, they argue that the nature of what is triggered is different. For the ABC model, what is triggered is a belief or series of beliefs which are characterized as being dysfunctional and of a black or white nature (B). Such thinking naturally leads to consequences of an emotional and behavioural nature (C), which provide the symptoms for anxiety cluster disorders as described above.

As can be seen from the Figure 4.1, the APET model sees the situation slightly differently.

APET or ABC?

- **A**ctivating trigger
- **P**attern F[1]
- **E**motional arousal
- **T**hinking (belief) F[2]

- **A**ctivating trigger
- **B**elief (thinking)
- **C**onsequence (behavioural and emotional)

Figure 4.1 The APET model (Griffin and Tyrell 2000)

NLP believes that the trigger will activate a first order information processing system that is sensory in nature and is characterized by a cluster of representations. In NLP this is known as First Access, or F^1. This information works through the process of association or anchoring in NLP. It is very similar to classical conditioning as demonstrated by Pavlov. As pioneers in the study of unconscious information processing, Libet *et al.* (1964) tell us that these associations can occur in well under the magic half-second needed to bring the processes into conscious awareness. Indeed, modern sports research suggests even though full consciousness may take 500 milliseconds to develop, the rapid pre-conscious processing needed to deal with responses to a late swerve from a tennis or cricket ball consistently takes at least 200 milliseconds and are by no means instantaneous as they may seem (McLeod, 1987). The NLP model believes it is the synaesthetic anchoring together of representations from the various sensory systems that represents the initial unconscious response to any environmental trigger.

The mind–body system, having registered this initial response to a trigger, sets the context and the frame for what comes next and this is an emotional response. Le Doux (1996) makes the point that the experience of an emotion is in proportion to the relative mass of cerebral cortex. So the lower animals, even though they may respond as though they are experiencing emotion (anger, fright, happiness), they are probably not, because reflexive conscious processing is needed for this. As the human body responds to the unconscious sensory-based representation of an action or percept, various cortical areas become involved. It is at this time that beliefs, as prior complexes of perception and response, begin to arise in an attempt to make sense of the event. This is done in such a way that the mind–body system can remain a stable entity and a functional self-organizing entity. When the mind–body system is successful in this venture, it may be sealed into a single-loop system of learning.

Figure 4.2 illustrates several levels of learning that are consistent with Bateson's (1972) model. The most basic level, the level just described, must been seen as part of a larger system, a perceptual and behavioural ecosystem. As the figure illustrates, changing behaviour is useful, however, if the new behaviour is not commensurate with underlying thinking and perception, such behavioural change will not be supported systemically and consequently will not be sustainable. For NLP it is not just the behaviour that needs to change. It is not even the behaviour and the thinking that need to change. What needs to change is the whole system. This is termed generative growth. Ideally, in a successful NLP intervention, the locus chosen for the change work will cascade through the system so that the patient will not only experience the alteration of the initial behavioural pattern, but that change will trigger further changes in emotion, thinking, language and behaviour. In the process she will have also assimilated an understanding of the NLP model and the patient will be able to develop the ability to respond flexibly and appropriately in the future.

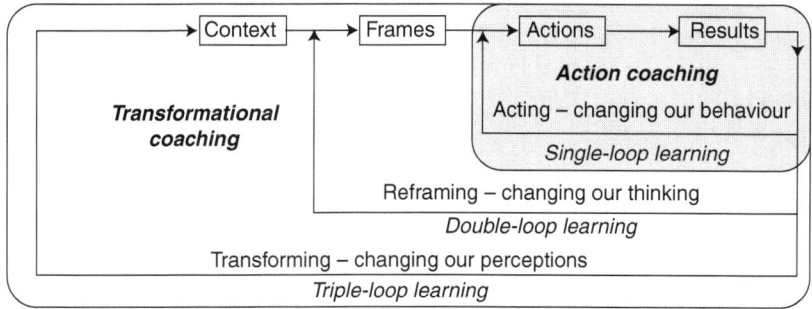

Figure 4.2 Systemic change. Diagram reproduced from www.mikethementor.com, with permission

As with many cognitive analyses, the APET model provides several intervention points where an NLP strategy might be applied to change the structure of the system. Recognizing that the anxious response often has a trigger that is linked to an associated image in one or more systems that evokes an emotional response, it does not take long to understand that, like other models, APET is cyclical. After a few experiences, the trigger evokes not only the image and the associated emotional response, but it now evokes a set of irrational beliefs or expectations about the client's inability to act or respond appropriately in the face of the problematic feelings. As those beliefs come to control the client's behaviour, they tend to become self-fulfilling prophecies: as they insure that negative affect deepens, the associative chain becomes more streamlined and the system becomes increasingly self-referential. As noted when discussing interventions in the TEAMS model of depression (see infra), the first task is to decide how to approach structural change and which element in the system is most likely to generate a change that will reverberate through the belief system.

Our previous discussion of Vasey and Borkovec's (1992) de-layering technique immediately suggests the mirror-image NLP technique, core transformation (Andreas and Andreas, 1994). Both techniques trace the overt behaviours to some core belief, but as is so often the case, the cognitive process seeks a problem content which can then be dealt with, whereas the NLP approach seeks an experience that is capable of reframing the structure of the problem and in so doing, resolve it.

Core Transformation begins by identifying the problem belief or behaviour and, assuming, in line with the basic presuppositions of NLP, that every behaviour has a positive intention for the individual, begins to find that outcome for each level of behaviour as it 'ladders down' the chain of outcome sequiturs. With each belief or question, it asks, 'What would that do for you?' Then, having received an answer, it continues down the ladder asking, 'How that would make you feel?' and 'Having that, fully and completely, what would that do for you?' Assuming that those feelings would be expressed by some other behaviour or perception, it continues to ask the same series of questions, obtaining deeper and more meaningful answers down to the ultimate positive end of the chain of behaviours and perceptions. At last, the series of outcome sequiturs reaches a level of oceanic positive affect beyond which the client is unable to go. After taking time to fully experience what is ultimately a deeply spiritual place within, that feeling is now applied to each of the outcomes elicited on the way down the ladder so that each behaviour and percept is touched and redefined in terms of that core spiritual state. In the end, the original eliciting stimulus becomes associated with the core state and ceases to evoke the chain of anxious behaviours. In some cases, one session of Core Transformation is enough to break apart the anxiety structure. In other cases, several iterations using different stimuli and beliefs are necessary before the elicitation structure can no longer hold.

Returning to Figure 4.2, we may observe that the Core Transformation process does not simply seek to solve the limited problem of the situational evocation of anxiety. Passing through the other levels and beyond, it creates a new affective context and in that context generates the possibility of transformative change.

This means not only are the gains made in therapy sustainable, but also a more resilient human is created as they now experience the world through a different set of process filters which are more effective at creating internal models which generate appropriate emotional states, physiological postures, cognitive orientations, linguistic models and behavioural responses. This allows the client to discover what is truly important to them, to create plans to achieve those ends and to recognize the wider ecology of the system of which they are a part.

The same kind of transformational change, approached through a different NLP technique is illustrated through the following case history. This case history nicely exemplifies the point that even though there are standard processes within NLP therapy, each client is different and these differences need to be noticed and made use of in the intervention.

Case history

John was a fire and rescue officer with many years of experience at both the operational and support levels. He was referred to the author by occupational health as he was experiencing panic attacks and extreme anxiety. His Beck Anxiety Inventory (BAI) (Beck and Steer, 1993) score was 42 at the beginning of treatment. The BAI manual classifies scores of 26–63 as severe anxiety. From the below response set on the detailed assessment of post-traumatic stress (DAPS) (Briere, 2001), one can see the only dimension preventing a diagnosis of PTSD was avoidance (Figure 4.3). John had a belief that he had to face up to his fears and anxiety. He refused to run away either from his symptoms, which he did not understand, or many of the triggers that surrounded his every working day. However, his symptoms

82 Bruce Grimley

were preventing him from working and he could not understand how they could seemingly appear out of nowhere, without warning, and without a readily explainable trigger. John was suffering from trauma specific dissociation, re-experiencing and hyper-arousal.

In asking John what he wanted from these sessions, he said he wanted these symptoms to stop. It appeared that what caused him anxiety more than the horrific accident scenes he had to attend was the internal pressures

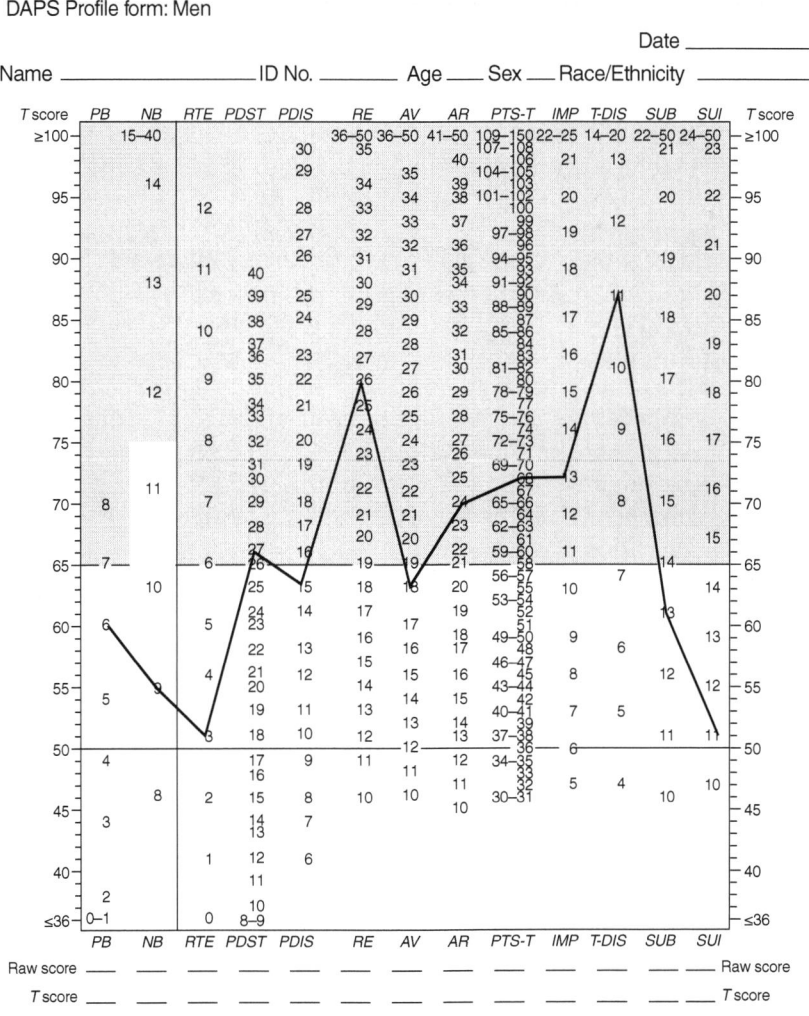

Figure 4.3 DAPS profile for John pre-treatment (01.01.2011)

within the service and the consequences for his family should he not be up to the mark. Interestingly, he first started developing panic attacks 14 years before treatment and he could find no reason as to why he should have them.

From an NLP perspective, more especially in terms of NLP meta-programmes (Charvet, 1997), I could recognize that he was operating from an away-from motivational orientation. This is a motivational trait (in NLP; meta-programming) that describes people who are motivated to use their resources when they are near something they really do not wish for and want to 'get away'. This is to be compared with the towards meta-programme, where individuals are characterized by being motivated through the setting of positive goals and being motivated towards achieving those goals, only letting up once accomplishment is forthcoming (Charvet, 1997). I fed this back to John and encouraged him to frame his responses in terms of what he wanted. He filled in further questionnaires, which allowed us to discuss his present pressures and how he was responding in terms of meta-programmes (Grimley, 2012). During these initial sessions, rapport was built up and an internal model of how John created this anxiety was developed and tested. For instance, whenever he was encouraged to relax using progressive muscular relaxation, he found himself automatically experiencing a stress response. His heart began to beat faster, his head began to spin, and he felt a knot in his stomach that expanded up towards his chest area.

During the fourth session, John was invited to participate in the NLP pattern called a six-step reframe. This pattern was chosen because the only characteristic that prevented a diagnosis of PTSD in this case was that the client did not engage in avoidance behaviour of any kind. In fact, he was totally characterized by the opposite; he wanted to 'face his demons' and understand them. Rather than use a dissociative technique, the six-step reframe actively makes use of the unconscious mind to identify the part responsible for the present behaviour and then make use of the creative unconscious in developing ecological alternatives to move the client forwards. This pattern thus maximized the utility of John's non-avoidance as a resource that John possessed. It also maximized his involvement in creating the change he was after and ensured his understanding of the process.

This pattern has six steps:

1 Identify the response to be changed.
2 Establish communication with 'the part' responsible for the behaviour.
3 Separate the positive intention from the behaviour.
4 Communicate with 'the creative part' and generate an alternative set of behaviours which achieve the same intention.
5 Ask 'X' part if it will agree to adopt the behaviours generated by the creative part which fulfils the same intention over the next week.
6 Check for ecology in the whole mind–body system and see if all other parts are in agreement with a trial of one week with the new behaviours.

John clearly explained the internal and external behaviours to be changed and by now he was used to identifying their positive counterparts. For instance, slow, relaxed breathing rather than holding his breath, and muscular relaxation rather than muscular tension.

In communicating with the 'part' responsible for the symptoms, immediately the symptoms became apparent and John was encouraged to relax while the part responsible for symptoms established communications.

I asked whether this unconscious part could demonstrate a willingness to communicate by increasing the John's symptoms without John's conscious involvement. This increase occurred.

Interestingly, the positive intention of this part was to 'check for doubt' and 'to exist', and for John the part was almost Goblin-like in its mannerism. The positive intention of this checking was to ensure that John would 'not get anything wrong'.

It took quite a long time for 'the creative part' to establish what alternative behaviour would be appropriate. However, we finally came to the conclusion that 'doubt' was doing a great job, but once an initial check had been done there was no need for 'Goblin' (as we began to call him) to proceed. If there was something to be addressed, John could get on and address it, if there was not, then Goblin could retire until he was needed again.

A scenario developed when Goblin found a door called doubt, however, when he went through it, there was just blank white on the other side. John began to believe this was evidence there was nothing further to doubt, but Goblin would always re-appear on John's side of the door after walking through it.

The author encouraged Goblin to engage in this behaviour and work with the creative part till he was sure there was no need to 're-appear' and he was 'thanked' for his work to date. Over successive sessions Goblin made fewer and fewer appearances and when he did the need to re-appear was also dramatically reduced.

Other NLP techniques such as meta-stating (Hall and Duval, 2004) were used to facilitate this process. For instance, John was asked to express his feelings about doubting, he said he felt frustrated. He was then asked how he felt about being frustrated and he said he felt sad. This process continued with the instruction that he should feel supportive about being sad. The process continued until John reached an 'Ah ha' moment when his whole physiology changed and he said, 'I can do this; I am worrying about nothing'.

John began to sleep better and did not rely on distraction to allay his anxiety. He began to generate time during the day and on weekends to focus on tasks which involved his family more and he began to take time just for himself. He was tasked with practising experiencing the old symptoms and recognizing that, without the doubting cognitions, they just went away. As he began to replace unnecessary doubt with a more positive yet realistic orientation towards his resources and capabilities, his moments of anxiety first reduced in intensity and then in frequency.

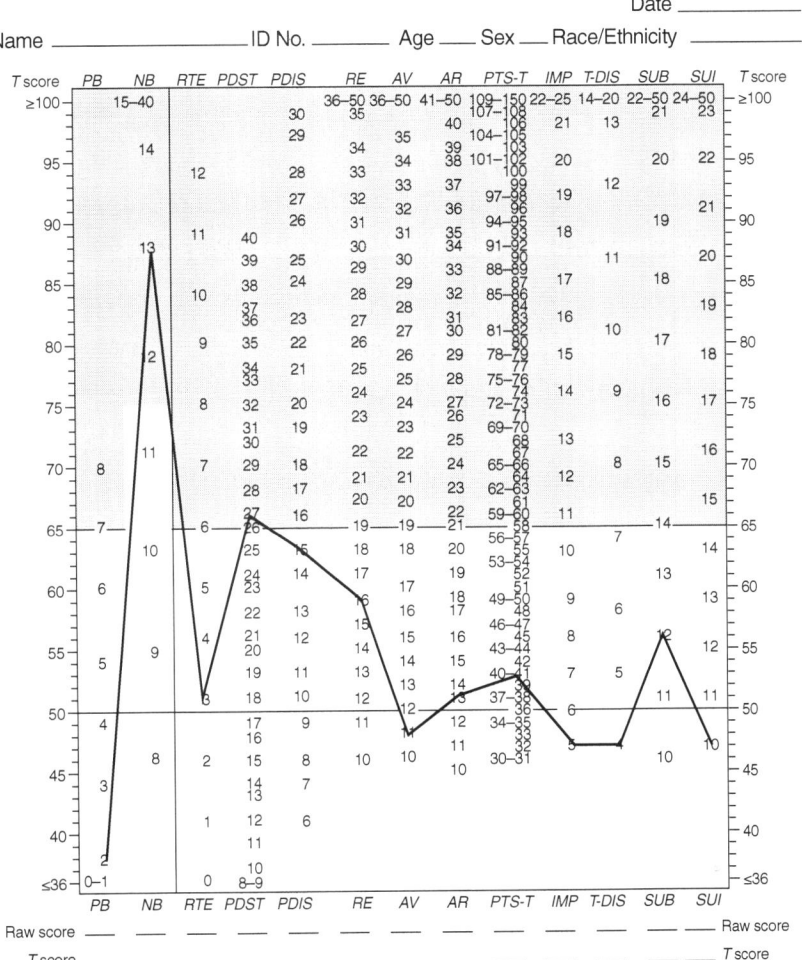

Figure 4.4 DAPS profile for John, post-treatment (13.06.2011)

John went from phoning me during the week in order for me to talk him down from panic attacks with weekly office sessions, to not phoning at all, and by the sixth session only needing to come and see me once a month.

Even though for John there was still residual anxiety after ten sessions, his subjective assessment demonstrated a move out of the clinical population:

> This counselling has been crucial to me in what was a very vulnerable time in my life, let alone my career. I fully expect I will still have my moments from time, but I have learnt some excellent coping strategies.

I never want to go back to those darkest of days and with what I have learnt, I will be OK. I have learnt a lot about myself and I have gained so much from the sessions. Just knowing help was a phone call was really supportive, whether I needed to call or not. I feel happy to go it alone at this time, but will certainly consider top ups from time to time, just to ensure I am on track. Although this has been a torrid 6–8 months at times, I very proud of what I have achieved because I really did wonder what was wrong with me and was I going mad. The sessions have given me the strength and knowledge to know that I will be ok and that I don't need to over analyse things. If I were to discover a colleague was showing signs of what I have been through, I would not hesitate to recommend this help. It has been invaluable to me. Thanks!!!

John's score on the BAI fell to 14, which is classified as 'mild' anxiety. His profile on DAPS, as can be seen in Figure 4.4, dramatically changed with no more trauma specific dissociation, re-experiencing or hyper-arousal.

Comments

Many points within this case history address the theoretical perspectives of the specific cognitive models in the first part of the chapter. This provides interesting convergent validity concerning what NLP has discovered about anxiety and what cognitive/behavioural researchers have discovered.

For instance, it is clear that John was different from the normal population in that he did have a predisposition to 'worry' and, as Rygh and Sanderson (2004) discovered, overestimated the benefits of worry as a strategy that has positive outcomes. His panic attack 14 years previously was just a symptom of this generalized anxiety disorder. Discussions with Goblin that were designed to bring to the surface the positive intention matched to a great extent the vertical descent technique of Vasey and Borkovec (1992). Consequently, John discovered himself that his worrying was excessive and not needed. These conversations also addressed his inability to deal with uncertainty, which Ladouceur *et al.* (1998) recognized was a key variable which prevented successful cognitive restructuring. John was encouraged to recognize that the physiological symptoms of anxiety were only one part of the equation. It was up to him, in their presence, to remain relaxed and generate internal dialogue, which would support his own outcomes rather than responding automatically thereby reinforcing the stress response. In accordance with the recommendations of Rygh and Sanderson, in order to obtain maximum effect this was done covertly in order to bypass any conscious resistance. As John created unconscious sensory representations that generated hyper-arousal, the author would fire an auditory anchor, 'and now you are in control' and then follow this with language full of sensory overlap providing alternative representations that previously were agreed represented positive and valued themes. This matched, to a great extent, the theme of response prevention that is used so successfully in OCD, however, it is delivered in a more covert fashion than would be expected within the traditional cognitive behavioural model.

Panic caused by systematic misconstruing of experiences leading to catastrophizing (Beck, 1976) was very much a theme of John's experience, and as the case history shows, learning to re-construe his physiological experiences as a trigger to generate positive cognitions in a relaxed way was a part of this successful intervention. Progressive muscular relaxation was also a continuing theme throughout the ten sessions to remind John he always had a *choice* to be tense or relaxed – with the 'relaxed' always being marked out with such analogue markers as tone, volume, pitch and pace in order to reinforce that 'choice'.

Research and NLP

Much of the research into NLP and anxiety cluster disorders follows the above anecdotal and qualitative style, using single or small clusters of cases as the sample base. Even when NLP practitioners make use of patterns discovered through NLP modelling projects, they do so in a manner that does not rigidly adhere to every jot and title of the protocol, but makes allowance for the dynamic interplay between therapist and patient. This is in-keeping with a paradigm which is much more fluid in its thinking compared with a strict positivist viewpoint which sees the world of people as a closed system with fixed labels, rules and generalizations which can be made on the basis of such rules.

A search on the PsycInfo, PsycArticles, PsychExtra and Medline databases returned 774 hits for NLP compared with 9,120 for CBT characterizing the present difference in the published research base for the two disciplines. When the searches were paired with anxiety the number of hits were reduced to 12 and 2456 respectively (21 July 2011).

Two of the NLP hits referred to something other than NLP, namely Neuroleptics and Needle Localization Procedure. The remaining papers as mentioned above were a mixture of case studies and small-scale empirical studies (N=17 maximum).

One difficulty in reviewing the research is not only are the NLP patterns operationalized in different ways according to the practitioner, but also NLP is often used as an adjunctive treatment, meaning it is not possible to understand the extent to which the NLP pattern was responsible for improvement and to what extent other modalities were. Osteopathy, holistic frameworks, self-hypnosis, eye-movement desensitization and reprocessing (EMDR), shamanic healing, and Buddhist meditation were all mentioned in the above search as being used in combination with NLP.

1 Effects of Neurolinguistic Psychotherapy on psychological difficulties and perceived quality of life (Stipancic et al., 2010)

In this first paper, NLPt (neurolinguistic psychotherapy) is regarded by the authors as a unique school of psychotherapy, starting in the 1980s, which draws upon the principles and techniques of NLP. The authors of this paper point out that there is a standard curriculum and a professional code of ethics based on the European Association for Psychotherapy.

One hundred and six participants who were psychotherapy clients were randomly assigned to either a therapy group or a control group. Their motivations to participate in psychotherapy were diverse; removal of distressing symptoms ($N=44$), altering disturbed patterns of behaviour ($N=12$), improving interpersonal relationships ($N=19$), improving coping with stresses of life ($N=12$) and personal growth and maturation ($N=19$). One can appreciate the theme of personal anxiety would permeate each of these categories.

What was important and characteristic of this study, making it stand out, was that all seven therapists were experienced (by 10–20 years), and were trained in NLPt and also trained to NLP training Master level. They all agreed to discipline themselves throughout this research to only make use of the NLPt 'goal model' in therapeutic work, meaning a clearly defined set of NLPt methods and techniques would only be used. Also significant is that the number of participants ($N=106$) is far greater than the norm concerning experimental research into the effects of NLP.

Outcome measures were the structured clinical interview for DSM-IV, personality disorders (SCID-II) and the Croatian Scale of Quality of Life (KVZ). These psychometric instruments had 118 items and 20 to 23 items (dependent on age group) respectively. Measurements were taken at times 1, 2 and 3. These were pre-therapy; t_1, immediately post-therapy; t_2 and at five-month follow-up t_3.

Table 4.1 Descriptive statistics of outcome variables

	SCID-II sum		KVZ predictor variables		KVZ criterion variables	
	Mean	SD	Mean	SD	Mean	SD
Therapy group						
Pre (t_1)	8.61	7.38	3.46	0.65	3.13	0.87
Post (t_2)	3.87	5.44	3.76	0.55	3.55	0.72
Follow-up (t_3)	1.83	4.74	3.86	0.49	3.73	0.78
Control group						
Pre (t_1)	7.10	5.86	3.42	0.49	2.99	0.72
Post (t_2)	6.27	5.91	3.36	0.56	3.02	0.83

Notes
Predictor variables = causes of satisfaction/dissatisfaction in life.
Criterion variables = perception of quality of life.

Anxiety disorders 89

As can be seen from Table 4.1, the results show significant movement in the 'right' direction for all measures. In the discussion, Stipancic *et al.* point out the only significant within group variable was length of therapy. It was found that the therapy effect size was related to the number of sessions. In terms of anxiety, this seems to be significant as the short fix can often produce quick positive effects and Stipancic *et al.* cite Morschitzky (2006) who points out that 'the contribution of longer therapies goes beyond resolving presented symptoms and enhances self-esteem, the capability to establish relationships, the ability to cope with everyday stress, and raises productivity in the workplace'. NLP, therefore, should not just be put into the category of brief therapy only, even though the authors concede that after six months there are usually diminishing returns (Howard *et al.*, 1986).

This research shows that NLPt can produce therapeutic effects on a par with the well-researched effects found within CBT (Grawe *et al.*, 2001; Renner and Platz, 1999).

2 Neurolinguistic programming used to reduce the need for anaesthesia in claustrophobic patients undergoing MRI (Bigley et al., 2010)

This next paper demonstrates the effectiveness of NLPt in a highly specific context. This paper is included as the NLP pattern used to resolve the anxiety of the patients was not the NLP phobia cure, but collapsing anchors, which is a pattern often used to resolve GAD and also specific stress responses within Acute Stress Disorder. Fifty patients who had failed to complete an MR (magnetic resonance scan) because of subjective claustrophobia were selected with eight of the 58 patients approached declining to take part. These eight patients subsequently undertook MRI scanning with the aid of a general anaesthetic, financially, a much more costly procedure.

The patients' level of anxiety was assessed by a questionnaire based on Spielberger's State–Trait Anxiety Inventory. This was assessed on two occasions: (i) on the same day as the NLP treatment and (ii) after NLP but before the MR scan.

The radiographer undertook 20 days of NLP training spread over a six-month period and the course was accredited by the International NLP Trainers Association. As mentioned above, a specific permutation of the NLP pattern 'collapsing anchors' especially tailored for phobias with an unknown origin was used. This was developed by Clare Rushworth (1994). It involves the integration of two states, usually a negative and a positive one in order to develop a third resourceful positive state which has within it the resources of both. The main differences from a straight collapsing anchors procedure are:

1 Two different systems are used for the anchors: visual (phobia) and kinaesthetic (resources).

2 A precise trigger for the phobic response is identified and then anchored.
3 A precise and ecological mix of 'antidote' states for the resource anchor is selected and a very powerful resource anchor is stacked with multiple resources.

Success was determined by three dependent variables:

1 Did the patient manage to have a complete examination?
2 Were the images adequate for clinical reporting as judged by a consultant radiologist not directly involved in the study?
3 Had the individual's anxiety levels reduced after the NLP counselling as measured by the psychometric?

Of the 50 patients who were recruited, 38 (76 per cent) completed the MR examination and all of those examinations were of sufficient quality for clinical reporting. MR examinations were not completed in 12 patients (24 per cent), including three who would not consider going onto the scanner and nine who went on the scanner bed but for whom no usable images were obtained. There was also a statistically significant reduction in anxiety scores post NLP counselling (collapsing anchors) for all patients.

As can be seen below from Figure 4.5, the 12 patients who subsequently failed to undergo the MR examination had statistically higher anxiety scores before NLP than the patients who tolerated the MRI ($p50.034, 0.05$).

What is significant about this study is that it unequivocally shows the financial savings that are created through the judicious use of NLP in specific contexts. The cost of an MRI under general anaesthetic (GA) is calculated at £488, compared with £169 for an MRI using NLP.

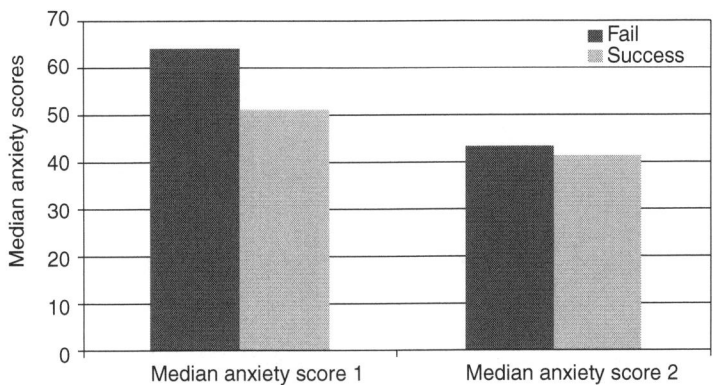

Figure 4.5 Median anxiety scores before NLP (left) and after NLP (right) in patients who subsequently had a successful MR (light grey) and those who failed (dark grey)

3 Neurolinguistic programming treatment for anxiety: magic or myth? (Krugman et al., 1985)

This paper's findings are not as positive as the above. Krugman *et al.* make the point that, as NLP apparently has clearly specified treatment instructions, unlike many therapeutic approaches it is possible to put the claims made for this therapy approach to an empirical test. As far as this assumption goes this seems quite reasonable. Public anxiety was chosen as the disorder as it is very prevalent in the general population.

Two graduate students in clinical psychology and one graduate student in counselling psychology served as therapists and were trained by a clinical psychologist who had been taught the NLP treatment for phobias in a workshop led by Bandler, one of the originators of the technique.

Fifty-five undergraduate psychology students responded to an advertisement for a programme to alleviate anxiety in public speaking situations. No mention was made of the experimental nature of the programme or of the availability of experimental credit until after subjects agreed to participate so as to increase the probability of obtaining a sample of genuinely anxious participants who were motivated to attend because of a desire to improve their public speaking. They were randomly assigned to an NLP group, a desensitization group or a waiting control group.

The pre- and post-test measures were:

1 Fear Expectancy Survey (12-item questionnaire drawn from Personal Report of Confidence as a Speaker; Gilkinson 1942).
2 During a four-minute speech, behavioral ratings of performance anxiety were made by three trained observers using Paul's (1966) Behavioral Checklist, as modified by Kirsch *et al.* (1975).
3 During a four-minute speech a global rating of subjects' speech anxiety on a ten-point scale.
4 Fear Survey (condensed version of Personal Report of Confidence as a Speaker; Gilkinson 1942).

The format for the NLP treatment was taken from a transcript of treatment by Bandler (Bandler and Grinder, 1979). Here, Bandler and Grinder suggest that therapists treat all psychological limitations as phobias (p.109). This was a 'structured regression' (p.116) known in NLP as the 'change personal history pattern' (p.108). This introduces the concept of time as well. The process sets up a resource anchor and an anchor for the 'phobic' response. Making use of the natural capacity to dissociate, the therapist encourages the patient to go back in time and experience viewing of the phobic response from a dissociated perspective. Making use of the resource anchor facilitates this process and encourages a reorganization of the representation and thus of the experience, so it now becomes a resourceful response rather than a 'phobic' one.

The experimental control was a condensed version of the self-control desensitization procedure (Goldfried, 1971). First, subjects received 20 minutes of progressive relaxation training. They were then instructed to imagine themselves giving a speech and to signal the therapist as soon as they experienced any tension or anxiety. When anxiety was signalled they were instructed to 'relax away' the anxiety while maintaining the image of speaking in public. This treatment was designed to last as long as the NLP intervention.

The wait-list control group received the same pre- and post-treatment assessments as were administered to the treatment groups. Between assessments the control subjects waited in a waiting room for the same amount of time that treated subjects spent in therapy. Following post-treatment assessment, these subjects received the same treatment that had been provided to subjects in the self-control desensitization group. This was offered to fulfill the promise of treatment upon which their participation was initially secured and was not part of the experimental study.

The results of the research are summarized in the Table 4.2.

Table 4.2 Mean pre- and post-treatment scores

Variable	Pre-treatment		Post-treatment				
	M	SD	M	SD	T	Df	P<
Fear expectancy							
NLP	38.28	6.21	32.89	6.94	3.15	17	.006
Cog-beh	41.74	7.49	32.63	10.13	4.87	18	.001
Control	39.27	4.92	36.13	6.17	2.91	14	.011
Fear survey							
NLP	39.37	7.12	28.16	7.90	7.11	18	.001
Cog-beh	39.68	10.00	27.26	6.67	7.13	18	.001
Control	38.00	9.86	27.06	8.00	5.47	16	.001
Behavioural checklist							
NLP	25.48	3.96	23.13	4.67	2.87	18	.010
Cog-beh	27.63	6.87	22.89	5.78	3.56	18	.002
Control	23.54	4.51	20.98	4.88	2.83	16	.012
Global rating							
NLP	6.72	1.18	6.06	1.06	3.48	17	.003
Cog-beh	7.09	1.51	5.93	1.66	4.67	18	.001
Control	6.62	1.19	5.61	1.54	3.90	16	.001

As can be seen, all three groups obtained significant improvements in their scores on all four measures. One-way Analysis of Variance (ANOVA) analysis revealed that the fear differences between groups in pre-treatment scores was not significant. ANCOVA analysis revealed that there were no significant differences between groups in reducing fear in public speaking. Statistically we could therefore conclude that waiting for treatment is as effective a treatment as either NLP or CBT. The researchers conclude that, as there was no significant difference between the two experimental groups and the control group, the significant improvements for each group are due to common factors namely pre-treatment assessment and habituation to the experimental setting. The authors point out this research replicates the findings of Mathews *et al.* (1985).

Matthews tested Bandler and Grinder's claim that, based on their observation and modelling of Erickson's use of two levels of communication and his interspersal technique, a double hypnotic induction procedure that they developed was 'one of the most powerful induction and deepening techniques' (Bandler and Grinder, 1975b, p.196). They found that this was not the case, however, they did point out that utilization of feedback from the participants was not possible as would normally be the case in an Ericksonian induction, as the double induction was conducted via a recording device.

The authors suggest that their findings argue strongly for continued study of NLP. They concede that the failure to find significant differences between both experimental groups and the wait-list control is probably a function of the brevity of treatment. Just as research has shown self-control desensitization to be effective over multiple sessions (Goldfried and Goldfried, 1977; Jacks, 1973; Spiegler *et al.*, 1976), so too it is likely that NLP as well would show better results over multiple sessions.

Conclusions

The initial literature search showed, compared with CBT, a paucity of research into the effectiveness of NLP. Of the 12 papers that were found concerning anxiety, none of the papers were particularly robust and consequently internal and external validity was essentially non-existent.

However, this has to be offset against thousands of NLP practitioners worldwide who can produce Level-D case histories, clinical and observational evidence which show significant reduction in symptoms for persons suffering from anxiety disorders. Such practitioners will point to the fact they have used NLP patterns and have done so in the therapeutic context of the NLP presuppositions. The majority of these practitioners will be professional psychologists or therapists who have a considerable amount of training, supervision and experience in NLP therapy.

There are many criticisms of DSM and scientist/practitioner methodologies. However, such methodologies do attempt to make observational assessments of what works and what does not less subjective. They do so by being clear about language and assigning verbal labels and processes in an accurate and precise manner. Whether this is the appropriate paradigm to adopt when assessing the effectiveness of a dynamic process that often makes use of covert communication is the subject matter for a book in itself.

There are many plusses to be taken away concerning NLP. There are *some* researchers who are sufficiently impressed with what NLP claims to suggest further research is advisable.

As is the case in the first paper (Stipancic *et al.* 2010), there is a standard curriculum for NLP psychotherapy in Europe and a professional code of ethics based on the code of ethics of the European Association for Psychotherapy already in place. Training of researchers is clearly an issue. In Stipancic *et al.* (2010), the therapists had between 10–20 years experience and were trained NLP therapists. Also in Bigley *et al.* (2010), the radiographer had 20 days' NLP practitioner training with an accredited provider. In the one paper where results were inconclusive the therapists had no NLP training apart from that imparted by a clinical psychologist who only had attended one NLP workshop. This may be significant and certainly needs to be addressed in future research into the effectiveness of NLP therapy.

There is research, such as two papers that have been discussed in this chapter, that show NLP therapy is highly beneficial. It is very important that as NLP is developed further as an alternative and tested treatment that such papers be referenced. It is also imperative that we appreciate, as far as experimental validation is concerned, that NLP is still a 'young' discipline and responsible practitioners will hold their hands up to this. Finally, there is a theoretical base upon which NLP stands which generates therapeutic patterns which are tried and tested in other modalities. These patterns include clinical hypnosis, Socratic questioning, cognitive framing and reframing, vertical descent/pyramid questioning, tasking, perceptual positioning, time lines, visualization, goal setting and many more.

NLP therapy and its ability to reduce anxiety effectively and sustainably is more than a possibility, it is a fact, albeit one supported by largely anecdotal reports. What would be useful over the next decade is the emergence of NLP trained researchers who are prepared to put in the time to engage in experimental work. This will demonstrate to the clinical community how NLP patterns work and the circumstances in which they work. Such research will more clearly control for intervening variables and will work with larger samples. If dual diagnosis and co-morbidity are factors as often as they are these will be identified and taken into consideration. NLP therapists will demonstrate experience and appropriate training. Most importantly, the research will be falsifiable, and NLP knowledge and practice will respond appropriately to research that does not support the claims which have been made. Such a future is possible; let us hope that it will also become probable.

5 Addictions

Richard M. Gray

One of the central difficulties in thinking effectively about drugs and addictions lies in the fact that the whole topic is dominated by propaganda, outdated information and superstition. Whenever people begin to talk about drugs (including alcohol) the following ideas are trumpeted as fact:

- Addiction is a progressive chronic disease that ends in death or abstinence.
- There is some single identifiable entity called addiction.
- All drug use inevitably leads to addiction.
- Certain drugs have the specific property of being addictive.
- Certain people are born with addictive personalities.

In a real sense, not one of these ideas is 'true'. Each of them is a generalization or distortion that proceeds from the medical and moral models of addiction that have framed most of our thinking about drugs and alcohol. They have also crippled our capacity to deal effectively with the concept of addictions.

Anciently, and far into the twentieth century, addiction was treated as a moral failing. It was a sin or error of excess. It was proof positive of the presence of some lack of personal virtue, self-control or will power. Addicts were sinners or idiots. Through most of American history, the addict's ruin was viewed as just desserts but the toll taken on long-suffering family members and business associates was scandalous (Shattuck, 1994).

In the 1930s, when Bill Wilson and his associates put together the basic ideas of Alcoholics Anonymous, they decided that alcoholism (and later, drug addiction more generally) should be treated as a disease of the spirit. They held that alcoholism, while rooted in moral failings and character defects, had its final manifestation as disease.

Although the disease concept was originally designed *as a metaphor* with the intent of saving addicts from humiliation, in 1956 the American Medical Association (AMA) accorded alcoholism the medical status of disease. From then on the idea of addiction-as-disease gained momentum and was finally concretized through the growth of the huge business concerns that developed around it. The medicalization of addiction came to full fruition in the Minnesota Model, which immortalized the definition of addiction as a chronic, progressive disease that ultimately ends in death (Doweiko, 1996; Laundergan, 1983; Mann et al., 2000; Peele, 1989; Peele and Brodsky, 1991).

There are multiple reasons for arguing against the idea that addictions are diseases. Here, however, we will focus only on the fact that the disease concept implies a level of brokenness and biological stasis that limits creative thinking about the problem. From an NLP perspective, and from the perspective of a growing body of neuroscience, it may be useful to think of addictions as a set of over-learned and over-valued behaviours that have the impact of disease.

The thing we call addiction

Nominalizations are powerful distortions of reality. By turning a set of actions or symptoms into a static label we often miss the dynamic reality of the problem itself. In the case of addictions, we are often so blinded by the label that we miss the underlying utility of the behaviour and the fact that it serves or has served some practical use in the life in question. In NLP these are described as positive intentions (Dilts and DeLozier, 2000; O'Connor and Seymour, 1990).

Over the course of a lifetime, 'addictions' ebb and flow. For some persons, allegedly chronic, progressive addictions disappear for years and then suddenly reappear. For others, a terrible addiction suddenly goes away forever. These are not the behaviours of *things*. They are qualities of concepts; expressions of personal behaviours that are active in some contexts and dormant in others. Like other behavioural preferences, addictions are bound to contexts. Contexts may relate to persons, places, things, environments, self-definitions and mood.

Stanton Peele reports how the Veterans Administration prepared huge resources to meet the anticipated flood of addicted GIs returning from Vietnam. They knew that many of our soldiers had developed significant heroin addictions while in the service and expected that they would need a great deal of help when they returned home to the US. When they returned, however, levels of addiction dropped dramatically to the precise levels appropriate to the communities in which the GIs lived. Diseases do not respond to social context (Peele et al., 1991; Robins et al., 1974).

The NLP perspective on addiction

For our purposes, it may be useful to think about 'addictions' as reifications of patterns of behaviour. They are not real things, but things that are solidified into illusory realities by the words we use. They are conjured into existence by the labels we apply to them. What happens when we begin to think of preferences and skills instead of diseases?

If we think of an addiction as a set of (often unconscious) preferences, we may then be able to discover another set of preferences that are more valuable than the problem substance or behaviour. If we know the utility of the problem behaviour, it may be possible to find behaviours that are more useful, more immediate and more intuitive than these others. This analysis was suggested by Bandler and Grinder in the mid-1970s. If we can find an ultimate set of criteria, we stand the chance of 'outframing' the entire problem (Bandler and Grinder, 1979, 1983; Hall, 1996).

If we begin to think of addictions as learned skill sets that come to be preferred patterns of action that have generalized into multiple contexts, what happens if we find a generalized pattern of behaviour that works more effectively for that individual? If we create a new set of behaviours, beliefs or experiences that serve the purposes of social integration, positive self-regard, transcendence, etc., what happens to the addiction? This perspective is reflected by three studies cited by Peele *et al.* (1991) and Gray (2008a, b).

After urinalysis and interviews revealed that more than 40 per cent of returning Vietnam veterans had significant drug problems, the United States' Veterans Administration prepared huge resources to meet the anticipated flood of addicted GIs. They expected that they would need a great deal of help when they returned home to the US. When they returned, however, levels of addiction dropped dramatically. In fact, the actual level of addicted veterans dropped by 95 per cent with most of them needing no treatment at all (Gray, 2008a, b; Peele *et al.* 1991; Robins *et al.*, 1974).

A study conducted with rats (Alexander *et al.*, 1981) and the effect that environment can have on opiate addiction goes some way towards explaining why these veterans reverted to their pre-combat behaviour on return to their normal environment. The rat experiment concluded that there may be natural preference hierarchies that are organized in terms of the opportunities that they afford. Rats given access to an environment that tended to support self-reinforcing 'instinctive' behaviours were less likely to choose morphine solutions than were the rats that had no such opportunities. Early stress made the choice of opiates more likely for rats that had moved to the colony situation; all of the rats living in the positive environment were less likely to choose opiates than the rats in cages.

The most important piece of information provided by these studies may be that addictions are controlled less by the drugs than they are by the opportunities that an individual perceives beyond the drugs. If there are options of value to the individual, s/he may be less likely to begin or to continue drug consumption.

Although the idea of human (and to some extent, animal) instincts has passed from favour, we can still understand humans as having needs and tendencies to respond. Like most organisms we respond to pleasurable stimuli – tastes, petting, variety, sex, warmth, etc. We respond to the same kinds of conditioning behaviours as other mammals and it would appear that these preferences or needs are arranged hierarchically under the influence of immediate states of deprivation and satiety.

In 1998, the World Health Organization (WHO) published a survey of research regarding the use of opioids for palliative care in pain treatment. Colleau (1998), the editor of the survey, examined 11 studies regarding the incidence of addiction in medically supervised palliative care contexts. Her research indicated that addiction is exceedingly rare for patients receiving long-term opioid treatment for cancer pain and among those patients with no history of substance abuse, it does not occur. An examination of studies accounting for 24,000 patients with no previous history of substance abuse who had received opioid treatment for pain found that only seven out of the 24,000 had become addicted. They also reported that cancer patients who received long-term opiate treatment could stop the drugs when the pain ended. That equates to an addiction rate of two one-hundredths of one per cent.

One of the interesting facets of the interface between the concepts of addiction-as-disease and addiction-as-skill-set is that you never really lose a skill. Once it's learned, it can always be revived. It may take a little practice but, like bicycle riding, it is always there. How does this differ from the chronic nature of addictions? If addiction is the skill of solving every problem by artificially, and momentarily transcending it, is it unreasonable that when other strategies fail, the problem behaviour recurs? Just so, if the new behaviours are sufficiently rewarding, the old skill may never be needed again.

The idea that drug use inevitably leads to addiction is conceptually the same as saying that kissing makes you pregnant. While it is necessarily true that you have to have the first drink in order to become an alcoholic, it does not follow that having a drink will inevitably lead you to alcoholism. Robinson and Berridge (2003) report that, while as many as 32 per cent of Americans use illicit substances regularly, even for as highly addictive a substance as cocaine, only 15 to 16 per cent of users become addicted in the first ten years of use. Addiction is a long-term skill.

Modern neuroscience has also shown clearly that addicts do not necessarily pass through the stages of use, abuse, dependence and addiction. Addiction is not a property of chemical agents; it is about how people use the substances and behaviours. One of the key things that modern neuroscience tells us is that addiction is a property of brains that are functioning normally.

Neuroscience and addiction

In recent years, cognitive neuroscience has shed significant light on the problems of addiction and substance abuse. These researchers have uncovered a close relationship between drug addictions, behavioural addictions, compulsions and more normal patterns of reward and motivation. Central to this information are the ideas that drug and behavioural addictions are not problems with the 'hedonic impact' of the reinforcing agent ('liking' the drug), but they are problems related to 'wanting' or 'craving' the agent. They have called the measure of wanting, incentive salience. A second important discovery is that the mechanism of craving or incentive salience is mediated by neurons in the midbrain that produce dopamine. The midbrain dopamine tract runs from the ventral tegmental area at the base of the brain; through the nucleus accumbens, at the base of the ventral striatum; and finally ends in the frontal cortex with high concentrations of terminals in the orbito-frontal cortex, an apparent control centre for motivation and wanting in general (Canales, 2005; Diekhof *et al.*, 2008; Robinson, 2004; Robinson and Berridge, 2001, 2003; Ruden, 1997; Schultz *et al.*, 1997; Waelti *et al.*, 2001; Tobler *et al.*, 2005).

For some time it was believed that people became addicted because the behaviours or substances made them feel good. While this is certainly part of the reason, it doesn't explain why, even after substances or behaviours cease to produce the same 'whack', people continue to seek them out. The 'feeling good' interpretation of behavioural addiction violates some of the cardinal principles of behavioural psychology. Every addictive drug, every behavioural addiction, and every learned behaviour is subject to habituation. This means that the more exposure you have to something, the less effective it becomes. When a behaviour ceases to be rewarding, the behaviour becomes less probable. At some point, the stimulus stops evoking the trained response and the response is said to have been extinguished.

By this rule, most substances of abuse and most behavioural addictions should disappear on their own as they become less and less rewarding. However, even though, over time, addicts report lessened pleasure from the drug or behaviour (decreased hedonic impact), they complain that they still want the drug. This has led researchers to focus not on the pleasure that drugs impart (hedonic impact) but on their ability to create craving or wanting (incentive salience). It is this factor, craving or wanting, that is mediated by the midbrain dopamine system (O'Brien and Gardiner, 2005; Robinson and Berridge, 2001, 2003).

Incentive salience connects to neurophysiology through a series of experiments on single dopaminergic neurons and neural implants measuring the response of the neurons to various stimulus conditions. In general, researchers found that the midbrain dopamine system responds in very specific and predictable ways. First, it responds powerfully to novel rewards. Whenever rewards appear in an unexpected context, these neurons respond vigorously. Second, the brain seeks 'the difference that makes a difference'. If a stimulus fully predicts a reward or if it predicts decreasing reward, the neuronal response decreases and often disappears (this is one of the neural roots of habituation.). Third, if the stimulus predicts a reward that appears reliably but increases in value relative to other recent rewards, the neurons again increase the intensity of their response (Diekhof *et al.*, 2008; Robinson, 2004; Robinson and Berridge, 2001; Schultz *et al.*, 1997;

Waelti et al., 2001; Tobler et al., 2005). This data relates to addiction in the following ways:

- *Novelty* is a crucial part of the value accorded to addictive behaviours and substances (Diekhof et al. 2008; Robinson, 2004; Robinson and Berridge, 2001; Schultz et al. 1997; Tobler et al. 2005; Waelti et al. 2001). There is significant literature on relapse prevention pointing to boredom and stress as crucial predictors of relapse. In standard behavioural literature, animals that have suffered sensory deprivation will perform for rewards consisting of nothing more than exposure to novelty (Daly et al., 2002; NIDA, 2002).
- *Inconsistency of reward* reflects the standard behavioural idea of schedules of reinforcement. Once behaviours have been established through simple reinforcement, their probable repetition can be enhanced by changing the frequency or schedule of reinforcement. That is, instead of rewarding every correct trial one might reward every third correct response or every response that happens ten seconds after the first. This kind of reinforcement schedule is associated with persistent and sometimes compulsive behaviours (Ferster and Skinner, 1953; Skinner, 1957). In the world of addiction, the initial encounters with the drug providers do not always provide access to the expected intensity or quality of the high. The contexts of the problem behaviours do not always reliably predict access (the wrong company, the wrong place, nothing available). Drug cues in general set up an expectancy that is not always fulfilled. This very inconsistency increases the power of expectation. This is more an explanation of the consistency of the response, its relative probability within the behavioural repertoire but it does not fully explain the *wanting* aspect (Diekhof et al., 2008; Robinson, 2004; Robinson and Berridge, 2001).
- *The relative intensity of addictive behaviours*, as compared to normal experiences, leads the substance abuser to anticipate and prefer them over more mundane rewards. One of the important things about this observation is that the comparisons made by the dopamine systems are short term. Behavioural preferences are established when there is a sharp difference in intensity between problem reinforcers and other recently experienced stimuli. Positive experiences from last month are not remembered in the context of a drug or behaviour that that is overwhelmingly better than anything in the last hour (Diekhof et al., 2008; Schultz et al., 1997; Tobler et al., 2005; Waelti et al., 2001).

Addictive behaviours tend to appear after intense exposure to the substance or behaviour. Although there may be such things as one-shot learnings of addictive responses (even though this is highly unlikely), the compulsive behaviours called addictions tend to be established over multiple experiences, especially when those experiences are repeated with great frequency over time. Addictions are rarely established in less than a year of intense use and more often take several years to establish (Canales, 2005; Inaba and Cohen, 2007; Robinson, 2004; Robinson and Berrridge, 2003).

Another important insight from neuroscience should be familiar to practitioners of NLP. Preferences and values are experienced hierarchically. That means that we accord more or less value (incentive salience) to various actions and experiences. In NLP we describe these preference hierarchies in terms of value criteria. According to most researchers, the problem of addiction consists most centrally in the fact that the addictive behaviour or substance is so far over-valued that it 'outframes' normal response systems (Berridge and Robinson, 2003; Dilts and DeLozier, 2000; Goldstein and Volkow, 2002; McClure *et al.*, 2003; O'Connor and Seymour, 1990).

As noted previously, the midbrain dopamine system responds to the most impactful stimulus in recent neural history. Drugs, risky behaviour, shoplifting, chocolate and sex often provide a significantly more powerful experience than many other behaviours that we encounter daily. As a result, they are promoted to the top of the preference hierarchy. This promotion happens in two ways: with addictive substances, the primary means by which using behaviours are accorded increased incentive salience is through the direct or indirect chemical action on the midbrain dopamine system. Whether directly (e.g. amphetamines) or indirectly (e.g. alcohol or heroin), substances of abuse create an inordinate concentration of intracellular dopamine that promotes the behaviour to the head of the salience hierarchy as if it were a more vital need. This is termed incentive sensitization (Chambers *et al.*, 2007; Robinson and Berridge, 2001, 2003). The second way that behaviours are promoted in the hierarchy is through behavioural adaptations. The same midbrain dopamine system is activated whenever a particular outcome or behaviour can be used in the following three ways.

1. As an integral part of different behavioural sequences ('I always have a drink before I go out, just to loosen up.' 'Whenever I have to face John's mother, I have a drink.'). In the language of behavioural science we would say that the behaviour is present in multiple schemas.
2. It is found to be useful or available in multiple contexts (cigarettes and alcohol become powerfully addictive because they are so well integrated into the contexts of everyday life).
3. A behaviour becomes important when it seems to represent an easy answer, the path of least resistance. Drugs and behavioural problems work quickly and effectively to remove the stressors of the moment. They are easy, if impermanent, answers (Austin and Vancouver, 1996). In effect, the short-term utility of the behaviour and its generalization into multiple contexts increases its overall behavioural salience. In the presence of the increased concentrations of dopamine that occurs with the use of drugs, these generalized networks become central nodes in a growing network of drug-related responses (Chambers *et al.*, 2007).

Recent work in neuroscience has indicated that substance abusers also suffer from inhibitory deficits related to malfunctions in the frontal cortex, including the dorso-lateral prefrontal cortex, where target behaviours are identified and attention is focused; the ventro-medial prefrontal cortex (VMPFC), where responses are evaluated and automated responses inhibited; the orbito-frontal cortex where negatively valenced hierarchies in the right OFC are deactivated in favour of the approach valenced addictive patterns in the left and which also, in its dorso-lateral aspect, seems to support negative reinforcement; and the anterior cingulate cortex (ACC), which monitors performance and risk. Each of these centres project glutamatergic neurons into the accumbens-related circuitry and affect its sensitivity to various stimuli. Some of those same studies suggest that reactivation of the frontal cortex can ameliorate some of the problems associated with addictive cravings (Bechara, 2005; Bechara and Damasio, 2002; Bechara et al., 1999, 2000, 2002; Bechara and van der Kooy, 1985; Craig, 2009; Davidson, 1993; Diekhof et al., 2008; Feil et al., 2010; Kringelbach, 2005; Kringelbach and Berridge, 2009).

It is interesting to note that the same circuits that are deactivated in the addicted brain (ACC, OFC, DLPC) are essential elements in what has been termed the 'default mode network' (DMN) – the part of the brain that is active in introspection, self reflection, internally generated self-talk and meditation. In a later section we discuss the DMN as a candidate for a possible off-switch for addictive behaviour (Buckner et al., 2008; Feil et al., 2010; Greicius et al., 2003; Smallwood et al., 2012)

The nature of addictions summarized

Motivations are ordered into preference hierarchies through the action of several structures in the mid-brain dopamine pathway. Addiction develops as behaviours associated with substance abuse are artificially promoted in the preference hierarchy through the direct and indirect action of addictive drugs on intracellular concentrations of dopamine. The increased dopamine targets the brain circuits associated with the evaluation and prediction of reward and the behaviours leading to them. This action affects wanting the drug (incentive salience) not necessarily liking it (hedonic impact) (O'Brien and Gardiner, 2005; Robinson and Berridge, 2001, 2003; Volkow et al., 2002).

Drug-related behaviours are artificially streamlined and accorded high-incentive salience. This class of behaviours and percepts includes behaviours associated with drug contexts, people, places and things. These experiences and behaviours are organized as networks and are evoked by drug-related stimuli as preferred response systems instantiated by neural networks in the basal ganglia that direct behaviour by inhibiting competing pathways. Early drug-related responses are dominated by the action of the motivational properties of structures in the ventral striatum with special reference to the nucleus accumbens. Later-stage responses are dominated by ritualized automatic behaviours organized in the dorsal striatum. Once these networks are established they tend to become self-maintaining, independent of reinforcement (Berke and Hyman, 2000; Canales, 2005; Chambers *et al.*, 2007; Feil *et al.* 2010; O'Brien and Gardiner, 2005; Robinson and Berridge, 2001, 2003).

The behaviours in question can be either conscious or unconscious. Unconscious responses relate to preferences, moods and various automatisms related to substance use (the automatic reach for a pack of cigarettes by an ex-smoker). Conscious responses include the obsessive search for, and efforts to obtain and use substances of abuse (Berke and Hyman, 2000; Canales, 2005; Chambers *et al.*, 2007; Milner *et al.*, 1998).

At the same time that drug-related behaviours are promoted to the head of the salience hierarchy, the increased presence of extracellular dopamine reduces the number of dopamine (d_2) receptors in circuits that are not related to drugs or drug contexts. Besides natural reinforcers, the major brain circuits that suffer from these depletions are the circuits that are primarily concerned with the evaluation of behavioural outcomes and the inhibition of unwanted behaviours. These include the following circuits: circuits in the dorsolateral prefrontal cortex which choose behaviours and percepts, focus attention, plan for their execution and allow for flexible transition from one focus or outcome to another; circuits originating in the anterior cingulate cortex which evaluate behaviour, predict errors and override inappropriate behaviours; circuits originating in the right ventromedial prefrontal cortex and orbitofrontal cortices which modulate automatic behaviours, limit impulsivity and socially inappropriate behaviours, and provide contextually appropriate evaluative feedback. Addictions dominate the user's life through this combination: the increased valuation of the addiction related substances and contexts, and the decrease in evaluative capacities centred in the dorsolateral prefrontal cortex, anterior cingulate cortex, right ventromedial prefrontal cortices and orbitofrontal cortices (Bechara, 2005; Bechara and Damasio, 2002; Bechara *et al.*, 1999, 2000, 2002; Bechara and van der Kooy, 1985; Canales, 2005; Craig, 2009; Davidson, 1993; Diekhof *et al.*, 2008; Feil *et al.* 2010; Goldstein and Volkow, 2002; Gu *et al.*, 2010; Kringelbach, 2005; Kringelbach and Berridge, 2009; Volkow *et al.*, 2002).

Dissociation of behavioural networks

LeDoux (Brockman and LeDoux, 1997) has pointed out that neural systems tend to exist independently of one another. Wolpe (1958) showed that there are neural response systems that cannot be expressed at the same time. The literature of extinction and inhibition in classical conditioning has also shown that one set of associations tends to dominate a response network while excluding the influence of other possible associations.

State-dependent memories reflect the almost absolute dissociation between contextually bound behavioural systems. Chambers *et al.* (2007) have suggested that behavioural networks exist independently of one another and that the evocation of one network can effectively render another temporarily inaccessible. Craig (2009) has argued for the functional division of forebrain structures into those sub-serving sympathetic and parasympathetic activities as major subdivisions of emotional control. He also suggests that the anterior cingulate cortex is capable of significantly affecting subjective perception of well-being through direct connections with the anterior insula (Bouton, 1994; Bouton and Moody, 2004; Brockman and LeDoux, 1997; Canales, 2005; Chambers *et al.*, 2007; Craig, 2009; Rescorla, 1988; Rossi, 1986; Rossi and Cheek, 1988; Wolpe, 1958).

This is relevant to addiction in that drugged states, as altered states of consciousness, are often inaccessible to normal, waking contexts and often lead to behaviours that are segregated into specific drug related contexts. Lyvers (2000) reports that alcoholics, assumed to be persons who have lost control over drinking, have been observed to moderate their drinking under specific incentive conditions. Smokers, moreover, are often observed to become so engaged in some other activity that smoking is essentially forgotten for the time being. The author, Gray, over 20 years' time working with substance abusers in the federal and local courts, has had the not-uncommon experience of having substance abusers time their abuse so that they are least likely to be detected. The classical preclinical test for addiction is a place preference association. In the context of addictions, the assertion of a novel context, not associated with addictive response systems, may be crucial to recovery.

Target problems

There are three problems that need to be dealt with in answering the problem of addiction. The first is the overwhelming incentive salience of the addictive behaviour. The second is restoring the active capacity of attentional and evaluative mechanisms in the orbitofrontal cortex, the ventromedial prefrontal cortex, the anterior cingulate cortex and the dorsolateral prefrontal cortex. The third problem is ensuring that alternate behavioural networks are in place that are independent of the drug-centred behavioural networks and that are sufficiently self-reinforcing and salient that they will maintain sober behaviour over time.

NLP approaches to addiction

In the early history of NLP, Bandler and Grinder made several suggestions about the treatment of addiction. In *Reframing* (1982), they suggested that addictions could be treated by providing the client with a response option that was more powerful, more accessible and more immediate than the drug itself. In several sources, Bandler suggests making the state of being high available as an anchor or intensifying the urge to use to the point where it becomes preferable to the use itself (Bandler, 1999). Andreas suggests using the compulsion blow-out to solve the immediate problem of craving. He also suggests using the guilt-resolution process and other techniques for clean-up of motivations and secondary gain (Andreas and Andreas, 1989, 2002).

One of the early applications of NLP to the treatment of addictions was the six-step reframe (Bandler and Grinder 1979, 1982). This technique was promulgated specifically for use in addictions by Sternman (1990) *Neuro Linguistic Programming in Alcoholism Treatment.*

The six-step reframe, as one of the old NLP standbys, continues to be used for the treatment of addictions and works by enlisting the aid of the unconscious mind, as personified in the 'part' responsible for the presenting problem, to generate more useful alternatives that will realize the original positive intent of the behaviour. The process has been critiqued in terms of its tendency to artificially fragment the personality and its generally allopathic orientation. Beyond some case material provided by Sternman and her associates, there is no published research on the technique.

Another, more elegant approach to addictions was provided by Connirae and Tamara Andreas in their 1994 book, *Core Transformations.* This approach looked to uncover a series of outcome sequiturs from the problem behaviour that would eventually lead to deep, core-level values and experiences. These core values could be understood as the ultimate positive intent of the behaviour. Once conscious, the core value could become the active outcome towards which organismic energies would be directed.

From a Jungian and generative perspective, both of these approaches reach down to access an archetypal level of experience that can be used to redirect conscious and unconscious energies in a direction that is much more aligned with archetype of the deep self – the centre and goal towards which each life tends to grow (Gray, 1996, 1997). In the six-step reframe, the approach is accomplished outside of consciousness with the expectation that all of the parts (presumably Jungian complexes – behavioural and perceptual habit centres) will be able to negotiate an effective, alternative answer to the problem behaviour and then replace it. The approach of core transformation works from the problem behaviour to reach one of several possible conscious experiences of wholeness, a core value that serves to provide a new direction for the behaviour. In this approach, something much closer to a conscious experience of the deep self is awakened and acknowledged.

From an evolutionary and behavioural perspective, both approaches may be understood as providing access to essential – survival level – organismic motivations for the problem behaviours; e.g. safety, nourishment, sociality, sexual expression, etc. By accessing the content-free state associated with satiation of those needs, they provide an alternative experience to which the triggering stimuli can now be associated. On a neurological level, there is reason to believe that core transformation activates the DMN in that it accesses internally oriented, transcendent states that are framed as desired outcomes.

It is unfortunate that, although each of these interventions has fairly extensive anecdotal support, there has been no empirical testing of either. With the exception of Sternman's work, a search for the term 'six-step reframe' failed to return any results in Lexis-Nexis Academic, Jstor, ProQuest Dissertations and Theses: Sciences and Engineering, PsychInfo, Sage Journals, Science Direct and SocINDEX. The responses for Sternman were articles from her book with no associated analysis or testing. The search term, 'Core Transformation' received a brief précis in PsycINFO excerpted from Hoyt (1996), but no substantive analysis. There was no mention in the other databases.

The Brooklyn Program

The only NLP intervention for addiction that has any coverage in the academic journals is The Brooklyn Program by Gray. Unfortunately, those reports consist exclusively of Gray's reports of his own results. The search term [addiction AND 'Brooklyn Program' AND Gray AND 'Neurolinguistic programming'] in SocINDEX recovers his report in the *Journal of Social Work Practice in the Addictio*ns (Gray, 2001a). PsychInfo returns that and his 2002 report in the *Federal Probation Journal* (Gray, 2002).

Gray reports a 29.6 per cent abstinence rate one-year post-treatment, but indicates that this rate was not statistically different from a control group composed of programme dropouts who were later referred to other treatment. He notes, however, that, whereas the standard treatment cost an average of $3,600 per client and required large time commitments, the NLP-based intervention required a weekly investment of approximately four hours of the facilitator's time (he was on payroll at the time) and only two hours (exclusive of homework assignments) of each client's time. This, he noted, makes the programme worthy of further attention.

In a later report of the programme (Gray, 2010), Gray reports that participants in the last two programme groups completed the Positive and Negative Affect Scale (Watson *et al.*, 1988) as pre- and post-measures for the month immediately preceding the evaluation. When compared to the norming data, participants at the start of the programme scored below the norming mean on the positive scale and near the mean on the negative scale. Post-treatment, the positive scores increased by more than one full standard deviation, while the negative scores decreased by one half standard deviation. Gray interprets this data to mean that, while participants gained in positive outlook, the relative stability of the negative scores meant that they were not unrealistic about their prospects.

In the two reports cited in the academic indexes, Gray (2001a, 2002) relies upon Jungian and Maslowian concepts of calling and self-actualization as root concepts in the programme. He indicates that the programme aims to create feelings of *self-esteem*, understood as knowing one's calling or place in the universe; *self-efficacy*, understood as developing as a result of learning to control feeling states with NLP-based tools, and *futurity*, conceptualized in terms of Prochaska's (Prochaska, 1994; Prochaska *et al.*, 1994) strong principal of change and the development of a positively desired future using tools from NLP. In later descriptions of the programme (Gray 2008a, 2010, 2011b), he makes a more straightforward appeal to functional neuroanatomy and relates the programme procedures to incentive salience and the capacity of learned affective skills to challenge the salience of addictive behaviours; a reawakening through the use of NLP-based tools of frontal processes that had been diminished by the action of substances of abuse; and the creation of personally meaningful futures.

The programme is described as a 16-week treatment programme that meets once a week for two hours per week. It also requires two one-on-one sessions for each participant. It is notable in that after the first session, drugs and problem behaviours are never officially mentioned. The programme is manualized with the original version appearing in 2008 and an updated version appearing in 2011.

NLP tools used in the programme

Gray relies on four basic tools from NLP. These are: submodality analysis/amplification, anchoring, future-pacing/pseudo-orientation in time and the NLP well-formedness conditions for outcomes.

Submodality analysis/amplification refers to the amplification or modification of a remembered resource by focusing upon and manipulating the fine-grained details of the experience across sensory modalities so as to increase or decrease the intensity of the present-time experience of the resource. These details include: amplitude, intensity, complexity, distance, direction and other features (Andreas and Andreas, 1987; Bandler, 1985; Bandler and MacDonald, 1987; Gray, 2011d).

Anchoring is a general term for conditioning in NLP that can mean almost anything from a structured classical conditioning procedure using multiple iterations to produce the association between stimulus and response to a simpler mnemonic that may represent a species of one-shot learning with the client's conscious approval and cooperation (Andreas and Andreas, 1989; Bandler and Grinder 1979; Dilts and DeLozier, 2000). Rescorla (1988) indicates that this represents a reasonable understanding of the range of classical conditioning phenomena. In the Brooklyn Program, anchoring is understood as a specific instance of Pavlovian delayed conditioning executed by the participant as she repeatedly makes a specific repeatable gesture during multiple elicitations of a practiced resource state. Stacking anchors refers to chaining multiple conditioned responses to a single conditioned stimulus or anchor (Gray, 2011a).

Future pacing is imaginal practice. It consists of imagining a context where an anchor or resource state would be useful while evoking the resource or firing off the anchor. It is rooted in Milton Erickson's pseudo-orientation in time (Erickson and Rossi, 1989). Insofar as imagined stimuli activate much of the same neurology as the original stimulus, practice of an anchor or resource in an imagined context effectively transfers some of the practice to the imaginal context (Andreas and Andreas, 1989; Bodenhamer and Hall, 1988; Cade and O'Hanlon, 1993; Dilts and DeLozier, 2000; Gray, 2011a; Linden and Perutz, 1998).

Well-formedness conditions for outcomes, refers to a standard NLP procedure used to design or evaluate outcomes. Based on Chomsky's concept of well-formedness conditions for language, these conditions require that the outcome be stated in the positive, under the participant's personal control, verifiable in sensory terms and evaluated in terms of the client's personal ecology (Andreas and Andreas, 1989; Bodenhamer and Hall, 1988; Cade and O'Hanlon, 1993; Dilts and DeLozier, 2000; Gray, 2011a; Linden and Perutz, 1998).

Description of the Brooklyn Program (based on Gray, 2011b)

The Brooklyn Program is implemented over 16 weeks for one two-hour session per week. It teaches specific behavioural and cognitive skills and, as noted, it never discusses drugs or problem behaviours, but works to build emotional and cognitive resources that will ultimately out-frame them. Gray notes that, while the programme could be implemented in a shorter time period, the 16-week duration allows for overlearning of the target behaviour and ensures that it will be taken seriously by persons unused to the speed of NLP techniques.

Insofar as the programme does not discuss addictive behaviour, in the initial meeting, three promises or representations are made to the participants. These are that: the participants will learn how to enhance their memory; the participants will learn how to control their feelings; and that, if they do the exercises each week, they will find the programme the most rewarding two hours of their week. If however, they do not do the exercises, it will be the most boring two hours.

In the first several sessions, participants are taught how to access and enhance a series of positive resource states using standard NLP submodality techniques. As is well known in the NLP community, this submodality work begins with a striking enhancement of the remembered experience. This validates an early promise made to all participants, that they will be taught memory enhancement techniques.

During the same several sessions, the participants are taught to focus more and more on the feelings associated with a series of resource experiences so that they discover a series of deeply pleasurable transcendent states. These pseudo-meditative states are designed partly to provide feelings of self-efficacy, but they are also intended to provide powerful positive experiences that are strong enough to challenge the salience of the problem behaviour.

Next in sequence, the participants are taught to anchor several predefined states that they have accessed and enhanced during the preceding sessions. These include:

- the experience of focused attention
- a single, good decision made in a systematic fashion
- a moment of skill consolidation or streamlining of a learned behaviour – riding a bike, driving a manual car
- an experience of pure fun or enjoyment
- an experience of confidence or personal competence.

These resources are enhanced to ecstatic levels – to the point where there is virtually no shadow of the original content or context. Each state is anchored to a distinct hand gesture. According to Gray, the anchoring process, the creation of conditioned access points for immediate and automatic evocation of the states, has the following advantages:

1   They make the resource transportable and accessible in multiple contexts.
2   They create a relatively mechanical means for evoking and enhancing the anchored state.
3   They enhance self-efficacy perceptions by providing an affective tool that is totally under the client's control.
4   They create an automated access for later integration of these preliminary anchors into a more complex state (stacking anchors).

Once the anchors have been practised and enhanced several times, participants are encouraged to practise them in multiple situations so that they generalize into other life contexts. This ensures that the new behaviour – access to the resource states – generalizes beyond the confines of the weekly session. A strong emphasis on homework and independent practise serves the same end. Participants are also encouraged to create several of their own anchors to ensure that they understand that all of this is under their personal control and that the resource states are theirs and theirs alone. A crucial element here is an emphasis on the development of efficacy tools and beliefs about the participants' own efficacy perceptions (Bandura, 1997).

At about the seventh week, the anchors are stacked into a single anchor which has been labelled 'NOW' and which, according to the author's understanding, creates a basic felt experience (constellation) of Jung's deep self. Jung (Edinger, 1972; Gray, 1996; Hillman, 1996; Jung 1965, 1977) indicated that every person was being moved by unconscious processes towards the realization of a whole, integrated expression of all that they could be as psychological and spiritual beings. This inner potential served as a life compass, in those able to use it, for personal development on all levels. This sense of personal direction is evoked to provide an affective basis for creating a truly meaningful and compelling set of outcomes. This is done in the last sessions where the NLP well-formedness conditions are used to create a future that matches the function of the positive outcome in Prochaska's strong principle of change (Prochaska, 1994) and in light of his observation that movement through the stages of change is propelled most significantly by the identification of a meaningful and compelling future (Gray, 2011a, 2011b).

The process continues with the collection and anchoring of another series of resources from various time periods in the participant's life. These consist of times when the participants felt good about themselves; things that they did well; things that they learned easily; meaningful jobs and roles that they held; and things they wanted to be when they were kids. These are again anchored, enhanced and integrated into the NOW anchor.

Finally, the felt state associated with NOW is used to create well-formed outcomes across several life domains: home life, occupation, spiritual life, relationships, intellectual life and health practices. Each outcome is created by accessing the NOW anchor and imagining life in each of these domains through the affective window of the felt state 'NOW'. This results in future outcomes that are consistent with a deep, felt sense of personal identity. Superficial outcomes such as wealth, sex and possessions are discarded in favour of behavioural outcomes that give expression to the constellated sense of the deep self. Remaining exercises are devoted to enhancing the vision of the future and consolidating the learnings.

The process

Gray (2010, 2011b) indicates that the core of the programme is to be found in exercises 1–3, 5, 6 and 10. This discussion will be limited to those exercises. They are fully scripted in the most recent version of the manual (Gray, 2011c). The bulk of the following process description is adapted from his most recent formulations (Gray, 2011a, 2011c).

The programme begins with the amplification of positive resources using submodality analysis. This occupies the bulk of exercises 1 and 2. These exercises require each participant to identify positive past experiences that were clean, sober and legal. The memories should be pleasurable, empowering, positively spiritual or loving. Participants are instructed to find a single memory resource, one in which all of the action is complete in the past and is not subject to change. Participants choose one experience for exercise one and five experiences, as noted below, for exercise 2.

Once the exemplar has been identified, participants are instructed to review their experience of the memory through each sensory system (most often the visual, auditory and kinaesthetic elements) while imagining changes in various dimensions (submodalities) of that memory. These dimensions include: size of the image or stimulus, proximity of the source to the subject, intensity of the stimulus, complexity of the stimulus (timbre for sound, hue for vision), focus (field ground dimensions and clarity of source), etc. With each change they are asked to consider the effect of the change on their experience of the exemplar. The participants are led through multiple repetitions of enhancing and evaluating their experience of the chosen memory. They are asked to keep any change that enhances the experience and to discard any that lessens the experience or has no effect. Crucially, the process of modifying the resource experience begins by ensuring that the participants are experiencing the exemplar in an associated fashion, that is, from the perspective of being there, in their own bodies as they relive the experience.

Participants are reminded regularly not to force their attention, but to 'gently turn' their attention to the best part of their experience. If attention waivers, they are to note the wavering and gently turn their attention back to the experience. The exercise is executed in an instructional tone without special hypnotic techniques. In the process, the memory is reported to increase in detail, ease of access and intensity of emotional impact.

Towards the end of the exercise, invoking the limited capacity of short-term memory (Miller, 1956), Gray begins to ask participants to pay attention more and more to the feeling associated with the experience and to focus more and more intently on possible and impossible dimensions of the feeling. These dimensions include: the movement of the feeling, whether it moves within the body or moves beyond the body, the speed of the feeling's movement, the texture of the feeling, the colour of the feeling, whether the feeling makes a noise and other possible dimensions of the experience. In the process, he claims, the content and context of the memory are abstracted out of the experience and clients find themselves floating in a pleasant, sometimes ecstatic trance state that is devoid of content and context. Special emphasis is placed on ensuring that the end states are completely divorced from the original source memories. He indicates that in this exercise, clients are taught to use a memory to access a feeling and then use the feeling to access a powerful altered state of consciousness.

In the first exercise, clients are allowed to choose their own resource without divulging its content. Gray explains that this encourages participation in the exercise. In the second exercise the same process is followed with the exception that the types of resource memories are dictated by the programme materials. For exercise 2, the memories must exemplify the following five states.

1   Focus: the experience of focused attention.
2   Solid: a single, good decision made in a systematic fashion.
3   Good: a moment of skill consolidation or streamlining of a learned behaviour – riding a bike, driving a manual car.

4   Fun: an experience of pure fun or enjoyment.
5   Yes: an experience of confidence or personal competence.

According to Gray, the first two exercises should have the effect of providing a very specific experience of self-efficacy in creating a strongly positive felt experience; they also provide practice in focusing conscious attention. On a neurological level this is expected to increase frontal activation, increase parasympathetic and (positive) limbic activation and enhance the incentive salience of the exercise through its hedonic impact, novelty and self-reinforcing aspects. He claims that the intensely pleasurable affect, novelty and surprising element of self-efficacy together increase the likelihood that the new behaviours will compete against addictive behaviours. He also repeatedly makes the point, citing Rossi (2000), that such activities take about 20 minutes to build to peak but can continue to affect mood and attitude for up to three hours. Gray also makes an explicit connection to meditative states and although he avoids mentioning meditation or spirituality to participants he characterizes the state as a pseudo-meditative state created with Western psychological tools (2002, 2008a, 2010, 2011b, 2011c).

In exercise 3, participants re-access and amplify the five states from exercise 2 and then they are led through the anchoring procedure. This is a classically conditioned association of the affects originally associated with the resource memory. More especially, it employs a delayed conditioning paradigm in which the anchor or neutral stimulus is presented after the onset of the unconditioned stimulus and terminates while the unconditioned stimulus is still present (2011a).

The procedure is as follows: after practicing the five resource states (Focus, Solid, Good, Fun, Yes) to the point where they are easily accessed and immediately give rise to a content-free altered state of consciousness, participants are taught how to associate those responses to five distinct physical gestures. For convenience they are five simple gestures that run, in order, down the first three fingers of either hand: Focus – tip of thumb to tip of index finger; Solid – tip of thumb to first joint of index finger; Good – tip of thumb to tip of middle finger; Fun – tip of thumb to first joint of middle finger; Yes – tip of thumb to tip of ring finger. These gestures are illustrated several times, and each time the participants are reminded to use these gestures. Other gestures will work, but later, when facilitators are checking for behavioural competency, they will be looking for these specific gestures. The anchoring process is simple and is described in detail in an earlier chapter.

After one or two more iterations the process is modified so that when every participant has the clear sense that the gesture is adding to the power or depth of the experience, step four is repeated with the following difference: As the participant notices the change that flows out of making the gesture, they are to quickly break and remake the gesture. They are then to hold the gesture again until they become aware of the return of the experience and then again, break and remake the gesture. This pumping action is continued until the experience becomes pleasurably intense. After several minutes for practice, participants are called back to the present context, asked to shake out the state (physically shake their bodies) and discuss their experience.

After several repetitions of this last implementation, the anchor is tested for automaticity. The participants are instructed to test the state as follows:

> Clear your mind. Sit or lie comfortably and make the gesture. As you notice the rush of feeling that flows out of making the gesture, begin to pump the gesture by breaking and remaking the gesture repeatedly. Do your best to make the gesture at the first hint of a bodily feeling. Repeat this pumping action as you find yourself enjoying the growing intensity of feeling. With each pump, allow your attention to discover something better or deeper in the feelings. As you do this, enjoy more and more aspects of the feeling itself. Let your attention move into the feeling ... Keep pumping until you have an intense experience of pure feeling. Shake out the state (shake your body) and return to the present.
> (Gray 2011a, p. 70)

Gray reports (2001a, 2002, 2008a, 2010, 2011b, 2011c) that at about this time, participants begin to spontaneously report places where they have discovered personal uses for the anchors. On a very uniform basis, clients return to report that they have used the anchors to counter road rage and to otherwise reclaim emotional control. This represents a significant validation of the techniques for the participants and suggests something about the underlying mechanism that Gray has not previously considered in his reports of the technique (see below).

In his published materials, Gray notes that the first experiences of anchoring often produce such dramatic responses as people being startled, pleasantly surprised and positively overwhelmed. Gray would suggest, once again that the experiences of novelty, agency and intensity move these behaviours to a preferred position in the salience hierarchy and that this enhanced salience persists through the session and into the temporal frame after the two-hour session and surrounding any practice in other contexts. He also indicates that the anchored states may be used to interrupt unwanted affects, change focus and jumpstart meditative and trance states.

We will later suggest that these responses also shift consciousness from the dorsal attentional networks to the default mode network, serving as a metaphorical off-switch for active, external attentional processes.

After the initial creation of the anchors, the participants are instructed to begin to use the anchored resources in contexts beyond the place where they were learned. Although in sequence, this begins in exercise 6, Gray suggests that the need to generalize the behaviour into other contexts is sufficiently important that it can be started as soon as the skills are acquired. This entails the use of the Positive Resource Day Planner (2011c).

In the exercise, Pacing the Future (exercise 6), each participant is instructed to practice one anchor each day. They are to start off each morning by firing off the anchor and end each night by again firing the anchor. Upon arising, after firing off the anchor and from within the anchored resource state, participants are to identify three places during the day where they anticipate the anchored feeling will be useful. They are to write these down and give them no further attention. They are also required, before continuing the day, to make three appointments with themselves through the day. At each of the appointed times (they should vary from day to day) they will:

1. Fire off and enjoy the anchor (eyes open or closed, privately or publicly).
2. Take a few minutes to review how *well* the day has gone to this point.
3. Make a few notes on their accomplishments and then get on with business.

At the end of the day they will again fire off the anchor, review the day and make some progress notes. Finally, they are instructed to drift off to sleep firing off the day's anchor.

Exercise 5 stacks the five anchors created in exercise 3 into a single complex resource. Gray indicates that this is designed to instantiate a felt experience of Jung's deep self (2001a, 2002, 2008a, 2010, 2011b, 2011c). According to Gray, this instantiation is designed to provide a foundation for designing a compelling, personally meaningful future in exercise 10.

Beyond the utility of creating a foundational state for use in exercise 10, the state is thought to awaken pre-addictive identities and directions. These are alternate but continuing identities that are not associated with the addicted identity patterns. It is also thought to open the participants to what Gray characterizes as the *sine qua non* of spiritual experience (2008a, 2011b, c).

Stacking anchors is a standard NLP procedure in which conditioned responses are chained to create a composite state. Gray invokes the system property of emergence and indicates that the NOW anchor, as it is called, should evoke a deep sense of personal identification, centeredness and positive self-regard. In brief, the anchors are fired off one at a time. As each begins to arise in consciousness, attention is focused on its features while the next anchor in sequence is fired off. As that arises and mixes with the initial state, the state that they evoke in combination becomes the focus of attention as the next is added. After all five states have been added, and as the combined state coalesces, the anchor gesture for NOW (a gentle fist) is pumped until a conditioned association is established. The procedure is fully scripted in Gray (2011c).

After the creation of the NOW anchor, participants are encouraged to practise it at home and to use it in the context of the Positive Resource

Day Planner as noted above. This is part of a consistent effort throughout the program to generalize the gains realized in the sessions to the world at large.

Exercise 10 applies the NLP well-formedness conditions for outcomes in the context of the NOW anchor. The technique is normally used to structure or evaluate pre-existing outcomes. Here, however, it is used to create outcomes rooted in the affective tone of the NOW resource. Assuming that the NOW resource represents an instantiation of Jung's deep self, Gray indicates that building an outcome rooted in this state will inevitably produce an intrinsically motivating outcome that represents one version of a personal calling. He suggests that just such a future direction meets the needs of Prochaska's (1994) strong principle of change and will be sufficient in many cases to drive positive behaviour away from the addictive patterns that have brought the participant to the programme.

Proposed mechanism

Earlier in this discussion it was pointed out that there are three problems that need to be dealt with in answering the problem of addiction: the overwhelming incentive salience of the addictive behaviour; restoring the active capacity of attentional and evaluative mechanisms in the frontal cortex; ensuring that alternate behavioural networks are in place that are independent of the drug-centred networks and that they are sufficiently self-reinforcing and salient that they will maintain sober behaviour over time. These issues are addressed as follows.

The incentive salience of addictive behaviours is a dynamic element; drugs and other destructive behaviours move to the top of the salience hierarchy and they can be reduced in salience by more immediate, more rewarding and more intuitive reinforcers (Bandler and Grinder, 1979, 1982; Hall, 1996). Miller and C'de Baca (Miller, 2004; Miller and C'de Baca, 1994) report a survey of spontaneous, life-altering experiences that, whether spiritual or non-spiritual, resulted in the self-identification of previous alcoholics and addicts simply as non-drinkers. The experiences had the effect of re-ordering personal priorities and asserting deeply personal and meaningful life-directions. Prochaska's strong principle of change relies tacitly on just such a reorganization of the salience hierarchy (Prochaska, 1994; Prochaska et al., 1994). Gray (2008a, 2008b, 2011a, 2011b, 2011c) reports anecdotal accounts of just such transformations. He further indicates that the states created in the exercises are equivalent to Maslow's peak experiences, various kinds of meditative states and spiritual experience without the religious content. He reports multiple instances of participants spontaneously identifying the states engendered in the programme as spiritual. He also holds that the novelty of the experiences in combination with their capacity to build self efficacy with regard to feelings and subjective experience further amplify the subjective value of the states.

Re-assertion of frontal capacities is a function of the rigorous concentrative activities entailed in the early part of the program. The development of the new skills of manipulating attention and the submodality structure of the resource experiences marshalls canonical functions of the frontal lobes (Smallwood *et al.*, 2012). Moreover, once the altered states have been conditioned and enhanced, it is believed that they activate the DMN in the context of a highly pleasurable self-reinforcing state. This network is associated with just the elements of frontal function and inhibitory control that addictive behaviours have down-regulated (Buckner *et al.*, 2008; Canales, 2005; Craig, 2009; D'Argembeau *et al.*, 2010; Diekhof *et al.*, 2008; Feil *et al.*, 2010; Goldstein and Volkow, 2002; Greicius *et al.*, 2003; Gu *et al.*, 2010; Kringelbach, 2005; Kringelbach and Berridge, 2009; Raichle and Snyder, 2007; Schooler *et al.*, 2011; Spreng and Grady, 2010; Volkow *et al.*, 2002).

The DMN was originally identified in attempts to define a baseline for brain-imaging studies during a time when scholarly attention was focused exclusively on active, externally oriented perception and behaviour that was expected to create functional changes in brain circuits. As researchers persisted in their efforts, they became aware of a central network of cortical structures that increased its activation during internally focused attention and decreased its activity during externally focused, attentionally demanding tasks. Although subject to some variation, the central nodes in the network include the ventromedial prefrontal cortex, the dorsomedial prefrontal cortex, the anterior and posterior cingulate gyrus, the inferior parietal lobule and the medial temporal lobe (Buckner *et al.*, 2008; D'Argembeau *et al.*, 2010; Greicius *et al.*, 2003; Raichle and Snyder, 2007; Schooler *et al.*, 2011; Spreng and Grady, 2010).

The DMN is active when individuals are engaged in internally focused tasks that are often referred to as stimulus or task independent thought. Such tasks include: autobiographical memory retrieval, planning or envisioning the future, imagining other's perspectives (theory of mind), engaging in internal dialog and imagining various scenarios. It is also associated with self-talk or task-unrelated talk. Importantly, one of the striking features of the DMN is its capacity to limit access to external perception. That is, it appears to act as a perceptual off-switch (Buckner *et al.*, 2008; Greicius *et al.*, 2003; Schooler *et al.*, 2011; Smallwood *et al.*, 2012).

The nodal elements of the DMN integrate biographical memory and past experiences from the medial temporal lobe. The ventromedial prefrontal cortex allows for the flexible integration of past experience and the evaluation of subjective scenarios. The dorsomedial prefrontal cortex selects targets of attention and processes conscious awareness of the subjective experience itself. The anterior cingulate allows for the modelling of subjective actions while the posterior cingulate integrates multiple subcortical systems. The inferior parietal lobule is subdivided into areas that regulate the control of movement and perception, stimulus salience and aspects of reflexive cognition (Buckner *et al.*, 2008; Greicius *et al.*, 2003; Hongkeu 2010; Schooler *et al.*, 2011; Smallwood *et al.*, 2012).

Smallwood *et al.* (2012) discuss the DMN in terms of its capacity to 'decouple' attentional processes from the external environment in order to refocus it on imaginative thought. It allows the individual to attend almost exclusively to internal states and cognitions including desires and feelings.

Spreng *et al.* (2008) relate the DMN to reflexive meta-cognition, including the development of a self-directed theory of mind. These authors found that functional activations involving self-directed thought and theory of mind showed considerable overlap. This may suggest that the DMN is a crucial element in empathic understanding and self-evaluation in the context of a life that extends beyond the individual. It has implications for empathy-based treatments for both substance use disorders and predatory crime.

It is striking that D'Aquili and Newberg (2000) have associated these same neural centres with spiritual and aesthetic experiences along with other varieties of trance and altered states of consciousness. Relying on their work, Gray (2001a, 2002, 2008a, 2008b) has repeatedly referred to the states engendered in the programme as pseudo-spiritual or pseudo-meditative.

The third element, the production of self-reinforcing behaviours that retain sufficient incentive salience over time, is presumed to be created by the mechanisms already discussed but is specifically implemented through the use of the NLP well-formedness conditions for outcomes. These outcomes, rooted in the structure of intrinsic motivation, once again re-assert frontal function through planning, self-reflection, imagining the future and participation of the DMN as an organizing and self-directing mechanism. Insofar as the pattern evokes a truly well-formed set of intrinsic motivations it fulfils Prochaska's (1994; Prochaska *et al.*, 1994) criteria for an outcome that will motivate change.

At their most basic level, the NLP well-formedness conditions for any given outcome specify that:

1 The outcome must be stated as a positive thing or experience; something wanted, not something unwanted or ended.
2 The outcome must be something that is under the goal seeker's personal control which also implies that the task should not be stated too broadly.
3 The outcome must be specified in terms of multiple levels of sensory experience; it must be described in terms of what can be seen, heard, felt, tasted or smelled.
4 The outcome should be evaluated for ecology; what it will change in the person's life and the lives around them?
5 The outcome should be imagined and experienced in fantasy as fully as possible (Andreas and Andreas, 1989; Bodenhamer and Hall, 1988; Cade and O'Hanlon, 1993; Dilts and DeLozier, 2000; Linden and Perutz, 1998).

Major support for these criteria are found in the psychology of intrinsic motivations. Intrinsic motivations are desired for their own sake. They are meaningful to the individual independent of external pressures or rewards. They are contrasted with extrinsic motivators, which include things such as money, sex, power, fame and popularity: stuff. Extrinsic motivators are well known for their capacity to sometimes weaken intrinsic motivations. When, however, they are simply the fruit of a deeply held personal direction or outcome, they present no such problem (Deci and Ryan, 2008; Hullerman et al., 2008).

The NLP well-formedness criteria require first that the outcome be desired positively – it is something wanted and the outcome is stated as a positive intention. Intrinsic motivators are desired positively (Deci and Ryan, 2008). This criterion is also supported by the finding by Wegner et al. (1987) to the effect that injunctive commands, which easily translate into negative outcomes, create a paradoxical increase in the salience of the problem behaviour.

The second criterion, that the behaviour be under the client's personal control is supported by findings that intrinsic motivators are characterized by choice and personal autonomy – they often include strong self-efficacy beliefs (Baumeister and Heatherton, 1996; Deci and Ryan 2008; Hullerman et al., 2008; Koestner, 2008; Notz, 1975).

The third criterion, that the outcome be specifiable in sensory terms, is supported by findings by Baumeister and Heatherton (1996), that, because intrinsically motivating outcomes are often rooted in previous or vicarious experiences, they can be specified in sensory terms (often with special emphasis on kinaesthetic elements – 'this is how I will feel'). The criterion receives further support from research into the motivational and attentional mechanisms in the orbitofrontal cortex and the superior-colliculus to the effect that multi-sensory representations of outcomes are more highly motivating and focus attention more effectively than uni-modal or abstract outcomes (Kringelbach, 2005; Sparks, 1999).

The criterion for imaginal practice is supported by a broad array of authors. Research into the impact of imagined movement supports the position that future performance is enhanced by the imagined performance of the process (Driskell et al. 1994; Martin and Hall, 1995; Pham and Taylor, 1999; Wohldmann et al., 2007).

The utility of clearly specified goals is strongly supported by Prochaska's principle of change (Prochaska, 1994; Prochaska et al. 1992, 1994). Prochaska discovered that a great many of his most successful changers had one thing in common: each of them had identified a positively valued outcome that was more important to them than the problem behaviour. The identification of a positively valued outcome increased positive attitudes towards change by one full standard deviation. Simultaneously, the positive outcome decreased the valuation of the problem behaviour by one half standard deviation. Problems are generally overcome by finding something more valuable.

A fourth element that impacts the capacity of the program to evoke new patterns or to revive and reinforce pre-existing sober patterns is supported on a neurological level (Dilts and DeLozier, 2000) by observations by Morris (2006) and confirmatory work by Tse *et al.* (2008). Morris theorizes that all experiences, whether the focus of attention or not, are stored on some basis in neural structures. One of the distinctive features of long-term memory is the selection of specific memories from day-to-day experience for long-term retention. Although long-term storage can take a relatively long time through canonical hippocampal mechanisms, the concurrent revivification of relevant, pre-existing memory schemas can facilitate the consolidation of new memories through their incorporation into those pre-existing memory structures. Significantly, Morris also points to novel stimuli as preferentially subject to facilitated long-term consolidation.

Most new memories go through a long period of cortical consolidation. Tse *et al.* (2008) reported that a stable cortical network of place associations took approximately a month to develop, a time period historically supported across multiple species. If, however, the new material is learned in the context of a stable long-term memory schema – usually thought to be distributed in cortical networks – they can be incorporated into that schema in short order. According to Tse, learning under the influence of a stable cortical schema may be accomplished in timeframes approaching real-time. This suggests that with regard to the programme exercises, the same process may be understood as facilitating the incorporation of the NLP-enhanced perceptions into the older pre-drug schemas and identities and that they, in turn, are rendered more salient as they have incorporated the novelty, positive affect and self-efficacy perceptions into their own structures.

Mechanism applied to the Brooklyn Program

In his original formulations, Gray indicated that the programme operates on the assumption that there are root organismic states that are so intrinsically rewarding that they can compete with addictive behaviours for primacy of place in the salience hierarchy. Essentially, he appeals to Jungian and Maslowian patterns of individuation and self-actualization as behavioural patterns that carry sufficient biological impact to compete with addictions (Gray, 2001a, 2002, 2008a, 2008b).

More practically, the programme was designed to provide multiple, overlapping modes of action that include experiences of self-efficacy, the control of emotions, the reawakening of frontal function, the creation of patterns of behaviour that are incompatible with addictive responses and sufficiently rewarding to compete with those behaviours. It also included the structuring of positive outcomes that are sufficiently meaningful that they can reorient the individual to new or previously-held goals and outcomes and support positive change outside of the treatment context.

The original inspirations for the programme were the Jungian and Maslowian elements. It was originally believed that, following the pattern of Wolpe's *Psychotherapy by Reciprocal Inhibition* (1959), the elicitation of the strong positive affects occasioned by the patterns of individuation and self-actualization would block the expression of the negative behaviours. It was assumed that as these developmental pathways represented deeper and more fundamental patterns of being in the world, that they would necessarily overwhelm other behaviours and assert a more fundamental personality structure. These insights were partly inspired by the Jungian concept that the assertion of the archetype of the self was often disruptive to normal ego patterns and was the real explanation for sudden personal transformations and redemption experiences (Edinger, 1972; Gray, 1996; Hillman, 1996; Jung 1965, 1977). From the Maslowian perspective, Gray came to understand that development towards self-actualization did not always entail the fulfilment of all of the preceding stages of need satisfaction as originally put forth by Maslow, but could be accelerated by the conscious appreciation of peak experiences that typically drove the path of self-actualization (Maslow, 1970, 1971).

While formulating the programme, Gray became aware of the stages of change model (DiClemente, 2003; Prochaska *et al.*, 1994) and more especially Prochaska's strong principle of change (Prochaska, 1994; Prochaska *et al.*, 1994). This insight was understood as supporting the developmental insights of Jung and Maslow and provided an added dimension in that it suggested that a concrete outcome created from a deep archetypal sense of self in accordance with the NLP well-formedness conditions for outcomes would produce not only a felt direction, but a concrete outcome toward which that developmental pathway could clearly point (Gray, 2001a, 2002, 2008a, 2008b).

Early experiences in exercises 1 and 2 were designed to provide experiences of self-efficacy as they provide real-time experience of the clients' ability to alter emotional states, enhance memories and create positive focus. Self-efficacy is further enhanced by experiences of unsuspected capacities for concentration. These experiences are connected to the training context as a matter of simple, contextual conditioning.

Insofar as the early exercises include focused attention and the conscious manipulation of subjective content as a new skill, they entail the activation of frontal capacities which often suffer as a result of addictive mechanisms (Bechara, 2005; Bechara and Damasio, 2002; Bechara *et al.*, 1999, 2000, 2002; Bechara and van der Kooy, 1985; Canales, 2005; Craig, 2009; Davidson, 1993; Diekhof *et al.*, 2008; Feil *et al.*, 2010; Goldstein and Volkow, 2002; Gu *et al.*, 2010; Kringelbach, 2005; Kringelbach and Berridge, 2009; Volkow *et al.*, 2002). The activation of frontal function is enhanced by the pleasurable experience of the altered states generated by the process and this increases the incentive salience of an already self-reinforcing or autotelic set of behaviours (Kringelbach and Berridge, 2009).

Insofar as the exercises are linked to pre-addictive or non-addictive contexts, these behaviours and the positive effects associated with them become associated with non-drug-related behaviours and memories and reinforce a context dependant enhancement of those memories and response patterns. This can be understood as a valorization of sober experience as contrasted with the 'awfulization' of sobriety documented by Gorski and others (Inaba and Cohen, 2007).

In exercise 3, the programme takes advantage of simple Pavlovian conditioning in creating the anchors, operant conditioning in reinforcing the behaviour of accessing and anchoring the states as positive effects from the exercises both reinforce the behaviours and the emotional context of the program itself.

Morris (2006) reports that novelty increases the probability that a new behaviour or memory will be encoded into long-term memory. Lee (2009) and Pedreira et al. (2004) have indicated that novelty also preferentially invokes reconsolidation in long-term memory schemas. Further, evidence ranging from the analysis of individual neurons to the response of the entire system has pointed to the preferential activation of the midbrain dopamine system in response to novel rewarding stimuli (Diekhof et al., 2008; Robinson, 2004; Robinson and Berridge, 2001; Schultz et al., 1997; Tobler et al., 2005; Waelti et al., 2001). Gray reports that responses to the novelty impact of the early exercises are often dramatic (Gray, 2001a, 2002, 2008a, 2008b). This data suggests that the novelty of the individual responses to the anchoring and enhancement exercises makes them not only easier to learn and more worthy of attention but also more likely to be used (Gray, 2001a, 2002, 2008a, 2008b).

According to Chambers et al. (2007), the persistence of addictive behaviours is partially a result of the organization of addiction-related perceptions and behaviours as a major associative route in a small world pathway. Because so many behaviours and perceptions are linked to addiction related nodes, the behaviours are very resilient. In their view, an essential element in overcoming addictive patterns is the establishment of alternative functional networks that do not link preferentially to the substances and behaviours associated with drugs or other problem behaviours.

It is suggested that, by this time in the programme, as the anchoring exercises have become well practiced, streamlined behaviours and have come to be generalized into other contexts, that there has been established, or revivified, a functional circuitry that is associated with the programme, the exercises and past-positive resources that is not linked to drugs or problem behaviours but to past, pre-drug or non-drug experiences, positive feelings of personal efficacy and the reawakening of deeper patterns of motivation towards positive outcomes.

In support of the presumed creation of these positive networks, the clients are encouraged to practice and use the anchors in contexts outside of the place where the programme-related behaviours have been learned.

It should be emphasized that here, as throughout the programme, a significant effort is made to separate the new behaviours and the programme more generally from any mention of drugs or problem behaviours. It is also to be noted that the participants are never told to specifically attempt to use the anchored responses to overcome substance-related urges. These precautions are intended to build strong, independent sets of neural associations that have no relationship to drugs or problem behaviours. In previous descriptions this was logically expressed in terms of the desire to separate the behaviours from drug treatment so that they were not viewed as *only* exercises for drug treatment (Gray, 2001a, 2002, 2008a, 2008b). It is believed that the current network hypothesis represents a more robust justification for creating that separation.

Exercise 5 links the resources already anchored to conditioned stimuli into a chained or stacked resource, which is thought to instantiate a deep sense of the Jungian self. It is proposed that the NOW state represents a conditioned response that evokes activity in the DMN.

Exercise 12 uses the NOW resource as an affective template for generating personally relevant outcomes for each participant. Insofar as the outcomes are structured as intrinsically motivating and rooted in a structured affect that is presumed to instantiate a deep sense of personal capacities and life-directions, it is believed that they will be accorded overwhelming incentive salience and will provide the level of motivation identified by Prochaska in his strong principle of change (Prochaska, 1994; Prochaska *et al.*, 1994) that will sustain positive behaviour over time.

Research directions

The preceding material leads to multiple testable and falsifiable hypotheses which, in and of themselves, represent a programme for the evaluation of the claims made and the procedures used by the Brooklyn Program. Any implementation of the programme should be able to implement a test of all of the listed hypotheses at minimal expense with the exception of those requiring MRI or other tests. The hypotheses are as follows.

1 There is a set of consciously manipulable sensory distinctions (submodalities) that individuals can learn to use to alter their subjective experience of an event. The results of that manipulation can be measured in the short term by their subjective response and in the longer term (several hours) by standard inventories such as the PANAS). The long-term effects should be assessable after the states have been practiced over a twenty minute period.
2 The effects of those submodality manipulations (altered states of consciousness) may be associated to conditioned stimuli that are under the participant's personal control and practiced so that the states can be evoked at any time and in any context.

a The conditioned states will produce measurable changes in physiology including GSR, cardiac rhythm. The longer the period during which the states are used, the more pronounced the measurable effect.
3 With sufficient practice, generally lasting a month or more, those conditioned responses will constitute a novel, highly rewarding and highly salient behaviour that can compete successfully with other behaviours in a counter conditioning paradigm.
b This implies that a well-practiced consolidated anchor should produce better and more permanent changes in a desensitization paradigm than the standard Jacobsen technique.
c It also suggests that the technique would be successful in an anger management protocol.
d In either case, for reasons not discussed here, the anchored positive stimulus should follow an evocation and interruption of the target behaviour.
4 When created in such a way that the resulting anchors are devoid of content and context, the anchors will activate the DMN, instantiating a behavioural 'off switch' resulting in a decoupling of outward-oriented perceptions and behaviours and the possibility of reorienting behaviour in a direction characterized by the positive affect carried by the CR. After a period of several minutes, that decoupling will be observable via brain imaging devices.
5 The creation and practiced use of the anchors will increase frontal function such that persons who have participated in the program for one month or more will show increased activity in DLPFC, VMPFC, ACC and MTL independent of DMN activation or temporally proximal use of the anchors.
e After one month's practice of the anchors and procedures from the Brooklyn Program, participants will score more positively in an affect inventory (e.g. PANAS) and will improve scores over pre-tests or matched controls in depression inventories (e.g. BDI).
6 When the anchors are practised in multiple contexts they will become more readily available in all contexts. Practice in multiple contexts will enhance their incentive salience.
7 After a period of one month's practise of the anchors, during activation of the anchors as taught in the Brooklyn Program, without instructions for their direct application to craving states, the perceived salience of addictive drugs and problem behaviours will decrease. In persons who apply them to counter cravings, the period of craving will end, be foreshortened or decreased in intensity. In persons currently using drugs, programme-related changes will be reflected in decreased frequency of use and less intense cravings.
8 The anchored NOW state will, like the other anchors, evoke increased responsivity from the DMN, matched by lessened responses from

sensory and motor cortices. It will also act as a behavioural 'off-switch'. After several minutes of activation by firing-off the anchor (or the CS), those changes will be observable via brain imaging.
9 The practiced creation and activation of the anchors, during the course of one month or more, will result in improved access to sober and pre-problem memories. The behaviours associated with those memories will be more valued than they may have been before treatment.
10 Outcomes based on aspirations rooted in the NOW state that have been subjected to the NLP well-formedness criteria for outcomes, will become highly salient and capable of motivating further sober behaviour and behaviours supportive of non-problematic choices. They will fulfil the function of outcomes noted in Prochaska's strong principle of change (Prochaska, 1994; Prochaska et al., 1994).

More simply, we would suggest that premises set forth here would be most efficiently tested in a drug treatment context with voluntary subjects randomly assigned to 16 weeks of treatment. Three suggested treatments would be the Brooklyn Program, Motivational Interviewing or Cognitive Behavioural Treatment and a drug education or wait-group control. All treatments should be manualized, applied by trained therapists and the therapists trained in each technique to a predefined level of competency. All subjects should be subject to urinalysis. The test would exclude persons with serious health complications and serious psychological comorbidities. These would be assessed by pre-treatment interviews and the application of appropriate, standardized clinical assessments. Pre- and post-tests would include an assessment of addiction severity, the Beck Depression Inventory and the PANAS. They should be administered at intake, immediately post-treatment and six months, one year and three years post-treatment.

From this design we would predict that the Brooklyn Program would equal or surpass the results of the comparison treatment and both would be superior to the educational or wait-group control.

Summary

This chapter has examined the Brooklyn Program, a 16-week substance use treatment programme that was operated under the aegis of the US Federal Government for seven years, ending in 2004. The programme produced abstinence rates of 28.6 per cent at one-year follow-up. Unfortunately, the programme has never been replicated and this needs to be done in order to validate the findings reported here.

The Brooklyn Program operated on assumptions drawn from NLP, Jungian and Maslowian practice and theory and relied on tools from NLP. Although the results were not statistically significant, and the programme suffered from an inadequate control condition – programme drop-outs assigned to alternate treatments – comparable results were achieved with minimal investments of time and money using NLP tools.

Here, the authors present a two-tiered validation approach. First, they present a series of testable hypotheses that derive from the program's exercises. Second, they offer a brief experimental design that replicates the initial programme, but that adds randomly assigned treatment and control groups, consistent evaluation, assessment and follow-up.

6 Depression symptom clusters

Lisa Wake, Karl Nielsen, Nandana Nielsen, Cătălin Zaharia

In this chapter we review the depressive disorders as categorized by the Diagnostic and Statistical Manual of Mental Disorders 4^{ed} Text Revision (DSM-IV-TR, 2000). We review the specifics of the disorders and currently recognized treatments, including parallels between CBT, an evidence-based treatment for depression, and NLP. We then discuss how NLPt can be utilized to help aid the symptoms of depressive disorders, research evidence to date, and provide a clinical case example.

Current context of depressive disorders

The World Health Organization (WHO) (2011) estimates that 850,000 lives each year are lost through suicide in individuals with depression. Depression is recognized as the leading cause of disability globally and the fourth contributor to the global burden of disease in Disability Adjusted Life Years (DALYs). It is reported to be the second cause of DALYs in 15–44 year olds. Depression affects approximately 121 million people worldwide and, although it can be diagnosed and treated in primary care, less than 25 percent of individuals with depression are in receipt of effective treatment (WHO, 2011).

The US Center for Disease Control and Prevention reports that more than 26 percent of the US adult population have depression, with 6.7 percent of US adults experiencing a major depressive episode in the previous 12 months.

In the UK, the Depression Report (Layard et al., 2006) indicated that up to 50 percent of all people in receipt of incapacity benefits receive them due to mental illness as either a primary or secondary factor. There are over a million people in receipt of benefit and not working, yet the Depression Report identifies that the cost of treatment for those suffering anxiety or depression is only £750 per person.

The DSM-IV-TR lists a range of depressive disorders:

- Major Depressive Episode (296.2) is a general mood disorder represented by a depressed mood that has existed for a minimum period of

time, is accompanied by a minimum number of symptoms and results in some disability.
- Recurrent Major Depressive Disorder (296.3) which is thought to arise in up to half of all individuals who have experienced one major depressive episode.
- Dysthymic Disorder (300.4), where individuals are chronically depressed, experiencing low mood, fatigue, hopelessness, difficulty concentrating, problems with appetite and sleep. Six percent of all adults are thought to experience Dysthymic Disorder, with the condition often being under-diagnosed because the individual perceives their low mood as normal.

In general, mood and affect in depression are not influenced by circumstances, however some individuals may experience diurnal variations in mood, with the evenings frequently better than the mornings. Symptoms include irritability, tearfulness, social withdrawal, muscle tension that can lead to increased pre-existing pain, lack of libido, fatigue, agitation, reduced sleep, changes in appetite, loss of interest in everyday life, feelings of guilt, low self-esteem, poor concentration, negative thought patterns, self-harm, and suicidal ideation. Occasionally, individuals with severe depression may develop psychotic symptoms that may or may not be related to low mood.

The aetiology of depression is thought to be multi-factoral, including social, biochemical, genetic, neurophysiological and psychological elements. However, Nuechterlein and Dawson (1984) and Harris (2000) propose that there is increased vulnerability to depression when social and physical triggers interact with stressful life events, making talking therapy a useful adjunct to any pharmaceutical intervention.

The NLP perspective

From the perspective of NLP, such diagnostic designations, in and of themselves, are often not viewed as useful. They tell us little to nothing about the problem at hand and tend to reify the active problem of how the person participates in the creation of the problem called depression and concretizes it into something that is understood as real in itself and that exists beyond the confines of the living person who acts it out. This is not to say that there are not very real problems rooted in real physiology and that some of these may indeed be beyond our reach. This does not imply that pharmacological remedies will solve such problems (for a review see Ecker and Toomey, 2008). It does say, however, that we might profit far more by describing what the client is doing when he says that he is depressed than by just finding the right label.

So, the first questions that we need to ask are: When do you find this happening and when do you find yourself doing this? How do you do this and what is the sequence of behaviors that you engage in to set this problem in motion?

This is not blaming the victim, but it is restoring a frame that allows the client to participate in changing the behavior. It is the discovery of personal agency in contexts where agency is often no longer considered. It begins to open the individual to a new belief about what is possible for them. Moreover, it gives us, as treatment providers, clear descriptions of the process involved in the expression of the problem behavior so that we can design an appropriate response.

In those cases where the precipitating voices or images or stimuli are unconscious, there is the added task of making the driving stimulus conscious. Where it extends across contexts, uniting the behavior across those contexts can make the change-work more efficient.

Steve and Connirae Andreas, two of the founding lights in NLP and its most well-known interpreters, warn that all such work must be careful to honour the positive intent of the perceived problem and that any perceived resistance must be taken into account. The intention of such work must always be to add options, not to eliminate possible responses (Andreas, 2009; Andreas and Andreas, 1989, 2002).

As in cognitive behavioral models, NLP does not view depression as a single phenomenon but as the expression of what may be many possible triggers, stimuli and patterns of response. From the perspective of NLP, however, mood disorders are generally to be approached in terms of the structural patterns that maintain the behavior, not their content. Thus, whether depression finds its source in grief, loss, distorted perceptions and memories, or repeated, unconscious self-referential patterns, the task is most often viewed as a modification of the structure of the behavior.

NLP begins with the assumption that any behavior can be described by sequences of behavioral and sensory elements: visual, auditory, kinesthetic, olfactory, and gustatory. Each of these elements may be subdivided into multiple modes of expression: internal, external, digital, etc., and each may operate on the others as context or precondition. Further, each element has a range of submodalities—the small-grained dimensions of perception such as intensity, distance, movement, complexity, locus, and magnitude—that code for valence and intensity of emotional impact. As a result, their combinations can give rise to the full range of human experience. These basic elements are assembled into strategies or sequences of behavior. That is to say, simple behaviors and sensory expressions combine into patterns (schemas) that operate to reach some personally relevant goal or outcome.

As an example, take an internal picture that is being repeated obsessively with strong feelings of sadness, like a boyfriend/girlfriend lost a year ago. Along with labeling the obsession as harmful (insight in CBT) one NLP intervention could be changing the specific remembered picture size, distance, physical location, or context (happy in heaven) until these new changes of the previously unconscious parameters (submodalities) produce a painless, sadness-free picture. This would be constructed by the client with the therapist's help so that the new version no longer produces the strong feelings of depression. At first, the new representation is consciously inserted when the client feels the sadness and finds that the cause is the sad picture. After practice, however, the new representation arises automatically (Andreas and Andreas, 1987, 1989; Bandler and Grinder, 1975a, b, 1979; Bandler and MacDonald, 1987; Dilts et al., 1980).

One of the formative influences on NLP was the cybernetic thinking of Bateson (1972) through whose work the concepts of self-regulation in the form of feed-forward and feedback loops entered the field. The feed-forward mechanism of self-regulation allows for limitless potential but in its unregulated form leads to loss of control. The feedback loop allows for active control of growth in ecological balance with a wider system (Andreas 2006; Bandler and Grinder, 1975a, b; Dilts et al., 1980). An individual who is successful in relationships will use feedback to expand their relationships to become ever more fulfilling and self-actualizing, equally they may use their experience of relating well to inform their work with others, e.g. in counselling or therapy settings where the therapist is using their own personal experience of therapy to inform and influence their clinical work.

In addition to the older analogue visions of self-regulation, early on, NLP adopted Miller et al.'s (1960) TOTE heuristic that allowed for such systems to become self-regulating with regard to a specific goal or outcome. The TOTE heuristic stands for Test, Operate, Test, Exit. In general it is a pattern of self-regulation that sets a criterion for success, operates upon the environment or the organism itself, tests for satisfaction of the criterion and if successful, exits the sequence. If the test fails, if it is unsuccessful, the pattern repeats until the criterion is met.

From linguistics, NLP drew upon the works of Korzybsky and Chomsky. Crucially, both were influenced by Korzybsky's (1994) early description of errors in logic that flowed out of current Biology and Arostotelian logic. These same errors became the root of the cognitive distortions later claimed by Beck and Ellis as being at the heart of depression and other mental disorders. NLP, however, emphasized what came to be known as the meta-model, a more general linguistically oriented classification of the deletions, distortions, and generalizations made by people as they sought to express their experience of the world. Both models were used in NLP to discover the places where a client's model of the world had been impoverished and as way-markers for understanding their progress through treatment (Bandler and Grinder, 1975a, b; Lewis and Pucelik, 1990; Sherman and Skinner, 1988).

NLP and depression

As previously noted, NLP views cognitive depression in all of its specific complexities as behaviors that are, for the most part, subject to change through operations on the structure of the problem perceptions or behaviors involved. Simple depressions may arise from a compelling negative voice, a persistent image of dire consequences or failure, or the misinterpretation of internal states. More serious episodes may rely upon the perpetuation of false beliefs or the recycling of negative feed-forward systems and TOTES that result in deepening feelings of loss, helplessness, or incapacity. In most cases, a structural intervention that changes the process or the structure of the perception characterizes the NLP approach (Andreas and Andreas, 1987, 1989; Bandler and Grinder, 1975a, b, 1979; Bandler and MacDonald, 1987; Dilts et al., 1980).

A search of Medline, PsychArticles, PsychInfo, Science Direct College Edition, and Sage Journals found one controlled randomized study regarding the use of NLP for the treatment of negative affect (McMorran, 1988) but none for depression per se. A further review of those databases found several case reports and treatment reports indicating that NLP had shown some success in the treatment of depression (Hossack and Standidge, 1993; Stanton, 1993; Taylor, 2004). Most of these interventions were rooted in changes in the structure of the problem behavior or perception rather than the content. In this group, neither Miller (1997) nor Taylor (2004) was found relevant to the present inquiry. Another group of books and articles were descriptions of specific techniques with anecdotal reports interspersed (Andreas, 2009, 2012).

Unlike CBT, NLP focuses upon the structure of the problem, not its content. While, like CBT it acknowledges various linguistic dimensions of cognitive distortions which reflect the presence of the problem, changes to those patterns are often viewed as diagnostic of progress in treatment, rather than being essential to the treatment itself (Grinder and Bandler, 1975a, b; Sherman and Skinner, 1988).

McMorran (1988, abstract only) described a study that compared an experimental group using submodality manipulations to provide relief from the feelings associated with unpleasant memories to a control group using a light trance induction, with no manipulation of the memory as a control. The study was understood as a test of NLP's claims that submodality manipulations of unpleasant memories could provide quick and permanent relief from the associated feelings.

Participants were 16 male and 38 female volunteers from a large church. Treatments were provided by trained psychologists who were also experts in NLP and hypnosis. Measures included a Target Complaint Box Scale, which was administered before and after treatment as well as two weeks post-treatment. Other measures included a Client Post-Therapy Questionnaire, administered immediately post-treatment and at the two-week follow-up. Two other measures, the Global Improvement Rating Scale and the Counsellor Rating form were completed immediately post-treatment.

Results of the treatment found that the submodality treatment resulted in significantly lower symptom scores and significantly higher counsellor ratings than those provided for the control group ($p<.05$ in both cases). Global Affect scores were also significantly higher for the submodality group.

Author conclusions indicate that the predicted efficacy for NLP was partially supported but the prediction of permanent change was not sustained.

In 1993, Hossack and Standidge presented a case study of an elderly patient who had just emerged from a period of clinical depression. The depressive episode developed over a period of several years following his retirement and a series of tragic life events. The current treatment followed a three-month stay in an inpatient geriatric facility that included multiple sessions of electro-convulsive shock therapy. After three months, he released with a continuing anxiety, agoraphobia, and feelings of worthlessness. Consistent with previous research the client found it difficult, post-recovery, to reassemble a coherent account of his own successes, worth, and positive identity.

The authors—relying on a suggestion by Beck that, in such cases, assisting the client in reviewing pictorial representations of positive events and achievements from their past can be useful in restoring positive identity and a sense of self-esteem—noted that there are some people who may have an impoverished capacity to access visual images, but that submodality concepts from NLP can be used to enhance access to the positive memory scenarios recommended by Beck. This process can be done using a scrapbook, which is a set of chronologically ordered representations of emotionally significant accomplishments, chosen by the client to serve as present time resources for combating negative emotions. Because the resource memories are chosen by the client as particularly significant examples of specific positive experiences, and because they are accessed in chronological order and access to them is practiced with the assistance of the therapist over multiple sessions, they become powerful, well-practiced counter-examples to present negative feeling states.

The procedure depended upon choosing representative images that were consistent with the client's preferred representational system (PRS) in order to ensure that he had vivid access to them (for a critique and analysis of the PRS please see Chapter 8). The patient was determined to be primarily kinesthetic with a weak capacity for visual imagery and little or none for auditory. As a result, his access to the imagined book began in primarily kinesthetic terms. The therapist would then overlap to the visually modality, by using the felt experience of the book or image as a means to access visual information about the resource. As sessions went on, the therapist would go through each of the images beginning with kinesthetic information, proceeding to visual images and then adding in auditory data.

It is to be noted that this practice is consistent with the use of the PRS noted by Grinder and Bandler in the *Structure of Magic II* (1976), where they indicate that the presence of the PRS often represents an impoverished representation of the world making it the therapist's task to expand the client's capacities to experience more of reality using a broader set of sensory experiences.

The scrapbook was developed over six sessions, with the client sitting with his eyes closed in a relaxed state as the therapist described the content, one image at a time, and adding one image at the end of each session. After completion of the scrapbook, the client was sent home with instructions to imaginally review the scrapbook, daily at first, and then weekly as his condition improved.

By the end of the fifth session the client reported alleviation of most of his symptoms. He was able to go out, drive his wife to work, return to his part-time job, and had even played a round of golf. By the sixth session he reported alleviation of all symptoms and requested a decrease in medication. At the six-month follow-up he reported continued progress and continued enjoyment of life.

The patient was formally assessed using the New Personal Disturbance Scale (DSSI/sAD) which was derived from the Delusional Symptoms States Inventory (DSSI). Before treatment he scored significantly above the depression threshold. At the nine-month follow-up his scores were significantly below threshold for both anxiety and depression.

Stanton (1993) describes three NLP submodality manipulations used to counteract the emotional impact of negative perceptions in three adolescent subjects. He notes that Bandler discusses how submodalities impact the intensity and present-time experience of various remembered stimuli and that, by modifying the structure of the memories, their emotional impact can be modified. In each case, he began by asking the client what their experience was of the problematic vision, voice, or feeling.

In the first of the three cases, Stanton describes an adolescent whose confidence in approaching girls was impacted by an intrusive visual image of a memory of having been rejected by a specific girl. Whenever he considered approaching a girl, the image would intrude into consciousness and he would not even make an attempt to talk to the girl.

The client described the image as dissociated, large, close, bright, sharply focussed, and colorful. In accordance with standard practice, the client was instructed to vary each of the submodality dimensions, one at a time, and then to return it to its original state until he found one or more that significantly changed the emotional impact of the image. In order, he modified the picture by shrinking the image, pushing it into the distance, defocusing the image, turning down the brightness, extracting the color, framing it, and associating into it. The modifications that worked best were defocusing the image, pushing it into the distance, framing it, and hanging it on the wall. These changes de-potentiated the image and he immediately replaced it with a close, sharply focused, unframed picture of himself after winning a tennis tournament. Six months later the problem with approaching potential dates had disappeared and he had entered an appropriate relationship.

Stanton's second client was a 14-year-old girl who was a talented speaker and debater who, when doing well in a debate, would hear her mother's critical voice telling her that she was hopeless. Whenever the voice spoke, the client's confidence would fail, her train of thought would become jumbled and she would be unable to succeed at the task at hand.

As with the previous example, this client was instructed to vary the submodalities—this time of sound—one by one, noting which had the most impact on the voice and then returning the voice to its original condition. When none of the standard submodalities—volume, distance, tone, timbre, location, etc.—had the expected effect, it was suggested that she give the voice the qualities of Donald Duck, speaking underwater. The change was so ridiculous, that the voice could no longer affect her and she emerged as a champion debater.

Stanton's third client was an unemployed 17 year old who awakened every morning with a feeling of absolute dread. The feeling was not accompanied by a picture or sound of any kind. As had been done previously, the client was asked to describe the sensation as fully as possible. He indicated that it was a large, cold, heavy, black circular feeling located in his abdomen.

Following similar techniques to those previously described, he shifted the position of the feeling to a place outside of his body and changed its color to a pleasant green. He then warmed it by the radiator, compressed it into a cube and threw it out of the window. He experienced immediate relief. At a six-month follow-up he reported that the feeling had returned on two occasions but that he had dealt with it effectively as described.

Stanton notes that, although most adolescents were easily able to accept the submodality distinctions—they are reflected in natural language—those suffering from depression were found to be less able to accept the fact that they had probably experienced as many positive experiences as others. Nevertheless, he reports that when depressed clients were taught to enhance the intensity of their positive experience it often resulted in positive mood changes.

It might be argued here that none of the studies mentioned has actually dealt with clinical depression per se. It is to be noted, however, that each of the intrusive thought patterns discussed may serve as an element in a vicious cycle that, in many persons, resolves into a pattern of clinical depression. In light of this, the patterns discussed, both the problems, and the interventions, may become crucial parts of an integrated approach to a feed-forward loop that maintains deep levels of depression and hopelessness. In general, both NLP and CBT focus on just such perceptions as the source of major clinical depressions.

The remaining literature consists of NLP texts, and include *Help with Negative Self Talk* (Andreas, 2009), *Resolving Shame* (Andreas and Andreas, 2002), and *Resolving Grief* (Andreas, 2012).

Help with Negative Self Talk (Andreas, 2009) is a detailed text focused on the submodality manipulation of negative auditory, visual, and kinesthetic images and describes the various ways in which the structure of those experiences can be changed in order to change the client's experience. The descriptions of the techniques are peppered with reports of interventions and variations provided by other NLP trainers and therapists. In general, the basic techniques have been described above.

Mechanism

NLP holds that the submodality structure of perceptions and beliefs determine, to a large extent, their meaning and their impact. From this perspective, words and perceptions act as anchors or classically conditioned stimuli for the felt states and other associations that constitute their meaning. In a depressive sequence, words or perceptions may become associated with internal state changes, which, in their turn, become associated with beliefs about the feelings. The beliefs often reflect negatively on the individual or their state and so enhance negative affect. This produces a self-perpetuating cycle of sadness, dysthymia, or depression. The pattern analysis is common to both NLP and CBT (Andreas, 2009; Bandler and Grinder, 1975a, b; Dilts et al., 1980; Mansell et al., 2007; Searson et al., 2012).

As long ago as 1927, Pavlov recognized that conditioned associations were remarkably sensitive to the fine details of stimulus, context, and the condition of the organism. One report from his early experiments with dogs found that a change in the color of the room required all of his experimental subjects to be retrained. Other research has shown that conditioning is exquisitely sensitive to changes in stimulus properties (Domjan, 2005; Rescorla, 1988).

The current understanding of perception in all of the senses indicates that images, sounds, words, and other percepts are first analyzed by feature detectors in the various systems. Combinations of these details assemble into larger, more meaningful units and these assemble into recognizable percepts that later may be associated to specific labels, affects, and categories. Reciprocal connections between, the identities of the percepts and the higher levels of feature detection in such hierarchical systems are involved in feedback loops that determine the relevance of the label to the percept or the response to the percept. When the feedback system fails, the association breaks down. This hierarchical organization has been illustrated for language (Chomsky, 1972), vision and reading (Glezer et al., 2009; Kanwisher, 2010), the perception of faces and objects (Kanwisher; 2010), and the mirror neuron system (Kilner et al., 2007, see also Damasio, 1999 and Kandel, 2009).

Insofar as the manipulation of submodalities alter the cues that give the percepts their unique qualities with regard to salience and impact, their manipulation interferes with the neural construct at one of the levels below associative categories and breaks the associative chain. When one of the elements in a chain of negative feed-forward associations is compromised, the vicious cycle will end.

CBT, NLP, and variations on a theme

In other disciplines, such as Cognitive Behavioral Therapy (CBT), Cognitive-Bias Modification (CBM), and Neuroscience, there exist scientific findings for procedures that are used in NLP under different names. These other disciplines usually do not refer to or mention NLP.

Butler et al. (2006) indicate that CBT is defined by the concept that psychological symptoms and dysfunctional behaviors are mediated by cognitive behaviors and can be impacted through the conscious modification of dysfunctional thinking and beliefs. It is distinct from behavioral therapies in that they proceed on the belief that volitional cognitive behavior is neither important for explaining aberrant behavior nor is it a specific target for treatment. Cognitive methods used in CBT include role play, Socratic questioning, and imagery. While early on, NLP focused upon the role of the unconscious and the power of emotion and motivation, in many cases CBT is just catching up. CBT has long been recognized as NLP's closest relative in mainstream psychology. In fact, with his strong emphasis on verbal behavior and conscious action, the work of Hall (2003) comes closest to CBT as an NLP strategy. NLP enables clients to become more aware of their internal state, including behaviors that reinforce a negative state or self-perception. By understanding the finer distinctions of the internal coding of thought processes and how these relate to states, the client is presented with tools that enable dissociation from negative states by changing the submodalities of an experience—people who are depressed tend to be associated into the negative experience and dissociated from positive experiences—by altering the quality of internal dialogue, e.g. changing the harshness of an internal voice.

Role play, especially in its imaginal use and in the NLP tool called future pacing, is also an element in the NLP intervention, the New Behavior Generator. The manipulation of imagery is used in the NLP world through both future pacing and submodality manipulation. Socratic questioning bears a strong relationship to the meta-model and is a central part of the Sleight of Mouth technique. The meta-model parallels the aberrant thinking styles identified by Beck and Ellis.

Role playing in CBT: future pacing and the New Behavior Generator in NLP

Role playing is related to the NLP process of future pacing and is especially relevant to the New Behavior Generator. Imaginal practice is supported by a broad array of authors. Research into the impact of imagined movement supports the position that future performance is enhanced by the imagined performance of the process (Driskell et al., 1994; Martin and Hall, 1995; Pham and Taylor, 1999; Wohldmann et al., 2007). Before neuroscience had confirmed that imaginal practice activated many of the same neural pathways as actual movement, NLP had incorporated imaginal practice and role plays into goal setting, future pacing, and the New Behavior Generator (Andreas and Andreas, 1989; Bandler and Grinder, 1975a, b; Epstein and Dilts, 1991; Dilts and DeLozier, 2000).

In goal setting, the client imagines a first position or self-perspective on what they will see, hear, and feel on achievement of the goal, and a second position or other person perspective on what they will observe at a multisensory level in the client on achievement of the goal. In future pacing, the client utilizes multisensory modes to imagine performing or practising a role in the imaginary context where she hopes to make it available. In the New Behavior Generator, the client imagines performing a new, resourceful behavior in place of one that represented a stuck state (Bandler and Grinder, 1975a, 1979, 1981; Andreas and Andreas, 1987, 1989); the technique is also extensively used in timeline work (James and Woodsmall, 1988).

In each situation, the client repeatedly imagines himself in the context where the behavior is needed, performing the desired behavior in front of himself in a way that appears both motivating and attractive to him. When the subject then goes to the time, place, or situation where he imagined himself acting out the desired behavior, the likelihood of his actually performing the behavior there is enhanced and many clients act out the practiced role. In this process, the imagined—and later real—context becomes a conditioned stimulus or anchor that evokes the imaginally practiced behavior. This provides mental support for adopting new behaviors. Role playing in CBT uses a similar approach. In either case, the role and the context may be practised in imagination or the role may be physically acted out in the imagined situation.

A study conducted in 2004, "Fluoxetine, Comprehensive Cognitive Behavioral Therapy, and Placebo in Generalized Social Phobia" (Davidson et al., 2004), compared CBT and pharmacotherapy in a randomized, double-blind, placebo-controlled trial. The research found that all active treatments were superior to placebo on primary outcomes. One of the central methods used in this example of cognitive behavioral group therapy was role playing. In a direct application of Bandura's (1997) Social Modeling, the role-playing exercise required a therapist to act out appropriate reactions to different situations. The patient then modeled the behavior illustrated by the therapist. Modeling is a core element of many NLP interventions, with the client modeling out what has already worked well for themselves in other contexts, the therapist or coach using self-modeling of what they think might work, using their own strategy and adapting this for the client, or using modelled behavior from "experts." NLP techniques also recommend that, if there is no current memory access to a relevant resource experience, the patient may be encouraged to model a character from television or the theatre (Andreas and Andreas, 1989; Grinder and Bandler 1975a).

A meta-study (Beck and Fernandez, 1998) of CBT techniques included findings from 50 studies with over 1,500 subjects and included cognitive reframing, relaxation training, *in vivo*, and imaginal role playing in order to enhance the clients' ability to cope with difficult situations. Results found that 76 percent of the participants were better off after the treatment than the untreated subjects. Like many NLP-based interventions, the studies examined included various combinations of the performance-based interventions already mentioned. Each of these interventions, reframing, state change, role playing, and future pacing are standard NLP practices that are often combined in treatment strategies (Andreas and Andreas, 1987, 1989; Bandler and Grinder, 1975a, 1979, 1981).

Socratic questioning and cognitive distortions in CBT: the meta-model and Sleight of Mouth in NLP

Socratic questioning begins with the idea that the answer to the question is already available to the client and that appropriate questioning will elicit the correct answer. Instead of providing direct answers, the Socratic method uses thought-stimulating questions, which allows one to discover new paths of thinking (Paul, 1993). In NLP, the Socratic method has a strong parallel in the use of the meta-model to uncover information that has been deleted, distorted or generalized from a more complete deep structure representation. The structure used by Bandler and Grinder finds its most significant roots in the work of Noam Chomsky. In NLP this is further developed by Dilts in the NLP intervention called Sleight of Mouth (Bandler and Grinder, 1975a, 1979, 1982; Dilts, 1999; Dilts and DeLozier, 2000; Lewis and Pucelik, 1990).

Results from King (1995) and Taba (1966) suggest that, using the Socratic method to challenge the cognitive distortions and what NLP calls meta-model violations in students, impacts the depth and quality of thinking across many grade levels. A study by Yang et al. (2005) assessed the performance of university students from three different universities regarding the development of their critical thinking skills promoted through Socratic questioning. The results strongly indicate that the teaching and modeling of Socratic questioning increased students' critical thinking skills. Insofar as Socratic questioning has some scientific support for its effectiveness, the results may be understood as supporting both the meta-model and Sleight of Mouth interventions.

The NLP meta-model was introduced in 1975 by Bandler and Grinder as an implementation of language patterns often challenged by Perls and Satir, and which had been previously recognized by linguists as common violations of well-formedness constraints (Bandler and Grinder, 1975a, 1979, 1982; Bostic St. Clair and Grinder, 2002; Dilts and DeLozier, 2000; Lewis and Pucelik, 1990). A complimentary set of cognitive distortions was identified by Beck and Ellis in their formulations. Although the matches are not perfect, an examination of the two groups shows clearly that the CBT categories exemplify specific subcategories of the more inclusive meta-model violations. In general, CBT recognizes 12 errors (Allen, 2003) which correspond to the NLP meta-model violations as shown in Table 6.1.

Table 6.1 A comparison of linguistic patterns from CBT and NLP

CBT distortions	NLP meta-model violations
Emotional reasoning	
Overgeneralization	Universal quantifier
	Lost performative
Jumping to conclusions (or arbitrary inference)	Complex equivalence
	Mind reading
	Cause effect
Dichotomous reasoning	Complex equivalence
	Cause effect
Should statements	Modal operator
	Lost performative
Fortune telling or mind reading	Cause effect
	Mind reading
Selective abstraction	Nominalizations
	Unspecified noun
	Unspecified verb
Disqualifying the positive	Presupposition
	Complex equivalence
Maximization and minimization	Lost comparative
Catastrophism	Complex equivalence
	Cause effect
Personalization	Mind reading
	Lost performative
Labeling	Complex equivalence
	Unspecified verbs unspecified nouns Unspecified adjectives

Imagery in CBT and submodalities in NLP

NLP provides a more intricate relationship regarding internal imagery than CBT. NLP differentiates between motivating and non-motivating mental images in terms of the small grained structure of the images: color, distance, complexity, movement, size, etc. The resourceful structuring of otherwise demotivating, depressing, or disgusting images is often done by mapping the submodalities of an experience possessing the desired emotional qualities on to the image of the problem state. That is, if the problem state is bright, it may be darkened; if it is close, it may be placed further in the distance; if it is loud, the volume may be lessened or its tonality distorted (make the voice sound like Mickey Mouse). Such changes can be used to often permanently alter the impact of stuck states or to affect the belief structure of a possible action.

CBT differentiates between hot and cold—emotionally impactful and non-impactful ideas—correct and incorrect evaluations of ideas and automatic or non-automatic responses. These dimensions impact the importance and clinical relevance of the thought distortions already noted (Allen, 2003; Franceschi, 2007; Leahy, 1996). In NLP, each of these distinctions can be affected by meta-model challenges and submodality shifts. Like NLP, CBT also uses guided imagery, direct suggestion, visualization, metaphor, story-telling, and other treatment approaches which allow co-operation between the conscious and unconscious minds.

There are multiple validation studies that document these techniques from CBT, however, many have been combined with light medication. CBT techniques with strong parallels to NLP-based interventions have been shown to be effective, among others, for: situational anxiety and test-taking (Wachelka and Katz, 1999); fear of flying (Aitken and Benson, 1984); pain, anxiety, and mood disorders in cancer (Deng and Cassileth, 2005); and infertility (Chan et al., 2006).

The tools and techniques used in guided imagery as paralleled in NLP and CBT may improve people's ability to cope with mental distress such as depression, and supports people's ability to influence their mood in a positive manner (Goldbeck and Schmid, 2003). These aspects lead to a better quality of life in the course of medical treatment and more general well-being.

Joystick treatment in CBM: submodalities and future pacing in NLP

Although CBT focuses upon cognitive, conscious, and often language-based interventions, CBM practises behaviors which are expected to appear automatically in the imagined context. This is an exact compliment to NLP Future pacing.

In a recent study (Wiers et al., 2011), alcoholic patients were taught to imagine physically pushing away alcoholic beverages and to replace them with images of non-alcoholic drinks. In NLP the action is an example of future pacing, while the change of distance between the patient and the drink is a submodality shift that weakens the attractive power of the image. More specifically, the technique partially duplicates the NLP swish pattern (Bandler, 1985; Bandler and McDonald, 1987). In the swish pattern a full-color, three-dimensional representation of the subject expressing the trigger for the problem behavior is held in the foreground of the client's visual screen, and the same client expressing the desired behavior as a small, colorless background image is held in the lower, left-hand corner of their visual screen. At a specific moment, the client, as quickly as possible, moves the desired image into the foreground and into the same space with the same qualities as the problem image while she simultaneous moves the problem representation into the distant, colorless position originally occupied by the other image. The swish is practiced several times until the client is confident that a change has occurred.

Complex patterns of perception and response

We have already noted that NLP recognizes that behaviors are often organized in loops. We have noted that early on, NLP adopted the cybernetic conceptions of Bateson (1972) and Korzybski (1994) and that they adopted the TOTE strategy of Miller et al. (1960). Dilts (1993, 1994–5) discusses the relevance of recursive patterns for the structure of beliefs and the structure of extraordinary behavior.

In a similar fashion, CBT took some of its formative constructs from linguistics, general semantics, and computer science. More generally, cognitive science draws extensively from the work of Chomsky in linguistics, Shannon in communications theory and Turing in artificial intelligence (Boeckx, 2010). Needless to say, cognitive science and NLP have much in common.

In a series of articles exploring the structure of bipolar disorders, cognitive therapists have outlined a recursive structure named Think Effectively About Mood Swings (TEAMS) that provides an explanatory mechanism regarding intervention points for the treatment of bipolar disorders and depression more generally (Mansell et al., 2007; Searson et al., 2012).

According to the TEAMS model, the process begins with a triggering event that creates a change in internal state. The trigger might be a conditioned stimulus, a tone of voice, a smell, an interaction, or an imagined image. The response could be an internal change in mood, physiology (pain, discomfort), or cognition (confusion, racing thoughts, blankness, perception of social conditions). These changes are interpreted in terms of a distorted belief system. Those beliefs lead to an extreme, distorted understanding of the change that may be rooted in past personal experiences or past experiences of increased loss of control during similar episodes. Importantly, the distorted interpretations are multiple and contradictory. Even though they occupy consciousness one at a time, they can alternate quickly and unpredictably. In the case of depression, they lead to catastrophic negative interpretations; in the case of hypomania, they are interpreted positively in an unrealistic and exaggerated fashion.

In an effort to suppress the expected consequences—based on the distorted beliefs—the individual engages in behaviors that they believe will restore balance and control. Those behaviors, intended to provide safety from the predicted consequences, paradoxically contribute to the downward spiral. In depression, the behaviors may include withdrawal, sleeping, and self-criticism. While engaged in those efforts, the individual becomes more unable to resolve contradictions, deal effectively with the distortions or attend to helpful or meaningful information from outside of themselves.

Mansell (2007) explains that the protective behaviors tend to avoid reality testing and, by avoiding a confrontation with the problem, confirm the distorted beliefs about the problem state. With the confirmation of the beliefs provided by the safety behaviors, whether ascending or descending, the problem continues to cycle out of control.

The direction of the spiral, whether ascending to hypomania or descending into depression, is partially determined by internal and environmental stimuli and preconditions. In the case of racing thoughts, the person moving into depression interprets them as precursors of some extreme negative consequence: "Whenever this happens, I end up in hospital." In the hypomanic pattern, that same change in cognition might be understood as good thing: "Whenever this happens it means that I am entering a creative phase when everything I do is worthwhile." In both cases the responses are not only irrational and extreme, but they have the effect of shutting out moderating external influences.

These sequences build up over time and attain the status of automatic, unconscious behavior systems. Each repetition of the cycle typically results in more extreme distortions of reality and more intractable patterns of belief.

As this structure emerges from the CBT literature, the interventions flow from the same source. One intervention calls for working with the client to create a continuum of states that extend from depressed to manic. The states are to be described in detail, while not caught up in the cycle. Thereafter the descriptions can be used to describe a continuum of healthy states that the patient can use to evaluate their own progress toward a healthy self-concept. It is envisioned that the descriptions would be evaluated in terms of their pros and cons in assisting the patient to achieve his or her personal goals. Mindfulness exercises might be used to allow the client to become aware of their internal states and making the decision to consciously accept the state without making specific efforts to manage them. This technique would have the advantage of not allowing the cycle to proceed to the stage of the paradoxically self-defeating, self-protective behaviors and the acceleration of the problem that they imply.

From the perspective of NLP, the TEAMS model presents several significant points in the cycle where structural interventions would be effective. NLP might also reconceptualize the model in terms of the structures and processes that arise in the NLP literature.

The cycle begins with intrusive thoughts that change internal states. From an NLP perspective, these thoughts and state changes are anchors—conditioned stimuli. When the conditioned stimuli are known, their intensity and valence can be changed using a collapse anchors procedure, or by changing their submodality structure.

The TEAMS pattern continues when the internal state change is reinterpreted in terms of an irrational belief. This is most likely to result in a restructuring of the submodalities of the representation associated with the internal state. Although the belief itself might be challenged using the NLP meta-model, that tool is best used to identify the problematic belief while a collapse anchor, belief change or swish technique might be used to change the structure of the representation.

The NLP swish technique was first described by Bandler (1985). The technique was refined and re-described by Andreas and Andreas (1989) and is generally considered to be one of the standard elements of the NLP toolkit. It is a technique that can be used to replace negative beliefs, expectations, or behaviors with more positive options. In this case, it should be practised while the client is neither in the midst of an episode nor moving into mania or depression. The pattern involves the replacement of an associated image of the problem state with a dissociated image of the individual in a state of having the desired capabilities and choices. At this stage in the development of depression or mania, the internal state that evokes the distorted belief typically evokes an internal representation of the expected result of the change of state. This might be a representation in any or all of the senses. While the swish may be executed for any or all of these possibilities, the primary focus is usually on an internal visual representation. When structuring a swish based on an internal representation, it is important that the problem image represents that internal image as closely as possible. In dealing with the development of bipolar or depressive cycles, the pattern should be applied to enough examples of the triggering internal state and the belief representation so that the behavior spontaneously generalizes to neutralize the cycle. Andreas and Andreas emphasize that the positive image should be a dissociated image that is observed from without, not experienced from within. They explain that an associated image indicates that the change has already been made—you already have the trait. A dissociated image, to the contrary, represents a goal toward which the client may aspire.

The irrational beliefs about the internal states might usefully be transformed using a belief change technique. Robert Dilts (1993) has described several such techniques.

Andreas (2009) describes a verbal affirmation for restructuring limiting beliefs and critical thoughts that takes the form, "Even though I (statement of problem or difficulty) I (statement of a positive outcome)" (p. 52).

In this case, the verbal reframe might take the form, "Even though (statement of the irrational interpretation of the internal state), I (statement of positive outcome)". So, "Even though this fast thinking usually means that I am going to lose control and be hospitalized, this time I can choose to observe my behavior and see what actually happens. Even though these feelings usually mean that I'm no good, I can discover something of my own value by waiting until the feeling dissipates".

An NLP model of change for depressive disorder

While it must be acknowledged that certain levels of depression may be non-amenable to behavioral interventions, for many cases of depression, NLP techniques can be very useful. Recalling that every remembered experience and every imagined experience is a potential resource, many clients can be taught to model their own or other's behaviors (Andreas and Andreas, 1987, 1989; Bandler and Grinder, 1975a, b).

From the client's perspective, NLP can model the perspective of clients who have managed to resolve their depressive state or disorder, which can then be mapped across for clients who are unable to resolve their depression. Equally, a client can be encouraged to model their own strategy for how in the past, they have changed from a depressed mood to normal emotional modulation, from diminished interest/pleasure in almost all activities to a motivated and active person; from not controlled to a balanced diet and weight; from sleep disorder to a normal sleep; from fatigue or loss of energy to an energetic active life; from feelings of worthlessness or inappropriate guilt to assertive communication; from impaired ability to concentrate or indecisiveness to focused and appropriate decision-making behavior; and from recurrent thoughts of death and suicidal ideation to enjoying life and value oriented actions.

From the therapist's point of view, many of the strategies and intervention frames in NLPt come from modeling the patterns of the therapists that managed to help their clients get rid of symptoms, including those of depression. As we have already demonstrated, there are components found in other therapies that either emerged from NLP or have influenced NLP. An NLPt psychotherapist sees every successful client as a possible model. Pure observation of such intervention patterns like dissociation used in phobia techniques, the outcome intervention, adaptation of sensory experience, the utilization of eye patterns, were then used in clinical fields for psychotherapeutic interventions for depression. Modeling enables a cognitive description of a process that therapeutically happens over a number of sessions. No therapist would apply the reframing interventions without having a good relationship and a basic understanding of the client's history. The therapeutic relationship and relationship interventions are mandatory for the therapeutic process even if it is not described per se in the technique manuals.

NLPt provides a perspective on depression that is based not on what is not working and a specific diagnosis, but on the success strategies related to energy, negative thoughts and beliefs, relationship patterns, identity and self-esteem, resource management, successful outcome work, positive visualizations, etc. NLPt as an intervention in depression can be effective when the needed resources are in place in order to balance the depressive patterns. In an ideal situation the client is encouraged to access an excellence state: in which the mind and its expression in linguistic and sensory representation is influencing the body and physiology. This is the "state goal" leading to better physiological and psychological health.

The criteria for therapeutic outcomes in NLPt include the following:

- A clear therapeutic goal that the client is motivated to achieve.
- The client agrees to formulate a course of actions that are self-initiated.
- The client is informed of and agrees to any work that he is expected to do during therapy, e.g. accepting body touch for anchoring, moving to different chairs for perceptual positions, visualization processes.
- The client maintains the positive by-products of the therapeutic work through exercises, homework, or other agreed upon modalities.
- The client has family or social support.

In some cases, short-term interventions and techniques may be relevant. However, the earlier and the more frequent the traumatization or neglect occurred, the more necessary it is to focus on relational work as a baseline.

Relationship here is understood as:

1. The relationships of the patient and therapist to themselves individually and their own past, present and future.
2. The relationship of patient and therapist to each other.
3. The relationship of the client and therapist individually and together towards the outside world.

NLP views depression linguistically as a nominalization, the transformation of a process into a substantive. As "cancer" is a label for multiple diseases that lead to the uncontrolled proliferation of cells ending in a major dysfunction in the normal regulation of the body, "depression" is the end point of multiple processes that end with the characteristic symptomatology described by DSM or The International Classification of Diseases. Symptoms of depression are seen as possibly a dysfunctional result of the person's coping strategy in the face of an imbalance of forces, neglect of or an excessive need for attention, love, appreciation, challenge, information, stimulation, bonding, and often a disregard of basic stability and safety.

The most prominent symptom is depressive mood (mixed sometimes with anxiety) and a lack of energy, accompanied by inhibition of thinking and psychomotor activities. The main goal of therapy is to regain the energy necessary for the therapeutic process to continue. Contrary to the common belief in simple NLP approaches, in this stage, activation of the energy within the client cannot be obtained by anchoring processes or positive thinking. The recommended steps for restoring the energy for change include a detailed history and medical diagnostic for exclusion of possible causes for the condition. When all medical factors are excluded, extensive rapport can be established and a positive frame for understanding the purpose of the symptom can be found.

As we have already mentioned, the therapeutic relationship is key to successful therapy. Rapport has been modeled as one of the key behaviors of a successful therapist. We differentiate rapport at behavioral, emotional, and meaning/contextual levels. At a behavioral level, the person is mirroring external behaviors that may be enough to trigger mirror neurons, and then moving to leading, encouraging self-care behaviors, and awakening a more positive state. At an emotional level, the therapist will become sensitive, both unconsciously and consciously, to the emotional state of the client. At a meaning and context level, the therapist will work with the client to identify the level to which the problem lies with problem behaviors or problem states.

When it is possible and appropriate, the relationship intervention can be extended by giving the task of being close to a supportive family or social network.

The depressive state can be compared to the normal healthy state, in which the client has certain inner resources that they can call on to fuel that state. The depressive state has a different quality that may reflect a lack of family or peer contact, an underlying physical or medical condition, money or other external resources are not available, or a belief that they are not worth having these things. It may also be that the client may have had resources in the past that they are unable to access in the present. One of the inner resources needed for normal life is the capacity to have normal relationships, appropriate bonding with others, and established boundaries. If the relationship patterns previously established with parents or parental figures in childhood are not available in the present, this can affect the sensory or cognitive experiences possibly leading to a depressive state.

NLP would see this re-emergence of previous relationship patterns as a positive intention, which may not be in the cognitive awareness of the client. This attachment disruption can be enabled through the establishment of an appropriate narrative of the past situation, and a congruent description of the inner state. If this experience is well supported by the therapist, and associated with a here-and-now rapport from the therapist's side, it is likely to induce the experience of a congruent state for the client (Wake 2010b).

Multi-level interventions

One theoretical framework used in NLPt for treating depressive disorder is based on an NLP model proposed by Dilts' Neurological Levels. A brief description of the model and its application follows.

Spiritual

Is the mind having an impact on the body and the whole-system state: mind–body–spirit? Spiritual crisis can be present in someone with depression. Dilts proposed that the spiritual level is the connection with the outer world, where human experience is not just encapsulated in the body, rather the body provides a systemic feedback loop that contributes to its formation and lived experience. The reflection of this spiritual level can be traced through the identity and beliefs of the individual. Race, ethnicity, gender, cultural norms, prejudice, stigmas, economic conditions, and so many other aspects of social life affect the life of the depressive client. Understanding and alignment with such aspects can help both patient and therapist to adapt and integrate the psychotherapy in real life (Butcher, 1986; Cardemil et al., 2002; Chentsova-Dutton and Tsai, 2010; Dressler, 1992; Gaviria, 1988; Hernandez et al., 2006; Keitner et al., 1991; Kim et al., 2011; Kleinman, 2004; Lopez and Guarnaccia, 2000; Raguram and Weiss, 2004; Redmond et al., 2006; Schreiber et al., 1998; Stewart et al., 2004; US Department of Health and Human Services [DHHS], 1999).

Identity

When you listen to the self-definition of clients with depression, you can hear the footprint of self-definition: "I am not worthy." They believe that "I am depressed" is something that cannot be changed. Their identity includes perceptions and definitions about the self that are shaped by physiology and experience and that act to define the borders of self with the external world. These definitions are also reflected in changes in the endocrine and immune systems.

There are two different concepts of identity in NLPt. One is the wider Anglo-American approach, which is focused on roles and professional identities. The other is the more narrow central European approach, which focuses primarily on non-changeable biological and some cultural features (age, gender, family structure, and region).

At a conscious level a whole narrative of these clients is developed, about themselves, about their bodies, their history, about connections with others, about everything related to them. In depression, the representation of the self becomes distorted, is usually minimized, and represented as a deficit (Satir, 1972). Satir would talk about "gaining trust," "making contact," "building positive self-worth," and the importance of the "human connection" and an "I–thou relationship"; a whole approach toward identity that is nowadays used in neurolinguistic psychotherapy in the form of positive affirmations and visualization of identity.

In relationship with others, the metaphoric representation of the self is often held with a lack of emotional congruence, being expressed through abstract words or lack of empathetic feelings toward the younger self or the significant parental figure. These life stories are charged with a low level of energy that is then reflected into the body and contributes to further negative ideation (Carroll and Coetzer, 2011; Freed, 1987; Kraus, 1995; Lewis, 2001; Lidz and Parker, 2003; Lutz, 1982; Zinbarg et al., 2008).

Beliefs

NLP has developed extensive work in the domain of exploring and changing beliefs (Andreas, 1992; Bandler and Grinder, 1982; Dilts, 1990, 1993, 1999).

Depression is a disorder underpinned by many beliefs relating to sense of worth, feeling useless, and hopeless about the future. In every aspect of life the beliefs of a depressed person are usually represented linguistically in the form of meta-model violations including cause–effect, presupposition, or complex equivalence. A depressive person can have negative beliefs about himself, causing identity and self-esteem problems, about the environment, his own behavior or capability.

Capabilities

NLP sees depression as not something that you have (the end-result process), but something that you do—the leading process and the end result process. The patient "is capable of making" depressive process and symptoms. This would include strategies, chains, and other capability level factors (learning, sequences and events, etc.).

There are several strategies or patterns that people use that result in depressive symptoms. One very common strategy would be the Ad–K loop. Someone talks about how bad things are then feels bad. This loops back to more discussion, even worse, with worse feelings to follow, in an endless loop. The obvious intervention here is to modify the loop, usually with some kind of visual interruption, e.g. splicing in images of a positive future. It can be difficult to access a positive resource before modifying the state, because people stuck in this loop have created a state devoid of positive images and lack any images of a future (hazy, blank, etc.). Usually there are belief issues attached, so effective treatment becomes a combination of interventions based in precise resonance work.

Another common pattern is an internal polarity strategy. Typically it works like this: V_c-A_d-K. The person imagines something good in the future then goes into an explanation about how it won't happen, then feels bad. It usually then collapses into something similar to the A–K loop strategy described above.

Another strategy or pattern is based on past positive memories. In this strategy, which can take several forms, a person remembers a past good experience, then runs the movie until it ends, and feels bad about either the ending itself, or how it ended (for example a painful breakup of a relationship). This can turn into a consistent strategy for all good memories. Similarly, people can have a chain that effectively does the same thing, i.e. all good experience leads to bad experience.

A more severe variant on the above strategy occurs when the person not only goes to the end of the good memory, but then goes into an A–K loop based on the belief that the good experience can never happen again. This belief is usually based on first- or second-position experience based. This means that the person has experienced the unpleasant situation himself and deduced from it the conclusion that no such future is possible again, or has just observed the situation with sufficient identification, and made the deduction. When the good experience is believed to be lost forever, it can also be identified as the only good thing, making the loss even more devastating. This can be expanded to the belief that nothing good can ever happen again, which is the basis of total hopelessness and despair.

Behavior

NLP codes human experience that is represented at the mind–body level as a linguistic-neurological connection. The linguistic part is the surface structure representation of a deeper neurological process. The reflection in consciousness of the neurological processes is related to cortical arousal involving the anterior cingulate cortex, the thalamus, and the pontomesencephalic brainstem results in sensory-based experience. The quality of this sensory-based experience can be adjusted using submodalities, as described in previous chapters. The negative submodality changes in those kinds of representations are well known in depressive patients. When these are coupled with a disconnection from the outer world, they can become uncomfortable negative visualizations or interpretations of the person, their future or other situations (DePaulo et al., 2002).

From an NLP perspective it is important to consider the effect or influence of conditioned responses or anchors, both conscious or unconscious, that can trigger negative memories or states. The first, most obvious and frequently confirmed observation, is that people who are depressed have adjusted their submodalities so that they have increasing intensity of feeling around unpleasant thoughts and memories, and decreasing intensity around pleasurable ones. The sensory experience of symptoms by the client can include dramatic changes in mood, often characterized by a sense of numbness rather than sadness, a depletion of vitality, an inability to concentrate, which is accompanied by slowness in thinking, and a loss of self-regard or self-esteem. Depression is also marked by troubling changes in appetite, sleep, and sexual drive. In many cases, anxiety, panic disorder, and burn-out can occur as manifestations of the depression and disappear when the depression does. Many people with depression also experience hallucinations and delusions. In addition to these symptoms, there are signs of depression that express themselves physically, in a slowing down of speech or movement, or in certain instances in stupor or immobility.

The most dramatic example at a sensory level is that all negative memories are experienced as fully associated, present/future oriented, while all pleasurable memories are dissociated, located in the distant past, and no longer operative.

General activity level is something to be addressed. It is now established that exercise changes (neuro) physiology and often lifts depression. Clients are encouraged to improve their physical condition and to care for their ailments, since most ailments and illnesses, besides depressing bodily functions, add to psychological depression.

Conversely, it's easily observed that people, who are very depressed, almost by definition, are relatively inactive, even beyond the physical compared to how they were before or after their experience of depression: "Am I not doing the things I enjoy, that keep me active, healthy and alive because I'm depressed?" Or, "Am I depressed because I'm not doing the things that keep me active, healthy and alive?"

Environment

A central feature in depressive disorder is the lack of energy. In subjective experience the feeling of being energized is often physically experienced in the body. The experience is usually associated with distorted visual perceptions (the sub modalities) related to colour, movement and so on. Through this particular lens, perceptions of the self, the future, possible success, and their own abilities are distorted. All these contribute to the amplification of the negative sensations and feelings around unpleasant thoughts and memories, and decreasing intensity around the pleasurable ones. A specific submodality which has a great impact on the overall depressive state is association into all negative memories and dissociation from all pleasurable memories.

As studies on fitness have demonstrated over many years, the overall activity a person has influences their neurophysiology and consequently impacts their energy level and the level of serotonin in the brain. This, associated with balanced food, vitamins, and nutrients creates a solid basis for good health. In depressive disorder, the overall level of energy is decreased with a lack of personal health care including nutrition, hydration, and neglected medical conditions. The end result is inactivity, and even more than physical activity, lack of initiative, which will increase the awareness of discomfort and reinforce it at the belief level with negative thinking. At the surface level we can hear, at the tip of the iceberg, the expression of this inner, bodily experience, actually and selectively distorted towards the negative, as limiting beliefs and chains of thought.

Directions for future research

Currently there is just one study that supports the effectiveness of NLP interventions in improving depressive symptoms (Stipancic et al., 2010). Stipancic's study, discussed in Chapter 4, has demonstrated that NLPt can have a significant positive impact on self-esteem and quality of life, both significant factors in depressive illness.

We propose that controlled studies be developed to measure the effectiveness of NLPt in the treatment of depression using a combination of rebalancing resources using relationship and parts integration, the professional outcome model and goal setting, reframing and belief change, anchoring and submodality interventions.

Part II
Neurolinguistic programming contemporary research

7 Indirect research into the applications of neurolinguistic programming

Richard M. Gray, Lisa Wake, Steve Andreas, Richard Bolstad

Introduction, by Steve Andreas

I am often asked whether there is any "hard science" academic research that supports NLP. There is some good news and some bad news.

First, the bad news

Most of the research that is focused directly on NLP concepts was done in the 1980s and 1990s; little or no research has been done directly in the past decade or so. The vast majority of studies that were done earlier addressed the concept of a primary representational system (PRS)—that people are primarily visual, auditory, or kinesthetic—or the impact of matching sensory predicates on rapport (Carbonell, 1985; Dowd and Hingst, 1983; Gallo, 1985; Paxton, 1980; Rebstock, 1980; Schneider, 1984; Sperber, 1983).

There's a problem with this. Bandler and Grinder had introduced the idea of a PRS primarily as a teaching tool in the 1970s, to direct students' attention to people's sensory predicates and eye accessing. Soon after, they pointed out that the idea of a PRS was a deliberate and gross oversimplification, only somewhat true in a particular problem context. Despite this, the bulk of research, supposedly "on NLP" at that time was done in an attempt to verify or disconfirm this concept.

As those with significant NLP training will already know, whether or not people have a PRS is not in any way central to the field of NLP. Andreas notes that he and co-author Connierae Andreas didn't even mention it in the book *Heart of the Mind* (1989) introducing people to the field, because they didn't consider it important or useful. PRS doesn't have anything to do with the effectiveness of the many methods that NLP relies upon to get results for people who want change in their lives.

At the same time, it *is* often useful to notice what sensory channel the client is using *at the moment*, or what sensory channel underlies the "problem." For example, it can be useful to notice that someone's unpleasant feelings result from a critical inner voice, or to notice that many large and close movies of things to do leads to feeling overwhelmed.

Investigating PRS is a bit like Nasrudin looking for his lost keys under the street lamp "because the light is better here," even though he lost them somewhere else. PRS was perceived to be an "easy" thing to study, but the results of those studies don't tell us anything about the field of NLP.

It's also worth noting that the studies themselves were often full of research errors. The questionnaires used in an attempt to assess PRS often had confusing self-report questions such as, "Do you see yourself as a feeling person," or "Do you feel you are an auditory person?" As that kind of question clearly reveals, most experimenters were not trained in NLP, did not understand what they were researching, and did not use anyone extensively trained in NLP to review their experimental protocols. As a result, there was no control of the language used in the studies, nor control of non-verbal confounding variables such as gestures or voice tone.

For instance, when matching a subject's visual predicate with a sentence such as, "I see what you mean," a higher pitched voice, looking up, or a pointing gesture in the upper visual field will be congruent with visual processing, and be more likely to result in rapport. However, a lower pitched voice, looking down, or a palm-up gesture in the lower visual field will be incongruent, and be less likely to lead to rapport. (Visual processing is typically accompanied by a high voice tone, looking up, and pointing gestures, while kinesthetic processing is often accompanied by a lower voice tone, looking down, and palm-up gesturing) (Andreas and Andreas, 1989; Andreas and Faulkner, 1994; Bandler and Grinder, 1975a, 1979; Bodenhamer and Hall, 2001; Brooks, 1989; Dilts and DeLozier, 2000; Lewis and Pucelik, 1990; Linden and Perutz, 1998; O'Connor and Seymour, 1990).

As a result of these types of mistakes, most of the research was of a very poor quality. Not surprisingly, there is very little direct academic experimental support for NLP. A research committee working for the United States National Research Council in 1988 found little if any evidence to support NLP's assumptions or to indicate that it was effective as a strategy for social influence. "It [NLP] assumes that by tracking another's eye movements and language, an NLP trainer can shape the person's thoughts, feelings, and opinions. There is no scientific support for these assumptions" (Druckman and Swets, 1988).

To summarize, the research that has been done was on the wrong questions, by people who did not understand what they were trying to measure, ignoring linguistic and behavioral confounding variables, so of course the results were negative or inconclusive.

Although researching NLP is definitely doable, effective research in the field of NLP is a challenge for a number of reasons.

Psychological research costs quite a lot of money, which most NLP-ers do not have. Furthermore, if research is not done in a recognized academic institution, it is usually ignored, even if the controls and protocols are impeccable.

NLP's focus on sensory process parameters makes it extremely hard to communicate with academics and mental health professionals, because it is so different from the typical psychiatric focus on content. For instance, cognitive behavioral therapy (CBT), a recognized therapy that is most similar to NLP (and which has the strongest experimental support) focuses almost entirely on the content of internal auditory dialogue—the words that people say to themselves. CBT ignores the volume of the internal voice, its location in personal space, its direction, its tonality, and tempo, etc. Usually changing these process parameters has a much greater impact on experience than changing the content, and it is much easier. This is something that Andreas has explored in great detail.

Advocating rigorous research has not been easy or without resistance from within the field itself. The original developers and a number of others in the field—some of them widely respected—have explicitly said that NLP is inherently unverifiable by scientific research. One widely regarded leader in the field has even said that since NLP is about subjective experience, it is inherently untestable.

This ignores the fact that dreams—the most subjective experiences that most of us will ever have—have been researched scientifically for decades. A variety of new methods of brain scanning make it possible to do experimental work on internal mental events, some of which are not even subjective experiences. For instance, brain scans have been used to detect when a decision is about to be made by a subject several seconds *before* the subject becomes aware that they have made a decision (Haynes and Rees, 2006; Soon et al., 2008).

The near-universal lack of support for securing research grants from within the field of NLP has made it difficult to approach potential researchers. Even more of a problem is that many who "do NLP" have combined NLP with reflexology, remote viewing, crystal healing, aromatherapy, aura reading, and a host of other "new-age" methods. Most of these do not make specific claims that would be testable by the scientific method; associating NLP with them makes NLP appear to be only another get-rich-quick scam or even a cult.

Now for the good news

All NLP processes include specific testable outcomes, detailed systematic protocols for different kinds of problems, and clear operational tests in sensory-based experience to determine when a client has reached their outcomes. In addition, many NLP processes can be completed in a single session of an hour or less. Because of this, NLP would be *much* easier to research than most therapies which are much less structured and usually take place during many sessions over a period of weeks or months. Scientific research needs to be done in order to confirm (or disconfirm) the various processes and understandings that are typically included in the term "NLP."

A diverse group of dedicated NLP-trained people have joined together in establishing the NLP Research and Recognition Project (http://nlprandr.org)

in an effort to propose, develop, and support relevant research by academic institutions, with the goal of doing high-quality research that tests NLP principles and methods. This could do a great deal to establish the legitimacy of NLP methods, as well as advance the practice of psychotherapy generally. The director of the project, Frank Bourke, a clinical psychologist with a strong research background, has been a tireless advocate, working with members of the NLP community and those in government organizations and universities, in efforts to establish studies. So far these efforts have just begun to obtain funding for large-scale studies. This is really quite a testament to Frank's diligence and persistence, because it is not an easy thing to get through all the levels of "hoops" to gain this approval.

Although little is currently being done directly on NLP processes, there is quite a lot of academic research that supports NLP indirectly. NLP methods and principles are being "rediscovered" in bits and pieces in a wide variety of research studies.

Evidencing the neuro of neurolinguistic programming

In considering the history of the development of NLP, when Bandler, Grinder, Cameron, Megus, Gordon, Dilts and DeLozier (DeLozier, 1985), among others, developed the patterns that became known as NLP, very little attention was paid to the neurological aspects of psychological processing. This was predominantly because there was little in the way of tools to measure specific neurological processes and the popular view of neural function focused almost exclusively on cognitive function without regard to emotion.

In more recent years investigative processes such as fMRI (functional magnetic resonance imaging), MEG (magneto encephalography), MRI (magnetic resonance imaging), and PET (positive emission tomography) have opened up opportunities for understanding psychological processes and how these directly relate to the structural and functional aspects of the brain. Science is now beginning to report on what Bandler, Grinder et al. postulated. Dilts and DeLozier defined one of the goals of NLP as being "to better understand and utilize the way that processes within our nervous systems and language ability join together to form the 'programs' which are responsible for our behavior in the world" (2000, pp. 840–1).

Direct and indirect research to support NLP techniques

There is a number of basic NLP concepts that have received significant validation in mainline research. The ideas that information is processed in separate sensory streams and integrated at multiple levels and that the subjective dimensions of sensory information (submodalities) impact the valence and intensity of experience are not only foundational to most NLP interventions but are well supported in the literature of mainline psychology and neuroscience. The imaginal representation of desired outcomes has received significant support from sources as disparate as imaginal role playing and exposure therapies for phobias and PTSD. In the emerging field of cognitive linguistics we find that metaphor, as practiced in NLP since Gordon's (1978) signal contribution, lie at the very heart of what it means to make sense of the world around us. NLP, finding its roots in Chomskian linguistics, early on emphasized the ideas of syntax and well-formedness. It adopted Miller et al.'s (1960) TOTE model, and continues to model optimal outcomes in terms of well-formedness conditions. Rooting its approach in the commonalities among the techniques used by the great therapists of the time, they identified rapport skills as a crucial part of the therapist's toolbox. That insight has now been supported by research ranging from standardized measurements of trust and co-operation to the physiology of the mirror-neuron systems. In a time where psychology was primarily focused upon cognitive models, NLP recognized the importance of more general affective states and their capacity to affect behavior globally, an idea not fully appreciated until LeDoux's (1995, 1997) groundbreaking work on the ubiquity of emotion in every human enterprize, Pert's (1997) insight that the body is the unconscious and the final demise of the Cartesian divide between mind and emotion, body and soul.

These and other insights linking NLP to mainline research are discussed below. It is important, however, to note that the list is not exhaustive and the level of concordance between what we do and what already stands as well established psychology grows every day.

Modalities and submodalities

Sensory accessing and representational cues

As a person goes through their daily activities, information is processed in all the sensory modalities, continuously. However, from context to context, the person's conscious attention tends to focus on one modality or sequence of modalities at a time. It is clear that some people have a strong preference for "thinking" (to use the term generically) in one sensory modality or another, while others show no strong preference beyond contextual demands.

As early as 1890, William James defined four key types of "imagination" based on this fact. He says:

> In some individuals the habitual "thought stuff," if one may so call it, is visual; in others it is auditory, articulatory [to use an NLP term, auditory digital], or motor [kinesthetic, in NLP terms]; in most, perhaps, it is evenly mixed. The auditory type ... appears to be rarer than the visual. Persons of this type imagine what they think of in the language of sound. In order to remember a lesson they impress upon their mind,

not the look of the page, but the sound of the words ... The motor type remains perhaps the most interesting of all, and certainly the one of which least is known. Persons who belong to this type make use, in memory, reasoning, and all their intellectual operations, of images derived from movement ... There are persons who remember a drawing better when they have followed its outlines with their finger.

(James, 1950, Volume 2, pp. 58–61)

In NLP, eye movements are clues to the sensory system from which a person is getting (accessing) information and the sensory modality in which they then "process" or "re-present" that information. Accessing and representing are not always done in the same sensory system. A person may look at a beautiful painting (visual accessing) and think about how it feels to them (kinesthetic representation). The person's representation of their experience in a particular language can be identified by the words (predicates) they use to describe their subject. For example, someone might say "I see what you mean" visually, "I hear you" auditorally, or "Now I grasp that" kinesthetically. The person who looks at the beautiful painting and represents it to themselves kinesthetically might well say "That painting feels so warm. The colors just flow across it". They experience the painting as temperature and movement.

It is important to understand that recognizing the sensory system that a person is using is not a way of typing a person. People are generally not "visuals" or "auditories" or "kinesthetics", even though some may have strong preferences in one context or another. These are tools that allow the interviewer to create increased empathy and the modeler to discern patterns of perception and action. They are best discerned in terms of a conversational gestalt in which context, breathing rate, posture, predicates, eye movement and repetitions reveal the operative senses (Bandler and Grinder, 1975a, 1979; Dilts et al., 1980; Dilts and DeLozier, 2000).

Research identifying the neurological bases for these different types of "thought" began to emerge in the mid-twentieth century. Much of it was based on the discovery that damage to specific areas of the brain caused specific sensory problems. Luria (1966) identified separate areas associated with vision, hearing, sensory-motor activity, and speech (the latter isolated on the dominant hemisphere of the brain).

By the time NLP emerged in the 1970s, researchers already understood that each sensory system had a specialized brain area. In their original 1980 presentation of NLP, Dilts et al. (1980, p. 17) point out that all human experience can be coded as a combination of internal and external vision, audition, kinesthesis and olfaction/gustation. The combination of these senses at any time (VAKO/G) is called a 4-tuple.

The developers of NLP noticed that we also process information in words and that words too have a specific brain system specialized to process them, as if they were a sensory system. They described this verbal type of information as "auditory digital", distinguishing it from the auditory input we get, for example, in listening to music or to the sound of the wind. In thinking in words (talking to ourselves) we pay attention specifically to the "meaning" coded into each specific word, rather than to the music of our voice.

> The digital portions of our communications belong to a class of experience that we refer to as "secondary experience". Secondary experience is composed of the representations that we use to *code* our primary experience—*secondary* experience (such as words and symbols), are only meaningful in terms of the *primary* sensory representations that they anchor for us.
>
> (Dilts et al., 1980, p. 75)

When we talk to you in words about "music" for example, what we say only has meaning depending on your ability to be triggered by the word *music* into seeing, hearing or feeling actual sensory representations of an experience of music.

Words (auditory digital) are therefore a meta-sensory system. Apart from words there are other digital meta-representation systems. One is the visual "digital system" used by many scientists, by composers such as Mozart, and computer programmers. This system has a specific area of the brain which manages it (Bolstad and Hamblett, 2000). In visual digital thinking visual images or symbols take the place of words. Hence, Einstein says:

> The words or the language, as they are written or spoken, do not seem to play any role in my mechanism of thought. The psychical entities which seem to serve as elements in thought are certain signs and more or less clear images which can be "voluntarily" reproduced and combined.
>
> (Dilts, 1994–5, pp. 48–9)

Digital senses do not just meta-comment on "stable" primary representations of course. They actually alter those representations. By learning the word "foot" and the word "leg", you actually perceive those areas of your body as visually and kinesthetically distinct units.

The developers of NLP claimed to have identified a number of more easily observed cues which let us know which sensory system a person is using at any given time. Among these cues are a series of largely unconscious eye movements which people exhibit while thinking (1980, p. 81). These "eye-accessing cues" (EACs) have become the most widely discussed of all the NLP discoveries.

In general, EACs are upwards for visual information, from side to side for auditory information and, with some variation, down and to the left for auditory digital and down and to the right for kinesthetic. A further distinction held that EACs to the left-accessed remembered information, and those to the right constructed information (Bandler and Grinder, 1979).

Tests of EACs, mostly focused on the now abandoned concept of the PRS, have for the most part failed to confirm the intuitions of NLP. The bulk of these studies have been criticized for their failure to employ adequately trained personnel to assess the presence or absence of the predicted eye movements (Einspruch and Forman, 1985; Diamantopoulos et al., 2009).

A serious problem with most of these experiments is their presupposition that a naturalistic phenomenon, like EACs, can be reliably recreated using a standardized procedure. That is to say that although eye movements may represent possible correlates of spontaneous mentation, especially when they occur in the presence of similarly correlated predicates and physiology, this does not imply that constructed attempts to evoke sensory specific responses will evoke the gestalt that is observed in the naturalistic context from which the observations are normally taken. Thus, a person speaking naturally will shift from sensory system to sensory system (Hammer, 1983; Graunke and Roberts, 1985) and that flow of sensory access will be followed short term by spontaneous eye patterns and predicates and over longer periods by patterns of breathing and voice tonality. NLP does not posit an absolute one-to-one relationship between these systems and does not suggest that a constructed access paradigm will or should evoke them. Moreover, because we cannot ascertain whether the subjects in most of the classic experiments are actually accessing the experimental target, are attempting to access it from a different modality, or are experiencing frustrations regarding difficulty in accessing it, the effort to assess the NLP prediction outside of a naturalistic setting is invalid unless backed up by brain imagery that might conclusively determine the course of internal processing.

Another subtlety that appears in the research is that the NLP research on predicate matching and empathy shows some sensitivity to the measure used. Studies using the Barrett-Lennard Relationship Inventory (1962) as a measure of rapport have provided results supporting NLP rapport skills with some consistency (Brockman, 1980; Ehrmantraut, 1983; Schmedlen, 1981).

Buckner et al. (1987) tested EACs against sensory specific accessing questions. For example, for a visual task, "Which is the brightest room in your home?" for an auditory task "Listen to one of your favorite songs in your own head" and, for a kinesthetic task, "Which of your feet is warmer right now?" (p. 284). Responses were evaluated independently by pairs of NLP-trained judges who had been re-assessed for their ability to identify NLP EACs and had passed pre-tests with better than 90 percent accuracy. These judges evaluated silent videos of the responses. Their assessments agreed with each other and with the verbal content of the spoken responses on a significant level ($p<.001$) for both the visual and auditory measures. Kinesthetic measures were non-significant ($p<.85$).

One of the indicia of visual access tested by Buckner et al. was staring into space. Sharot et al. (2008) have shown that, compared to persons remembering a less impactful scene, persons remembering an emotionally charged visual memory are more likely to limit their gazes to a cluster of fixation points centred on salient elements of the remembered scene. That is, they stare into space.

Although the direct evidence for EACs is not well developed, a series of studies that depend upon reciprocal interconnections between eye position and access to specific behavioral effects have been noted. These applications of the visual EACs are suggestive of a more robust neurological connection than has been established more directly. Specifically, looking up to the left (for most people) will help them recall images they have seen before.

Dilts and Epstein (1995) report that Loiselle selected 44 average spellers, as determined by pre-tests in which they memorized nonsense syllables. In the experiment, the subjects were required to memorize another set of nonsense words that were presented on a computer screen. The 44 were divided into four subgroups for the experiment: group one were told to visualize each word in the test while looking up to the left; group two were told to visualize each word while looking down to the right; group three were told to visualize each word (without reference to eye position); and group four were simply told to study the word in order to learn it. All groups were given the same amount of time to study the materials and there was no difference in the speed of recall for any of the groups. The results were reported to be significant but no measure was given.

The results on testing immediately following the memorization trials were: group one increased their success in spelling by 25 percent; group two worsened their spelling by 15 percent; group three increased their success by ten percent; and group four scored the same as previously. This strongly suggests that looking up and towards the left (visual recall) enhances the recall of words for spelling and is twice as effective as simply teaching students to picture the words. Furthermore, looking down and towards the right (kinesthetic), damages the ability to visualize the words. In a follow-up test some time later (testing retention), the scores of group one remained constant, while the scores of the control group, group four, declined by a further 15 percent, a drop which was consistent with standard learning studies.

Malloy (1995) completed a study with three groups of spellers, again pre-tested to find average spellers. One group were taught a version of the NLP "spelling strategy" in which they were instructed to view a word, visualize the word while looking up, to mark the word visually in way that would let them know it was correct and to attend to a feeling of confidence that let them know that the word was spelled correctly and later to look up while recalling how to spell the word. A second group were taught a strategy of sounding out the words using phonetics and auditory rules. The control group were given no new information. In this study the tests involved words from a standardized list of frequently misspelled words. Again, the visual recall spellers improved 25 percent, and had near 100 percent retention of those gains one week later. The group taught the auditory strategies improved 15 percent but this score dropped five percent in the following week. The control group showed no improvement. The differences in scores between the visualization group and the standard group were significant at the .05 level in the immediate test and at the .025 level at the two week test.

These studies support the NLP spelling strategy specifically, and the NLP notion of EACs indirectly.

NLP specific research

In the earliest formulations of NLP, Bandler and Grinder (1975a, 1979) set forth the idea of a PRS. That is, a system with which the client oriented themselves to a new stimulus or memory and then moved on to other systems for further processing. As noted by Andreas above, the idea did not last beyond the 1970s and was so inconsequential to the work of NLP that it was not even mentioned in the seminal work, *Heart of the Mind* (Andreas and Andreas, 1989). Whereas many early investigators made an erroneous assumption that the PRS was an essential foundation of NLP, it was no such thing.

There are, however, a number of studies that support the practice of dynamically matching representation systems to establish rapport in ongoing communication and they will be discussed in that section.

Although NLP originally insisted that the left–right distinctions in EACs have a neurological basis, this has been difficult to confirm (Bandler and Grinder 1975a, 1979; Dilts, 1983). Recent research, however, provides evidence for a temporal distribution of associations that would explain the same phenomenon. That is, in the West, memories associated with the past or causal elements are imagined to the left, while results and future events are imagined to the right. Moreover, consistent with the relative context dependency of other perceptual system related cues, it appears that the distinction is culturally determined and associated with the direction in which the subject's native language is read (Ouellet et al., 2010; Santiago et al., 2010; Tversky et al., 1991; Weger and Pratt, 2008). While this is not exactly the remembered/constructed division proposed in the NLP materials, it is congruent with their observations.

Weger and Pratt (2008) asked subjects to identify whether the names of actors presented on a computer screen were either current stars or stars from a previous generation by pressing buttons on the left or right side of a computer keyboard with their left or right index finger. In one series they were told to press the left-hand button with their left index finger for actors from before their time, and to press the right hand key with their right index finger to indicate current actors. In the next series, the fingers and sides were reversed. Results found that subject responded more quickly when the older actors were to the left and the younger to the right (on both measures

$p <.05$). This was interpreted to mean that participants had responded in terms of an internal timeline in which the past was imagined to the left and the future to the right. In two other experiments, the same authors found that prospective and retrospective time words, biased responses to the right and left in subsequent responding (Weger and Pratt, 2008).

Santiago et al. (2010) report that English speakers show a bias towards representing actors to the left and objects to the right. Pushing and pulling actions are imagined as proceeding from left to right. Native speakers of Arabic, however, which is written right to left, experience an opposite temporal orientation. Tversky et al. (1991) showed that when children were asked to place stickers on a timeline to indicate when meals occurred, English-speaking children placed them in accordance with a left-right temporal bias, but Arabic speaking children placed them from right to left.

Ouellet et al. (2010) tested responses to 48 Spanish words denoting either past or future time; half of the words were presented to the left of a computer screen and half to the right. The words were presented in such a way that past and present words were distributed equally in the left and right portions of the screen. Participants were to respond with a press to the left of a computer keyboard with the left index finger and to the right of the keyboard with the right index finger. In one set of trials the finger press on the left was to be used in response to the past-oriented words and the right finger in response to the future. In another set, the instructions were reversed. Ouellet et al. also found that participants responded more quickly when the past-oriented words were towards the left and future oriented words to the right. Results were significant at the .05 level.

The most recent comprehensive study of eye-pattern research in NLP has been conducted as a critical review by Diamantopoulus et al. (2009). They studied ten research papers and of these, six were found to have unsupportive results with poor validity and reliability. They conclude that there is no "research that directly proves or disproves the EAC model and there is substantial ground for further research" (2009, p. 7). In their wider conclusions they recommend that questions used for elicitation of eye patterns should be subject specific and refined to take into account representational systems. They noted that all eye patterns are potentially relevant with some generic and some idiosyncratic movements, all of which should be measured by a machine rather than human observation which is subjective, however, if they are elicited by a human, then rapport is an essential condition for accurate elicitation. They were able to identify that distinctions can be made between visual and non-visual movements, and that when an individual stares this equates with either visual access or to trans-derivational search. All eye patterns that occur when a physiological response is present are considered significant. They also noted that cultural differences are important considerations.

Further complications are introduced by the relatively new understanding that the direction of gaze often represents access to a submodality space where specific qualities of personal experience seem to be subjectively stored. With this complication, the difficulty of verifying the EACs is multiplied considerably (Bandler and LaValle, 1996).

Directions for further research regarding representational systems

Although supported by extensive anecdotal evidence but lacking an abundance of what can be considered well-designed experimental confirmation, we would suggest that this technique be subjected to rigorously controlled experiments based upon the design used by Buckner et al. (1987). Whereas prior designs have suffered serious problems in definition, execution, the criteria used, and the validity of the training that raters received, Buckner et al.'s procedure provides a significant improvement over the others.

Consistent with Buckner, we would suggest that experienced NLP practitioners or trainers who pass a pre-test for their ability to identify the EACs at a 90 percent accuracy rate would show considerable agreement as measured by Cohen's Kappa. As done by Buckner et al., we would further suggest that the EACs be scored in later multi-rater evaluations of soundless recordings of subjects responding to sensory-based questions designed to evoke the predicted EACs. Those questions would be designed and submitted by experts in the field to ensure the absence of linguistic confounds. The evaluations would use written forms detailing the specific patterns observed using check lists.

While Buckner et al. obtained highly significant responses for right-handed subjects in the visual and auditory modes, their results for kinesthetic and auditory digital responses were non-significant. We note that the original predictions made by Bandler and Grinder indicated that hemispheric laterality for left-handed persons is often indeterminate and thus would predict that results from a mixed right- and left-handed group would be indeterminate. For this reason the auditory digital and kinesthetic accessing cues should either be eliminated from the initial study or specific secondary hypotheses regarding their differentiating characteristics should be generated. For the purposes of this study, separation of the results from left-handed participants should be subjected to separate statistical analysis to determine whether the responses are consistent with right-handed responders or are reversed. A separate analysis should consider the direction in which their native language is written. We would predict that when separated based on the original observation, a better differentiation of kinesthetic and auditory digital (self-talk) responses would become apparent. We note that Buckner et al. suggest that the eye movements associated with kinesthetic cues are complex. For this reason, we suggest that just as eye movements include fixations along with the upward, the list of possible kinesthetic accessing cues include the specific movements suggested by Buckner's group including a lead to another system followed by the eyes moving down and to the right.

Submodalities

Modalities are the sensory-based representations that we use to code our experience. The five senses use finer coding processes to provide an experience of differentiation. These are referred to as submodalities or qualities that give meaning to the internal coding of our experience (Andreas and Andreas, 1989; Bandler, 1985, 1993; Bodenhamer and Hall, 1998; Gray, 2008a; Linden and Perutz, 1998; O'Connor and Seymour, 1990, Wake, 2010).

Inside the visual cortex, there are several areas which process these "qualities" or submodalities, such as color. Color is one of the first 14 visual submodalities listed by Bandler (1985, p. 24). The others are distance, depth, duration, clarity, contrast, scope, movement, speed, hue, transparency, aspect ratio, orientation, and foreground/background.

Submodalities occur neurologically in every sense. Different kinesthetic receptors and different brain processing occur for pain, temperature, pressure, balance, vibration, movement of the skin, and movement of the skin hairs (Kalat, 1988). Even in what NLP has called the auditory digital sense modality (language), there are structures similar to submodalities. For example, the class of linguistic structures called presuppositions, conjunctions, helper verbs, quantifiers, and tense and number endings (words such as "and", "but", "if", "not", "being") are stored separately from nouns, which are stored separately from verbs. Broca's aphasia (Kalat, 1988) is a condition where specific brain damage results in an ability to talk, but without the ability to use the first class of words (presuppositions). The person with this damage will be able to read "Two bee oar knot two bee," but unable to read the identical sounding "To be or not to be." If the person speaks sign language, their ability to make hand signs for these words will be similarly impaired.

When we change a person's experience in a visual submodality, submodalities in all the other senses are also changed. This process is known technically as "synaesthesia." Synaesthesia is technically the linking of one sense to one or more other senses. Synaesthetes often report that words may have colors or musical tones shapes and colors as well (Ramachandran and Hubbard, 2006).

More common instances of synaesthesia include office workers in a room repainted blue who will complain of the cold, even though the thermostat has not been touched. When the room is repainted yellow, they will believe it has warmed up, and will not complain even when the thermostat is actually set lower (Podolsky, 1938). A thorough review of such inter-relationships was made by NLP developer Gordon (1978). These cross-modality responses are neurologically based and not simply a result of conscious belief patterns. A recent article (Spector and Maurer, 2009) examines synaesthesia as a universal and neurologically based aspect of intersensory development, which updates much of what Gordon postulated in 1978.

Submodalities, as small-grained details of experience, have been known since at least the time of Galton (Wake, 2010) and have been the subject of research in mainstream psychology for many years. One such list is described by psychology pioneer James as early as 1890:

> The first group of the rather long series of queries related to the illumination, definition and coloring of the mental image, and were framed thus: ... think of some definite object—suppose it is your breakfast table as you sat down to it this morning—and consider carefully the picture that rises before your mind's eye.
>
> 1 *Illumination.* Is the image dim or fairly clear? Is its brightness comparable to that of the actual scene?
> 2 *Definition.* Are all the objects pretty well defined at the same time, or is the place of sharpest definition at any one moment more contracted than it is in a real scene?
> 3 *Coloring.* Are the colors of the china, of the toast, bread-crust, mustard, meat, parsley, or whatever may have been on the table, quite distinct and natural?
>
> (James, 1950, Volume 2, p. 51)

Modern NLP-ers will identify these examples as the submodalities of brightness in its general aspect and brightness as an aspect of focus. The second is focus more specifically. The third is hue and saturation as they apply to the scene in general and the attentional features of some aspect of the scene.

The first research on the neurological basis of visual submodalities was done by Hubel and Wiesel in the 1950s and 1960s working with cats. They found that there are cells which respond to lines, squares, rectangles, more that respond to orientation and still others that respond only to the submodality of motion. In later research they illustrated that monkeys who were blindfolded or had their vision restricted during a critical period of physiological development suffered enduring impairments (Hubel and Wiesel, 1959; Kandel, 2009).

Similar cells were also found in the prestriate visual cortex of monkeys' brains in the early 1970s. When the monkey watched a moving object, the motion cells were activated as soon as movement began. In 1983, the first clinical cases were found of people with these specific cells damaged, resulting in central motion blindness (akinetopsia). A person with akinetopsia can see a car while it is still, but once the car moves, they see it disappear and reappear somewhere else. They see life as a series of still photos (Sacks, 1995).

In 1976, Moore, Mischel and Zeiss, in an early version of Mischel's (Mischel and Mischel, 1983) marshmallow test, provided a perspective on how children use submodalities to alter their motivation to delay gratification. Mischel showed that the ability of small children to exert self-control when presented with marshmallows and pretzels correlated with success later in life (age 32), including college completion and a lessened likelihood of using illicit drugs or of being imprisoned. When the children were asked how they were able to put off eating the marshmallow for the appointed period, they said that either they deliberately distracted their attention from temptation by looking somewhere else, or they did something else. In the earlier study, children instructed to pretend that the real marshmallow was only a *flat picture* of a marshmallow or pretzel, were more easily able to wait for the reward than those confronted by the real target or an imagined image of the "real" target—an explicit submodality shift that is used in a number of NLP patterns.

Standard psychological and neurophysiological sources have validated many of the visual submodalities. We will focus on these insofar as many researchers find them primary for most humans (Williams and Bargh, 2008; Mandler, 2010). Stimuli that are closer or seem to be moving toward us evoke more powerful responses, while those that are far away or receding, evoke lessened responses. Williams and Bargh (2008) report that nearby stimuli are perceived as more concrete while more distant stimuli are viewed as more abstract.

These same authors showed that spatial priming—whether an object was near or far—had a significant impact on subject's responses to potentially embarrassing reading materials. Subjects primed with the near stimulus found the reading more embarrassing while those prompted with the distant stimulus found it more entertaining. Another experiment in the same series showed that subjects primed with a distance cue found a story that had been previously evaluated by others as extremely disturbing, was less disturbing than those primed with a proximal cue. In two more experiments they found that distance led to the underestimation of the calorie content of unhealthy food and that spatial primes also affected perceptions of emotional closeness (Williams and Bargh, 2008). They also report the well-established observation that on an ethological level, distance is equivalent to safety. This change in distance is reflected in a physiological shift from forebrain (cognitive) to midbrain (affective) dominance.

When a feared stimulus is far off, it creates a freezing response that may support detection avoidance or determine the most appropriate action. Closer to the feared object, our response is to run away and still closer we fight. These patterns are deeply ingrained in the mammalian nervous system and are reflected in our general response to distance (Blanchard et al., 1977; Muhlberger et al., 2008). We can translate this into non-aversive responses as stopping for a better look, running toward the desired object. It is interesting that the close-up response is fighting. This is associated with anger, an approach-valenced emotion. It suggests that if the object is really desired, we seek to consume it (Davidson, 1993).

When visual stimuli move, whether the movement seems natural to the object or not, the simple fact of movement awakens stronger emotions than do static stimuli. As a result, we find speakers who move about the stage more dynamic, animated signs more interesting, and sudden cinematic scene shifts attention-grabbing. Mandler reports that motion is the primary stimulus for neonatal attention during the first five to seven months of life and that this is a crucial foundation for later kinds of perception (Mandler, 2010; Simons et al., 2000: Simons et al., 1999).

De Cesarei and Codispoti (2006; Codispoti and De Cesarei, 2007), showed that larger emotional stimuli evoked stronger responses than did smaller. This held true, independent of the emotional value of the stimuli. The same authors (De Cesarei and Codispoti, 2008) have also shown that focus, or the availability of fine-grained detail, affects emotional impact in the visual system. Pictures lacking fine-grained detail were perceived as less impactful than those containing high levels of detail. They also found that the ability of an object to arouse an emotional response was dependent more on our capacity to recognize it than on how much detail was available. Consider the impact of the cinematic technique of suddenly zooming-in to a tight focus. Awe is often associated with size. Imagine the Grand Canyon or the open sea. Studies of babies find them looking longer at familiar faces than unfamiliar ones (Brigham Young University, July 21, 2009).

Research into the functions of the orbito-frontal cortex, where the brain creates hierarchies of value, indicates that motivations reflected there are ordered preferentially in terms of the amount of detail that they provide and the richness of their representation across multiple sensory systems. Objects that are more fully represented across multiple sensory systems are perceived as more valuable or more threatening (Kringelbach, 2005). Data emerging from studies of the superior colliculus—where spontaneous eye and head movements are controlled and one of the places where visual, kinesthetic, and auditory information is integrated—indicate that when auditory and visual impressions move together across the perceptual field, the neurons in the superior colliculus fire more intensely. This has the effect of increasing the amount of attention paid to the object in question (Bell et al., 2005; Gray, 2008c; Sparks, 1999).

Direct research on submodalities

Most research into the applications of submodalities has been conducted with clients experiencing phobias (Allen, 1982; Einspruch and Forman, 1988; Kammer et al., 1997; Liberman, 1984), trauma (Koziey and McLeod 1992), and anxiety (Hale, 1986; Ferguson, 1987; Field 1990).

Koziey et al. (1992) provide an overview of two case reports where the VK/D technique was used. The specific submodalities involved were distance (dissociation) and color (making the representation black and white). Assessment tools utilized were the SCL-90-R (Derogatis, 1983), the Veronen-Kilpatrick Modified Fear Survey (Veronen and Kilpatrick, 1983), the Profile of Mood States (McNair et al., 1981), and the State-Trait Anxiety

Inventory (Spielberger, 1983). Clinical observation, interview data, and independent measures showed a marked improvement in both clients, with client one showing a significant increase in positive affect in 18 independent measures and a subjective drop in her level of distress. Client two showed a significant positive effect in 22 independent measures and although the client presented with two instances of rape, she only needed to use the VK/D technique with one of the incidences with the other appearing to be resolved spontaneously. The authors comment on the limited empirical data from this study.

Gray (2009) conducted research using a combination of submodalities, outcome-setting processes, and anchoring to facilitate a 30 percent abstinence from drug use, determined by urinalysis in a program for drug offenders in Brooklyn, NY. Submodalities, including size, intensity, position, complexity, distance, and others were used across sensory systems to enhance positive resource states which were later made available as conditioned responses. Participants obtained equivalent results to those in intensive outpatient treatment despite the fact that the NLP intervention was significantly less expensive in time and cost. Program completers showed increased self-efficacy and overall participant satisfaction.

Masters et al. (1991) describe the swish pattern visualizing technique within NLP. Specific steps for using the swish include identifying the context, creating a desired self-image, checking ecology, swishing, and testing. Two case studies using the swish technique to alleviate stress and help a batterer are presented to illustrate its versatility and effectiveness. The visual swish pattern involves changes in size, distance, color, position, intensity, and movement of an imagined visual stimulus.

Visualization and imagery

Visualization of desired future states and goals is one of the key principles of the outcome oriented process of NLP. Within the goal-setting process the client is asked to describe what they will "see, hear, and feel" when they have achieved their goal. When a client visualizes their goal, the reticular activating system directly links to the arousal and attention responses of the client, causes a release in neuropeptides and an increase in blood and oxygen flow to the areas of the brain and body responsible for attainment of the goal (Pert, 1997; Wake 2008, 2010). Kosslyn et al. (2001) reviewed the neural foundations for imagery and found that imagery of emotional events leads to activation of the autonomic nervous system, resulting in the body experiencing the same effects as if the individual were actually seeing the object.

One other technique within the methodology of NLP that uses visualization processes is metaphor. Metaphors are symbolically loaded stories that are used to access states and resources within a client's unconscious processing that are then directly linked through the use of abstract and sensory based descriptions. Through neuroscientific investigation we are able to see that it is the right brain that processes metaphors and language that is characterized primarily by symbolic meaning (Beeman et al., 1994; Coulson and Van Petten, 2003; Rapp et al., 2006; Titone, 1998). Damage to the right hemisphere is shown to affect an individual's ability to interpret metaphorical and non-specific language (Bihrle et al., 1986; Hirst et al., 1984; Winner and Gardner, 1997). There is one Cochrane randomized control trial focused on visualization techniques (Bowers, 1996) that demonstrates the effectiveness of NLP-based hypnosis, guided imagery, and visualization, alongside other holistic therapies as an intervention for holistic healing and pain control. The author used the Visual Analogue Scale as the assessment tool and demonstrated that the treatment group experienced an average reduction of 6.2 points over 2.1 NLP sessions, compared with a reduction of 1.7 in the control group. Conclusions recommend NLP as an adjunctive treatment for chiropractic patients in acute pain. Limitations of the study included group size, lack of control on degree of patient participation, and therapeutic judgment. Bowers makes recommendations for further research into specific NLP techniques.

NLP specific research

Hossack and Standidge (1993) reported on a single case study utilizing NLP to facilitate the development of positive self-identity in an elderly male client with clinical depression. The process involved using recall of positively rewarding past experiences and collating these into an imaginary book. The authors report that this process enabled the development of continuity within chaotic and fragmented memory recall during the recovery phase. The patient experienced alleviation of anxiety and depression and the realization of functional goals. Research has also been conducted on the relationship between hypnotisability, internal imagery, and the efficiency of NLP (Kirenskaya et al., 2011), which found that, in high-hypnotizable subjects, NLP was found to decrease negative emotional intensity and autonomic activity.

Strategies

To achieve any result, such as relaxation, each of us has a preferred sequence of sensory "representations" which we go through. For some people, imagining a beautiful scene is part of their most effective relaxation strategy. For others, the strategy that works best is to listen to soothing music. Others simply paid attention to their breathing, slowing down as the feeling of comfort increased.

The concept of strategies was defined in the book *Neuro-Linguistic Programming, Volume 1*:

> The basic elements from which the patterns of human behavior are formed are the perceptual systems through which the members of the

species operate on their environment: *vision* (sight), *audition* (hearing), *kinesthesis* (body sensations) and *olfaction/gustation* (smell/taste) ... We postulate that all of our on-going experience can usefully be coded as consisting of some combination of these sensory classes.

(Dilts et al., 1980, p. 17)

Thus, human experience is described as an ongoing sequence of internal representations in the sensory systems. When assembled into ordered patterns of perceptions and actions, these sequences are known as strategies.

These senses were written in NLP notation as V (visual), A (auditory), K (kinesthetic), O (olfactory), and G (gustatory). To be more precise, the visual sense included visual recall, where I remember an image as I have seen it before through my eyes (V^r); visual construct, where I make up an image I've never seen before (V^c); and visual external, where I look out at something in the real world (V^e). So if I look up and see a blue sky, and then remember being at the beach, and then feel good, the notation would express this sequence: $V^e \rightarrow V^r \rightarrow K$. I have all my senses functioning (I could still feel my body while I looked up), but my *attention* shifted from sense to sense in a sequence. The digital senses (thinking in symbols such as words) have also been incorporated into this NLP strategy notation, so that we can describe one of the common strategies people use to create a state of depression as $K^i \rightarrow A_d \rightarrow K^i \rightarrow A_d$ ... (Feel some uncomfortable body sensations (K^i); tell themselves they should feel better (A_d); check how they feel now, having told themselves off (K^i); tell themselves off for feeling that way, (A_d) and repeat.)

The developers of NLP used the TOTE model to further explain how we sequence sensory representations. The TOTE was developed by Miller et al. (1960) as a model to explain how complex behavior occurred. Pavlov's (1927) original studies had shown that simple behaviors can be produced by the stimulus-response cycle. After training, when Pavlov's dogs heard the tuning fork ring (a stimulus; or in NLP terms, an "anchor"), they salivated (response). But there is more to dog behavior than simple stimulus–response associations.

For example, if a dog sees an intruder at the gate of its section (stimulus/anchor), it may bark (response). However, it doesn't go on barking forever. It actually checks to see if the intruder has run away. If the intruder has run away, the dog stops performing the barking operation and goes back to its kennel. If the intruder is still there, the dog may continue with that strategy, or move on to another response, such as biting the intruder. Miller et al. (1960) felt that this type of sequencing was inadequately explained in Pavlov's simple stimulus–response model. The mechanistic understanding of Pavlov's original observations was concretized in Sherrington's model of the relatively hard-wired reflex arc. In response to the disconnect between organismic flexibility and these mechanistic perspectives, these authors determined that there was a need to add a realistic level of flexibility to the conditioning model as it was then understood.

In Miller et al.'s model, the first stimulus (seeing the intruder) is the Trigger (the first T in the TOTE; Pavlov called this the "stimulus," and in NLP this is an "anchor") for the dog's "scaring-intruders-away" strategy. The barking itself is the Operation (O). Checking to see if the intruder is gone yet is the Test (second T). Going back to the kennel is the Exit from the strategy (E). This might be written as $V^e \rightarrow K^e \rightarrow V^e/V^c \rightarrow K^e$. Notice that the checking stage (Test) is done by comparing the result of the operation (what the dog can see after barking) with the result that was desired (what the dog imagines seeing—a person running away). In the notation, comparison is written using a forward slash "/".

To revisit the strategy for depression mentioned above, we can now diagram it as $K^i \rightarrow A_d \rightarrow K^i/K^c \rightarrow A_d$. The first K^i is the *trigger, stimulus*, or *anchor* which starts the strategy. The person feels a slightly uncomfortable feeling in their body. The next step, the A_d, is where they talk to themselves and tell themselves off for feeling that way. Next, they compare the feeling they get internally now (after telling themselves off) with the feeling they got before. (K^i/K^c). Noticing that it feels worse, they tell themselves off some more (the final exit A_d). The feeling of depression can be thought of as the result of repeatedly running this strategy, called "ruminating" by other researchers (Seligman, 1997, pp. 82–3).

Once we understand that every result a person achieves is a result of a strategy which begins with some trigger and leads them to act and test the results of that action, then we have a number of new choices for changing the way they run their strategies and the results obtained.

Miller et al. (1960) had recognized that the simple stimulus–response model of Pavlov could not account for the complexity of brain activity. Of course, neither can their more complex TOTE model. The TOTE model suggests that each action we take is a result of an orderly sequence A-B-C-D. In fact, as we go to run such a "strategy," we also respond to that strategy with other strategies; to use another NLP term, we go "meta" (above or beyond) our original strategy.

The developers of NLP noted that:

> A meta response is defined as a response about the step before it, rather than a continuation or reversal of the representation. These responses are more abstracted and disassociated from the representations preceding them. Getting feelings about the image (feeling that something may have been left out of the picture, for instance) ... would constitute a meta response in our example.
>
> (Dilts et al., 1980, p. 90)

Hall has pointed out that such responses could be more usefully diagrammed using a second dimension (Hall, 1995, p. 57), for example:

$$K^i$$
$$\downarrow$$
$$V^e \to V^c \to V^c$$

Here, the internal kinesthetic (K^i) response constrains the meaning of the remainder of the sequence ($V^e \to V^c \to V^c$); it stands as a context for the whole. This emphasizes that the TOTE model is only a model. It is a linear, sequential representation of dynamic, multi-dimensional process. Real neurological processes are more network-like (O'Connor and Van der Horst, 1994). Connections are being continuously made across levels, adding "meaning" to experiences. The advantage of the TOTE model is merely that it enables us to discuss the thought process in such a way as to make sense of it and enable someone to change it.

Resources and state-dependent memory

Resources may be thought of as any experience or any memory of an experience that the individual has had. They are as likely to be imagined experiences or role plays as actual experiences. The idea that people possess these kinds of resources was central to Erickson's approach and forms one of the basic presuppositions of NLP (Andreas and Andreas, 1989; Bodenhamer and Hall, 1998; Bandler and Grinder, 1975a; Dilts et al., 1980; Haley, 1973; James and Woodsmall, 1988; Linden and Perutz, 1997; Robbins, 1986; O'Connor and Seymour, 1990).

A "state" is the neurophysiological response that arises from a combination of mental and physical processes. Our state affects how we relate to ourselves and others.

Erickson (1980) reflects the basic understanding of resources in the following passage:

> *Hypnosis is not some mystical procedure, but rather a systematic utilization of experiential learnings—that is, the extensive learnings acquired through the process of living itself* ... For example, mention may be made of hypnotic anesthesia or hypnotic amnesia, but these are no more than learnings of everyday living organized in an orderly, controlled and directed fashion. For example, nearly everyone has had the experience of losing a painful headache during a suspense movie without medication of any sort. Similarly, everyone has developed an anesthesia for the sensation of shoes on the feet, glasses on the face, and a collar around the neck ...
>
> (p. 1325)

Every individual has a tremendous number of these generally unrecognized psychological and somatic learnings and conditionings, and it is the intelligent use of these that constitutes an effectual use of hypnosis (Erickson and Rossi, 1989, p. 224).

Cade and O'Hanlon provide the following listing of potential resources that may not be immediately obvious:

> Central to the solution-focused approach is the certitude that, in a person's life, there are invariably exceptions to the behaviors, ideas, and interactions that are, or can be, associated with the problem. There are times when a difficult adolescent is *not* defiant, when a depressed person feels *less* sad, when a shy person is *able* to socialize, when an obsessive person is *able* to relax, when a troubled couple *resolves* rather than escalates conflict, when a bulimic *resists* the urge to binge, when a child does *not* have a tantrum when asked to go to bed, when an over-responsible person *says* no, when a problem drinker *does* contain their drinking to within a sensible limit, etc.
>
> (Cade and O'Hanlon, 1993, p. 96)

State-dependent memory generally refers to the tendency to more accurately remember events that occurred in physiological conditions that are more or less similar to the current state of the organism. Thus drunks, while they are drinking, are more likely to remember things learned while drunk; happy people are more likely to remember happy times; depressed persons are more likely to remember being depressed. By the same token, depressed persons find it difficult to remember being happy, addicts find it difficult to remember managing without drugs and happy people tend to forget that they were sad or depressed. Erickson and Rossi suggest that post-hypnotic and traumatic amnesias are just such state dependent effects. Individual states of mind/body dependent upon the level of cortisol and other stress related substances have a similar effect. When we are stressed we tend to remember stressful events (Rossi, 1986; Rossi and Cheek, 1988). State-dependent memory is described by Rossi as a form of memory that is more diffuse than either classical or operant conditioning. It is a function of the state of the body with regard to hormonal flux and neuro-modulators. It provides the physiological context that frames other kinds of learning (Rossi, 1986).

State-dependant memories may be evoked either by directly recreating the neurophysiological context of the desired type of experience or by the evocation of memories which will in their arising, recreate that physiology. As a result, the new event will be connected to the previous one, and there will even be a tendency to conflate the new event with the previous one. If my childhood caregiver yelled at me and told me that I was stupid, I may have entered a state of fear, and stored that memory as a highly salient neural network. When someone else yells at me as an adult, if I access the same state of fear, I may feel as if I am re-experiencing the original event, and may even hear a voice telling me "I'm stupid."

This is called "state-dependent memory and learning" or SDML. Our memories and learnings, our strategies, are *dependent* on the state they are created in.

> Neuronal networks may be defined in terms of the activation of specifically localized areas of neurons by information substances that reach them via diffusion through the extracellular fluid ... In the simplest case, a 15-square mm neuronal network could be turned on or off by the presence or absence of a specific information substance. That is, "the activity of this neuronal network would be 'state-dependent' on the presence or absence of that information substance".
> (Rossi and Cheek, 1988, p. 57)

LeDoux (1997) has pointed out that neural systems tend to exist independently of one another. Wolpe (1958) showed that there are neural response systems that cannot be expressed at the same time. The literature of extinction and inhibition in classical conditioning has shown that one set of associations tends to dominate a response network while excluding the influence of other possible associations. State-dependent memories reflect the almost absolute dissociation between contextually bound behavioral systems. Chambers *et al.* have suggested that behavioral networks exist independently of one another and that the evocation of one network can effectively render another temporarily inaccessible (Bouton, 1994; Bouton and Moody, 2004; Brockman and LeDoux, 1997; Canales, 2005; Chambers et al., 2007; Rescorla, 1988; Rossi, 1986; Rossi and Cheek, 1995; Wolpe, 1958).

At times, the neural networks laid down in one experience or set of experiences can be quite "cut off" (due to their different neurochemical basis) from the rest of the person's experience. New brain-scanning techniques begin to provide more realistic images of how this actually looks. According to Adler (1999), psychiatrist Condie and neurobiologist Guochuan Tsai used an fMRI scanner to study the brain patterns of a woman with "multiple personality disorder." In this disorder the woman switched regularly between her normal personality and an alter ego called "Guardian." The two personalities had separate memory systems and quite different strategies. The fMRI brain scan showed that each of these two personalities used different neural networks (different areas of the brain lit up when each personality emerged). If the woman only pretended to be a separate person, her brain continued to use her usual neural networks, but as soon as the "Guardian" actually took over her consciousness, it activated clearly different areas of the hippocampus and surrounding temporal cortex (brain areas associated with memory and emotion) (Adler, 1999, pp. 29–30).

Freud based much of his approach to therapy on the idea of "repression," an internal struggle for control of memory and thinking strategies. This explanation of the existence of "unconscious" memories and motivations ("complexes") can now be expanded by the state-dependent memory hypothesis. No internal struggle is needed to account for any of the previously described phenomena. The "complex" (in Freudian terms) can be considered as simply a series of strategies being run from a neural network which is not activated by the person's usual chemical states. Rossi and Cheek note:

> This leads to the provocative insight that the entire history of depth psychology and psychoanalysis now can be understood as a prolonged clinical investigation of how dissociated or state-dependent memories remain active at unconscious levels, giving rise to the "complexes" ... that are the source of psychological and psychosomatic problems.
> (Rossi and Cheek, 1988, p. 57)

Baxter (1994) showed that clients with obsessive compulsive disorder (OCD) have raised activity in specific neural networks in the caudate nucleus. He could identify these networks on PET scan, and show how, once the OCD was treated, these networks ceased to be active. Research on post-traumatic stress disorder (PTSD) has also shown the state-dependent nature of its symptoms (van der Kolk et al., 1996). Sudden re-experiencing of a traumatic event (called a flashback) is one of the key problems in PTSD. Medications which stimulate bodily arousal (such as lactate, a by-product of physiological stress) will produce flashbacks in people with PTSD, but not in people without the diagnosis (Rainey et al., 1987; Southwick et al., 1993). Other laboratory studies show that sensory stimuli which recreate some aspect of the original trauma (such as a sudden noise) will also cause full flashbacks in people with PTSD (van der Kolk, 1994).

People come to psychotherapists and counsellors to solve a variety of problems. Most of these are due to strategies which are instantiated in neural networks that are dramatically separate from the rest of the person's experience. This means that the person has all the skills they need to solve their own problem, but those skills are localized in neural networks which may not be able to connect with the networks from which their problems arise. The task of NLP change agents is often to transfer skills from functional networks (networks that do things the person is pleased with) to less-functional networks (networks that do things they are not happy about).

PTSD may arise in part because of the neural tendency to function under the influence of one or another competing circuit. Diamond et al. (2007) indicate that under conditions of extreme stress, which create high levels of amygdalar activation, the hippocampus cannot function as integrator of time, place, and sequence and is driven to a simpler focus on the immediate context. Stress initiates a brief period of facilitated long-term potentiation (LTP) which is followed by a longer refractory period in which the hippocampus has limited response potentialities. This refractory period isolates the memory and creates a near indelible trace of the dangerous circumstance that is not subject to interference from subsequent stimuli (in the immediate context) and may be useful for protecting the organism from similar threats in the future. These are the flashbulb memories that accompany trauma and that are often characterized by what Loftus has called *gun focus* and others have described as tunnel vision (Loftus and Yuille, 1984). The continued lowered sensitivity of the hippocampus explains the disorientation, amnesia and the perception that the event is not connected in time and not susceptible of integration into the continuing narrative of the patient's life.

In experiences of extreme stress, the pre-frontal cortex (PFC) which normally modulates amygdalar function almost immediately falls into a state of long-term depression (LTD). Insofar as it is no longer capable of modulating amygdalar function, the amygdala becomes the driving force in the current state of the organism. Moreover, because the PFC is the centre of executive function and is responsible for most higher-level functions—including evaluations, decision making, and divided attention tasks—when it enters a state of lessened responsivity, the capacity for creating a coherent narrative of the stressful circumstance is lost. Under the influence of extreme amygdalar dominance, both the PFC and the hippocampal editing and organizing functions are impaired, resulting in emotionally driven but often inaccurate memories of the circumstances. These disordered recollections of the event may later give rise to fabricated memories, rationalizations and various psychological and psychiatric responses that contribute to the inability to make sense of the traumatic event.

States and strategies

The NLP term "state" is defined by O'Connor and Seymour (1990, p. 232) as "How you feel, your mood. The sum total of all neurological and physical processes within an individual at any moment in time. The state we are in affects our capabilities and interpretation of experience." Many new NLP practitioners assume that an emotional state is a purely kinesthetic experience. A simple experiment demonstrates why this is not true. We can inject people with noradrenalin and their kinesthetic sensations will become aroused (their heart will beat faster, etc.). However, the emotional state they enter will vary depending on a number of other factors in their environment. They may, for example, become "angry," "frightened," or "euphoric." It depends on their other primary representations and on their meta-representations—what they tell themselves is happening, for example (Schachter and Singer, 1962). The same kinesthetics do not always result in the same state.

Two classic experiments reflect this capacity of expectation and context to affect or "metastate" internal experience. Schacter and Singer (1962) gave naive subjects injections of adrenaline. One group was warned about side effects while two other groups were exposed to rooms full of ecstatic or angry people. When examined, each group reflected the response that the priming or context required. Those warned about side effects became frightened or concerned while those exposed to angry and ecstatic groups reflected the emotional tone of the group.

Dutton and Aron (1974) found that when two groups of men had gone through fear-inducing and non-fear-inducing experiences (a dangerous vs. a safe bridge crossing) the fearful group was more likely to judge a female experimenter, acting as a survey taker, more attractive and were more likely to take her phone number. Their level of arousal, originally derived from fear or simple physical arousal was transformed into attraction by the female survey taker.

These studies illustrate the impact of context, priming, and situational demands on how we understand the impact of state. States are not mere physiological responses; they are responses that arise within a meaning frame that may be determined by the set, setting or the source of the arousal itself.

Gray (2008c, 2010, 2011c) indicates that the states created in his drug program become powerfully reinforcing precisely because his clients were guided to perceive them that way. The demand characteristics of the exercises, the frame or context, required that they choose *positive* experiences that will always be *positively* remembered and that they should focus on the *very best part*. This frame ensures that even weak arousal is intensified in a positive direction.

Dilts suggests that a person's state is a result of the *interplay* between the primary accessing, secondary representational systems, and other brain systems (1983). Older theories assumed that this interplay must occur in a particular place in the brain; a sort of control centre for "states." It was clear by the time of Dilts' writing that this was not true. A state (such as a certain quality of happiness, curiosity or anxiety) is generated throughout the entire brain, and even removal of large areas of the brain will not stop the state being able to be regenerated. The state has a chemical basis and this specific chemical mix exists throughout the brain (and body) as we experience a particular state.

States, as Dilts originally hypothesized, are still best considered as "meta" to the representational systems. They are vast, brain-wide commentaries on the entire set of representations and physiological responses present. Our states meta-comment on *and* alter the representations (from the primary senses as well as from the digital senses) "below them." For example, when a person is angry, they may actually be physically unable to hear their partner or spouse telling them how much they love them. The interference from the state reduces the volume of the auditory external input. This often results in a completely different strategy being run. Put another way, the "state" determines which strategies we find easy to run and which we are unable to run well (Duncan and Barrett, 2007).

States that regulate states

Psychotherapist Satir noted that, during those times when a person is feeling sad, frustration, fear, and loneliness are fairly predictable consequences of being human. In most cases what creates serious problems is not so much the fact that people enter such states rather what creates disturbance is how people feel *about* feeling these states. Satir says, "In other words, low self-worth has to do with what the individual communicates to himself about such feelings and the need to conceal rather than acknowledge them" (Satir and Baldwin, 1983, p. 195). The person with high self-esteem may feel sad when someone dies, but they also feel acceptance and even esteem for their sadness. The person with low self-esteem may feel afraid or ashamed of their sadness.

Such "states about states" are generated by accessing one neural network (e.g. the network generating the state of acceptance) and "applying it" to the functioning of another neural network (e.g. the network generating the state of sadness). The result is a neural network which involves the interaction of two previous networks. Hall calls the resulting combinations "meta-states" (1995). Our ability to generate meta-states gives richness to our emotional life. Feeling hurt when someone doesn't want to be with me is a primary level state that most people will experience at some time. If I feel angry about feeling hurt, then I create a meta-state (which we might call "aggrieved"). If I feel sad about feeling hurt, a completely different meta-state occurs (perhaps what we might call "self-pity"). If I feel compassionate about my hurt, the meta-state of "self-nurturing" may occur. Although in each case my initial emotional response is the same, the meta-state dramatically alters and determines the results for my life.

Hall (1996) has formulated this process as meta-stating; bringing one state to bear upon another. He made the observation that self-reflection, recursion, is a crucial part of what it means to be human. He noted that part of the richness of what it means to be human is rooted in: (1) our self-reflexive consciousness; (2) our awareness of our awareness; and (3) our feelings about our feelings, what he called meta-states. In this groundbreaking work he points to how we can learn to apply feelings to feelings in order to take control of present states.

Hall makes the following statement about the effects of the recursive practice of meta-stating:

> Sometimes a state about a state will *negate* the first; sometimes it will create a *paradox* and send a person into a state of *confusion*; sometimes it will *amplify* the first state; sometimes it will *distort* the first state and turn it into something wondrously useful or destructive (fear about fear—paranoia, belief in belief—fanaticism).
>
> (1996, p. 44, original emphasis)

NLP specific research

There are two unpublished theses that support the use of anchoring for state management. Brandis (1986) reports on a treatment model for reducing anger responses, and Olson (1985) on the application of pacing and anchoring in pain management.

Brandis (1986) applied anchoring to parental anger and found indications that collapsing resourceful anchors with anger predictive responses has some effect in reducing parental anger as measured by a scale of typical anger-inducing experiences. Parents apparently had more success in modifying angry responses when the collapse anchors protocol was supplemented by self-anchored evocations of the resource state. Although there were clinical indications of treatment effectiveness, the results were non-significant. The study was marred by small samples and an inadequate anchoring procedure but may deserve revisitation with a larger sample size and a more robust anchoring procedure that will evoke the state changes necessary to counteract parental anger.

Gray (2011a) reports that a consistent outcome of his drug treatment program was the spontaneous and regular use of anchored resource states to overcome anger and road rage. He indicated that after several weeks of practising anchored resource states—enhanced using submodality manipulation—program participants began to report that they had tried the anchors in anger provoking situations and found that their anger dissipated quickly. Gray reports that his clients practise the enhancement of resource states to the point that they are no longer related to the original memory but evoke altered physical and emotional states. The anchors are practised in group session and as homework assignments so that they are robust, over-learned behavioral systems.

Swets and Bjork (1990) report on a non-empirical study of a range of "new-age" techniques being considered by the US Army. A range of speakers and "experts" were invited to present their "theory" to a panel representing the army. NLP was presented through a background paper and a report of a workshop attended by army representatives who also interviewed Bandler. A visit to an army base was also conducted to review the expert modeling process of NLP used in marksmanship. It is interesting to note that Pribram was also interviewed for his theories on "neuromuscular programming." The committee reported positively on the applications of mental practice, including a meta-analysis of relevant literature that demonstrated mental practice achieved a gain in performance by half a standard deviation compared to control groups.

There are a number of studies that review NLP as one of a range of techniques included in an integrative and often alterntive approach.

The management of dyslexia has provided a focus for NLP interventions. Bull's two studies (2002, 2007) report on a combined approach through a randomized controlled trial with 70 children with dyslexia. One of the central aims of the studies was to show the impact of improved health and affect—just feeling better—on children's learning abilities. The study found positive results, but Bull herself challenges the validity and reliability of the studies. Mathews et al. (2009) also challenge her studies, highlighting the methodological flaws that include failure to acknowledge the integrative and holistic nature of the therapeutic approach, or to include existing research studies verifying the complex nature of children with dyslexia.

Rapport: the work of the mirror neurons

Rapport is a process of responsiveness that facilitates trust in another. It was "modeled from Erickson's matching of his clients' physiology, language, and voice qualities" (Wake, 2010, p. 43). A number of studies are quoted that highlight the emphasis and influence that certain aspects of our communication have on others, all of which point to the importance of non-verbal communication (Argyle et al., 1970; Birdwhistell, 1970; Mehrabian and Ferris, 1967; Mehrabian 1971).

In 1995 a remarkable area of neurons was discovered by researchers working at the University of Parma in Italy (Rizzolatti and Arbib, 1998; Rizzolatti et al., 1996). Although the cells are related to motor activity (i.e. they are part of the system by which we make kinesthetic responses such as moving an arm), these are also activated by visual input. When a monkey observes another monkey (or even a human) making a body movement, the mirror neurons are activated (Aziz-Zadeh and Ivry, 2009; Bandler and Grinder, 1975a, 1979; Chartrand and Bargh, 1999; Fabbri-Destro and Rizzolatti, 2008; Gallese et al., 1996; Maurer and Tindall, 1983; Neumann et al., 2009; Rizzolatti and Craighero, 2004; Sanchez-Burks et al., 2009; Sandhu et al., 1993).

Strikingly, like the work of Hubel and Wiesel in the visual cortex, Gallese et al. (1996) found that individual populations of mirror neurons work as feature detectors and that their summative action results in the recognition of complex acts. Lyons et al. (2006) suggest that mirror neurons allow us to understand the intentions of others as they act. This is reflected in the observation by Gallese et al. that macaques' mirror neurons only fired in response to goal-oriented or purposive acts. In fact, these systems fired preferentially to an inferred goal as compared to non-descript action. Minimally, the mirror-neuron system consists of areas of the ventral premotor cortex, the inferior parietal lobule and the superior temporal sulcus. It is organized hierarchically (Kilner et al., 2007) into elements that encode long-term action outcomes, proximal or intermediate goals, kinematics or gross reflections of movement, and specific patterns of muscular activity. (Gallese et al., 1996; Kandel, 2009; Kilner et al., 2007; Lyons et al., 2006). This suggests that, through the instrumentality of mirror-neuron system, the visualization of personally meaningful outcomes is more fully embodied than other kinds of imaginal practice.

In human subjects, when parts of the pre-motor cortex are exposed to transcranial magnetic stimulation (TMS), reducing neural activation in that area, then merely showing a movie of a person picking up an object will cause activations of the muscles used in the task in their own hands (Fadiga et al., 1995). This ability to copy a fellow creature's actions as they do them has obviously been very important in the development of primate social intelligence. It enables us to identify with the person we are observing. When this area of the brain is damaged in a stroke, copying another's actions becomes almost impossible. Furthermore, there is increasing evidence that autism and Aspergers syndrome are related to unusual activity of the mirror neurons. This unusual activity results in a difficulty the autistic person has understanding the inner world of others, as well as a tendency to echo speech parrot-fashion and to randomly copy others' movements (Williams et al., 2001).

Mirror neurons respond to facial expressions as well, so that they enable the person to directly experience the emotions of those they observe. This results in what NLP researchers call rapport (Hatfield et al., 1994).

Rapport: predicate matching

Sensory-based predicates and predicate matching were some of the earliest evidences evoked by Grinder and Bandler and directly contributed to the insight that all behavior could be understood in terms of the flow of sensory information. It consists of the simple observation that most people under various circumstances reveal a sensory preference in their patterns of speech. People who are processing visual information tend to talk about what they see. Those processing auditory information talk in terms of what they hear while those processing feelings, talk in kinesthetic terms. When these patterns are fed back to the subject in conversation, they often create an enhanced feeling of rapport. This, combined with postural mirroring and sensitivity to EACs, helps to create and maintain a powerful sense of rapport. This is a claim that has been well validated by other researchers (Asbell, 1983; Brockman, 1980; Day, 1985; Ehrmantraut, 1983; Frieden, 1981; Green, 1979; Hammer, 1980; Palubeckas, 1981; Pantin, 1982; Sandhu, 1993; Schmedlen, 1981; Shobin, 1980; Thomason, 1984).

NLP specific research

Grinder and Bandler (Bandler and Grinder, 1975a, 1979; Bostic St. Clair and Grinder, 2002; O'Conner and Seymour, 1990; Lewis and Pucelik, 1990) began to teach their students that postural mirroring could enhance the sense of rapport between them and their clients. They suggested, however, that one of the important facets of the technique was the complementary dance of movements between the counsellor and client, not the possible static meanings of the gestures. They suggested, after observing the behavior of psychotherapeutic greats such as Erickson, Satir, and Perls, that this was one of the key variables in creating a sense of trust between therapist and client.

For many years before NLP made its introduction, psychologists, psychiatrists, and social workers were concerned about therapeutic relationships and how to establish and maintain them. More especially they were concerned about rapport and empathy as key indices of that relationship. However, beyond the specific work of Erickson and his followers in hypnosis, there was little in terms of the dynamic principles outlined by Bandler and Grinder (1975a). A review of several discussions of the relationship between posture and rapport or empathy finds that the bulk of research in the time surrounding the publication of *The Structure of Magic* was concerned with decoding the meaning of various gestures and postures, not with their dynamic interplay and its effect on empathy and rapport (Bayes, 1972; Buchheimer, 1963; Fretz, 1966; Fretz et al., 1979; Gladstein, 1974; Maurer and Tindall, 1983; Smith-Hanen, 1977).

Mirroring of posture and linguistic patterns was one of the first elements of the NLP tool set to receive scientific examination. In several studies (Ehrmantraut, 1983; Palubeckas, 1981; Sandhu, 1984; Sandhu et al. 1993) the value of postural mirroring was validated as enhancing the client's perception of empathy.

More recently, the discovery of mirror neurons has provided a neurophysiological basis for this phenomenon. Several groupings of neurons have been identified in the pre-motor, parietal, temporal and the inferior frontal areas of the brain that actively respond to actions performed by others. These neurons, the mirror neurons, fire when the individual watches some behavior performed by another organism. The neurons are associated with similar movements in the observer and fire in a nearly identical fashion, but more intensely, when the observing organism performs the same actions. There are specific sets of mirror neurons that scan facial expressions. Mirror neurons are particularly sensitive to goal-oriented behaviors. Observed actions are thus primed by observation and so become more probable. Here is a basis for mirroring and imitation. It also represents the physiological basis for Bandura's imitation-based social learning theory. Mirror neurons also respond to the sound of an action performed out of sight and this sound responsiveness suggests a level of physiological confirmation for the importance of tonal cues in developing trust. Other researchers have also noted that the mirror system is responsive to sound (Ramachandran, 2003; Rizzolatti and Craighero, 2004; Sonnby et al., 2003).

The technology of rapport more generally has been a centrepiece of the basic NLP toolkit. Rapport is established and maintained not only by postural mirroring, but by the dynamic mirroring of conversational predicates as the interaction proceeds. Rapport is often enhanced as participants support their sensitivity to the flow of sensory patterns in the language of their partners by paying attention to EACs. Research on rapport as perceived warmth, empathy, and trustworthiness has been well supported by multiple studies (Asbell, 1983; Brockman, 1980; Day, 1985; Ehrmantraut, 1983; Frieden, 1981; Green, 1979; Hammer, 1980; Palubeckas, 1981; Pantin, 1982; Sandhu, 1993; Schmedlen, 1981; Shobin, 1980; Thomason, 1984).

Studies researching the effect of predicate matching divide into two groups: those seeking to test a presumed PRS (falsely believed to be a foundational tenet of NLP), and those focused on the mirroring of the predicate language employed in present time. Those seeking the elusive PRS usually failed to find a significant relationship between the PRS and empathy (Carbonell, 1985; Dowd and Hingst, 1983; Gallo, 1985; Paxton, 1980; Rebstock, 1980; Schneider, 1984; Sperber, 1983). To the contrary, those testing the more dynamic predicate mirroring hypothesis typically showed a strong relationship between predicate matching and perceived empathy (Brockman, 1980; Day, 1985; Falzett, 1979; Frieden, 1981; Hammer, 1980; Hillin, 1982; Schmedlin, 1980; Shobin, 1980).

It should be noted, however, that one of the major thrusts of NLP is the provision of content-free interventions (Andreas and Andreas, 1989; Bandler and Grinder, 1975a, 1979). As a result, the rapport skills that emerge from NLP should be evaluated in terms of warmth, trustworthiness, trust, and even compliance, but not self-disclosure. We would suggest that future evaluations of NLP rapport skills should be mindful of the specific purposes, definitions, and presuppositions implied by the literature of NLP.

Syntax and language

Large components of NLP consist of linguistic patterns. They were first modeled by Bandler and Grinder as way of understanding how therapists used the linguistic representation of a client's subjective experience as a clue to deeper understanding. Each therapist also developed their own particular linguistic style to gain therapeutic change.

One of the essential foundations of NLP is the idea that syntax is fundamental to all behavior. The concept flows directly from Chomsky's work on the structure of language. Syntax is the ordering principle that creates for each language a uniform set of linguistic patterns that is recognizable by every native speaker of the language (Bandler and Grinder, 1976; Chomsky, 1972).

The prerequisite for a syntactical environment is a group of primitive elements that may be recombined into a broader inventory of more complex units and that these units may in turn be sequenced to create virtually unlimited numbers of combinations. According to Chomsky, the genius of language is its capacity to use a limited number of phonemes and, using a few basic rules of combination, generate an almost infinite capacity for expression (Chomsky, 1972). The root insight from NLP is that the same general principle can be applied to behavior and that the root elements are sensory perceptions: every behavior can be modeled in terms of a syntax composed of a sequence of sensory elements, visual, auditory, kinesthetic, olfactory and gustatory (Andreas and Andreas; 1980; Bandler and Grinder, 1975a; Lewis and Pucelik, 1980).

The idea is not new, it was espoused by Hume, Galton, and James (Wake, 2010). Skinner suggested that language and behavior might be fully explained by the chaining of stimulus associations (1957). Cognitive psychology has identified a similar phenomenon as action schemas.

Syntax is a fundamental property of human experience. Beyond the ordering of linguistic elements in speech, it is crucial to effective movement and action. The syntax of movement is what differentiates meaningful speech from gibberish, effective action from disorganized flailings. The incapacitation of syntactical mechanisms in the basal ganglia is responsible for movement and motivational problems in Parkinson's disease and obsessive compulsive disorder (Aldridge et al. 1998; Frank, 2005).

NLP sees behavior as built from incremental increases in complexity. This is chunking, an idea that leads back to Chomsky and is also reflected in patterns of sensory neurons in the neocortex. Chomsky indicates that the smaller elements of linguistic structure defined by the structure of the vocal tract and shaped by the demands of the linguistic environment, phonemes, are assembled into the characteristic building blocks or morphemes that are used to construct words. Words in turn construct phrases, phrases, sentences, and so on (1972). As applied to behaviors, this chunk-wise assembly proceeds as individual movements and perceptions build to create purposive modules that further assemble into chained or streamlined behaviors and schemas.

Chomsky also indicated that the process of chunking was often recursive so that a phrase (a verb phrase or a noun phrase) in a complex sentence might stand in for a single word (a lexical unit with a specific grammatical function—a verb or a noun). Just so, NLP understands the modularity of behavior and that one sequence of behaviors (a strategy) might take the place of a simple unitary action.

We have previously summarized the work of Hubel and Weisel (Kandel, 2009) who determined that the raw visual image is analyzed by feature detectors, whose output combines to allow the perception of different, more complex visual elements. These elements are further combined into larger elements. Whole objects, in turn, come to be recognized for themselves independently of their component parts in different parts of the brain. This pattern has been established for word perception as:

> a hierarchical organization in the ventral visual pathway … for the visual word form, leading to the proposal that running posterior to anterior along this pathway, neurons are tuned to increasingly complex word features, viz. from oriented bars, to letters, bigrams, and finally quadragrams.
>
> (Glezer et al., 2009, p. 199)

These finally give rise to word forms that are recognized as individual units. This hierarchical and modular mechanism is complemented by a top-down process that relates individual parts to already recognized wholes. This allows the organism to construct new perceptions from novel information as well as recognizing previously experienced wholes from significant parts (Lerner et al., 2008).

In a similar manner, we find mirror-neuron systems organized hierarchically into elements that encode specific patterns of muscular activities, gross movement patterns or kinematics, proximate goals (composite behaviors), and long-term action outcomes (Kilner et al., 2007).

This hierarchical organization of behavior and perceptions is ubiquitous and it is essential to understanding and modeling how people function. Andreas (2006a) has noted that if any behavior is broken down into small enough pieces, it becomes replicable.

Syntactical structures in NLP can be divided into two types, those derived from specific exemplars and their specific expertise and those rooted in biological or neurological principles, independent of the conscious process of modeling. Those derived from the analysis of exemplars are known as strategies and those derived from innate patterns—even if they were identified through the process of modeling—are known as well-formedness conditions.

NLP has classically defined two sets of well-formedness conditions: the well-formedness conditions for language in therapy and the well-formedness conditions for outcomes. The initial statement of well-formedness conditions for language in therapy appears in Bandler and Grinder (1975a) and the well-formedness conditions for outcomes first appears in *Frogs into Princes* (Bandler and Grinder, 1979).

The well-formedness conditions for language in therapy

The following list systematizes the criteria established by Bandler and Grinder. Although it is normally presented as a list that does not imply sequence, we note that the first two items are sequential and the last five represent specific criteria for meeting the second condition. A sentence or expression alerts us to missing information when it violates these conditions.

1 The sentences are well formed in English. That is they are grammatically correct and convey some meaning.
2 If there is information left out, the missing information is the result of their not knowing it. It is not missing because they have chosen to leave it out or leave it out because it may be too disturbing. In general, these holes in the story limit the client's choices.
  a The sentences do not replace verbs with their nominalized forms. Replacing "my deciding" with "my decision."

b All of the words and phrases used refer to a specific person, action or thing. They do not generalize to an unspecified "someone" or eliminate the actor all together: "The bank was robbed."
c All of the verbs refer to specific actions. "He walked down to the bank," not "He went somewhere."
d The statements are not based on presuppositions that limit choice for the client, "I can't do that," "I'm not allowed."
e They do not refer to actions or abilities that are impossible, "She *made* me angry," "I already know what you are thinking."

(Bandler and Grinder, 1975a)

The NLP meta-model, a series of violations of the above well-formedness conditions, was introduced in 1975 by Bandler and Grinder as an implementation of language patterns often challenged by Perls and Satir and were recognized as common violations of well-formedness constraints commonly observed by linguists (Bandler and Grinder, 1975a, 1979, 1982; Bostic St. Clair and Grinder, 2000; Dilts and DeLozier, 2000; Lewis and Pucelik, 1990). A complimentary set of cognitive distortions was identified by Beck and Ellis in their formulations and have become mainstays of CBT. Although the matches are not perfect, an examination of the two groups shows clearly that the CBT categories exemplify specific sub-categories of the more inclusive meta model violations. In general, CBT recognizes 12 errors (Allen, 2003) which correspond to the NLP meta-model violations. These correspondences are presented in tabular form in Chapter 6 of this book.

NLP direct evidence

There are a number of unpublished dissertations that provide some evidence of the effectiveness of the language patterns within NLP.

Curreen (1995) provides a two case study report on the use of NLP and Ericksonian language patterns with two clients, both of whom were within the criminal justice system and were serving sentences for aggressive behavior. Her case reports demonstrate that NLP that is enhanced with Ericksonian language patterns can be used to achieve successful outcomes.

Macroy (1978) at Utah State University did a detailed study of 31 families, whose members were asked to rate their level of satisfaction with the family. Next, a family session was held for each family and recorded on audiotape. The audiotapes were analyzed for the occurrence of 150 specific meta-model patterns. In those families where people were less satisfied, substantially more violations of meta-model patterns were being used, especially deletions and unspecified nouns. This study supports an association between the frequency of meta-model violations and the level of family dysfunction.

Moines (1981) used multiple raters to examine 45-minute long audio-cassette recordings of insurance salespeople for the use of specific NLP patterns from the meta-model. His sample included top producers from their companies, as well as "average" producers of sales. The highly successful salespeople used far more embedded suggestions, complex equivalences, mind reading, metaphors, pacing, and modal operators of possibility. This artfully vague and suggestive language was part of their skill in enabling others to change. Strikingly, the patterns of highly successful salesmen were structured in such a way that they gradually built the number and quality of patterns through the sales pitch, starting with few and slowly building them in frequency while calibrating the response of the customer. It would appear that the successful salesmen took advantage of a syntax of persuasion. Less successful sales-persons used many of the same patterns but began almost immediately to use them with high frequency. In this study, the important difference appears to have been in the structuring of the pattern use rather than the patterns alone.

Well-formedness conditions for outcomes

At their most basic level, the NLP well-formedness conditions for any given outcome specify that:

1. The outcome must be stated as a positive thing or experience; something wanted, not something unwanted or ended.
2. The outcome must be something that is under the goal seeker's personal control which also implies that the task should not be stated too broadly.
3. The outcome must be specified in terms of multiple levels of sensory experience; it must be described in terms of what can be seen, heard, felt, tasted, or smelled.
4. The outcome should be evaluated for ecology; what will it change in the person's life and the lives around them?
5. The outcome should be imagined and experienced in fantasy as fully as possible (Andreas and Andreas, 1989; Bodenhamer and Hall, 1988; Cade and O'Hanlon, 1993; Dilts and DeLozier, 2000; Linden and Perutz, 1998).

Major support for these criteria is found in the psychology of intrinsic motivations. Intrinsic motivations are desired for their own sake. They are meaningful to the individual independent of external pressures or rewards. They are contrasted with extrinsic motivators which include things such as money, sex, power, fame, and popularity: stuff. Extrinsic motivators are well known for their capacity to sometimes weaken intrinsic motivations. When, however, they are simply the fruit of a deeply held personal direction or outcome, they present no such problem (Deci and Ryan, 2008; Hulleman et al., 2008).

The elements outlined in the NLP well-formedness criteria require first that the outcome be desired positively—it is something wanted and the outcome is stated as a positive intention. Intrinsic motivators are desired positively (Deci and Ryan, 2008). This criterion is also supported by the finding by Wegner et al. (1987) to the effect that injunctive commands, which easily translate into negative outcomes, create a paradoxical increase in the salience of the problem behavior.

The second criterion that the behavior be under the client's personal control is supported by findings that intrinsic motivators are characterized by choice and personal autonomy; they often include strong self-efficacy beliefs (Baumeister and Heatherton, 1996; Deci and Ryan 2008; Hulleman et al., 2008; Koestner, 2008; Notz, 1975).

The third criterion, that the outcome be specifiable in sensory terms, is supported by findings by Baumeister and Heatherton (1996), that because intrinsically motivating outcomes are often rooted in previous or vicarious experiences, they can be specified in sensory terms (often with special emphasis on kinesthetic elements—this is how I will feel). The criterion receives further support from research into the motivational and attentional mechanisms in the orbito frontal cortex and the superior colliculus to the effect that multi-sensory representations of outcomes are more highly motivating and focus attention more effectively than unimodal or abstract outcomes (Kringelbach, 2005; Sparks, 1999).

The criterion for imaginal practice is supported by a broad array of authors. Research into the impact of imagined movement supports the position that future performance is enhanced by the imagined performance of the process (Driskell et al., 1994; Martin and Hall, 1995; Pham and Taylor, 1999; Wohldmann et al., 2007).

The utility of clearly specified goals is strongly supported by Prochaska's strong principle of change (Prochaska, 1994; Prochaska et al., 1992, 1994). Prochaska discovered that a great many of his most successful changers had one thing in common: each of them had identified a positively valued outcome that was more important to them than the problem behavior. The identification of a positively valued outcome increased positive attitudes towards change by one full standard deviation. Simultaneously, the positive outcome decreased the valuation of the problem behavior by one half standard deviation. Problems are generally overcome by finding something more valuable.

Well-formedness conditions for behavioral change

A third set of well-formedness criteria is suggested by Dilts' work with the NLP allergy cure and his general report of a procedure for collapsing anchors. Collapsing anchors is an NLP technique with strong parallels with Wolpe's psychotherapy by reciprocal inhibition (1957) in which positive and negative conditioned stimuli (anchors) are evoked in succession—negative first and then positive—resulting in the negation of the problem affect or behavior (Bandler and Grinder, 1979; Dilts, 1983; Dilts and DeLozier, 2000; Dilts et al., 1980). Dilts introduced the refinement of introducing an anchor for a neutral or dissociated state between the negative and the positive anchors as a means of enhancing the efficacy of the procedure (Dilts and DeLozier, 2000; Dilts et al., 1990). Later research into the reconsolidation of long-term memory reveals the same pattern: evocation of the problem memory, interruption of its expression, and introduction of an amnestic or conflicting stimulus as a means of transforming or erasing traumatic or otherwise problematic memories.

Gray and Liotta (2012) and Gray (2011b) have adduced this pattern to explain the mechanism of the RTM technique for the treatment of traumatic memories. Briefly, when a memory is created, it passes through several stages, after varying time frames, including as little as 24 hours for emotional memories (in higher organisms), the "memory trace" becomes solidified as an assemblage of synaptic connections throughout the brain. This is basic memory consolidation (Amaral et al., 2008; Kandel, 2001; Schiller et al., 2010).

Each time the memory is activated after its consolidation as a long-term memory trace, the chemical processes that created the neural trace are reactivated. If the circumstances are similar to the original event, the synaptic connections are maintained or strengthened. If, however, the situation has significantly changed, the connections themselves can change. In the first case the memory is strengthened or unaffected, in the second it may be modified or erased. The repeated strengthening or weakening of the memory connections through the reactivation of protein synthesis is called reconsolidation because it repeats the original process by which the trace was consolidated (Alberini, 2005; Hupbach et al., 2008; Labar, 2007; Lee, 2009; Loftus and Yuille, 1984; Tronel et al., 2005).

When the memory has been activated for a sufficiently short period and interrupted before its full expression, the reconsolidation phenomenon opens a temporal window during which new versions of the experience may be introduced, the emotional impact of the event can be changed or (theoretically), the memory may be erased completely (Kindt et al., 2009; Schiller et al., 2010).

This mechanism gives rise to a pattern that consistently appears in NLP interventions from the basic pattern interrupt, to the simple protocol of collapsing anchors and the RTM procedure: evoke the problem state; interrupt it before it is fully expressed; introduce the amnestic or transformative stimulus (Gray, 2011c). We believe that this constitutes a well-formedness condition for emotional memory-based interventions.

Table 7.1 is based on Gray (2011b).

Table 7.1 A syntax for behavioral change in emotional memory: well-formedness conditions for memory-based interventions

Formulation	Stage 1	Stage 2	Stage 3	Stage 4	Stage 5
Behavioral/ neurological	Reminder of previous learning	Termination of response	Pause	Apply amnestic stimulus	Test
NLP	Briefly evoke problem state	Pattern interrupt	Pause	Elicit desired or alternate behaviour	Test
NLP allergy procedure	Briefly evoke allergic response	Evoke neutral anchor	Pause	Elicit similar non-allergenic response	Test
RTM PTSD protocol	Briefly evoke phobic response	Dissociate or evoke dissociated anchor	Pause	Dissociated movie Reversed movie	Test

Given the understanding that emotional memories can be permanently changed by observing these constraints, the reconsolidation paradigm provides a syntax for designing interventions with a firm neurological base.

The brain and NLP: a summary

A number of the factors discussed in this article create choices for an NLP practitioner wanting to help a client transfer functional skills to the neural networks where they are needed. The points below summarize what we have said about the brain with this in mind.

- The brain responds to visual, auditory, kinesthetic, olfactory-gustatory, and auditory digital (verbal) cues.
- Each of these modalities affects one or more sensory specific centers in the neo-cortex.
- The sensory organs are only indirectly connected to the areas of the cortex that analyze their data. On the way, the deeper areas of the brain where emotion and memories are stored influence the results of perception.
- Within each modality (sensory system) in the cortex, there are specific smaller areas which adjust the qualities of that sensory experience (the "submodalities"). For vision, these include such qualities as color and distance. When these submodalities change, the person's "feeling state" about the experience will change.
- Memories and imagined experiences stimulate and are analysed by the same sensory areas of the brain as new experiences. The submodalities of our memories and our imaginings are altered by our emotional state as we think of those memories or imagine those possibilities.

- All the outcomes that people generate are the result of a series of internal sensory "representations." In NLP such a series is called a strategy.
- As people execute a strategy and access information from the different modalities, there are a number of ways we can observe their thinking in these modalities. By watching their eye movements, and listening to their words, we can determine which sensory system they are using to present and re-present the information to themselves.
- Strategies can be thought of as having a trigger that starts them (also called an "anchor" in NLP), an operation where the person acts and collects information in some sense, a test where the person checks whether the results they got are the results they wanted, and an exit parameter that defines the end of the process. This sequence is known by the acronym TOTE.
- In real life, strategies are not simple sequential operations. The brain is able to meta-respond to a strategy.
- Each strategy is instantiated as a neural network (a series of interconnected neurons supported by the flux of intra- and extra-cellular neurotransmitters).
- The extra-cellular chemical mix which supports a specific neural network is a key ingredient of what we call an "emotional state," which is a brain-wide experience.
- When a neural network is dependent on a state which is very different to those usually occurring, then the person's usual coping skills may not be available while that state is active.
- Social skills including language use and empathy are dependent on the use of mirror neurons in diverse cortical areas. Mirror neurons give rise to a tendency to involuntarily copy the movements and facial expressions of others and to thus build an internal representation of their experience. This is the root of physical rapport.
- Helping someone change involves helping them access or trigger useful neural networks (running useful strategies) at the times they need them (often times just in those places where, in the past, they responded by using unresourceful strategies).

Most significantly, this chapter has shown a great deal of concordance between mainline psychology, neuroscience, and the insights of NLP. The breadth of scholarship that has been amassed in the past 35 years, independently of NLP, has confirmed many of its basic assumptions on cognitive, behavioral, perceptual, and neurophysiological levels. This should inspire researchers from NLP to seek out the neurological and psychological principles that confirm what our experiences have shown us and use them for the construction of vertically integrated theories that may be tested scientifically and to find new subtleties of understanding and technique. The chapter also provides a rationale for researchers from outside of the discipline to re-examine the findings of NLP and to test them against the objective findings in academic research by designing, new and well-informed experimental analyses of the claims of NLP.

8 Research and the history of methodological flaws

Richard M. Gray, Richard F. Liotta, Lisa Wake, Joe Cheal

Since its emergence in the mid-1970s, NLP has received attention ranging from accolades in national magazines to condemnation from various sources. The central popular critiques of NLP rise from its perception as being variously, a cult, a guru therapy, and that its claims of efficacy in producing quick cures are "impossible." Some of these critiques have merit. Historically, some NLP practitioners have grossly exaggerated the capabilities of NLP for personal gain. We have the same reaction as the popular critiques to the manner in which NLP has been presented and *sold* by some.

More relevantly, this chapter addresses the academic critiques that include the complaints that NLP is lacking a theory and that it has been disproven by extensive research in the 1980s. Research results from these studies and particularly the interpretation of those findings have discouraged continued empirical examinations of NLP. In many circles NLP has been dismissed as a field not warranting further study. Historically, most practitioners of NLP were not researchers. As a result, not only has limited research been done but little rebuttal has been offered regarding the negative findings in the literature. In this chapter we will systematically examine the reviews in the literature that purported to examine the root concepts of NLP and their validity. Many of the current critiques of NLP, like much material found in scientific journals, rely heavily on historical research. Literature reviews, as a standard element of scientific and psychological research, have their benefit in ensuring that successive generations of researchers do not have to reinvent the wheel. They also, at least in theory, provide a clear conceptual foundation for the material to follow. From the outset, there are two recurring problems that the standard model encounters. First, bad research is promulgated as the received wisdom. Second, there is the tendency to uncritically rely upon the interpretations and conclusions made about the research that has been done, despite significant misinterpretations of the material reviewed and the subsequent misrepresentation of findings.

An example of how misrepresentation occurs comes from mainline psychology in the story of Little Albert and John Watson; the bulk of this narrative is derived from Harris (1979).

In 1920, Watson and Rayner reported a conditioning experiment with "Little Albert." The experiment was designed to determine whether a child who was unafraid of small animals could be conditioned to fear a white rat when its presence was followed by the loud startling sound of a metal pipe being hit with a hammer, and whether that fear would generalize to other stimuli. The original literature gives a very clear and concise description of the process that Watson and Rayner followed, including the specifics of the items that Albert was exposed to, the length of time between the stimulus situations and the follow-up of Albert.

Harris reports that a survey of introductory psychology texts found that a majority misrepresented the experiment. Some reflected minor errors, including the child's name, age, and whether he was initially conditioned to a rat or a rabbit. More significantly, many texts claim that the fear generalized to a fur pelt, a man's beard, a cat, a pup, a fur muff, a white furry glove, various relatives who wore fur, and a teddy bear. Some failed to include a second conditioning event that was an essential part of the procedure. Yet other texts indicated that, at the end of the experiment, Watson extinguished the fear responses when, in fact, Albert was removed from the hospital where the experiments were performed and was never seen again (Harris, 1979).

Harris supposes that there are two main reasons for these inaccuracies: a desire to show Watson in a favorable light, and, more importantly for our purposes, an over reliance on secondary texts.

In the case of NLP, while there have been ill-intentioned popular reviews, many of the myths have been perpetuated by the continual reliance on a series of ill-informed studies that proceeded on the belief that the preferred representation system (PRS) was some kind of theoretical foundation upon which the rest of NLP depended. Anyone who has carefully read the literature—beyond a few early texts (Bandler and Grinder 1975, 1979; Lewis and Pucelik, 1980)—would have discovered that the concept fell quickly from favor as unverifiable. Insofar as the PRS represented an observation whose currency in NLP was sufficiently brief that it was never included in authoritative descriptions of the field, the premise of most of these studies was spurious. Nevertheless, because of the presence of these studies in the peer-reviewed literature, they continue to exert inordinate influence on researchers who are otherwise ignorant of the field. Despite a fairly steady stream of research that supports many of the basic concepts of NLP, researchers return to the flawed data from 30 years ago. The root sources of the supposed experimental refutation of NLP essentially come from two reviews by one author.

Examination of reviews

In 1984, after noting the repeated appearance of NLP in popular literature, Sharpley decided to review the extant research on what he understood to be one of the central tenets of NLP, the preferred representational system

(PRS). He reviewed 15 published studies that focused on this phenomenon and evaluated them for design, method, and dependent measures. He divided the studies into four categories: those that test for the presence of the PRS as an actual phenomenon, those examining the validity of the construct using multiple measures, the use of matching PRS in non-counselling situations, and whether PRS matching is effective in counselling situations. He concludes, accurately—in harmony with the main point made by NLP regarding eye-accessing cues (EACs)—that matching the dynamic range of predicate responses in a clinical conversation is valuable for enhancing client empathy. Because, however, he had gone in search of the elusive or non-existent PRS with the assumption that it was somehow foundational to NLP, he rejects (correctly) the dynamic use of EACs as not relevant to the PRS issue and warns that the research that he has reviewed has not verified the existence of the PRS and that it needs further study.

This is a reasonable analysis of the research to date (1985). From the perspective of NLP, it highlights several serious problems with the research. These are: the assumed ubiquity of the PRS; its presumed centrality to NLP; the presumption that the indicators, EACs, and predicates always agree as to the conscious perceptual system; and that rapport implies something other than a set of observable changes in interpersonal responses. Having already focused on the first two problems, it is important to focus on the others.

Sharpley, and most of the studies he examines, appears to believe that the analysis of sensory modalities is a reductive exercise. It is related to one or two indicators (EACs and predicate usage) and that those elements will reveal the active sensory modality either independently or as co-varying dependent variables. Sharpley, and many of the authors that he cites, believes that the sensory modality revealed by these cues must necessarily arise on demand. That is, if we instruct an individual to think about a sound or a picture, they must access the auditory or visual centres and this access must be reflected in the predicates or the eye accessing cues or both. What this assumption misses is that the NLP sensory modalities are for the most part not demand characteristics. This means that in their most salient aspects, their signatures in predicates, or eye movements are not simply evoked by an instruction but they are observed in the course of naturalistic conversation. Moreover, rather than being an absolutely invariant reflection of neural processing that must also be observable under easily specifiable circumstances, they are more often highlighted against the background of or inferred from an entire gestalt that includes breathing rate, body posture, speaking tone, speech rate, and the sensory context. This gestalt provides a perceptual frame that allows the trained practitioner to discern what the simple procedure cannot evoke. Beyond this, the "simple" EACs are complicated by multiple levels of concurrent eye movements.

In general, Bandler and Grinder (1979) refer to representational preferences being determined as a pattern that recurs more often than other concurrent eye movements. They suggest that the proper way of learning how to evaluate representational systems is by asking multiple questions, one system at a time, and noticing which pattern appears most frequently. They also indicate that these vary as specific personal patterns and therefore must be detected by observing each person as an individual.

Complicating the issue is their statement that EACs reflect the entire process of making the content conscious. This typically involves multiple systems. They note:

> We've got to make a distinction now. The predicates, the words a person chooses to describe their situation—when they are specified by representational system—let you know what their consciousness is. The predicates indicate what portion of this complex internal cognitive process they bring into awareness. The visual accessing cues, eye-scanning patterns, will tell you literally the whole sequence of accessing, which we call a strategy. What we call the "lead system" is the system that you use to go after some information. The "representational system" is what's in consciousness, indicated by predicates. The "reference system" is how you decide whether what you now know—having already accessed it and knowing it in consciousness—is true or not.
>
> (1979, p.28)

Further, they emphasize the contextual nature of any such determination in the following passage:

> Our claim is that you are using all systems all the time. In a particular context you will be aware of one system more than another. I assume that when you play athletics or make love, you have a lot of kinesthetic sensitivity. When you are reading or watching a movie, you have a lot of visual consciousness. You can shift from one to the other. There are contextual markers that allow you to shift from one strategy to another and use different sequences.
>
> (p.36)

The other conceptual problem with Sharpley and the studies he examines is the definition of rapport against which various tests of the PRS and EACs are made. As is often done in bad research, the term is defined using a standard definition, a dictionary definition or a definition that is current in the researcher's sub-discipline. For the most part this leads to false negatives. Unless the phenomenon under question is tested as defined by its proponents, the test is invalid. In general the tests of rapport, except those that define it in terms of increased empathy, are bound to fail.

The consistent error regarding the overemphasis on the PRS appears to come from readings of the early chapters of *The Structure of Magic, Volume II* (Bandler and Grinder, 1976). According to Andreas (who was present at the time), the PRS was introduced as a teaching tool. This becomes obvious and makes sense with a close reading of *Magic II*.

In the first several sections, Bandler and Grinder do indeed talk about the utility of the PRS as a means of establishing rapport and as an important tool in therapy. They talk about how all of us have the capacity to experience the world in terms of all five senses and that for each of us one or more of these is more fully developed or preferred than the others. This is described as a *tendency*; it is an observed pattern, not a truth. What often passes unnoticed in this discussion is that it appears to progress from the description of a general tendency to the discussion of a problem and it ends with several means of solving the problem. The early discussion of detecting the PRS develops into a discussion of how the highly preferred sensory system can limit people's maps of the world and thereby their capacity to communicate with others and to enjoy the full range of human experience. In such cases, the therapist first paces the limitation and then seeks ways to open the client to new possibilities of perception and action. They note:

> As we repeatedly pointed out in *Magic I*, when people come to us in therapy with pain, feeling that they are stuck in that they don't have enough choices, we find that their world is rich and varied enough for them to get what they want, but that the way which they use to represent the world to themselves is not rich and varied enough for them to obtain it. In other words, the way that each of us represents our experience will either cause us pain or allow us an exciting, living and growing process in our lives. More specifically, if we choose (consciously or not) to represent certain kinds of experience in one or another of our representational systems, we will succeed either in causing ourselves pain or in giving ourselves new choices.
>
> (Bandler and Grinder, 1976, p.28)

Other than in this therapeutic context, as Andreas notes, the PRS appears more generally as a way of focusing attention on representational systems.

Despite these errors, Sharpley is perceptive and often gets it right. Constrained, however, by the hypotheses he is testing, he has to pass the observations by. One of the more striking and accurate statements that he makes is:

> However, the identification of this PRS (if it is a PRS and not merely current language style) by either eye movements or self-report is not supported by the research data. The cuing effect of client verbalizations is valuable, not to identify PRS but to alert counsellors to phrase their responses in such a way as to maximize empathy within the interview. The existence or stability of the PRS is irrelevant to predicate matching as a counselling process, and parsimony argues for the process rather than the as yet unverified theory.
>
> (p.247)

Had it not been for his early preconceptions about the PRS as central to the technique and had he not taken his study authors at their word, this might have been a much more valuable paper. Somewhat earlier, he says, correctly, that:

> if NLP is suggesting that counsellors who demonstrate high levels of reflection and empathy will be more effective than those who do not, then little new is being said. If NLP seeks to promote empathic responses from counsellors, then scales designed to measure empathy ought to, and do, show this (e.g. Hammer, 1983). Although this is a worthwhile procedure for counsellors, it does not justify NLP as a separate theoretical position (nor as the "magic" its proponents quote).
> (p.246)

This appears to be another important part of the problem. NLP clearly indicates that its aim is to discover patterns that provide results in treatment that have been part of the characteristic repertoires, first of the exemplars that they modelled and then others. It did not claim that these elements of technique in and of themselves would be transformative—they were a set of techniques that *could* be used for various purposes. There was no claim that its techniques were, "something new" or that it was espousing a specific theory (Bandler and Grinder, 1975a, 1979; Dilts et al., 1980).

Sharpley is often unfairly criticized for taking a position on NLP that was wrong. This is done from a perspective many years in the future when several consensus models of NLP have arisen, none of which hold forth the proposition that either the PRS or EACs are central tenets upon which NLP must stand or fall. It should further be recognized that Sharpley depended upon his sources, who, preceding him, made their own false assumptions about NLP. The problem is not Sharpley, but the uncritical acceptance of his findings by researchers who have not examined the status of NLP since the mid 1980s. As Bradbury has observed, all roads point to Sharpley (Bradbury, 2011a,b).

Gambardella et al. (1991) discuss some of the negative conclusions made regarding NLP by the National Research Council (NRC), as reported in Druckman and Swets (1988). They note that the NRC appeared to favor Sharpley's perspective, rather than rebuttals to Sharpley's criticisms. They postulate that, "This may have contributed, in no small part, to the NRC's unfavorable conclusions." This is also an example of the problems that reliance on secondary sources, and the interpretation of them, has created for the progression of research on NLP.

Shortly after Sharpley's publication, Einspruch and Forman (1985) published their reply: *Observations concerning research literature on neurolinguistic programming*. These authors systematically criticized the 15 studies used by Sharpley and extended their analysis to another 24 not reviewed by

Sharpley. They began by pointing out the errors concerning NLP made by Sharpley and his authors. Among the errors noted are the following:

> The authors ignored NLP models for defining patterns (and their highly individualistic nature) and the nature of therapeutic communication and interventions.
>
> There is a failure to recognize the impact of context and that information may coexist on multiple sensory systems, on conscious and unconscious levels simultaneously.
>
> They focused upon the PRS and reified it as a nominalization as opposed to a partial expression of an ongoing process.
>
> He mistakenly assumes that both the PRS and representational systems more generally only apply to right handed people.
>
> Contrary to the representations made in the literature of NLP, they identify matching the PRS as the key to effective counselling.
>
> None of the studies took into account the Meta Model of communication as a central means for parsing conscious and unconscious process.
>
> Procedural errors included a lack of adequate training in the NLP techniques being tested and a failure to understand the NLP position that words are anchors that evoke responses.
>
> (Adapted from Einspruch and Forman, 1985)

It should be remembered that patterns, as understood in NLP, have a special status (Grinder and Bandler, 1980a). Patterns intimately involve the perspective of the observer and other participants. They are dynamic sequences of perceptions and actions that are identified by the flow of sensory information through the procedure. As a result, no pattern has a single, static formulation. Like statements in mathematics and symbolic logic, they begin with a set of common elements (VAKOG and sub-modalities). These individual elements may vary in order and value but the more general pattern of their interactions remains. Again, Grinder and Bandler make the following clarification:

> Notice that since patterns must be represented in sensory grounded terms, available through practice to the user, a pattern will typically have multiple representation[s]—each tailored for the differing sensory capabilities of individual users. I point out in passing that this requirement immediately excludes statistical statements about patterning as being well-formed in NLP as statistical statements are not user oriented.
>
> (1980a, p.6.)

In the end, Einspruch and Forman make several recommendations for further research. These include that researchers studying NLP should be trained by competent trainers for an adequate time and to a certain level of competency. Their training needs to include training in the recognition of patterns and a serious appreciation of the underlying presuppositions of

NLP. Only this level of training will provide an adequate basis for testing the application of NLP to therapy.

One of the significant problems with many of the studies was that they attempted to study rapport as a matter of paper and pencil tests. These authors suggest that any test of rapport be tested using objective sensory-based criteria. They also indicated that the procedures tested should be scored individually and later combined for statistical analysis. Finally, they recommended that tests of therapeutic procedures, whether NLP-based or in a comparison treatment, should only be performed by thoroughly trained therapists who have illustrated mastery of the procedures.

In 1987, Sharpley responded to Einspruch and Forman in the *Journal of Counselling Psychology*. Echoing Einspruch and Forman's critique of the methodology used in the studies to date, he complains that: "There is little more that a researcher can do, however, to evaluate a theory than to test the veracity and strength of those principles of behavior that are held by the proponents of that theory" (Sharpley, 1987, p.103). Yet it is precisely here where the studies fail. Because the researchers lacked adequate training in NLP they misunderstood the nature of the PRS and EACs as patterns and overvalued their importance to NLP.

Sharpley then seeks to correct Einspruch and Forman for critiquing the studies that claimed that EACs and the elusive PRS only work for persons who are right handed. In his earlier paper Sharpley (1984) claimed that all of the patterns only apply to right handed persons. In fact it is only the left-right distribution of the EACs to which this caution was applied (Bandler and Grinder, 1979). In a further indication of the superficiality of his reading, Sharpley points to the EACs diagram (the NLP homunculus) on page 29 of *Frogs* as applying only to the PRS. The most casual reading of the passage, however, places the chart in the context of an exercise identifying EACs in a general sense, *not* the PRS.

Two other critiques offered by Einspruch and Forman, that the means of accessing the PRS in several studies was inadequate and that the therapists used were inadequately trained, are actually closely related. As already noted, EACs and the PRS, where present, are patterns. They are not simple responses like raising your right hand but they are relatively complex response systems that require some subtlety on the part of the therapist for their discernment. Einspruch and Forman's critique, that training in pattern recognition, not just watching for eye movements, seems more than reasonable.

Having gone through Einspruch and Forman's critique of the research and rejecting it, Sharpley proceeds to show that the vast preponderance of research to that point did not support NLP. As a matter of simple fact, that observation is true—as far as it goes. Importantly, it misses the point that few if any of the studies were reflective of the tenets or practices of NLP. Most seemed to rely on a superficial reading of the materials and misunderstanding of the central idea of patterns as noted above. As Einspruch and Forman note, the findings are largely irrelevant.

At last Sharpley turns to the fact that if NLP has any value, this is derived from techniques garnered from other sources. In terms of technique he finally gets close to the point of NLP and its founders. As primarily a technique for modeling excellence, NLP makes no claim to originality in process, only originality in modeling and in making the processes transportable.

In summary, Sharpley's understanding of NLP is flawed, as were the understandings of the researchers he cites. Had any of them had a more complete understanding of NLP, it might have been valuable research but as the bulk is based on false understandings and total, if innocent, distortions, the conclusions reached are without value.

In 1987, shortly after Sharpley's (1987) second article, Heap (1988) published his review, covering much the same ground and making all of the same errors. Like Sharpley and his forebears, he takes the PRS as a central tenet of NLP theory and praxis and proceeds to illustrate its near total lack of support. While fairly exhaustive, Heap breaks no new ground and continues to test a false conception of NLP.

This chapter began with the observation by Harris that psychological research is often flawed by its reliance on inaccurate reports of previous research that become immortalized in the peer reviewed milieu. We have already seen how Sharpley, as early as 1985, suffered from just this problem in taking at their word the false understandings of his informants and that this problem—with regard to NLP— has been reinforced by Heap.

A significant and more recent case in point is the relatively objective attempt by Witkowski (2010) to assess the state of NLP by examining 35 years of published research. But it too suffers from the intellectual game of telephone.

The author presents, as the central concept of NLP, the presupposition that the map is not the territory and that individual perceptions are formulated in terms of personal interpretations of sensory data through the five basic sensory systems (VAKOG). He then states:

> As they suggested, each of us processes the majority of information using one primary representational system (PRS). Following the example of the most outstanding therapists, to work effectively with a patient one should necessarily match the patient's PRS so as to be able to use their "map."
>
> (2010, p.4)

Witkowski then asserts, that not only is the PRS central but that a second crucial theoretical element of NLP is the observation that EACs are used most importantly to access the PRS so as to effectively guide all other interventions.

> Another discovery of which the NLP originators were particularly proud of was to realize that access to the representational systems is possible

through the so-called accessing cues that are precisely specified eye movements. Careful observation of these movements should enable the NLP therapist to unequivocally identify the PRS of the patient, interlocutor etc., and, in consequence, facilitate matching their PRS. All other hypotheses of the NLP system related to the arising of mental disorders, the type of therapy and communication, etc. stem from these basic assertions.

(2010, pp.4–5)

It is important to note that here Witkowski has turned the PRS into a typology, an error that even its earliest promulgators were careful to avoid (Bandler and Grinder 1975, 1979; Lewis and Pucelik, 1990). Einspruch and Forman (1985) characterize this error as a reification of the idea, turning its measurement into a meaningless exercise.

Proceeding from these presuppositions, Witkowski embarks upon a review of the 315 articles published in the Neurolinguistic Programming Research Data Base (http://www.nlp.de/cgi-bin/research/nlp-rdb.cgi) that was compiled over a period of 18 years by an international body of NLP researchers. His choice was made to ensure that his own biases did not affect the choice of articles and because he believed that this database would provide a more comprehensive collection of such articles than could be found in a search of PsychLit, PsychInfo, MEDLINE, or other such academic collections.

Continuing with his qualitative analysis, Witkowski then limited his analysis to studies that had been published by the most reputable of scientific journals. This was done by excluding any publication that did not appear in the Master Journal List of the Institute for Scientific Information in Philadelphia. Using this filter the list was whittled down to 63, or 20 percent of the original list.

This remaining 20 percent was further subdivided into three groups: those testing what he believed to be the basic tenets of NLP or hypotheses derived from those tenets—33 studies; those focused on "polemics, discussions, case analyses" or other elements that he determined were irrelevant to his main research goal—14 studies; and studies that he determined to be irrelevant on its face—16 studies.

Of the original 315 studies, Witkowski only examined the 33 from category one. From this sample, he found nine works supporting what he believed to be the central tenets of NLP or hypotheses derived from them; 18 that were non-supportive and six that were indeterminate.

With the single exception that his understandings of the main tenets of NLP were wrong, Witkowski's methodology in reviewing the literature is fairly exemplary. He does it, however, from a fatally flawed understanding of the main tenets of NLP, which makes his work invalid. He states criteria to be evaluated, goes to a reasonably objective source (the Neurolinguistic Programming Research Data Base), evaluates the source journals for their academic integrity by a well-respected source, and then evaluates the remainder for relevance to his research criteria.

On a qualitative level, three of the supportive works were viewed as methodologically acceptable. These were Kinsbourne's (1974) study of eye movements and brain lateralization, Yapko's (1981) investigation of the PRS and its relationship to hypnotic depth, and Dooley and Farmer's (1988) study of eye movement differences in aphasic and normal controls. The remaining studies were reasonably adjudged to be of lesser value because they reported general outcomes based on 21-day intensive NLP trainings and/or lacked controls.

Of the 18 articles reporting non-supportive results, Witkowski goes through them systematically. He begins with Thomason et al. (1980); Farmer et al. (1985), Poffel and Cross (1985), and Burke et al. (2003), all of whom examined the correlation between eye movement and assumed sensory access. Witkowski reports that, "They all provided unequivocally negative results" (p.13).

A review of those studies finds that for the most part there is an assumption that external instructions or specific tasks designed for the purpose will, of necessity, produce the effects observed by NLP. The NLP EACs, however, are typically reported as expressions of a larger communications gestalt in which they are embedded. Because those negative findings do not reflect the context in which NLP predicts their appearance, the conclusions are dubious at best. Moreover, as no one has ever claimed that these were foundational to NLP in any manner, the research could only possibly impact this one set of observations.

An interesting twist that arises from this first batch of studies is the observation by Burke et al. (2003) that although they could find no evidence of the PRS, there was evidence that EACs changed with the subject matter. Although they were not testing the actual position of NLP, they appear to have found confirmatory evidence. Two other studies (Gumm et al., 1982; Coe and Scharcoff, 1985) that set out to test the presumed validity of the PRS failed to confirm its existence. Witkowski again mistakenly characterizes these studies as not supporting the theory of NLP.

Passing on to more complex research, Witkowski presents the findings of Fromme and Daniell (1984), Elich et al. (1985) and Graunke and Roberts (1985).

Fromme and Daniell (1984) design a set of tasks with which to evaluate the PRS which are so laden with self-contradictory language that their results are as unsurprising as their methods naïve. In the first of their experiments, the alphabet imagery task for sensory (VAK) distinctions, they begin by having the subjects write out the lowercase alphabet and noticing whether the curved portions of the letters are made using clockwise or counter-clockwise movements. After actually practising writing the alphabet, the remaining tasks rely upon the visualization of the printed alphabet and noting whether the visualized letters are pronounced with a long "e" sound (auditory task); whether the letters extend above or below the line of the other letters (visual task); and then, as in the practice round, noticing whether the curved portions of the letters are made using clockwise or counter-clockwise movements (kinesthetic task). The tasks then, were to visualize the alphabet, individually see the rounded parts of each letter, the height of each letter, and whether the sound of the letter's name contains a long "e." For each task, the subjects timed themselves with a stopwatch. The experimenters predicted that their subjects would respond more quickly for tasks that were related to their actual PRS and although some of the scores should relate to the other kinds of sensory-based tasks—presumably allowing for secondary preferences—the researchers predicted that if there were a PRS, those correlations should be non-significant.

When they examined the response times, they found that the times for each of the sensory modalities correlated with the response times for the other sensory tasks. They suggest that if the PRS hypothesis were true these correlations would not be significant. On this basis they rejected the "PRS hypothesis." But they also found that the results of the alphabet test didn't provide predicted correlations with two tests of imagery. One of their tests of imagery should have correlated with the speed of response on the sensory matched task (visual with visual, auditory with auditory...) but these correlations did not appear as expected.

The high correlation of latencies in the alphabet task can be explained as follows. We begin with the fact that the theory under examination was wrong: NLP posits no foundational principle regarding the PRS. We follow with an analysis of the alphabet task that shows that it is biased strongly towards the visual and that its very complexity makes the determination of any preference impossible.

The root task is a highly complex visual exercise. In each subset of the task one might reasonably expect that the dominant sensory modality must be visual. Even if the direction of movement for writing the letter is determined by a kinesthetic access, the need to focus on the visual elements of the task are so demanding that they are likely to overwhelm any other element. For the kinesthetic task, however, because the task is so highly visual, it is as likely that the motion would be traced by visualizing the movement of a clock as it would be by a hand movement. As a result, there should be a visual bias in the kinesthetic task. The visual portion of the task asked the subjects to notice which elements were taller—above or below the line—than the other letters; fair enough. A reasonable visual element in a complex visual task should legitimately provide visual access.

For the auditory test, subjects had to assess whether the pronounced letter-name had a long "e" sound. While it might be assumed by a casual reader of NLP that this would lead to an auditory response, there are at least two other response possibilities. Most likely, because of the intensity of the visual task, that modality would be most salient on all levels.

From the literature of NLP we might also assume that because the task calls for a verbal response, that an auditory digital response might be expected—if it were not overwhelmed by the difficulty of the visual task itself. At last, the relative difficulty of the task would have slowed all of the response times leading to the highly significant ($p<.0001>$) correlations observed.

The alphabet test was then used to determine the supposed PRS for each subject and based on these findings they were subjected to two other tests to determine whether fast visualizers would communicate visual information more effectively than slow vizualizers (they did) and whether subjects would choose verbal expressions that matched their supposed PRS (they didn't). The experiment is invalid on its face.

Witkowski then turns our attention to Elich et al. (1985). From the outset, although the study is presented by Witkowski, as a test of the idea that eye movements and spoken predicates reflect the sensory modality of imagery, a review of the article (Elich et al., 1985) finds that the aim of the assessment is to test the PRS hypothesis. The authors seek to determine PRS by matching eye movements with predicates using trained raters (perhaps mis-trained) to assess eye movement recordings and standardized assessments of the sensory modality of the spoken elements of the experiment. The experiment appeared to be well designed, despite some serious conceptual and procedural issues (smell is identified as a kinesthetic sense and although the raters were trained to identify EACs, there is little information about how they were trained). The authors acknowledge that use of the word imagery throughout may have biased the results towards the visual modality and that the difficulty of differentiating between conversational eye fixation and staring as an EAC made scoring problematic. They failed to confirm either the relationship between eye movements and predicates and further found that any such matching did not reliably identify the PRS. What is striking is that, although the study fails to confirm that matched eye movements and predicates can validate or reliably assess the PRS (as it should have), the authors provide the following conclusion which is much more in line with the actual position of NLP than the reviewer might have understood:

> Much of the problem is with the concept of the PRS. It is pointedly apparent from the research of the last few years that the concept of PRS is as slippery and elusive as a greased pig at a country fair. Dorn et al. (1983) and Sharpley (1984) concluded that (a) there is no reliable method for assessing PRS, (b) PRS may change over time, (c) it is not certain that PRS even exists, and (d) if PRS does exist it may merely reflect current language style, and we would add that PRS may be heavily influenced by language.
>
> (1985, pp.624–5)

Witkwoski then examines Graunke and Roberts' (1985) study of the PRS and appears to misrepresent the findings in a significant fashion. Graunke and Roberts set out to test whether sensory modalities changed with context rather than persisting as a trait variable. While it is true that they rejected the PRS, their focus was on the more consistent claim of NLP that the use of sensory modalities would shift with context. In their own words:

> The major purpose of this study was to examine the impact of varied imagery tasks on individuals' usage of sensory predicates. The specific purpose was to test whether female volunteers significantly altered their use of sensory predicates across imaging tasks. The present study's results indicated that most subjects were auditory types during auditory imaging tasks and kinesthetic types during kinesthetic imaging tasks. Thus, the participants in this study were able to vary their use of sensory predicates according to the situational context or task demands.
>
> (1985, p.529)

Witkowski finally turns his attention to several previous reviews of the literature. He cites Sharpley's two reviews (1984, 1987) and Einspruch and Forman's (1985) reply to Sharpley. We have already examined Sharpley at length and discovered his studies to be ill informed and based on presuppositions that do not exist within NLP.

In all, the serious published research into the validity of NLP seems to be characterized by a series of false understandings dating from the early days and the early misconceptions of those writers. The preponderance of the published literature largely comes down on the side arguing against NLP but for entirely the wrong reasons, they never tested NLP, only their own maps of what they thought it was. As Witowski adeptly argues: "*Argumenta ponderantur, non numerantur*—the force of the arguments lies in their weight, not numbers" (p.12). We might suggest that arguments are to be weighed, not counted.

Summary of methodological flaws

- Researchers have assumed that the Preferred Representational System is a theoretical construct at the heart of NLP. It is not. It is part of the gestalt of communication that provides *clues* to how someone is subjectively experiencing their world in a given moment.
- Researchers have assumed that EACs are pre-determined constructs that directly relate to the PRS. EACs are contextual and give an indication, moment to moment, of how a person is bringing to consciousness portions of unconsciously stored information.
- The definition of rapport utilized in studies is restricted to dictionary definitions or the authors' definition and is not discretely defined as a process in the way that it is experienced in NLP.

- Subsequent researchers and reviewers have based their assumptions on Sharpley's flawed assumption of theoretical constructs.
- Researchers have lacked adequate training in NLP, thereby introducing inaccurately defined variables, and have therefore failed to operate as the "expert" practitioner as required in effective studies.

A research future for NLP

The preceding history leaves us with two separate problems, the problem of what legitimately may be researched in the field of NLP and how to research it. We have already reviewed Einsprung and Forman's (1985) program for pursuing NLP research, but we have not defined either a theoretical base, or concepts that are fundamental to NLP.

NLP, as originally framed, is not based on any set theoretical foundation, there is probably no single premise upon which the field will stand or fall. Each model within the field is essentially independently verifiable and if unverified, discarded. Designed as what may be understood as a vertically integrated discipline (techniques and procedures must be supported by observable results, both should be supported by an underlying set of behavioral principles and neurological structures and functions), we may expect coherent theory to emerge as neuroscience provides the tools to formulate and verify the presuppositions intuited by NLP in the mid-1970s.

We are still left with the question: what may legitimately be studied? The best answer is that NLP can be evaluated in terms of techniques, procedures and the outcomes specified for them. Some of these include:

- Rapport skills defined by the interpersonal dance of responsivity, reflected in the increased propensity for the subject to pace the lead of the interviewer, the development of empathy and perceived warmth, but not self-disclosure.
- Strategies as sequences of behavior in terms of VAKOG sequences that are usually context dependant, highly personalized yet discernible through the modeling process as variants of discrete models that can be transferred to others as skills.
- Anchoring as a technique that models Pavlovian delayed conditioning using observation of client responses and testing for the presence of the conditioned association. Such research must include respect for the limitations of the procedure as described in the NLP literature. These may be tested in the context of collapsing anchors and creating generalizable resource states.
- Significant techniques including the fast phobia cure or VK/D for phobias and the RTM procedure for the treatment of post-traumatic stress disorder (PTSD)—so long as the research follows the protocols and honours the exclusion criteria.

A brief perusal of the indirect evidence chapter will find many others. Crucially, all such research must make reference to the literature and to experts in the field to ensure that the definitions from the field of NLP are accurately represented, appropriately operationalized, and that the protocols are appropriately followed. Ideally, the research should be performed using NLP practitioners from the field who are intimately familiar with the procedure.

The final question becomes how is the research to be pursued? The following section addresses those issues.

Researching NLP

NLP, as an applied psychology or model of the "how to" of performance excellence, does not necessarily lend itself to the rigours of empirical quantitative research. Yet, to become accepted and credible as a methodology of psychological intervention and change it is required to at least address some of the challenges and concerns of commissioners, clinicians, and detractors.

There are increasing calls within the psychotherapy community to bring forward the more qualitative aspects of research both as an evidence based tool and to illustrate the potential that therapeutic inquiry has in facilitating positive psychological change (Holmes, 2000; McLeod 2001). McLeod (2001) highlights the difficulty that psychotherapy faces in that it is based within the field of social science and the specific approach taken within psychotherapy means that new phenomena leading to the development of new approaches often arise in practice rather than through empirical research. This has implications for the field of psychotherapy in general, and particularly in its verification. McLeod proposes that there are three reasons why verification in psychotherapy is important:

- Verification research is an effective strategy for building legitimacy.
- The academic disciplines of psychology and psychiatry, that have hosted the bulk of therapy research, have been dominated by hypothesis testing, experimental research design.
- The majority of therapists have received training that does not encourage or prepare the therapist to become involved in research.

In 2006, Norcross, Koocher, and Garofalo conducted a Delphi Poll with a panel of 101 experts that considered discredited psychological treatments and tests. NLP as a treatment approach for mental and behavioral disorders was one of the methodologies reviewed. The most discredited therapy was angel therapy (4.92 – poll 1/4.98 poll 2) and the least discredited was behavior therapy for sex offenders (1.97/2.05). NLP was scored by the panel at 3.57/3.87. EMDR (eye movement desensitization and reprocessing), an emergent therapy with roots in NLP (Shapiro, 1985) that now has a substantial empirical evidence base scored 2.88/3.06.

What equates with evidence?

Evidence-based medicine enables clinicians to make judicious decisions about the most effective treatment options based on expert opinion that is grounded in the clinical practice of individual practitioners alongside evidence gained from systematic research. For an NLP technique to be considered a viable treatment for a range of clinical and psychological conditions it would need to demonstrate evidence of its effectiveness. The Centre for Evidence Based Medicine (www.cebm.net) identifies five levels in considering the effectiveness of studies for treatment benefit (Table 8.1).

Within evidence-based medicine there is also an accepted model referred to as the Evidence Pyramid, which is sometimes used to develop literature within a field of enquiry, as well as providing a measure by which research can be assessed.

Figure 8.1 presents a standard evidence based pyramid (Sackett et al., 2000). On the right is a proposed pyramid as it might be structured for the examination of NLP.

The authors are proposing that this book will offer an *evidence summary* of NLP research within the research pyramid model. Comprehensive inclusion, consideration, and critique of the current literature in NLP has not been done before and is critical in order for NLP to establish itself as an evidence-based discipline.

It is important to revisit the view of McLeod (2001) in considering the place of psychotherapy research within the social sciences. The following section aims to go some way towards addressing this.

Science and the scientific method

Science can be broken down into hard (the natural and physical) sciences and soft (the social) sciences. Like psychology and linguistics, NLP would be regarded as a social science. Ironically, although this is obviously a "softer"

Table 8.1 Study levels and types

Study level	Study type
Level 1	Systematic reviews of randomized trials.
Level 2	Randomized trial or (exceptionally) observational studies with dramatic effect.
Level 3	Non-randomized controlled cohort/follow-up study.
Level 4	Systematic review of case control studies, historically controlled studies.
Level 5	Opinion without explicit critical appraisal, based on limited/undocumented experience or based on mechanisms.

Research and the history of methodological flaws 211

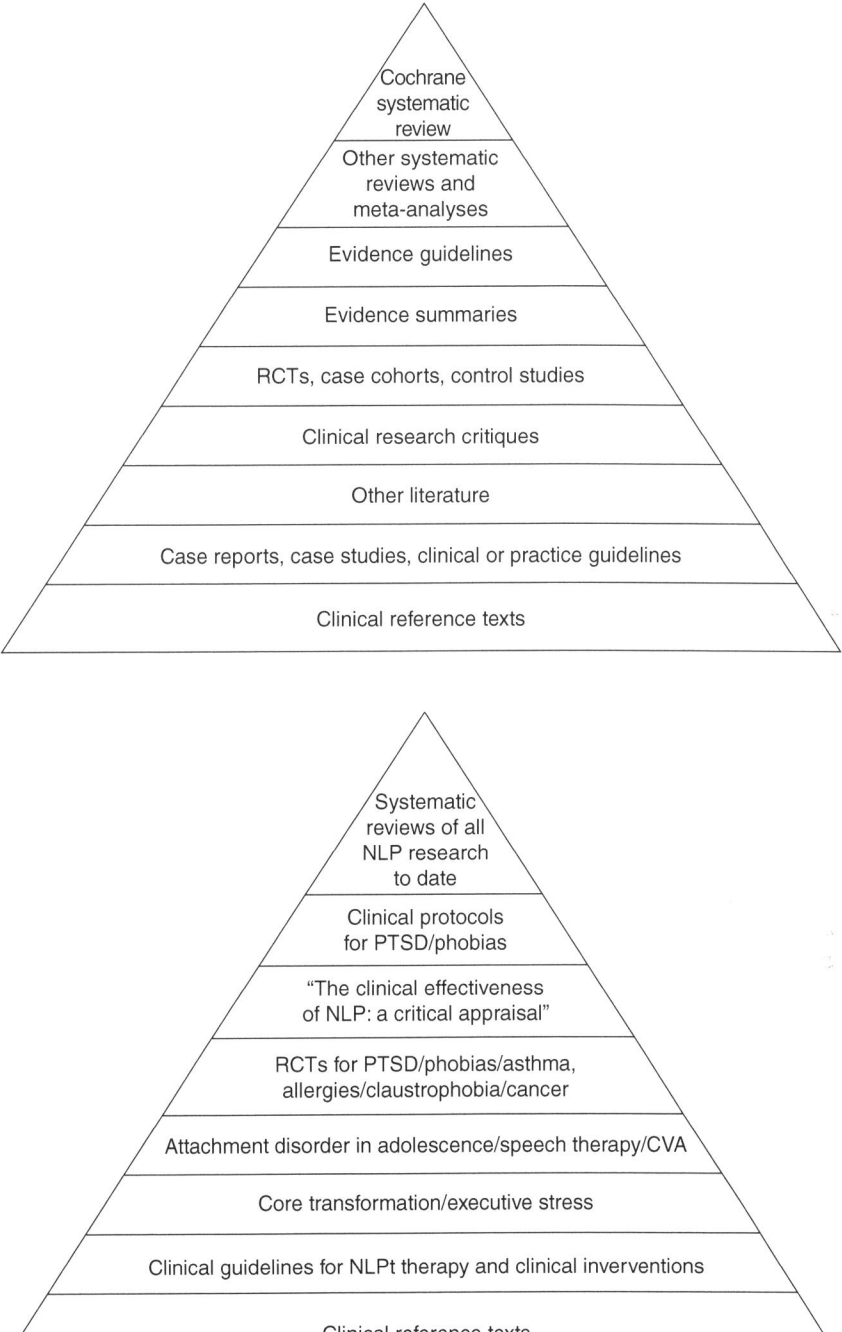

Figure 8.1 A proposed model for NLP clinical research

form of science, because the research is likely to be more open to misinterpretation, the researcher must take extra care to remain objective and "scientific." The foundation of science is carefully controlled experiments with carefully considered interpretation and rigorously defined variables and hypotheses. In common parlance, for something to be considered "scientific," it needs to be testable, reproducible, and refutable.

Can NLP be "proven to work" scientifically?

NLP is the study of subjective experience and it makes no claims for either an objective world or objective knowledge of a world (independent or otherwise). All the principles and techniques of NLP are designed to work with the subjective experience of the client. Subjective experience manifests in behavior that is observable and measurable. If NLP is conceptualized in a similar way to CBT, then the resultant behavior from changed or adapted cognitions can equally be measured. Einspruch and Forman indicated that although NLP is testable and verifiable, any previous research was methodologically inadequate. They concluded that it was not yet possible to determine the validity of either NLP concepts or whether NLP-based therapeutic procedures are effective for achieving therapeutic outcomes. They made recommendations that empirical investigations should be conducted to test the validity of NLP as a model of psychotherapy.

It could easily be argued that the researcher cannot take an objective "view from nowhere" (Nagel, 1986), and at best will only be able to take a meta, or "third perceptual position" (Dilts and DeLozier, 2000). This is the reason for rigorous definitions, clear and transparent design methodology, validity, and reliability reporting in quantitative studies. Where possible in qualitative research, the introduction of blind raters is required. It is recognized that information from any subjective research is likely to reflect the researcher/practitioner's biases and interpretations as it is simultaneously influenced by the subject/client's own biases and interpretations of their own subjective experience. As we highlight earlier, raters need to be trained regarding what they are observing.

As to whether NLP "works" or not, we need to consider what we are testing. NLP techniques are open to many confounding variables as are many —if not all—psychotherapies. They appear in the performance of the practitioner, the "readiness" of the client, the relevance of the treatment to the problem under consideration (inclusion and exclusion criteria), and the appropriateness of the environment. It is challenging to provide consistency across interventions and therefore difficult to "prove" that NLP works. As Carroll (ND) states:

> This is not to say that the techniques won't work. They may work and work quite well, but there is no way to know whether the claims are

valid. Perhaps it doesn't matter. NLP itself proclaims that it is pragmatic in its approach: what matters is whether it works. However, how do you measure the claim "NLP works"?

With current advances in technology (e.g. MRI brain scans), it is possible to add objective data to effectively develop structured randomized control trials that measure the concordance between physical brain changes and behavioral and emotional change over time. NLP also lends itself to qualitative research methodologies: to personal reports, interviews, surveys, case reports, and questionnaires. It is important that we also study the subjective nature of the interpersonal process of therapy through robust qualitative research that is empirically grounded through an interpretivist/constructivist scientific platform.

NLP can also be examined quantitatively through controlled research designs. NLP has protocols and interventions that would be quite amenable to examination of their effectiveness when compared to a control group or matched comparison subjects.

Further challenges for NLP researchers

Although NLP is a subjective approach, it does have models that apply to everyone. Some of the concepts in NLP are generalizable and independent of the individual and are therefore objective. For example, anchoring happens whether we believe in it or not; our ability to learn is based on the nervous system building a network of anchored associations. Modalities exist, based on our five senses and sub-modalities exist, based on the qualities of our five senses. So, although people may experience them subjectively, it is possible to demonstrate that a change in sub-modalities leads to a reported change in felt experience and responding behavior.

Yeager (1985) reports that NLP can fail for a number of reasons, including experimenters who have an inadequate understanding of NLP and setting up test conditions where the procedures do not fit the study of subjective behavior. As has already been demonstrated with CBT, it is possible to measure objective behavioral change in response to therapeutic input.

Hall (2001) points to the lack of distinction between primary states and meta-states as another reason for failure. This could be understood as a confusion of logical types with logical levels by practitioners where primary states and meta-states sit at different logical levels but are treated as the same level by the practitioner. An example would be in trying to use a simple kinesthetic anchor (which is a primary state technology) for proactivity (a meta-state) without creating a specific frame. "Without knowing about meta-levels or meta-states, an inexperienced researcher would not get the predicted response and would naturally draw the conclusion (a hasty and unfounded conclusion) that 'NLP anchoring does not work'" (Hall, 2001, p.107).

Beyond the problems raised in assessing the interactions between the practitioner and the client, there is the question of the presence or absence—not to mention the validity—of a theory of NLP itself. There is beginning to be an understanding of a core theory of NLP within psychotherapy (Wake, 2008). NLP consists of a methodology, tools, and techniques that are derived from systems theory, family therapy, learning theory, linguistics, and transformational grammar. More recently, evidence from neuroscience of how the brain works is now supporting what for years have only been the assumptions and observations of NLP—that language affects neurology and that both function together in a systematic fashion. Hall suggests that:

> Most of the techniques, if viewed as expressions of implicit models of human behavior and change, point in different directions. The model underlying anchoring is different from the model underlying parts which is different from the model underlying strategies … that we accommodate all these disparate models of human behavior and change, and can utilize them all in any one intervention, proposes the character of NLP as an "open theoretical system."
>
> (2001, p.15)

Tosey and Mathison (2009, p.384) concur that NLP is "certainly eclectic," that it "could be regarded as a trans-disciplinary knowledge" and that "there seems to be no evidence that writers on NLP aspire to make it a formal theory at all". We propose that now is the time to take a meta-perspective to the source literature for NLP and discover if there is a unifying structure that can bring together the processes under a new model of therapy (Tosey and Mathison, 2009; Bateson, 1972).

Einstein is famously quoted as having said "No problem can be solved from the same level of consciousness that created it". The emerging model of NLP will allow us to stand above and apart from the disparate techniques and our current understanding of how they work. We will then begin to see emerging patterns that come together in the form of a coherent picture of what NLP is and how it does what it does.

A number of NLP treatment protocols can be researched in accordance with the standard methods of randomized controlled trial (RCT) protocols, (Foa et al., 2000; Cuijpers et al., 2008a; Cuijpers et al., 2008b). These NLP protocols will provide measurable clinical results that exceed the clinical performance of other clinical treatment protocols applied to the same target variables. It is hoped that those results will generate sufficient professional and academic interest in NLP to encourage scientific research that will honor the constructivist position of NLP. While NLP has historically described itself as a "modeling process" unrelated to science, measured proof of the "model" is prescribed as the last step in "scientific modeling."

In that light, current research in NLP focused on NLP treatment protocols which produce consistent FMRI measures of changes in the amygdala and other neural structures for pre- and post-measures of veterans diagnosed with PTSD. These were accompanied by subjective reports of the cessation of associated nightmares, flashbacks, and hyper-vigilance symptoms. Together they will be the beginning of serious clinical research interest in NLP. Science properly done measures what "works" rather than what can be easily measured. Some of the components of NLP can be tested both subjectively and more objectively through physiological and psychometric tests and behavioral measurements.

Developing NLP research

We propose an epistemological perspective on the development of NLP research that uses the systemic patterns of perceiving, thinking, and learning as they are portrayed by Bateson (1972). NLP has developed to the point where there are some elements that are sufficiently robust that they can be delivered as standardized protocols and subjected to objective testing.

Tosey and Mathison (2009) posit three scenarios for the future of NLP: entropy with recycling of old and out-dated material; seeds of its own destruction, with greater and greater diversity of opinion in the field (this is already happening with the emergence of diverse standards for training and certification and the groups that uphold them); and renaissance through the development of research, evidencing efficacy, and most likely the development of a new or advancing model of therapy.

In Table 8.2 we present Bateson's levels and their relationship to NLP theory and practice at present.

We would suggest that NLP as a clinical application is experiencing a finely balanced tension at level III learning, with the tension occurring between renaissance and an emerging model of therapy. As researchers start to investigate whether or not NLP actually produces the predicted results, this in itself creates the risk that the field, as it is currently constituted, will cease to exist.

We propose, therefore, that the NLP research community develop a series of clinical protocols that can be researched in the RCT format. We recognize and appreciate our earlier concerns about the validity and biases in RCTs. We therefore propose that simultaneous work continue to be encouraged through the continued development of epistemological and phenomenological methodologies of understanding. We would advocate moving forward with both qualitative and quantitative strategies.

Table 8.2 Bateson's levels and their relationship to NLP theory and practice

Bateson's level	Description	Status of NLP
Level 0	Specificity of response with no judgment of right or wrong.	The original modeling work of Bandler and Grinder. This is "how" Satir, Perls, and Erickson communicate.
Level I	Changing the specificity of response to model out what works and what does not.	The testing of processes that appeared to work, and dropping the idiosyncratic for the elements that appeared to make a difference. This then becomes the "standard" of training offered to all.
Level II	Adapting and changing the processes from level I. Replicating the behaviors and transferring them to other contexts.	The transfer of the original therapeutic skill set into other contexts—sales, education, business, etc.
Level III	Changing the processes of level II such that each one is tested as a set or methodology rather than a method. Those that work are replicated and utilized further, those that don't are dropped or tested in other contexts.	Some of the research being conducted by Churches and West-Burnham (2009) in education; and Stipancic et al. (2010) in therapy has moved NLP to level III learning.
Level IV	Is changed in level III and defies linguistic representation, resulting in evolutionary change.	This has not been attempted before within the NLP community. Where it has occurred in other therapeutic communities, it has often resulted in fragmentation and splitting away from the original, which has resulted in new developments. This may be the process that enabled the development of new and adapted forms of therapy as Klein, Jung, and Adler moved away from the original ideas of Freud.

Part III
Towards the future

9 Certification and training

Lisa Wake, Frank S. Bourke, Peter Schütz, Richard M. Gray

Training is the foundation upon which any profession stands. Professional boards have typically set standards for law, medicine, nursing, social work, and psychotherapy. Crucially, training and the resultant license or certification to practice includes some level of competence testing, supervised internship and various degrees of specialization. All of these standards are set by professional boards and national or international government organizations to ensure a certain base level of knowledge, practice, competence, and ethical standards.

NLP training varies in its compliance to these standards, from professional standards matching those noted as found in Europe, to for-profit certifications on a par with mail-order ordinations that impart few skills, little knowledge, and minimal ethical oversight.

The existence of a recognized and standardized body of knowledge and praxis, professional oversight organizations, and a procedure for licensure and quality assurance are essential to the establishment of meaningful training standards. This book represents a significant effort to provide the first, a body of knowledge that conforms to and meets the criteria for evidence-based practice. The problem of this chapter, however, is to help define the course of NLP in providing standards for training and practice, the identification of pathways to professional oversight, and how we can create these standards in an atmosphere that will satisfy the needs of professional practice. It also seeks to protect ethical practitioners who have invested a great deal of time and energy in developing their businesses, practices, and training organizations.

As any internet search will show, there are over one million search results on *NLP Training* alone. Many of these programs are direct replicas of the very early training in NLP from the late 1970s and do not reflect the significant advances that have occurred in applied psychology, neuroscience, cognitive linguistics, and human relationships. NLP trainings range from certification as a purchasable distance learning commodity on websites such as eBay (2011), short practitioner programs of four or five days' length, accelerated programs that use DVDs as learning support materials, programs that occur over several months to one year, with full accreditation as an NLP psychotherapist with trainings in the UK and Europe involving more than four years of study, clinical practice, personal therapy, and supervision. Each of these programs leads to a loosely recognized industry certification as *Practitioner of NLP*, yet there is considerable difference in the quality, length, depth, and competency standards across the trainings. It should be noted that there is currently no regulation of non-clinical NLP based training. Some clinical practitioners, however, are recognized by national and international bodies that attempt some form of ethical framework for practice.

Status of NLP training

At the time of publication, NLP has little recognition, validation, or accreditation by bodies outside of the field of NLP. There are some programs available as part of a higher education framework within Europe.

Across the UK there are MA and MSc coaching, psychology, psychotherapy, and counselling programs that include NLP within the course content and learning outcomes. The world's first Masters degree in NLP was started at Portsmouth University by Sally Vanson. This has more recently moved to the University of Derby and is being offered as a Masters in applied coaching. Across Europe there are a significant number of coaching, counselling, mediation, and sports psychology degrees at undergraduate and postgraduate levels that incorporate NLP as a significant component. It is now also possible to earn PhDs researching NLP within the UK university system. Other programs are recognized by the Institute of Leadership and Management (www.i-l-m.com) at both Level 5 and Level 7 accreditation, which equates with undergraduate and postgraduate levels of study. In the wider context of Europe there are some NLP psychotherapy programs, but at publication there appear to be no degree programs that include NLP within the course content or as the primary focus of study.

The US university system is somewhat different in that there are some clearly private universities that have an interest in awarding degrees in NLP. Most of these are owned and operated by training companies with a vested interest in seeing NLP offered from a "University." None of them are accredited by nationally recognized accrediting organizations. In searching higher education degrees that are offered by state-accredited universities, there appear to be no degree programs that have a substantial component of NLP included in any of the degrees awarded. At a wider level within the US higher education system, there are two programs or activities that are affiliated to one or more universities. The NLP University, www.nlpu.com, has been based at a University of California Campus since 1991. This is a private enterprise and although based at the University, does not have any direct affiliation to the academic process of the University and does not share their academic credentials. NLPU provides a community focus whereby academics and serious students of NLP can connect and pursue academic discourse in a supportive educational environment. The second project that is gaining increasing academic and serious scientific support is the NLP Research and Recognition Project (NLP RandR), www.nlprandr.org. The project is primarily focused on developing and communicating research into the basic scientific validity of NLP and allied techniques. NLP RandR is closely linked to the Institute for Advanced Studies of Health (www.nlpiash.org). At present, it is neither a training nor a certification organization.

Continuing the global perspective, Linder Pelz (2010) reports on NLP programs in Australia that meet the government's competency based training standards at the postgraduate level.

Within each country there are some umbrella bodies for the recognition and accreditation of trainings, trainers, and practitioners. These vary considerably in levels of credibility, independence from training bodies or trainers, competencies required, and codes of conduct and ethics. The most rigorous associations are those linked to psychotherapy with some, such as The European Association for Neurolinguistic Psychotherapy (EANLPt), being legally recognized for the training of statutorily registered psychotherapists (www.eanlpt.org).

The UK has two totally independent umbrella bodies; one for generic NLP, the Association for NLP (ANLP), and one for NLPt (neurolinguistic psychotherapy), the Neurolinguistic Psychotherapy and Counselling Association (NLPtCA). ANLP is a community interest company and has an international focus in providing an impartial and independent voice for NLP. It supports the development and informal monitoring of standards, provides a robust and independent complaints process and supports research on NLP techniques and practice through its publications. NLPtCA is a not-for-profit company that is also a registered accrediting member organization of UKCP (UK Council for Psychotherapy). It provides a portfolio accreditation pathway for NLP psychotherapists and oversees codes of conduct and ethics for the profession as well as overseeing complaints and concerns related to the professional conduct of members.

There is only one independent umbrella body for Europe that is not attached to any NLP training school, this is EANLPt (European Association for Neurolinguistic Psychotherapy). EANLPt is a Europe-wide accrediting organization for NLPt within the European Association for Psychotherapy. At the time of publication the following European countries had member organizations or working groups within EANLPt: Germany, England, France ×2, Switzerland, Austria, Finland, Italy, Ireland, Hungary, Poland, Croatia ×2, Belgium, Latvia, Greece, Ukraine, Slovenia, Russia, Serbia, Romania, and Ukraine.

There are other associations across Europe, India, Asia, and North America, however, each of these is directly linked to training companies and therefore are not considered to be providing independent assessments of training and certification standards. Most do have a code of ethics and conduct. Some Australian trainings are extensive, 40 contact days and

33 hours of training accredited nationally through state bodies and are government recognized.

There is a multiplicity of NLP certification trainings across the globe, many of which award the title "NLP practitioner." As a result, if you meet people who describe themselves as NLP practitioners or trainers, it is not easy to discern what those titles represent in terms of competence, skills, and attitude.

NLP focuses on the structure of subjective experience, its change and development. It also focuses on meaning, thoughts, feelings, social roles, and—quite frequently—spiritual understandings. From the perspective of Bateson's (1972) levels of learning, NLP training partly focuses on knowledge, skills, and procedures (mainly Learning I), and partly on values, beliefs, and deep personal change work (learning II and III). There is, at present, no standardized criterion to determine whether any training will provide the rote formulaic applications of Level I learning, or the more sophisticated, professional-level meta-analytical applications consistent with Bateson's higher levels of learning.

This focus is then reflected across the entirety of NLP programs on offer. Some NLP courses and books promise instant healing and change procedures. Some seek these courses as "therapy in disguise". The field may attract both the power hungry and needy and others with underlying psychopathologies. Across a wider context, and beyond the "pyramid selling" style of some programs, many professionals, including those within the vocational caring professions, such as nursing, physiotherapy, social work, counselling, and psychotherapy, take up NLP as professional training that enhances their coaching, consulting, counselling, and therapy work.

As has already been noted, there are some courses that are offered within accredited state education systems for coaching, psychotherapy, or counselling licenses. These programs clearly identify their affiliation and accrediting bodies. They are always subject to external verification and assessment procedures and operate under clear codes of conduct and ethical standards. In some European countries they are under government supervision.

In the wider world of available programs, the following rule of thumb generally applies: the shorter the program, the more you pay per day, and the less professional the training. In such courses, there is also an increasing emphasis on "accelerated learning"—as both an argument for shorter courses versus longer courses. These are often sold as a marketing ploy with little or no objective validation of their efficacy. Despite the claims of such programs, NLP involves the acquisition of specific skills and skill-sets that take time to master and that can be objectively evaluated after training. Some well-meaning but naive or dishonest trainers do not distinguish between beliefs about the capacity to acquire the skills and the skills themselves; this may be a symptom of poor training, wishful thinking, or outright falsehood.

We accept that it is possible to gain personal benefit from any form of personal development training, including NLP, and to gain deep and valid experience from these processes. One of the key outcomes in NLP culture is to bring out the best in everyone and to emphasize the good features and the good intentions of behavior. Unfortunately, this philosophical position tends to discourage a more traditional objective standard of evaluation and assessment that focuses on competence in different types of training, as is common practise in other educational settings. In many countries, this has led to NLP's classification with cults like scientology, and its labelling in unfavorable political ways. More importantly, the failure to create and enforce training, performance and ethical standards and a similar failure to pace the criteria of the established scientific community, has led to NLP's inability to obtain respect for its real and potential contributions to the areas of therapy, coaching and personal development.

The requirements to reach "industry standard" trainer status in the NLP community as compared with that required of psychologists, psychotherapists, psychiatrists, and for some countries, coaches and certified management consultants, are often quick, shoddy, and without prior qualification. For some training schools, practitioner-level status and an installed belief that the practitioner can work with clinical conditions such as phobias, anxiety or more complex disorders such as PTSD and OCD is offered after less than a week's training. This inevitably creates a difficult public image for NLP. Compare this to the requirements of accredited NLPt therapists who complete over 1500 hours of training for a minimum four-year period. Such trainings often require frequent clinical supervision with a high supervision to client ratio and receive extensive personal therapy, paralleling other recognized and respected professions. However, as most of their work is pursued in a quiet professional manner, it also not so well known and has little impact on the public image of NLP.

One possible typology of NLP Institutes, from a socio-anthropological perspective, resembles the four types in Francis Bacon's (1887) typology of idols.

1 Fragmented esoteric NLP

In such institutes, the length of training varies, and may include dancing, singing, and a spiritual-animistic approach in the foreground. Semi-reflective quasi-spiritual work on self-esteem is given a much higher emphasis than methodology, solid psychological grounding, and behavioural testing. Occasionally, science-phobic notions are communicated as acceptable and realistic belief structures. The practical aim is a feel good experience and the installation of specific feelings of self-esteem and personal empowerment.

2 Power guru clubbings NLP

These are rather short courses led by a charismatic figure. The leaders display high levels of alpha characteristics. Trainings include large to very large groups. They are oriented towards young, power-seeking males and are characterized by short-term empowerment and enthusiasm. Such groups are often targeted to sales-persons. Scientific quotes taken out of context are used to legitimize otherwise untenable beliefs, and the groups are often led to levels of exuberance and enthusiasm, not supported by the tools supplied (Hooper, 2010).

3 Visionary spiritual dogmatic NLP

These providers usually block-out courses over a month, using well-structured and sound material, and a very positive attitude. While they are basically methodical, much of their emphasis is placed on relationship values and structured spirituality as a basis for growth.

4 Scientific pragmatic organized NLP

These include courses over a longer time frame of 8–12 months and providing 30–37 actual contact days. They are oriented to both personality development and evidence-based methodological competence within a framework of well-defined values and a strong emphasis on state of the art didactic tools (video). They generally include *in vivo* competence assessment. They are well connected to, or are accredited by traditional government and educational systems.

The main phenomenology of NLP practitioner courses

The following typologies of training standards are ideal types which of course are rare in their pure form but exemplify the general patterns.

Although beyond the scope of this chapter, correspondence courses are also offered as NLP trainings. On completion of such trainings you can gain membership in organizations such as The Society for Holistic Therapists and Coaches (e.g. http://www.opencollege.info/nlpcourse.html, accessed online January 14, 2012), or a NCFE Level 4 award which is the equivalent to an undergraduate qualification (http://www.stonebridge.uk.com/course/neuro-linguistic-programming-advanced, accessed online January 14, 2012). Despite the state-level recognition, such courses provide little in the way of hands-on application of the materials or any form of competency assessment.

- 0.3 days—Certified *mail order* NLP practitioner. A few manuals, tapes, sometimes a day of in person training for "certification."

- Standard *Speed* 5–7 days. These often include up to 300 participants, large group trances, rock music, and a motivational business emphasis. Such courses often emphasize the installation of beliefs rather than practical instruction.
- Standard *Quick* 130 hours (16–18 days). These take place in one or two blocks, often including trainers and assistants with little or no personal experience in coaching or therapy.
- Standard *Commercial* 180 hours, 24–27 days stretched over more than nine months. Trainers in such courses often have a variety of qualifications.
- Special form: *Standard or Commercial block* (holiday camps in the US and Europe). These trainings often present high quality didactics with well-experienced trainers. This level of training is provided with considerable variations in course design. Despite their high teaching standards and trainer expertise, these trainings are rarely credible according to standard educational criteria. Such programs frequently produce short-term psychological highs with little follow-up and reinforcement possibilities. They include medium to large groups. They are often interesting due to their multi-national presence and clients, multiple languages, and group dynamics.
- Standard *Solid* 200–250 hours (27–34 days), training often lasting longer than nine months with professional supervision, peer groups that are established and monitored by the training provider. High demands are placed on trainers' education and their supervision. Such programs regularly use three or four trainers. Emphasis is placed on personal development.
- Standard *Professional* 240–280 hours (35–40 days). These trainings include admission interviews to filter out students with sociopathic or psychoses and personality disorders. They generally include nine months training, professional supervision, structured pre-assessment outcome definitions, client competence video, or *in vivo* assessments as mandatory for certification. There is real-client testing, maximum group sizes of 25 or less, and terminal assessments of four days. Trainers are generally required to have many years' education before entering training plus sufficient personal experience and experience in the supervision of trainers, and accreditation in personal change work. Similar trainings use three or more master trainers, who also are fully accredited mediators, qualified psychotherapists, MDs or teaching counsellors.

Current standards of training

Taking into account the comments included from the European perspective above, Table 9.1 depicts the standards of training as they are practiced across the spectrum of NLP training.

Table 9.1 Current standards of training

Standard	EANLPt/EAP	UKCP	UKCP NLPt member organization	Non-accelerated practitioner training	Accelerated practitioner (CDs used)	Fast-track practitioner
Entry requirement	Postgraduate	Postgraduate	Postgraduate	No requirement	No requirement	No requirement
	Personal qualities	Personal qualities	Reference	No requirement	No requirement	No requirement
	Experience of working with people	Required	CV	No requirement	No requirement	No requirement
Minimum curriculum	Model of the person in mind	Model of the person in mind	• NLPt • TA attachment	• NLP definition • NLP presuppositions	• NLP definition • NLP Presuppositions	All conducted in trance
	Model of gendered and culturally influenced human development	Model of gendered and culturally influenced human development	• NLPt • TA • Attachment • Ericksonian	• Rapport • Outcomes • Sensory Acuity • Submodalities • Strategies • Anchoring	• Rapport • Outcomes • Sensory Acuity • Submodalities • Strategies • Anchoring	Content vague
	Model of human change	Model of human change	• NLPt • Prochaska and DiClemente	• Belief change processes • Emotional clearing processes	• Belief change processes • Emotional clearing processes	

Standard	EANLPt/EAP	UKCP	UKCP NLPt member organization	Non-accelerated practitioner training	Accelerated practitioner (CDs used)	Fast-track practitioner
Minimum curriculum	Clinical concepts linking theory to practice	Clinical concepts linking theory to practice	• NLPt • TA attachment • Ericksonian self-relations psychodynamic	No clinical concepts covered	No clinical concepts covered	No clinical concepts covered
	Extensive literature	Extensive literature	Students have to cover at least 3 other approaches as well as NLPt	No literature covered as essential reading	No literature covered as essential reading	No literature covered as essential reading
	Research methodology	Research methodology	3-day module	None	None	None
	Psychopathology	Psychopathology	2-day module plus taught at pract and MP levels	None	None	None
	Sexuality	Required	2-day module	None	None	None
	Ethics	Required	Ongoing throughout the 4-year training	Code of conduct and ethics from the umbrella body, if registered with one	Code of conduct and ethics from the umbrella body, if registered with one	Code of conduct and ethics from the umbrella body, if registered with one
	Social science	Required	On going throughout the 4-year training	None	None	None

Continued

Table 9.1 Continued

Standard	EANLPt/EAP	UKCP	UKCP NLPt member organization	Non-accelerated practitioner training	Accelerated practitioner (CDs used)	Fast-track practitioner
Training hours	3,200 which includes psychotherapy, client work, and supervision	Minimum 900	921	Minimum 130	Minimum 35 hours face-to-face	3–5 days
Length of time	7 years. First 3 years in a related degree, last 4 years specific to psychotherapy	4 years	4 years	4–9 months	5–9 days	3–5 days
Supervised Practice	Ratio of 1:5	Ratio of 1:6	Ratio of 1:6	None	None	None
Client contact hours	Minimum 600 hours	Minimum 450	Minimum 450, at least one client more than 20 hours	None	None	None
Personal development	380 hours of which minimum 80 hours must be personal therapy	Ongoing	250 hours of which 48 must be personal therapy	None	None	None
Range of psychotherapies and counselling	Range	Range	Minimum 4 approaches covered	None	None	None

Standard	EANLPt/EAP	UKCP	UKCP NLPt member organization	Non-accelerated practitioner training	Accelerated practitioner (CDs used)	Fast-track practitioner
Mental Health Placement	Required	Required	50 hours	None	None	None
Dissertation	Required, no set word count	Required, no set word count	15,000 words research project or extended case study and literature review	None	None	None

The level of diversity in training and certification criteria (shown in Table 9.1) makes it difficult for NLP to take its place alongside other recognized professional disciplines. In order to do so, it must not only standardize its training methods and certification criteria, but it must also become responsive to and reflective of current best practises. Over the past few years, with the increasing level of interest in the serious academic discourse that is occurring through the International NLP Research Conference, and postgraduate and doctorate level students critically investigating NLP, we are proposing an evidence-based stance.

Evidence-based clinical practice

For NLP to be taken seriously, we recommend that it conduct clear empirical studies within the context of the "hour glass" approach to psychotherapy and psychology research (Salkovskis, 1995). Paralleled with this is the need to pace the clinical psychology world in its development of training standards, ethics and practise.

Effective mental health care is almost exclusively determined by the "gold standard" randomized control trial. Before considering what this means for the world of psychological therapies, it is worth reflecting on the definition of evidence based medicine (EBM) as well as some of the debates about vested interests. Sackett et al. (1996) define evidence-based medicine as

> the conscientious, explicit, and judicious use of current best evidence in making decisions about the care of individual patients. The practice of evidence based medicine means integrating individual clinical expertise with the best available external clinical evidence from systematic research.
>
> (p.71)

The American Psychological Association defines evidence-based practice in psychology as "the integration of the best available research with clinical expertise in the context of patient characteristics, culture, and preferences" (APA, 2005). The Centre for Evidence Based Medicine at the University of Oxford defines the five steps of evidence-based practice as they were first described in 1992 (www.cebm.net):

- Asking focused questions: translation of uncertainty to an answerable question.
- Finding the evidence: systematic retrieval of best evidence available.
- Critical appraisal: testing evidence for validity, clinical relevance, and applicability.
- Making a decision: application of results in practice.
- Evaluating performance: auditing evidence-based decisions.

Although there appears to be comparability across the field of health care for the definition of EBM, there are some recent challenges to the impartiality of those that determine what constitutes evidence based medicine. Moynihan (2011) in the *British Medical Journal* (BMJ) suggested that panels which evaluate definitions and EBM are fraught with conflicts of interest. He refers to the DSM-IV, where

> 56 percent of panel members had financial ties to drug companies, although for some panels including that for mood disorders, the figures was 100 percent ... an analysis of the forthcoming fifth edition found that of those panel members who'd made disclosure statements, exactly 56 percent had financial relationships with pharmaceutical companies ... it was not just financial ties that were important, but intellectual conflicts too, where researchers pushed for greater recognition of their own pet conditions.
>
> (p.2548)

In an attempt to get beyond this problem, Norcross et al. (2006) conducted a Delphi poll using a panel of experts to determine which psychological treatments had been discredited. Ninety three percent of the panel members were psychologists who, it could be said, had a vested interest in discrediting treatments that were not recognized by the APA. Additional points that are highlighted by the authors are that only 20.5 percent were in clinical practice and of these 44 percent practiced cognitive or behavioral approaches. It is perhaps not surprising that cognitive and behavioral therapies are the only therapies suitable for the protocol requirements of an RCT, which is required for funding of the treatment. EMDR, which was introduced by Francine Shapiro and developed by her following her work with one of the co-founders of NLP who first described the use of eye patterns to effect "cognitive emotional" understanding, was listed by the Delphi poll as possibly discredited. EMDR now has six meta-analyses and 26 randomized studies that attest to its efficacy, and it is listed as a treatment of choice by the National Institute for Clinical Excellence (NICE) as an established treatment for PTSD.

EBM (evidence-based medicine) and psychological therapies

Stiles et al. (2006) proposed that all psychotherapy treatments will have equivalent outcomes despite the non-equivalent theories and techniques. Their study compared cognitive behavioral, person centred, and psychodynamic therapies and found that all therapies achieved similar outcomes, summarizing that it is the therapist, not the therapy that is more likely to determine outcome. Seligman's study (1995) gathered self-report data from 2,900 therapy clients and showed that psychotherapy works, yet there is no link between problem type and which therapy helped. Clients who are able to make active choices about the therapy tend to do better, however, this element of choice and control does not work in clinical trials. This conclusion is supported by Hubble et al. (1999) and Beyebach et al. (1996, 1997).

When it comes to evidencing the process of therapy by a therapist, which is thought to be the most accurate predictor of outcome, the field of psychotherapy does not lend itself to effective research and statistical measurement. Psychotherapy and many of the psychological approaches to change are based within the field of social science, which often results in new procedures or techniques arising from practice rather than through empirical research (McLeod, 2001).

This then places emphasis on ensuring that the training of therapists, and particularly those using NLP as a change tool, needs to include practice-based evidence and a set of training standards and assessment tools that facilitate the production of robust, ethical and rounded practitioners of the methodology.

Recommendations for training

- In the context of developing NLP further, particularly as an applied psychology and a grounded psychotherapy modality we appreciate that the journey forward from this point presents a number of challenges that make its final configuration "a work in progress." A majority of training programs in NLP have limited commonality in training, certification standards, or criteria with each other or with other disciplines.
- There is a high level of competence amongst some existing NLP practitioners that would nevertheless not meet the most robust training standards as they are laid out for psychotherapy practice in Europe and the UK.
- There is a financial challenge for the field in that many people are making a lot of money from the "get rich quick" attitude that exists in some parts of the NLP world.
- There is considerable success in the application of NLP in business, coaching, and sports contexts. This needs to be retained while at the same time providing differentiation between this career path and those wishing to utilize the methodology in clinical practice.
- There is some high-quality clinical work among some non-clinical practitioners. How do these practitioners become part of an integrated clinical field?
- The few umbrella bodies that exist are dependent on the fees paid by their members, which keeps the field operating at a base line standard that is determined by sales, popularity and other considerations but not by best practices.
- The typical "profile" of the standard NLP practitioner does not lend itself to the academic rigour required to pace the scientific community.
- Funding to support research into the efficacy and effectiveness of NLP will only be gained if there is rigorous clinical application by practitioners trained and qualified to work within those clinical protocols.

How, if, and when these challenges will be overcome and what the resultant training and certification developments would, or should, look like in final form is impossible to predict at this time. In addition to longstanding certification development programs in Europe and in the UK, as detailed previously, the NLP Research and Recognition Project, working with experts in the field and university faculties from the US and Europe, has committed to designing a modular approach to training that meets international requirements for the development and delivery of standardized individual clinical treatment protocols at the outset. It has further committed to the development of a university accredited Masters Degree in NLP clinical skills as time goes on. This modular approach will consist of step-by-step competency based, behaviorally evaluated, training certifications, of NLP process work and change techniques which would lend themselves to a professionally recognized toolbox of certified skills organized and researched for clinical effectiveness. The first step is in progress within a 2012 Department of Defense Contract to research both the clinical efficacy of the PTSD treatment protocol, Reconsolidation of Traumatic Memories (RTM), and its "manualized" training and certification materials. That "manualized" training and certification in RTM administration, on completion, will also be offered with professional continuing education credits for licensed psychiatrists, psychologists, social workers, and counsellors at certified university and institute locations. As more clinically effective NLP protocols, for additional clinical areas such as phobia and anxiety disorders, are brought through the steps to certification as evidence-based medicine, the format of the accompanying training and certification materials will become clearer and may provide more detailed future training and certification formats. Networking those developments with existing quality training and certification programs along with their differing curriculum materials and nationally recognized formats, is at the moment an obvious challenge. It will become an obvious fundable need, if and when the NLP clinical protocol research trials, which have begun, are completed and the results reflect their well-documented clinical efficacy.

10 Future directions

Frank S. Bourke, Richard M. Gray, Lisa Wake

In the 35 years that have elapsed since the founding of NLP, the field has matured significantly and now includes a large group of practitioners and trainers who are inspired by the commonalties between mainline science and the practical insights of NLP. These same practitioners and trainers have the training and sophistication to design, develop, and execute randomized controlled treatment studies.

This is not to say that this is new. Although they resisted a program of formal scientific investigation into the efficacy of NLP, Bandler and Grinder based many of their insights on the best science of the day. Andreas and Andreas, Dilts, Gordon, Hall, Hallbom and Hallbom, and Bolstad, have made it their business to link NLP with the findings of psychology, physiology, and neuroscience. Charvet, Merlevede, and the LAB Profile community have worked hard to validate the original insights of Leslie Cameron Lebow in the meta-programs, one of the most well-documented patterns in all of NLP. Wake and Gawler-Wright have taken a contemporary approach in their NLPt writings, providing a theoretical basis for human development and the notion of a co-created client/therapist relationship in psychotherapy.

Currently, the NLP Research and Recognition Project (RandR) is working to build bridges between NLP, the armed forces, and the scientific establishment in order to study and test the efficacy of the RTM model for the treatment of post-traumatic stress disorder (PTSD) and phobias. As a result of their efforts, NLP RandR has applied for two government contracts and submitted a research grant proposal in conjunction with Ohio University for just such an A-level study. Further, the NLP community across Europe and the UK has developed certification and training programs and standards that are recognized by mainline psychotherapy organizations. They have also established a regular NLP Research Conference and a peer-reviewed research journal.

These are exciting times. Information multiplies at untold rates, increasing at such a pace that no one person can master any one field. For us, in the field of NLP, it provides the opportunity to be not only artful practitioners of the skills provided by NLP, but to become collectors and integrators of scientific information so that we can continue to build and test scientifically informed behavioral interventions that work, and work well. Access to almost unlimited amounts of information means that we can build theoretical and analytical structures that integrate neurological, perceptual cognitive, behavioral, and subjective levels of information into coherent wholes that can open dialogue with academic and scientific psychology and allow the design of techniques that will withstand the most rigorous randomized control testing (RCT). Moreover, by taking advantage of our capacity to access this level of information, by working to carefully point out the correspondences, by nurturing the links between standard research and the structure of subjective experience, we can begin to invite researchers to test our patterns and hypotheses, according to our definitions, which they must now acknowledge and respect. Having matched their map of the world in our explanatory rigor, they must listen when we tell them that there is no Primary Representational System (PRS) and NLP does not stand or fall on this or that premise. As we can now speak the common language of science, we need no longer speak past each other (Kuhn, 1962) but can work together to solve the problems of psychic pain and human limitations.

The NLP research already discussed in the previous chapters provides testable treatments for PTSD, phobias, various levels of depression, substance abuse, and anxiety. It sets forth structured interventions that can inform the practice of motivational interviewing and motivational enhancement therapy (Gray, 2011d). Insights from NLP have already been used to good effect in the teaching of the spelling strategy now being employed internationally (Malloy, 1995). We note also that cognitive behavior modification techniques such as the joystick technique (Wiers et al., 2011) closely model the NLP swish pattern. Likewise, the clinical rapport skills developed in the NLP materials need to follow across the recent discovery of mirror neurons and their application to the treatment of children with Asperger's syndrome where the combination would be of great clinical value as social skill training. Moreover, those same techniques could help adolescents with conduct disorders to form more positive attachment relationships.

Needless to say this has not yet happened, but this book is a glimmer in earnest of the promise that NLP holds forth to its practitioners and its trainers and to the world of mainline science that we are working in this direction. As we move from a few B- and C-level studies, to a series of well-grounded A-level researches, others who carry the same care for understanding human behavior and ending human suffering will join us to test and, presumably, confirm what these techniques can do.

Future recommendations

The primary goal and first future recommendation of the authors of this book is to motivate rigorous future research of NLP clinical treatment protocols on DSM-IV-R diagnoses and symptoms. We believe that the related

NLP protocols presented in the previous chapters of this book, starting with phobias and PTSD, when researched in "gold standard" RCT fashion, will exceed the clinical performance of evidence-based clinical treatment protocols for the same DSM-IV-R diagnoses and clinical symptoms. We believe this conclusion is sufficiently supported by clinical need, research evidence, and the explanations of the NLP processes that were provided in the previous chapters to warrant the time, money, and effort necessary to continue the research/publication sequence through to the classification of a number of those protocols as evidentiary medicine. We hope that the initial A-level research study results from PTSD, phobias, and NLP practitioner outcome studies will awaken and validate interest in researching additional NLP clinical protocols; fund client centered designs more appropriate to NLP processes than RCT; and make clinically effective training certification in the evidence based NLP materials available both for continuing professional clinical education and a clinical specialization certification in NLP practice.

Initial specific research recommendations

Phobias

Future research on the NLP approach to the treatment of specific phobias should include the VK/D-RTM model, collapsing anchors, and a modified systematic desensitization model. Using the standardized versions of the three techniques as presented with hypothetical neurological and behavioral models, several testable hypotheses for the root mechanisms need to be studied with A-level research designs based on the outlines that were also included in the chapter.

Post-traumatic stress disorder (PTSD)

PTSD research should be conducted using the standardized Reconsolidation of Traumatic Memories Protocol (RTM). Given the neurological support offered by the recent research into the reconsolidation mechanism, the Gray and Liotta article in *Traumatology* and clinical evidence presented in Chapter 2, large-scale, A-level trials of this protocol are warranted. Such trials are also in great clinical need, given the large number of returning veterans afflicted by PTSD and the cost-effective nature of the current clinical findings. These studies should follow the recommendations for well-controlled studies set forth by the International Society for Traumatic Stress Studies (Foa et al., 2000) and outlined in the research recommendations in Chapter 2.

NLP psychotherapy

Chapter 9 clearly explains that there are huge differences in the quality and quantity of NLP training certifications around the world. However, as evidenced by studies in Chapter 4 (Stipancic et al., 2010), a number of NLP organizations have produced sufficiently skilled and motivated NLP practitioners to begin measuring their clinical abilities to treat a number of clinical areas. These studies range from validation of NLP as a psychotherapy to the effectiveness of NLP trained practitioners to clinically improve DSM-IV-R diagnostic categories and symptoms. Research in a number of these areas have shown significant C- and B-level results and, while the complexity and cost of these studies makes them the most difficult to design and complete, they should be continued to A-level research.

The Stipancic et al. (2010) study of the effects of NLPt on psychological difficulties and quality of life is a good example of an RCT Clinical Outcome B-level study done by NLPt certified practitioners. With improvements in design, including the addition of a control group, this study could serve as an exemplar for A-level, gold-standard research.

When reviewed in conjunction with the previous European NLPt Genser-Medlitsch and Schutz (1997, 2004) paper, it provides a clear example of sufficiently high-level training and organizational capability to warrant support for next generation, RCT, A-level research. There are many quality NLP training institutes in the United States, New Zealand, Australia, and the UK, whose certified practitioners should be organized to emulate this format, including comparisons made with established, evidenced-based techniques such as cognitive behavioral therapy (CBT) using gold-level research for outcome study designs.

While methodologically very different, studies of the clinical effectiveness of certified NLP practitioners should also be conducted using individual client outcome scales pioneered in the US by Scott Miller (Miller et al., The Outcome Rating Scale, *Journal of Brief Therapy*, 2003) and exemplified in the UK by CORE methodology. These short-outcome surveys are being used by therapists across the UK and the US in an attempt to gain comparative data on and benchmark clinical mental health services. In the UK, Weaver (2009) conducted a pilot study using the CORE Systems Research Tool to assess the effectiveness of neurolinguistic psychotherapy with clients in private practice. While the study was small and of pilot quality, it exemplifies an effective, affordable tool that can be used to begin collecting evidence of NLP practitioners' performance. This data can then be compared to the growing collections of clinical performance data from other professional disciplines. Enlargement of the designs to include standardized behaviorally based problem lists as well as session and treatment outcome scales for clients is a recommended tool for NLP training organizations when collecting evidence of certified NLP practitioners clinical performance.

"Manualized" clinical certification programs of individual treatment protocols

Without effective training and certification for using the protocols being proposed here and specific efforts made to follow them through the rigorous process for establishing them as "evidentiary medicine," there would be little hope of the clinical promise shown here making its way into widespread clinical use. As was often repeated in the previous chapters, NLP protocols are by design always behaviorally tested to ensure that the desired changes have been successfully accomplished. Because of this, they readily lend themselves to "manualized" training formats (Beutler, 1999) and easily administered clinical protocols. But manualization is insufficient without the development of basic NLP standards of "sensory acuity." For example, if a clinical protocol begins with the instruction, "after the client has become relaxed," an NLP practitioner would not begin the next step in the protocol until they had validated the client's self-report by their own observations, including vocal rate and pitch, physical posture, eye movements, changes in facial symmetry, the width of the lips, changes in facial, neck, and shoulder tensions, the rate and locus of the breath, and visible changes in the pulse, to the effect that the client was genuinely relaxed. In order to achieve this level of acuity, the practitioner would have been through weeks of written descriptions, supervised group exercises, and interactive group practice. Finally, they would have undergone testing by a training or therapist supervisor and received their certification that the practitioner had sufficient sensory acuity to administer the clinical protocols as written. NLP protocols, as written, usually contain sufficient behavioral specificity to ensure that all the steps are administered correctly. It would be relatively easy to add in the behavioral details necessary to ensure that the practitioner understands and can successfully guide the client through the necessary steps and test that the procedure has been successful.

University accredited Masters Degree in NLP Clinical Technology

If NLP is to continue to exist and develop, it must provide evidence that it works in a professionally and academically acceptable fashion. To that end we have stressed the development of research on the PTSD and phobia protocols in conjunction with certified training programs for their administration.

Because of the standardization necessary to produce A-level, RCT research, some of the basic rules of NLP clinical operation must be broken. NLP is most importantly a client-centered individualized change in "process" which achieves its high, clinical efficacy based on those principles and appropriate application of the technology within those parameters. A great deal of NLP's clinical efficacy would be lost if it were to be considered and used as a collection of evidence-based protocols alone. Charles Faulkner, an accomplished NLP trainer and writer in the field observed about NLP's early days that it was

> important to note in hindsight ... that a thorough education in NLP involved much more than attending the scheduled trainings and obtaining any of the offered Institutes certifications. Actually mastering NLP involved assisting several times on the trainings one had attended, participating in numerous practice groups, modeling something, working on one's own difficulties and development, and receiving at least occasional guidance from someone who had already done all these things. These activities deepened certain kinds of experiences until there were specific additions in cognitive skills, from content to process, from content to context, from being situated in oneself to having multiple perspectives, and from causal modeling to systemic. Few managed the time, resources and dedication to complete this process but those who did appear to have achieved remarkable clinical competencies, which because of the nature of the clinical technology, can be easily researched and duplicated.
> (Bourke, personal communication, 2011)

This technology has been clinically researched and put into sophisticated, well-documented training programs in NLP institutes and clinical organizations in Europe, the US, the UK, New Zealand, and Australia. The best of those curricula and training programs need to be assembled to create a university accredited Masters Degree in NLP Clinical Technology in the US and throughout the world.

Networking NLP Expertise with Universities

Chapter 7 provides a new basis for dialogue between NLP practitioners, researchers, and the world of mainline science. As a number of the areas in the chapter highlight, basic elements of NLP practice—like the use of sub-modality changes to clinically improve negative emotions and harmful perceptions—have evidence parallels in mainline published research. The list continues. There are significant parallels between the NLP well-formedness conditions for outcomes and motivational research from mainline investigators. Prochaska's Strong Principle of Change provides new depth to the NLP focus on specifiable outcomes. Neuroscience has confirmed multiple sets of hierarchically ordered perceptual systems that confirm the structures observed by Chomsky and adopted by NLP. The structure and impact of NLP sub-modalities have been confirmed by many individual researchers. Cognitive linguistics continues to open new windows onto the world of metaphors pioneered by David Gordon, while embodied cognition daily reveals the parallels between the insights of NLP and mainline science. CBT has created detailed maps of the cycles of depression and anxiety that correspond to the self-referential patterns found in NLP-based behavioral analyses as NLP provides the techniques to alter and disarm those same structures.

Relatively recent publications in peer-reviewed journals have established a "new field" in psychology—cognitive bias. On close examination it is working on protocols and practices that have been taught and worked on in NLP circles for 30 years. The findings and clinical evidence from this area of psychology need to be integrated with the pre-existing insights from NLP. To do this, scientific dialogue needs to be opened between the two fields.

The fields of cognitive psychology and cognitive linguistics provide significant contributions to the common ground between NLP and academic research. Cognitive research into priming and the structure of perception has confirmed much of the NLP work on sub-modalities. The cognitive behavioral analysis of patterns of behavior as discussed in the TEAMS model (Mansell, 2007; Mansell et al., 2007; Searson et al., 2012) provides a level of analysis that is easily adaptable to NLP strategies for breaking the cycles of depression and bi-polar disorder.

NLP needs to network and dialogue with researchers working in all of these areas to more clearly define, validate, extend, and integrate the body of working knowledge that NLP has accumulated over the past 30 years of practice.

References

Adler, R. (1999) *Crowded Minds.* New Scientist. 164(2217), pp.26–31, December 18.
Aitken, J. R. and Benson, J. W. (1984) The use of relaxation/desensitization in treating anxiety associated with flying. *Aviat. Space Environ. Med.*, 55(3): 196–9.
Akirav, I. and Maroun, M. (2006) Ventromedial prefrontal cortex is obligatory for consolidation and reconsolidation of object recognition memory. *Cerebral Cortex*, 16(12), 1759–65.
Alberini, C. M. (2005) Mechanisms of memory stabilization: Are consolidation and reconsolidation similar or distinct processes? *Trends in Neurosciences*, 28(1), 51–6.
Aldridge, J. W. and Berridge, K. C. (1998) Coding of Serial Order by Neostriatal Neurons: A 'Natural Action' Approach to Movement Sequence. *The Journal of Neuroscience*, 18(7), 2777–87.
Alexander, B. L., Beyerstein, P. F., Hadaway, B. K. and Coambs, R. B. (1981) Effect of early and later colony housing on oral ingestion of morphine in rats. *Pharmacology, Biochemistry and Behavior*, 15: 571–6.
Allen, K. L. (1982) An investigation of the effectiveness of neurolinguistic nrogramming procedures in treating snake phobics. Dissertation Abstracts International 43(3), 861-B, University of Missouri at Kansas City.
Allen, J. P. (2003) *An overview of Beck's cognitive theory of depression in contemporary literature.* Rochester Institute of Technology. Available online: http://www.personalityresearch.org/papers/allen.html (accessed 4 August 2006).
Allen, W. (1982) Programming procedures in treating snake phobics. *Dissertation Abstracts International*, 43(3): 861.
Amaral, O. B., Osan, R., Roesler, R. and Tort A. B. (2008) A synaptic reinforcement-based model for transient amnesia following disruptions of memory consolidation and reconsolidation. *Hippocampus*, 18(6): 584–601.
American Psychiatric Association (APA) (1994) *Diagnostic and Statistical Manual of Mental Disorders.* 4th edn. Washington, DC: American Psychiatric Association.
American Psychological Association (2005) *Policy Statement on Evidence-Based Practice in Psychology.* Available online: http://www.apa.org/practice/resources/evidence/evidence-based-statement.pdf (accessed 1 August 2011).
American Psychiatric Association (APA) (2010) *DSM-5 Development.* Available online: http://www.dsm5.org.
Andreas, C. (1992) *Advanced Language Patterns.* Moab, UT: Real People Press.
Andreas, C. (2002) *The Core Transformation Story: How the process came to be; Acknowledgements and History.* Available online: http://www.coretransformation.org/ct_story.htm (accessed 30 July 2008).
Andreas, S. (2006a) 'Imaginal Disc NLP Group' Workshop presented at The Institute for the Advanced Study of Health (IASH), September, World Health Conference: Well Being and Integrity for Our Lives Our Work and Our Communities, San Francisco, CA.

Andreas, S. (2006b) *Six Blind Elephants* (2 vols) Boulder, CO: Real People Press.
Andreas, S. (2009) *Help with Negative Self Talk. Vol. 1.* Boulder, CO: Real People Press.
Andreas, S. (2012) *Resolving Grief.* Denver, CO: NLP Comprehensive. Available online: http://www.nlpco.com/library/therapy/grief.
Andreas, S. and Andreas, C. (1987) *Change Your Mind—and Keep the Change.* Moab, UT: Real People Press.
Andreas, C. and Andreas, S. (1989) *Heart of the Mind.* Moab, UT: Real People Press.
Andreas, C. and Andreas, T. (1994) *Core Transformations.* Moab, UT: Real People Press.
Andreas, S. and Andreas, C. (2002) Resolving Shame. *Anchor Point.* March, 2002, p. 17.
Andreas, S. and Faulkner, C. (1994) *NLP: The New Technology of Achievement.* Morrow. New York.
Appleby, I. L, Klein, D. F, Sachar E. J. and Levitt M. (1981) *Biochemical indices of lactate-induced panic: a preliminary report.* In Klein D. F. and Rabkin J. (eds) *Anxiety: New Research and Changing Concepts.* New York: Raven Press.
Argyle, M., Salter, V., Nicholson, H., Williams, M. and Burgess, P. (1970) The communication of inferior and superior attitudes by verbal and non-verbal signals. *British Journal of Social and Clinical Psychology,* 9, pp. 222–31.
Asbell, H. C. (1983) Effects of reflection, probe and predicate matching on perceived counselor characteristics (psychotherapy, interpersonal attraction, Neurolinguistic Programming (NLP). Doctoral Dissertation, University of Missouri at Kansas City, *Dissertation Abstracts International,* 44(11): 3515.
Austin, J. T. and Vancouver, J. B. (1996) Goal Constructs in Psychology: Structure, Process and Content. *Psychological Bulletin,* 120(3): 338–75.
Aziz-Zadeh, L. and Ivry, R. B. (2009) The Human mirror neuron system and embodied representations. *In Progress in Motor Control,* pp. 355–76).
Bacon, F. (1887) *The Four Idols of Francis Bacon.* Available online: http://www.sirbacon.org/links/4idols.htm.
Baddeley, M. (1992) *The use of hypnosis in marriage and relationship counselling. Australian Journal of Clinical Hypnotherapy and Hypnosis,* 13(2): 87–92.
Bandler, R. (1985) *Using Your Brain for a Change: Neurolinguistic Programming.* Moab, UT: Real People Press.
Bandler, R. (1993) *Time for a Change.* Capitola, CA: Meta Publications.
Bandler, R. (1999) *Introduction to DHE.* Chicago (Audio).
Bandler, R. and Grinder, J. (1975a) *The Structure of Magic I.* Cupertino, CA: Science and Behavior Books.
Bandler, R. and Grinder, J. (1975b) *Patterns in the Hypnotic Techniques of Milton H. Erickson, MD, Volume 1.* Cupertino, CA: Meta Publications.
Bandler, R. and Grinder, J. (1976) *The Structure of Magic II.* Cupertino, CA: Science and Behavior Books.
Bandler, R. and Grinder, J. (1979) *Frogs into Princes.* Moab, UT: Real People Press.
Bandler, R. and Grinder, J. (1982) *Reframing: Neuro-Linguistic Programming and the Transformation of Meaning.* Moab, UT: Real People Press.
Bandler, R. and LaValle, J. (1996) *Persuasion Engineering.* Cupertino, CA: Meta Publications.
Bandler, R. and MacDonald, W. (1987) *An Insider's Guide To Submodalities.* Moab, UT: Real People Press.
Bandler, R., Grinder, J. and Satir, V. (1976) *Changing with Families. A book about further education for being human.* Science and Behaviour books.
Bandura, A. (1977a) Self-efficacy: Toward a unifying theory of behavioral change. *Psychological Review,* 84: 191–215.
Bandura, A. (1977b) Self-reinforcement: The power of positive personal control. In P. G. Zimbardo and F. L. Ruch (eds), *Psychology and Life* (9th edn). Glenview, IL: Scott Foresman.

Bandura, A. (1977c) *Social Learning Theory*. Englewood Cliffs, NJ: Prentice-Hall.
Bandura, A. (1977d) Social learning theory. In B. B. Wolman and L. R. Pomroy (eds), *International Encyclopedia of Psychiatry, Psychology, Psychoanalysis, and Neurology* (vol. 10). New York: Van Nostrand Reinhold.
Bandura, A. (1997) *Self-Efficacy: The Exercise of Control*. New York: Freeman.
Barlow, D. H. (1988) *Anxiety and it's Disorders: The Nature and Treatment of Anxiety and Panic*. New York: Guildford Press.
Batelann, N., Smit, R., de Graaf, R., Van Balkom, A., Vollebergh, W. and Beekman, A. (2007) Economic Cost of full blown and subthreshold panic disorder. *Journal of affective disorders*, December, 104(1–3) pp. 127–36.
Barrett-Lennard, G. T. (1962) Dimensions of therapist response as causal factors in therapeutic change. *Psychological Monographs*, 76, (43 whole no. 562).
Bateson, G. (1972) *Steps Towards an Ecology of Mind*. New York: Ballantine.
Bateson, G., Jackson, D. D., Haley, J. and Weakland, J. H. (1956) Towards a Theory of Schizophrenia. *Behavioural Science*, 1: 251–64.
Baumeister, R. and Heatherton, T. (1996) Self-regulation failure: An overview. *Psychological Inquiry*, 7(1), 1–15.
Baxter L. R. (1994) Positron emission tomography studies of cerebral glucose metabolism in obsessive compulsive disorder. *Journal of Clinical Psychiatry*, 55 Supplement: p. 54–9.
Bayes, M. A. (1972) Behavioral cues of interpersonal warmth. *Journal of Consulting and Clinical Psychology*, 39(2): 333–9.
Bechara, A. (2005) Decision making, impulse control and loss of willpower to resist drugs: A neurocognitive perspective. *Nature Neuroscience*, 8(11): 1458–63.
Bechara, A. and Damasio, H. (2002) Decision-making and addiction (part I): Impaired activation of somatic states in substance dependent individuals when pondering decisions with negative future consequences. *Neuropsychologia*, 40(10): 1675–89.
Bechara, A., Damasio, H., Damasio, A. and Lee, G. (1999) Different Contributions of the Human Amygdala and Ventromedial Prefrontal Cortex. *The Journal of Neuroscience*, 19(13): 5473–81.
Bechara, A., Damasio, H. and Damasio, A. R. (2000) Emotion, decision making and the orbitofrontal cortex. *Cerebral Cortex*, 10(3): 295–307.
Bechara, A., Dolan, S. and Hindes, A. (2002) Decision-making and addiction (part II): Myopia for the future or hypersensitivity to reward? *Neuropsychologia*, 40(10): 1690–705.
Bechara, A. and van der Kooy, D. (1985) Opposite motivational effects of endogenous opioids in brain and periphery. *Nature*, 314: 533–4.
Beck, A. T. (1976) *Cognitive Therapy and Emotional Disorders*. New York: International Universities Press.
Beck, A. T. and Clark, D. A. (1988) Anxiety and depression: An information processing perspective. *Anxiety Research Vol I*, 23–36.
Beck, A. T. and Steer, R. A. (1993) Beck Anxiety Inventory. *The psychological corporation*.
Beck, A. T., Laude, R. and Bohnert, M. (1974) Ideational components of anxiety neurosis. *Archives of General Psychiatry*, 31, 319–25.
Beeman, M., Friedman, R. B., Grafman, J., Perez, E., Diamond, S. and Beadle Lindsay, M. (1994) Summation priming and coarse semantic coding in the right hemisphere. *Journal of Cognitive Neuroscience*, 6: 26–45.
Bell, A. H., Meredith, M. A., Van Opstal, A. J. and Munoz, D. P. (2005) Crossmodal Integration in the Primate Superior Colliculus Underlying the Preparation and Initiation of Saccadic Eye Movements. *Journal of Neurophysiology*, 93(6): 3659–73.
Bem, D. J. (1967) Self-perception: An alternative tnterpretation of dissonance phenomena. *Psychological Review*, 74: 183–200.
Berke, J. D. and S. E. Hyman (2000) Addiction, Dopamine and the Molecular Mechanisms of Memory. *Neuron*, 25(3): 515–32.

References

Bertoli, J. M. (2002) The use of neuro-linguistic programming and emotionally focused therapy with divorcing couples in crisis. In Figley, C. R. *Brief treatments for the traumatized: A project of the Green Cross Foundation*. Westport, CT: Greenwood Press/Greenwood Publishing Group, pp. 207–25.

Beutler, L. E. (1999) Manualizing flexibility: The training of eclectic therapists. *Journal of Clinical Psychology*, 55(4): 399–404.

Beyebach, M. and Carranza, V. E. (1997) Therapeutic interaction and dropout: Measuring relational communication in solution-focused therapy. *Journal of Family Therapy*, 19: 173–212.

Beyebach, M., Morejon, A. R., Palenzuela, D. L. and Rodriguez-Arias, J. L. (1996) Research on the process of solution-focused therapy. In Miller, S.D., Hubble, M. A. and Duncan, B. L. (eds), *Handbook of Solution-Focused Brief Therapy*. San Francisco, CA: Jossey Bass, pp. 299–334.

Bigley, J., Griffiths, D., Prydderch, A., Romanowski, A. J., Miles, L., Lidiard. H. and Hoggard, N. (2010) Neurolinguistic programming used to reduce the need for anaesthesia in claustrophobic patients undergoing MRI, *The British Journal of Radiology*, 83: 113–17.

Bihrle, A. M., Brownell, H. H. and Powelson, J. A. (1986) Comprehension of humorous and nonhumorous materials by left and right brain-damaged patients. *Brain and Cognition*, 5: 399–411.

Birdwhistell, R. L. (1970) *Kinesics and Context – Essays on Body–Motion Communication*. Harmondsworth: Penguin.

Blanchard, R. J., Blanchard, D. C., Takahashi, T. and Kelley, M. (1977) Attack and defensive behavior in the albino rat. *Animal Behaviour*, 25: 622–34.

Blazer, D. G., George, L. K. and Hughes, D. (1991) *The epidemiology of anxiety disorders: An age comparison*. In Salxman, C. and Lebowitz, B. D. (eds) *Anxiety in the Elderly: Treatment and Research*. New York: Springer, pp. 17–30.

Bodenhammer, B. G. and Hall, L. M. (1998) *The User's Manual For the Brain: The Complete Manual for Neuro-Linguistic Programming Practitioner Certification*. Institute of Neuro Semantics.

Bodenhamer, B.G. and Hall, L.M. (2001) *The Users Manual for the Brain*. Carmarthen: Crown House.

Boeckx, C. (2010) *Language in Cognition*. Malden, MA: Wiley Blackwell.

Bokuro-Shafé, K., Kono, M. and Tamaki, H. (2011) *Medical Applications of NLP. Using NLP in the Holistic Treatment of Cancer*. Innovations in NLP for Challenging Times. Bancyfelin: Crown House Publishing, pp. 216–29.

Bolstad, R. D. (2002) *Resolve. A New Model of Therapy*. Carmarthen: Crown House Publishing.

Borkovec, T. D., Alcaine, O. M. and Behar, E. (2004) Avoidance theory of worry and generalized anxiety disorder. In Heimberg, R. G., Turk, C. L. and Mennin, D. S. (eds) *Generalized Anxiety Disorder: Advances in research and Practice*. New York: Guilford Press, pp. 77–108.

Bostic St Clair, C. and Grinder, J. (2002) *Whispering in the Wind*. Scotts Valley, CA: J & C Enterprises.

Bouton, M. E. (1994) Conditioning, remembering and forgetting. *Journal of Experimental Psychology: Animal Behavior Processes*, 20(3): 219–31.

Bouton, M. E. and Moody, E. W. (2004) Memory processes in classical conditioning. *Neuroscience and Biobehavioral Reviews*, 28(7): 663–74.

Bowers, L. A. (1996) An Exploration of Holistic and Ontratraditional Healing Methods including Research in the use of Neuro-linguistic Programming in the Adjunctive Treatment of Acute Pain. *Dissertation Abstracts International*, 56(11): 6379.

Bradbury, A. C. (2011a) *All Roads Lead to Sharpley – Part 1 (The First Journey to the Emerald City)*. Available online: http://www.bradburyac.mistral.co.uk/sharpley1.html.

Bradbury, A. C. (2011b) *All Roads Lead to Sharpley – Part 2 (Second Journey to the Emerald City)*. Available online: http://www.bradburyac.mistral.co.uk/sharpley2.html.

Brandis A. D. (1986) A neurolinguistic treatment for reducing parental anger responses and creating more resourceful behavioral options. *Dissertation Abstracts International*, 47(11), 4642-B California School of Professional Psychology (Order = DA8626141): 161.

Briere, J. (2001) *Detailed Assessment of Posttraumatic Stress*. Psychological Assessment Resources.

Brigham Young University (2009, July 21) Babies understand dogs, bark-matching study finds. *Science Daily*. Available online: http://www.sciencedaily.com/releases/2009/07/090720163559.htm.

Brockman, W. P. (1980) Empathy revisited: the effects of representational system matching on certain counseling process and outcome variables. Doctoral Dissertation, College of William and Mary. *Dissertation Abstracts International*, 41(8): 3421. Available online: from http://www.nlp.de/cgi-bin/research/nlp-rdb.cgi?action =res_entries (accessed 24 November 2006).

Brockman, J. (Interviewer) and LeDoux, J. (Interviewee) (February 1997) *Parallel Memories: Putting Emotions Back Into The Brain: A Talk With Joseph Ledoux* [Interview transcript]. Available online from The Edge Web site: http://edge.org/conversation/parallel-memories-putting-emotions-back-into-the-brain.

Brooks, M. (1989) *Instant Rapport*. New York: Warner.

Buchheimer, A. (1963) The development of ideas about empathy. *Journal of Counseling Psychology*, 10: 61–70.

Buckner, M. N. M., Reese, E. and Reese, M. (1987) Eye Movements as an Indicator of Sensory Components in Thought. *Journal of Counseling Psychology*, 34(3): 283–7.

Buckner, R. L., Andrews-Hanna, J. R. and Schacter, D. L. (2008) The Brain's Default Network. *Annals of the New York Academy of Sciences*, 1124(1): 1–38.

Bull, L. (2002) Parents Use of Complementary Medicine with their Children who have Learning Difficulties. *The Case of the Sunflower Method. Early Child Development and Care*, 172(3): 247–57.

Bull, L. (2007) Sunflower therapy for children with specific learning difficulties (dyslexia): a randomised, controlled trial. *Complementary therapies in clinical practice*, 13(1): 15–24.

Burke, D. T., Meleger, A., et al. (2003) Eye-movements and ongoing task processing. *Perceptual and Motor Skills*, 96(3, Pt2): 1330–8.

Butcher, J. N. (1986) Culture and Depression: Studies in the Anthropology and Cross-Cultural Psychiatry of Affect and Disorder. *PsycCRITIQUES*, 31(9): 719.

Butler A. C., Chapman, J. E., Forman, E. M. and Beck A. T. (2006) The empirical status of cognitive-behavioral therapy: A review of meta-analyses. *Clinical Psychology Review*, 26: 17–31.

Butler, G. Fennell, M. and Hackmann, A. (2008) *Cognitive-Behavioral Therapy for Anxiety Disorders. Mastering Clinical Challenges*. New York: The Guilford Press.

Brawman-Mintzer, O. and Lydiard, R. B. (1996) Biological basis of generalized anxiety disorder. *Journal of Clinical Psychiatry*, 58: 16–25.

Cade, B. and O'Hanlon, W. H. (1993) *A Brief Guide to Brief Therapy*. New York: W.W. Norton.

Canales, J. J. (2005) Stimulant-induced adaptations in neostriatal matrix and striosome systems: Transiting from instrumental responding to habitual behavior in drug addiction. *Neurobiology of Learning and Memory*, 83(2): 93–103.

Cao, X., Wang, H., Mei, B., An, S., Yin, L., Wang, L. P. et al. (2008) Inducible and Selective Erasure of Memories in the Mouse Brain via Chemical-Genetic Manipulation. *Neuron*, October, 60(23): 353–66.

Carbonell, D. A. (1985) Representational systems: An empirical approach to neurolinguistic programming. *Dissertation Abstracts International* 46(8): 2798-B DePaul University, p. 144.

Carbonell, J. L. and Figley, C. (1999) Promising PTSD treatment approaches: A systematic clinical demonstration of promising PTSD treatment approaches. *Traumatology*, 5(1): 32–48.

Cardemil, E. V., Reivich, K. J., Seligman, M. P. (2002) The prevention of depressive symptoms in low-income minority middle school in Chinese children and adolescents: parent, teacher, and self-students. *Journal of Affective Disorders*, 111: 291–8.

Carroll, R.T. (ND) Neuro-linguistic programming (NLP) *The Skeptic's Dictionary*. Available online: http://skepdic.com/neurolin.html (accessed 1 February 2007).

Chambers, R. A., Bickel, W. K. and Potenza, M. N. (2007) A scale-free systems theory of motivation and addiction. *Neuroscience and Biobehavioral Reviews*, 31(7): 1017–45.

Chan, C. H., Ng, E. H., Cha, C. L and Ho, C. T. H. (2006) Effectiveness of psychosocial group intervention for reducing anxiety in women undergoing in vitro fertilization: a randomized controlled study. *Fertility and Sterility*, 85(2): 339–46.

Charney D. S., Beninger G. R. and Breier A. (1984) Noradrenergic function in panic anxiety: effects of yohimbine in healthy subjects and patients with agoraphobia and panic disorder. *Archives of General Psychiatry*, 41, 751–63.

Chartrand, T. L. and Bargh, J. A. (1999) The chameleon effect: The perception-behavior link and social interaction. *Journal of Personality and Social Psychology*, 76: 893–910.

Charvet, S. R. (1997) *Words That Change Minds: Mastering the Language of Influence*. Dubuque, IA: Kendall Hunt Publishing.

Chentsova-Dutton, Y. and Tsai, J. L. (2010) Self-focused attention and emotional response: The role of culture. *Journal of Personality and Social Psychology*, 98: 507–19.

Chomsky, N. (1957) *Syntactic Structures*. The Hague: Mouton & Co.

Chomsky, N. (1972) *Language and Mind: Enlarged edition*. New York: Harcourt: Brace, Jovanovich.

Chugani, H. (1996) Neuroimaging of development nonlinearity and developmental pathologies. In: Thatcher, R. Lyon, G., Rumsey, J. and Krasnegor, N. (eds) *Developmental Neuroimaging. Mapping the Development of the Brain and Behaviour*. San Diego, CA: Academic Press, pp. 187–95.

Churches, R. and West-Burnham, J. (2009) *Leading Learning Through Relationships The Implications of Neuro-linguistic Programming for Personalisation and the Children's Agenda in England*. Current Research in NLP Volume – Proceedings of 2008 Conference, pp. 6–20.

Clark, D. M. (1986) A Cognitive approach to panic. *Behavior research and Therapy*, 24: 461–70.

Clark, L. A. and Watson, D.M. (1991) A tripartite model of anxiety and depression: Psychometric evidence and taxonomic implications. *Journal of Abnormal Psychology*, 100: 316–36.

Clark, D. A, Beck, A. T and Stewart, B. (1990) Cognitive Specificity and positive negative affectivity: Complimentary or contradictory views on anxiety and depression? *Journal of Abnormal Psychology*, 99(2): 148–55.

Clark, D. M., Salkovskis P. M. and Chalkley A. J. (1985) Respiratory control as a treatment for panic attacks. *Journal of Behavior Therapy and Experimental Psychiatry*, 16: 23–30.

Clark, D. A., Steer, R. A. and Beck, A. T. (1994) Common and specific dimensions of self-reported anxiety and depression: Implications for the cognitive and tripartite models. *Journal of Abnormal Psychology*, 103(4): 645–54.

Codispoti, M. and De Cesarei, A. (2007) Arousal and attention: Picture size and emotional reactions. *Psychophysiology*, 44: 680–6.

Coe, W. C. and Scharcoff, J. A. (1985) An empirical evaluation of the neurolinguistic programming model. *International Journal of Clinical and Experimental Hypnosis*, 33(4): 310–18.

Colleau, S. M. (1998) *Pain, opioid use and the incidence of addiction. Cancer Pain Release*, 11: 3. Available online: http://www.whocancerpain.wisc.edu/index?q=node/244 (accessed 25 June 2007).

Coulson, S. and Van Petten, C. (2003) A Special Role for the Right Hemisphere in Metaphor Comprehension? ERP Evidence from Hemifield Presentation. *Cognitive Science*, 31(5): 673–89.

Craig, A. D. (2009) How do you feel now? The anterior insula and human awareness. *Nature Reviews Neuroscience*, 10(1): 59–70. Available online: http://www.nature.com/nrn/journal/v10/n1/suppinfo/nrn2555_S1.html.

Cuijpers, P., van Straten, A. and Warmerdam, L. (2008a) Behavioral activation treatments of depression: a meta-analysis. *Clinical Psychology Review*, 27, 318–26.

Cuijpers, P., van Straten, A. Andersson, G. and van Oppen, P. (2008b) Psychotherapy for depression in adults: A meta-analysis of comparative outcome studies. *Journal of Consulting and Clinical Psychology*, 76: 909–22.

Curreen, M. P. (1995) A simple hypnotically based NLP technique used with two clients in criminal justice settings. *Australian Journal of Clinical and Experimental Hypnosis*, 23(1): 51–7.

Dadds, M.R., Bovbjerg, D.H., Redd, W.H. and Cutmore T. R. H. (1997) Imagery in Human Classical Conditioning. *Psychological Bulletin*, 122(1): 89–103.

Damasio, A. R. (1999) *The Feeling of What Happens: Body and Emotion in the Making of Consciousness*. New York: Harcourt.

D'Aquili, E. G. and Newberg, A. (2000) The Neuropsychology of Aesthetic, Spiritual and Mystical States. *Zygon*, 35(1): 39–51.

D'Argembeau, A., Stawarczyk, D., Majerus, S., Collette, F., Van der Linden, M., Feyers, D. *et al.* (2010) The neural basis of personal goal processing when envisioning future events. *Journal of Cognitive Neuroscience*, 22(8): 1701–13.

Daley, D. C., Mercer, D. and Carpenter, G. (2002) *The Collaborative Cocaine Treatment Study Model*. Bethesda, MD: NIDA.

Davidson, R. J. (1993) Parsing Affective Space Perspectives from Neuropsychology and Psychophysiology. *Neuropsychology*, 7(4): 464–75.

Davidson, J. R. T., Foa, E. B., Huppert, J. D., Keefe, F. J., Franklin, M., Compton, J. S., Gadde, K. M. (2004) Fluoxetine, Comprehensive Cognitive Behavioral Therapy and Placebo in Generalized Social Phobia. *Archives of General Psychiatry*, 61: 1005–13.

Davis, S. L., Davis, D. I. (1983) Neuro-Linguistic Programming and family therapy. *Journal of Marital and Family Therapy*, July, 9(3): 283–91.

Day, R. C. G. (1985) Students' perceptions of Neurolinguistic Programming strategies (counseling, communication, clients, therapy), Doctoral Dissertation, Florida State University, 1985. *Dissertation Abstracts International*, 46(4): 1333.

De Cesarei, A. and Codispoti, M. (2006) When does size not matter? Effects of stimulus size on affective modulation. *Psychophysiology*, 43: 207–15.

De Cesarei A. and Codispoti M. (2008) Fuzzy picture processing: effects of size reduction and blurring on emotional processing. *Emotion*, June, 8(3): 352–63.

Deci, E. L. and Ryan, R. M. (2008) Facilitating Optimal Motivation and Psychological Well-Being Across Life's Domains. *Canadian Psychology*, 49(1): 14–23.

DeLozier, J. (1985) Mastery, New Coding and Systemic NLP. *NLP World*, 2(1): 1.

Deng, G. and Cassileth, B. R. (2005) Integrative oncology: Complementary therapies for pain, anxiety and mood disturbances. *CA Cancer J Clin.*, 55(2): 109–16.

Denson, T. F., Spanovic, M., Miller, N. (2009) Cognitive appraisals and emotions predict cortisol and immune responses: A meta-analysis of acute laboratory social stressors and emotion inductions. *Psychological Bulletin*, November, 135(6): 823–53.

DePaulo, J. R. and Horvitz, L. A. (2002) *Understanding Depression: What We Know and What You Can Do About It*. New York: John Wiley and Sons.

Derogatis, L. R. (1983) *SCL-90-R Administration, Scoring and Procedures Manual-II*. Towson, MD: Clinical Psychometric Research.

Diamantopoulos, G., Wooley, S.I. and Spann, M. (2009) *A Critical Review of Past Research into the Neuro-linguistic Programming Eye-Accessing Cues Model*. Current Research in NLP Volume, proceedings of 2008 Conference pp. 6–20.

Diamond, D., Campbell, A., Park, C., Halonen, J. and Zoladz, P. (2007) The temporal dynamics model of emotional memory processing: A synthesis on the neurobiological basis of stress-induced amnesia, flashbulb and traumatic memories and the Yerkes–Dodson Law. *Neural Plasticity*, 1–33.

DiClemente, C. C. (2003) *Addiction and Change: How Addictions Develop and Addicted People Recover*. New York: The Guilford Press.

Diekhof, E. K., Falkai, P. and Gruber, O. (2008) Functional neuroimaging of reward processing and decision-making: A review of aberrant motivational and affective processing in addiction and mood disorders. *Brain Research Reviews*, 59(1): 164–84.

Dietrich, A. M. (2000) A review of visual/kinesthetic disassociation in the treatment of posttraumatic disorders: theory, efficacy and practice recommendations. *Traumatology*, 6(2): 85–107.

Dietrich, A. M., Baranowsky, A. B., Devich-Navarro, M., Gentry, J. E., Harris, C. J. and Figley, C. R. (2000) A review of alternative approaches to the treatment of post-traumatic sequelae. *Traumatology*, 6(4): 251–71.

Dillon, D. G. and Pizzagalli, D. A. (2007) Inhibition of action, thought and emotion: A selective neurobiological review. *Appl Prev Psychol.*, 12(3): 99–114.

Dilts, R. B. (1983) *Roots of NLP*. Cupertino, CA: Meta Publications.

Dilts, R. B. (1993) *Changing Belief Systems with NLP*. Cupertino, CA: Meta Publications.

Dilts, R. B. (1999) *Sleight of Mouth*. Cupertino, CA: Meta Publications.

Dilts, R. B. (1994–5) *Strategies of Genius, Volume I, II and III*. Cupertino, CA: Meta Publications.

Dilts, R. B. and DeLozier, J. (2000) *Encyclopedia of Systemic Neurolinguistic Programming and NLP New Coding*. California: California University Press. Available online: http://NLPuniversitypress.com (accessed December 2012).

Dilts, R. and Epstein, T.(1995) *Dynamic Learning*. Capitola, CA: MetaPublications.

Dilts, R. B., Grinder, J., Bandler, R. and DeLozier, J. (1980) *Neuro-Linguistic Programming: Volume I. The Structure of Subjective Experience*. Cupertino, CA: Meta Publications.

Dilts, R. B., Hallbom, T. and Smith, S. (1990) *Beliefs. Pathways to Health and Wellbeing*. Oregon: Metamorphous.

Domjan, M. (2005) Pavlovian conditioning: A functional perspective. *Annual Review of Psychology*, 56(1): 179–206.

Dooley, K. O. and Farmer, A. (1988) Comparison for aphasic and control subjects of eye movements hypothesized in neurolinguistic programming. *Perceptual and Motor Skills*, 67(1): 233–4.

Dowd, T. E. and Hingst, A. G. (1983) Matching therapists' predicates: an in vivo test of effectiveness. *Perceptual and Motor Skills*, 57(1): 207–10.

Doweiko, H. (1996) *Concepts of Chemical Dependency (3rd edn)*. Pacific Grove, CA: Brooks/Cole.

Dressler, W. W. (1992) Stress and Adaptation in the Context of Culture: Depression in a Southern Black Community. *Journal of Nervous and Mental Disease*, 180(3): 211.

Driskell, J., Copper, C. and Moran, A. (1994) Does mental practice enhance performance? *Journal of Applied Psychology*, 79(4): 481–92.

Druckman, D. and Swets, J. A. (eds) (1988) *Enhancing Human Performance: Issues, Theories and Techniques*, Commission on Behavioral and Social Sciences and Education National Academy Press.

DSM-IV-TR (2000) *Diagnostic and statistical manual of mental disorders 4th Edition*. American Psychiatric Association.

Duncan, S. and Barrett, L. F. (2007) Affect is a form of cognition: A neurobiological analysis. *Cognition and Emotion*, 21(6): 1184–211.

Duncan, R.C., Konefal, J. and Spechler, M.M. (1990) Effect of neurolinguistic programming training on self-actualization as measured by the Personal Orientation Inventory. *Psychological Report*. June, 66(3 Pt 2): 1323–30.

Dutton, D.G. and Aron, A.P. (1974) Some evidence for heightened sexual attraction under conditions of high anxiety. *Journal of Personality and Social Psychology*, 30(4): 510–17.

Duvarci, S. and Nader, K. (2004) Characterization of fear memory reconsolidation. *Neuroscience*, 24(42): 9269–75.

eBay (2011) http://cgi.ebay.co.uk/NLP-Practitioner-Home-Study-Training-12-DVD-2-CD-Crse-/300418001827?pt=UK_Health_Beauty_Natural_AlternativeTherapies&hash=item 45f24eeba3 and http://cgi.ebay.co.uk/NLP-HOME-STUDY-MASTER-PRACTITIONER-CERTIFIED-DVD-COURSE-/360370140872?pt=LH_DefaultDomain_3&hash=item53e7b bf6c8 (accessed 27 July 2011).

Ecker, B. and Toomey, B. (2008) Depotentiation of Symptom-Producing Implicit Memory in Coherence Therapy. *Journal of Constructivist Psychology*, 21(2): 87–150.

Edinger, E. F. (1972) *Ego and Archetype*. New York: Penguin.

Ehlers, A., Mauchnik, J. and Handley R. (2010) Reducing unwanted trauma memories by imaginal exposure or autobiographical memory elaboration: An analogue study of memory processes. *Journal of Behavor Therapy Experimental Psychiatry*, Dec 22 (Epub ahead of print). Available online: http://www.sciencedirect.com/science/article/pii/ S0005791610001242.

Ehrmantraut, J. E., Jr (1983) A comparison of the therapeutic relationships of counseling students trained in Neurolinguistic Programming vs. students trained on the Carkhuff Model. Doctoral Dissertation, University of Northern Colorado, 1983) *Dissertation Abstracts International*, 44(10): 3191-B.

Einspruch, E. L. and Forman, B. D. (1985) Observations Concerning Research Literature on Neuro-Linguistic Programming. *Journal of Counselling Psychology*, 32(4): 589–96.

Einspruch, E. L. and Forman, B. D. (1988) *Neurolinguistic Programming in the Treatment of Phobias*. Psychotherapy in Private Practice. 6(1): 91–100.

Elich, M., Thompson, R. W. et al. (1985) Mental imagery as revealed by eye movements and spoken predicates: A test of neurolinguistic programming. *Journal of Counseling Psychology*, 32(4): 622–5.

Ellis, A. (1962) *Reason and Emotion in Psychotherapy*. New York: Lyle Stewart.

Epstein, T. and Dilts, R. (1991) *Tools for Dreamers: Strategies of Creativity and the Structure of Innovation*. Capitola, CA: Meta Publications.

Erickson, M. H. (1980) *The Collected Papers of Milton H. Erickson on Hypnosis*. New York: Irvington.

Erickson, M. H. and Rossi, E.L. (1989) *The February Man. Evolving Consciousness and Identity in Hypnotherapy*. New York: Brunner Mazel.

Fabbri-Destro, M. and Rizzolatti, G. (2008) Mirror neurons and mirror systems in monkeys and humans. *Physiology*, 23, 171–9.

Fadiga, L., Fogassi, G., Pavesi, G. and Rizzolatti, G. (1995) Motor Facilitation during action observation: a magnetic stimulation study, *Journal of Neurophysiology*, 73: 2608–11.

Falzett, W. C., Jr (1979) Matched versus unmatched primary representational systems relationship to perceived trustworthiness in a counseling analogue. *Dissertation Abstracts International*, 41(1): 105-A. Marquette University. Text can also be found in: *Journal of Counseling Psychology* (1981), 28(4).

Farmer, A., Rooney, R., et al. (1985) Hypothesized eye movements of neurolinguistic programming: A statistical artifact. *Perceptual and Motor Skills*, 61(3, Pt 1): 717–18.

Feil, J., Sheppard, D., Fitzgerald, P. B., Yücelc M., Lubman, D. I. and Bradshaw, J.L. (2010) Addiction, compulsive drug seeking and the role of frontostriatal mechanisms in regulating inhibitory control. *Neuroscience and Biobehavioral Reviews*, 35: 248–75.

Ferguson, D. M. (1987) The effect of two audiotaped Neurolinguistic Programming (NLP) phobia treatments on public speaking anxiety. *Dissertation Abstracts International*, 49(4): 765. University of Tennessee.

Ferster, C. B. and Skinner, B. F. (1953) *Schedules of Reinforcement*. New York: Macmillan Free Press.

Field, E. S. (1990) Neurolinguistic programming as an adjunct to other psychotherapeutic/hypnotherapeutic interventions. *The American journal of clinical hypnosis*, 32(3): 174–82.

Figley, C. R. (ed.) (2002) *Brief Treatments for the Traumatized*. West Port, CT: Greenwood Press.

Foa, E. B. and Kozak, M. J. (1986) Emotional Processing of Fear: Exposure to Corrective Information. *Psychological Bulletin*, 99(1): 20–35.

Foa, E. B. and Meadows, E. A. (1997) Psychosocial treatments for posttraumatic stress disorder: A critical review. *Annual Review of Psychology*, 48: 449.

Foa, E. B., Keane, T. M. and Friedman, M. J. (eds) (2000) *Effective Treatments for PTSD*. New York: The Guilford Press.

Forcato, C., Pedreira, M. E, Maldonado, H. (2009) Human reconsolidation does not always occur when a memory is retrieved: The relevance of the reminder structure. *Neurobiology of Learning and Memory*, 91(1): 50–7.

Forcato, C., Burgos, V. L., Argibay, P. F., Molina, V. A., Pedreira, M. E. and Maldonado, H. (2007) Reconsolidation of declarative memory in humans. *Learning and Memory*, 14(4): 295–303.

Frank, M. J. (2005) Dynamic dopamine modulation in the basal ganglia: A neurocomputational account of cognitive deficits in medicated and non-medicated Parkinsonism. *Journal of Cognitive Neuroscience*, 17: 51–72.

Franzini, A., Messina, G., Gambini, O., Muffatti, R., Scarone, S., Cordella, R., Broggi, G. (2010) Deep-brain stimulation of the nucleus accumbens in obsessive compulsive disorder: clinical, surgical and electrophysiological considerations in two consecutive patients. *Neurological Sciences*, 31:353–9.

Freed, A. O. (1987) Psychotherapy with older women. *Smith College Studies in Social Work*, 57(3): 171–83.

Freeston, M.H. and Ladouceur, R. (1997) What do patients do with their obsessive thoughts? *Behaviour and Research Therapy*, 35(4): 335–48.

Freeston, M. H., Rheaume, J., Letarte, H., Dugas, M. M. and Ladeouceur, R. (1994) Why do people worry? *Personality and individual difference*, 17: 791–802.

Fretz, B. R. (1966) Postural movements in a counseling dyad. *Journal of Counseling Psychology*, 13:335–43. Retrieved from PsychArticles.

Fretz, B. R., Corn, R., Tuemmler, J. M. and Bellet, W. (1979) Counselor nonverbal behaviors and client evaluations. *Journal of Counseling Psychology*, 26: 304–11. Retrieved 25 November 2006 from PsychArticles.

Frieden, F. P. (1981) Speaking the client's language: the effects of Neurolinguistic Programming (predicate matching) on verbal and nonverbal behaviors in psychotherapy. A single case design. Doctoral Dissertation, Virginia Commonwealth University. *Dissertation Abstracts International*, 42(3): 1171-B.

Fromme, D. K. and Daniell, J. (1984) Neurolinguistic programming examined: Imagery, sensory mode and communication. *Journal of Counseling Psychology*, 31(3): 387–90.

Fuller, T, E. (1986) *Witchdoctors and Psychiatrists*. New York: Harper and Row.

Gallese, V., Fadiga, L., Fogassi, L. and Rizzolatti, G. (1996) Action recognition in the premotor cortex. *Brain*, 119(2): 593–609.

Gallo, F. P. (1985) Verbal synchrony and the maintenance of rapport between collegiate instructors and their students (NLP Teaching). *Dissertation Abstracts International*, 46(3): 624.

Gaviria, M. (1988) Culture and Depression: Studies in the Anthropology and Cross-Cultural Psychiatry of Affect and Disorder. *Journal of Nervous and Mental Disease*, 176(1): 58.

Gawler-Wright, P. (2004) *Intermediate Contemporary Psychotherapy, Volume 2*. London: BeeLeaf Publishing.

Gawler-Wright, P. (2006) *Wider Mind; Ericksonian Psychotherapy in Practice.* London: BeeLeaf Publishing.
Genser-Medlitsch, M., Schütz, P. (1997, 2004) Does Neuro-Linguistic psychotherapy have effect? New Results shown in the extramural section. Martina Genser-Medlitsch; Peter Schütz, ÖTZ-NLP, Wiederhofergasse 4, A-1090, Wien, Austria/Nowiny Psychologiczne. *Psychological News.* Issue 1.
Gerdes, A. B. M., Uhl, G. and Alpers, G. W. (2009) Spiders are special: fear and disgust evoked by pictures of arthropods. *Evolution and Human Behavior,* 30(1): 66–73.
Gershuny, B. S. and Sher, K. J. (1998) The relation between personality and anxiety: Findings from a 3-year prospective study. *Journal of abnormal psychology,* 107: 252–62.
Gilkinson, H. (1942) Social Fears as Reported by Students in College Speech Classes. *Speech Monographs,* 9: 141–60.
Gladstein, G. A. (1974) Nonverbal communication and, counseling/psychotherapy: A review. *Counseling Psychologist,* 4: 34–57.
Glezer, L. S., Jiang, X. and Reisenhuber, M. (2009) Evidence for Highly Selective Neuronal Tuning to Whole Words in the 'Visual Word Form Area'. *Neuron,* 62: 199–204.
Goldbeck, L. and Schmid, K. (2003) Effectiveness of autogenic relaxation training on children and adolescents with behavioral and emotional problems. *Journal of the American Academy of Child and Adolescent Psychiatry,* 42(9): 1046–54.
Goldberg, D. P. *et al.* (1978) *Manual of the General Health Questionnaire.* Windsor: NFER Publishing.
Goldfried, M. R. (1971) Systematic desensitization as training in self-control. *Journal of Consulting and Clinical Psychology,* 37: 228–34.
Goldstein, R. Z. and Volkow, N. D. (2002) Drug addiction and its underlying neurobiological basis: Neuroimaging evidence for the involvement of the frontal cortex. *American Journal of Psychiatry,* 159(10): 1642–52.
Goodrich, W.E. (1994) *Scientific validity of NLP?* Available online: http://www2.hawaii.edu/~lady/archive/phobia-research-2.html.
Gordon, D. (1978) *Therapeutic Metaphors: Helping Others Through the Looking Glass.* Cupertino, CA: Meta Publications.
Gradus, J. (2010) *Epidemiology of PTSD.* Washington, DC: National Center for PTSD. Available online: http://www.ptsd.va.gov/professional/pages/epidemiological-facts-ptsd.asp.
Graunke, B. and Roberts, T. K. (1985) Neurolinguistic programming: The impact of imagery tasks on sensory predicate usage. *Journal of Counseling Psychology,* 32(4): 525–30.
Grawe, K., Donati, R. and Bernauer, F. (2001) *Psychotherapy in transition. From confession to profession* (5th edn). Göttingen: Hogrefe.
Gray, R. M. (1996) *Archetypal Explorations.* London: Routledge.
Gray, R. M. (1997) *Ericksonian Approaches to the Ego-Self Axis: Establishing Futurity and a Sense of Self in Addictive Clients Seminar: Innovative Approaches to the Treatment of Substance Abuse for the Twenty First Century.* St. Francis College, Brooklyn, NY.
Gray, R. M. (2001a) Addictions and the self: a self-enhancement model for drug treatment in the criminal justice system. *The Journal of Social Work Practice in the Addictions,* 2(1): 75–91.
Gray, R. M. (2001b) *Pseudo-Orientations in Time: Outframing Addictive Behaviors.* National Association of Social Workers, Institute on Addictions, Fordham University, NY.
Gray, R. M. (2002) The Brooklyn Program: Innovative Approaches to Substance Abuse Treatment. *Federal Probation Quarterly,* 66(3): 9–16.
Gray, R. M. (2003) *The Brooklyn Program: Cognitive applications of the physiological correlates of spiritual experience.* The Dr. Lonnie E. Mitchell National HBCU Substance Abuse Conference, sponsored by Howard University, on 2 April.
Gray, R. M. (2004) *Incentive Salience, Meditation and the Neurobiology of Addiction* (Conference Workshop). Presented at The Dr. Lonnie E. Mitchell National HBCU Substance Abuse Conference. Baltimore, MD, 1 April.

Gray, R. M. (2006) Thinking About Drugs and Addiction, Boulder CO: NLP Comprehensive. September 2005. Available online: http://www.nlpcomprehensive.com/articles/AddictionsGray.html (accessed 1 April 2006).

Gray, R. M. (2008a) *About Addictions: Notes from Psychology, Neuroscience and NLP*. Raleigh, NC: LuLu Press.

Gray, R. M. (2008b) *Transforming Futures: The Brooklyn Program Facilitators Manual*. Available online: http://www.lulu.com/content/2267218.

Gray, R. M. (2008c) *The NLP Trauma Protocol*. The Dr. Lonnie E. Mitchell National HBCU Substance Abuse and Mental Health Conference, sponsored by the Morehouse School of Medicine, on 7 April.

Gray, R. M. (2009) *Applying NLP to Addictions*. Current Research in NLP (Vol 1)b, 86–96.

Gray, R. M. (2010) *The Brooklyn Program: Applying NLP to Addictions*. Current Research in NLP: Proceedings of 2008 Conference, 1(1), 88–98.

Gray, R. M. (2011a) *NLP and Addictions*. In Charvet, S. and Hall, L.M. (eds), *Innovations in NLP, Volume 1*. Carmarthen: Crown Publishing.

Gray, R. M. (2011b) *NLP and PTSD: The Visual-Kinesthetic Dissociation Protocol*. Current Research in NLP: Proceedings of 2010 Conference, 2(1).

Gray, R. M. (2011c) *Transforming Futures: The Brooklyn Program Facilitators Manual* (2nd edn). Raleigh, NC: Lulu Press.

Gray, R. M. (2011d) *Interviewing and Counseling Skills: An NLP Perspective*. Raleigh, NC: Lulu Press.

Gray, R. M. and Liotta, R. F. (2012) PTSD: Extinction, reconsolidation and the visual-kinesthetic dissociation protocol. *Traumatology*, 18(2): 3–16.

Greicius, M. D., Krasnow, B., Reiss, A. L. and Menon, V. (2003) Functional connectivity in the resting brain: A network analysis of the default mode hypothesis. *PNAS*, 100(1): 253–8.

Green, M. A. (1979) *Trust as effected by representational system predicates* (Doctoral Dissertation, Ball State University. *Dissertation Abstracts International*, 41(8): 3159-B.

Greenough, W. T. and Black, T. E. (1992) Introduction of brain structure by experience: substrates for cognitive development. In: Gunnar, M. R. and Nelson, C. A. (eds) *Minnesota Symposium on Child Psychology. Volume 24: Developmental Behavioural Neuroscience*. Hillsdale, NJ: Lawrence Erlbaum, pp. 155–200.

Griffin, J. and Tyrrell, I. (2000) *The Apet Model. Patterns in the brain*. The European Therapy Studies Institute.

Grimley, B. (2012) *Achieving-Lives Team profiler*. Available online: http://www.achieving-lives.co.uk/free-profiler.html (accessed 2 June 2012).

Grinder, J. and Bandler, R. (1980a) Forward. In Dilts, R., Grinder, J., Bandler, R. and DeLozier, J. (1980) *Neuro-linguistic Programming: Volume I. The Structure of Subjective Experience*. Cupertino, CA: Meta Publications.

Gu, H., Salmeron, B. J., Ross T. J., Geng, X., Zhan, W., Stein, E. and Yang, Y. (2010) Mesocorticolimbic circuits are impaired in chronic cocaine users as demonstrated by resting-state functional connectivity. *NeuroImage* 53(2): 593–601.

Guehl, D., Benazzouz, A., Aouizerate, B., Cuny, E., Rotge, J-Y., Rougier, A. *et al.* (2008) Neuronal correlates of obsessions in the caudate nucleus. *Biological Psychiatry*, 63(6): 557–62.

Gumm, W. B., Walker, M. K. et al. (1982) Neurolinguistic programming: Method or myth? *Journal of Counseling Psychology*, 29(3): 327–30.

Guy, K. and Guy, N. (2003) *The fast cure for phobia and trauma: evidence that it works*. Human Givens Publishing Limited. Available online: http://www.hgi.org.uk/archive/rewindevidence.htm (accessed 29 November 2009).

Hale, R. L. (1986) *The effects of Neurolinguistic Programming (NLP) on public speaking anxiety and incompetence. Dissertation Abstracts International*, 47(5).

Haley, J. (1973) *Uncommon Therapy*. New York: W. W. Norton.

Hall, L. M. (1995) The New Domain of Meta-States in the History of NLP. *NLP World*, November, 2(3): 53–60.

Hall, L. M. (1996) *Meta-States: A domain of Logical Levels*. Grand Junction, CO: Empowerment Technologies.

Hall, L. M. (2001) *NLP: Going Meta: Advanced Modeling Using Meta-Levels*. Clifton, CO: Neuro-Semantic Publications.

Hall, L. M. (2003) What's new, unique, or special about neuro-semantic coaching? Available online: http://www.equilibrio.com.au/inthenews/images/neurosemantic.pdf.

Hall, L. M. and Duval, M. (2004) *Meta-Coaching. Volume 1 Coaching Change. For higher levels of success and transformation*. Clifton, CO: Neuro-Semantic Publications.

Hammer, A. L. (1980) Language as a therapeutic tool: the effects on the relationship of listeners responding to speakers by using perceptual predicates. Doctoral dissertation, Michigan State University. *Dissertation Abstracts International*, 41(3): 991-A, 149.

Hammer, A. L. (1983) Matching perceptual predicates: Effect on perceived empathy in a counseling analogue. *Journal of Counseling Psychology*, 30(2): 172–9.

Hartley, C. and Phelps, E. (2009) Changing fear: The neurocircuitry of emotion regulation. *Neuropsychopharmacology*, 35(1): 136–46.

Harris, B. (1979) Whatever happened to Little Albert? *American Psychologist*, 34: 151–60.

Harris, T. (2000) *Introduction to the work of George Brown*. In Harris, T. (ed.) *Where Inner and Outer Worlds Meet: Psychosocial Research in the Tradition of George W. Brown*. London and New York: Routledge, pp. 1–52.

Hatfield, E., Cacioppo, J. and Rapson, R. (1994) *Emotional Contagion*. Cambridge: Cambridge University Press.

Haynes, J. and Rees, G. (2006) Decoding mental states from brain activity in humans. *Nature Reviews Neuroscience*, July, 7, 523–34.

Heap, M. (1988) Neurolinguistic programming: An interim verdict. In Heap, M. (ed.) *Hypnosis: Current Clinical, Experimental and Forensic Practices*. London: Croom Helm, pp. 268–80.

Hernandez, A. M. S. and Sachs-Ericsson, N. (2006) Ethnic differences in pain reports and the moderating role of depression in a community sample of Hispanic and Caucasian participants with serious health problems. *Psychosomatic Medicine*. 68(1): 121–8.

Hibbert, G. A. (1984) Ideational components of anxiety: their origin and content, *The British Journal of Psychiatry*, 144: 618–24.

Hillin, H. H., Jr (1982) Effects of a rapport method and chemical dependency workshop for adults employed in Kansas service agencies. *Dissertation Abstracts International*, 44(12), 3574-A Kansas State University.

Hillman, J. (1996) *The Soul's Code: In Search of Character and Calling*. New York: Random House.

Hirst, W., LeDoux, J. and Stein, S. (1984) *Constraints on the Processing of Indirect Speech Acts: Evidence from Aphasiology. Brain and Language*, 23: 26–33.

Hogue, C., Castro, C., Messer, S., McGurk, D., Cotting, D. and Koffman, R. (2004) Combat duty in Iraq and Afghanistan, mental health problems and barriers to care. *New England Journal of Medicine*, 351(1): 13–22.

Hollander, J. (1999) NLP and science: Six recommendations for a better relationship. *NLP World*, 6(3).

Holmes, J. (2000) Narrative in Psychiatry and Psychotherapy: The Evidence? *Medical Humanities*, 26: 92–6.

Hongkeun, K. (2010) Dissociating the roles of the default-mode, dorsal and ventral networks in episodic memory retrieval. *NeuroImage*, 50(4): 1648–57.

Hooper, J. (2010) Roman awayday lands firewalking estate agents in hospital, *The Guardian*, 6 July. Available online: http://www.guardian.co.uk/world/2010/jul/06/roman-firewalking-hospital-estate-agents.

Horowitz, M. J., Wilner, N. and Alvarez, W. (1979) Impact of Event Scale: A measure of subjective stress. *Psychosomatic Medicine*, 41, 209–18.

Hossack, A. and Bentall, R. P. (1996) Elimination of posttraumatic symptomatology by relaxation and visual-kinesthetic dissociation. *Journal of Traumatic Stress*, 9(1): 99–110.

Hossack, A. and Standidge, K. (1993) Using an imaginary scrapbook for neurolinguistic programming in the aftermath of a clinical depression: a case history. *Gerontologist*, 33(2): 265–8.

Howard, K.I., Kopta, S.M., Krause, M.S. and Orlinsky, D.E. (1986) The dose-effect relationship in psychotherapy. *American Psychologist*, 41: 159–64.

Hoyt, M. F. (ed.) (1996) *Constructive therapies, Vol. 2*. New York: Guilford Press.

Hubble, M. A. and Duncan, B. L. and Miller, S. D. (1999) *The Heart and Soul of Change: What works in Psychotherapy*. Washington, DC: American Psychological Association.

Hubel, D. H. and Wiesel, T. N. (1959) Receptive fields of single neurons in the cat's striate cortex. *J Physiol.*, 148: 574–591.

Hulleman, C. S., Durik A. M., Schweigert S. A. and Harackiewicz, J. M. (2008) Task Values, Achievement Goals and Interest: An Integrative Analysis. *Journal of Educational Psychology*, 100(2): 398–416.

Hupbach, A., Gomez, R., Hardt, O. and Nadel, L. (2007) Reconsolidation of episodic memories: A subtle reminder triggers integration of new information. *Learning and Memory*, 14: 47–53.

Hupbach, A., Gomez, R. and Nadel, L. (2009) Episodic memory reconsolidation: updating or source confusion? *Memory*, 17: 502–10.

Hupbach, A., Hardt, O., Gomez, R. and Nadel, L. (2008) The Dynamics of Memory: Context-Dependent Updating. *Learning and Memory*, 15: 574–9.

Hyman, B. M. and Pedrick, C. (2010) *The OCD Workbook 3rd edition: Your Guide to Breaking Free from Obsessive-Compulsive Disorder*. Oakland, CA: New Harbinger Publications.

Inaba, D. and Cohen, W. E. (2007) *Uppers Downers and All Arounders* (7th edn). Medford Oregon: CNS Press.

Jacks, R. N. (1973) Systematic desensitization versus a self-control technique for the reduction of agrophobia. *Dissertation Abstracts International*, 33, 394IB. (University microfilms no. 73-04, 521).

James, T. and Woodsmall, W. (1988) *Time Line Therapy and the Basis of Personality*. Cupertino, CA: Metapublications.

James, W. (1950) *The Principles Of Psychology (Volume 1 and 2)*, New York: Dover.

Jung, C. G. (1965) *Memories, Dreams, Reflections*. Princeton: Princeton University Press.

Jung, C. G. (1977) *Mysterium Conjunctionis*. Princeton, NJ: Princeton University Press.

Juhnke, G. A., Coll, K. M., Sunich, M. F. and Kent, R. R. (2008) Using a Modified Neurolinguistic Programming Swish Pattern With Couple Parasuicide and Suicide Survivors. *The Family Journal*, 16: 391.

Kahneman, D. (2011) *Thinking Fast and Slow*. New York: Farrar, Straus and Giroux.

Kalat, J.W. (1988) *Biological Psychology*. Belmont, CA: Wadsworth Publishing.

Kammer, D., Lanver, C. and Schwochow, M. (1997) Controlled Treatment of Simple Phobias with NLP: Evaluation of a Pilot Project. University of Bielefeld, Department of Psychology, unpublished paper.

Kandel, E. (2001) The molecular biology of memory storage: A dialog between genes and synapses (Nobel Lecture, 8 December, 2000) *Bioscience Reports*, 21(5): 569–611.

Kandel, E. (2009) An introduction to the work of David Hubel and Torsten Wiesel. *The Journal of Physiology*, 587: 2733–41.

Kanwisher, N. (2010) Functional specificity in the human brain: A window into the functional architecture of the mind. *Proceedings of the National Academy of Sciences*, 107(25): 11163–70.

Kaplan, G. B., Heinrichs, S. C. and Carey, R. J. (2011) Treatment of addiction and anxiety using extinction approaches: Neural mechanisms and their treatment implications. *Pharmacology, Biochemistry and Behavior*, 97(3): 619–25.

Keitner, G.I., Fodor, J., Ryan, C.E., Miller, I.W., Bishop, D.S. and Epstein, N.B. (1991) A cross-cultural study of major depression and family functioning. *Canadian Journal of Psychiatry (Revue Canadienne de Psychiatrie)*, 36(4): 254–9.

Kessler, R. C., Chiu, W. T., Demler, O. and Walters, E. E. (2005a) Prevalence, severity and comorbidity of twelve-month DSM-IV disorders in the National Comorbidity Survey Replication (NCS-R). *Archives of General Psychiatry*, June, 62(6): 617–27.

Kessler, R. C., Berglund, P. A., Demler, O., Jin, R. and Walters, E. E. (2005b) Lifetime prevalence and age-of-onset distributions of DSM-IV disorders in the National Comorbidity Survey Replication (NCS-R). *Archives of General Psychiatry*, June, 62(6): 593–602.

Kilner, J., Friston, K. and Frith, C. (2007) Predictive coding: an account of the mirror neuron system. *Cognitive Processing*, 8(3): 159–66.

Kim, G., DeCoster, J., Huang, C.H. and Chiriboga, D. A. (2011) Race/Ethnicity and the Factor Structure of the Center for Epidemiologic Studies Depression Scale: A Meta-Analysis. *Cultural Diversity and Ethnic Minority Psychology*, 17(4): 381–96.

Kindt, M., Soeter, M. and Vervliet, B. (2009) Beyond extinction: erasing human fear responses and preventing the return of fear. *Nat Neurosci*, 12(3): 256–8.

King, A. (1995) Designing the instructional process to enhance critical thinking across the curriculum: Inquiring minds really do want to know: Using questioning to teach critical thinking. *Teaching of Psychology*, 22 (1): 13–17.

Kinsbourne, M. (1974) Direction of gaze and distribution of cerebral thought processes. *Neuropsychologia*, 12(2): 279–81.

Kirenskaya, A.V., Novototsky-Vlasov, V.Y., Chistyakov, A.N. and Zvonikov, V.M. (2011) The relationship between hypnotizability, internal imagery and efficiency of neurolinguistic programming. *International Journal of Clinical and Experimental Hypnosis*, April, 59(2): 225–41.

Kirsch, I., Wolpin, M. and Knutson, J. L. (1975) A comparison of in vivo methods for rapid reduction of 'stage-fright' in the college classroom: A field experiment. *Behavior Therapy*, 6: 165–71.

Klein, S. B. (2008) *Learning: Principles and applications* (5th edn). Thousand Oaks, CA: Sage.

Kleinman, A. (2004) Culture and depression. *New England Journal of Medicine*, 351(10): 951–3.

Koestner, R. (2008) Reaching one's personal goals: a motivational perspective focused on autonomy. *Canadian Psychology*, 49(1): 60–7.

Korzybski, A. (1933) *Science and Sanity. An introduction to non-Aristotelian systems and general semantics.* The Institute of General Semantics.

Korzybski, C. (1994) *Science and Sanity* (5th edn). European Society for General Semantics. Available online: http://www.generalsemantics.org/store/all-books/413-pdf-version-science-and-sanity-an-introduction-to-non-aristotelian-systems-and-general-semantics.html.

Kosslyn, M., Ganis, G. and Thompson, W. L. (2001) Neural Foundations of Imagery. *Nature Reviews Neuroscience*, 2: 635–42.

Kostere, K. and Malatesta, L. (1990) *Maps, Models and the Structure of Reality. NLP Technology in Psychotherapy*. Portland, OR: Metamorphous Press.

Koziey, P. W. and McLeod, G. (1987) Visual-Kinesthetic Dissociation in Treatment of Victims of Rape. *Professional Psychology: Research and Practice*, 18(3): 276–82.

Kraus, A. (1995) Psychotherapy based on identity problems of depressives. *American Journal of Psychotherapy*, 49(2): 197–212.

Kringelbach, M. L. (2005) The Human Orbitofrontal Cortex: Linking Reward to Hedonic Experience. *Nature Reviews: Neuroscience*, 6: 691.

Kringelbach, M. L. and Berridge, K. C. (2009) Towards a functional neuroanatomy of pleasure and happiness. *Trends in Cognitive Sciences*, 13(11): 479–87.

Krugman, M., Kirsch, I., Wickless, C., Milling, L., Golicz, H. and Toth, A. (1985) Neuro-Linguistic Programming Treatment for Anxiety: Magic or Myth? *Journal of Consulting and Clinical Psychology*, 53(4): 526–30.

Kuhn, T. (1962) *The Structure of Revolutions*. Chicago: University of Chicago Press.

Labar, K. S. (2007) Beyond fear emotional memory mechanisms in the human brain. *Current Sirections in Psychological Science*, 16(4): 173–7.

Ladouceur, R., Blais, F., Freeston, M. H. and Dugas, M. J. (1998) Problem solving and problem orientation in generalized anxiety disorder. *Journal of Anxiety Disorders*, Mar–Apr, 12(2): 139–52.

Lakoff, G. (1990) *Women, Fire and Dangerous Things: What Categories Reveal About the Mind*. Chicago, IL: University of Chicago Press.

Lamberton, A., Oei, T.P. and Tian, P. S. (2008) A test of the cognitive content specificity hypothesis in depression and anxiety. *Journal of Behavior Therapy and Experimental Psychiatry*, March, 39(1): 23–31.

Lang, P. J. (1985) The Cognitive Psychophysiology of Emotions: Fear and Anxiety. In Tuma, A. H. and Maser, J. D. (eds) *Anxiety and the Anxiety Disorders*. Hillsdale, NJ: Erlbaum, pp. 131–70.

Lang, P. J. and Lazovik, A. D. (1963) Experimental desensitization of a phobia. *Journal of Abnormal and Social Psychology*, 66: 519–25.

Laundergan, J. Clark. (1982) *Easy Does It*. Minneapolis, MN: Hazelden.

Layard, R., Bell, S., Clark, D., Knapp, M., Meacher, Priebe, S., Thornicroft, G., Turnberg and Wright, B. (2006) *The Depression Report: A New Deal for Depression and Anxiety Disorders*. London School of Economics: The Centre for Economic Performance's Mental Health Policy Group.

Leahy, R. L. (1996) *Cognitive-Behavioral Therapy: Basic Principles and Applications*. New York: Jason Aronson Publishers.

LeBar, K. and Phelps, E. (1998) Arousal-mediated memory consolidation: The role of the medial temporal lobe in humans. *Psychological Science*, 9(6): 490–3.

LeDoux, J. (1995) Emotion: clues from the brain. *Annual Review of Psychology*, 46: 209–35.

LeDoux, J. (1997) *The Emotional Brain: The Mysterious Underpinnings of Emotional Life*. New York: Simon and Schuster.

Lee, J. L. C. (2009) Reconsolidation: maintaining memory relevance. *Trends in Neurosciences*, 32(8): 413–20.

Lee, J. L. C., Milton, A. L. and Everitt, B. J. (2006) Reconsolidation and extinction of conditioned fear: inhibition and potentiation. *The Journal of Neuroscience*, 26(39), 10051–6.

Lerner, Y., Epshtein, B., Ullman, S. and Malach, R. (2008) Class information predicts activation by object fragments in human object areas. *Journal of Cognitive Neuroscience*, 20(7): 1189–1206.

Lewis, B. and Pucelik, F. (1990) *Magic of NLP Demystified*. Portland, OR: Metamorphous Press.

Lewis, S. L. (2001) *Psychotherapy and spirituality: A paradigm for healing*. Dissertation Abstracts International: Section B: The Sciences and Engineering. Vol. 61 (10-B), p. 5570.

Ley R. (1985) Agoraphobia, the panic attack-and the hyperventilation syndrome. *Behaviour research and therapy*, 23: 79–82.

Libet, B., Alberts, W. W., Wright, E. W, Jr, Delattre, L. D., Levin, G. and Feinstein, B. (1964) Production of threshold levels of conscious sensation by electrical stimulation of the human somatosensory cortex. *Journal of Neurophysiology*, 27: 546–78.

Liberman, M. B. (1984) The treatment of simple phobias with Neurolinguistic Programming techniques. *Dissertation Abstracts International*, 45(6), St. Louis University.

Lidz, C.W. and Parker, L.S. (2003) Issues of ethics and identity in diagnosis of late life depression. *Ethics and Behavior*, 13(3): 249–62.

Linden, A. and Perutz, K. (1998) *Mindworks: NLP Tools for Building a Better Life*. New York: Berkley Publishing Group.

Linder-Pelz, S. (2010) *NLP Coaching. An Evidence-Based Approach for Coaches, Leaders and Individuals*. London: Kogan Page.

Loftus, E. F. and Yuille, J. C. (1984) *Departures from reality in human perception and memory*. In Weingartner, H. and Parker, E. S. (eds), *Memory Consolidation: Psychobiology of Cognition*. Hillsdale, NJ: Lawrence Erlbaum Associates, pp. 163–84.

Lopez, S. R. and Guarnaccia, P. J. J. (2000) Cultural Psychopathology: Uncovering the Social World of Mental Illness. *Annual Review of Psychology*, 51: 571–98.

Luria, A. R. (1966) *Higher Cortical Functions In Man*, New York: Basic Books.

Lutz, C. (1982) Sense or nonsense: The ego search of suicidal adolescents from the psychotherapeutic viewpoint. [German] "Sinn oder Un-Sinn"–die Selbstsuche des jugendlichen Suicidalen aus psychotherapeutischer Sicht. *Praxis der Psychotherapie und Psychosomatik*, 27(5): 209–16.

Lyons, D. E, Santos, L. R. and Keil, F. C. (2006) Reflections of other minds: How primate social cognition can inform the function of mirror neurons. *Current Opinion in Neurobiology*, 16(2): 230–4.

Lyvers, M. (2000) Loss of control, in alcoholism and drug addiction: A neuroscientific interpretation. *Experimental and Clinical Psychopharmacology*, 8(2): 225–45.

Macroy, T. D. (1978) Linguistic surface structures in family interaction. *Dissertation Abstracts International*, 40(2): 926-B, Utah State University, 133 pp.

Mahishika, K. (2010) Neuro-linguistic programming and application in treatment of phobias. *Complementary Therapies in Clinical Practice*, 16(4), 203–7.

Malloy, T. E. (1995) Empirical evaluation of the effectiveness of a visual spelling strategy. In K.H. Schick (ed) *Rechtschreibtherapie*. Pacherborn Junformann Verlaf.

Mandler, J. M. (2010) The spatial foundations of the conceptual system. *Language and Cognition*, 2(1): 21–44.

Mann, K., Hermann, D. and Heinz, A. (2000) One hundred years of alcoholism: The twentieth century. *Alcohol and Alcoholism*, 35(1): 10–15.

Mansell, W. (2007) An integrative formulation-based cognitive treatment of bipolar disorders: Application and illustration. *Journal of Clinical Psychology*, 63(5): 447–461.

Mansell, W., Morrison, A. P., Reid, G., Lowens, I. and Tai, S. (2007) The interpretation of and responses to, changes in internal states: An integrative cognitive model of mood swings and bipolar disorders. *Behavioural and Cognitive Psychotherapy*, 35(5): 515–39.

Martin, K. and Hall, C. (1995) Using mental imagery to enhance intrinsic motivation. *Journal of Sport and Exercise Psychology*, 17(1), 54–69.

Maslow, A. (1970) *Religions, Values and Peak Experiences*. New York: The Viking Press.

Maslow, A. (1971) *The Farther Reaches of Human Nature*. Esalen, CA: Penguin.

Massad, P. M. and Hulsey, T. L. (2006) Exposure Therapy Renewed. *Journal of Psychotherapy Integration*, 16(4): 417–28.

Masters, B. J., Rawlins, M. E., Rawlins, L. D. and Weidner, J. (1991) The NLP swish pattern: An innovative visualizing technique. *Journal of Mental Health Counseling* 13(1): 79–90.

Mathews, M. O., Thomasa, E. and Yeunga, A. (2009) Rebuttal paper to 'Sunflower Therapy for children with specific learning difficulties (dyslexia): A randomised, controlled trial'. *Complementary Therapies in Clinical Practice*, 15(1): 44–6.

Matthews, W. J., Kirsch, I. and Mosher, D. (1985) Double hypnotic induction: An initial empirical test. *Journal of Abnormal Psychology*, 94(1): 92–5.

Mattis, S. G. and Ollendick, T. H. (2002) *Panic Disorder and Anxiety in Adolescence*. New York: Wiley and Sons.

Maurer, R. E. and Tindall, J. H. (1983) Effect of postural congruence on client's perception of counselor empathy. *Journal of Counseling Psychology*, 30(2): 158–63.

McClure, S. M., Daw, N. D. and Montague, P. R. (2003) A computational substrate for incentive salience. *Trends in Neuroscience*, 26(8): 423–8.

McDowell, W. A. and McDowell, J. A. (ND) Neuro-Linguistic Programming Applied: The Use of Visual-Kinesthetic Dissociation to Cure Anxiety Disorders. *Brief Treatments for the Traumatized*.

McLeod, P. (1987) Visual reaction time and high-speed ball games. *Perception*. 16: 49–59.

McLeod, J. (2001) *Qualitative Research in Counselling and Psychotherapy*. London: Sage.

McMorran, P. R. (1988) Brief treatment of disturbing memory: A neuro-linguistic programming submodality procedure. *Dissertations Abstract International*, A 48 (7), 1710–11.

McNair, D., Lorr, M. and Droppleman, L. (1981) *EITS Manual for the Profile of Mood States*. San Diego, CA: Educational and Industrial Testing Service.

McNally, R. (2007) Mechanisms of exposure therapy: How neuroscience can improve psychological treatments for anxiety disorders. *Clinical Psychology Review*, 27(6): 750–9.

Mehrabian, A. (1971) *Silent Messages: Implicit Communication of Emotions and Attitudes*. Belmont, CA: Wadsworth.

Mehrabian, A. and Ferris, S. R. (1967) Inference of attitudes from nonverbal communication in two channels. *Journal of Consulting Psychology*, 31(3): 248–58.

Miller, F. C. (1997) *The NLP loss pattern: Imagery and experience in grief and mourning*. Academic Support Division: Faculty Publications. Paper 12. Available online: http://digitalcommons.wku.edu/bgcc_acad_supp_div_fac_pub/12.

Miller, G. (1956) The magical number seven, plus or minus two. *The Psychological Review*, 63, 81–97.

Miller, G.E. and Sheldon, C. (2001) Psychological interventions and the immune system: A meta-analytic review and critique. *Health Psychology*, 20(1): 47–63.

Miller, G., Galanter, E. and Pribram, K. (1960) *Plans and the Structure of Behaviour*. New York: Holt, Rinehart and Wilson.

Miller, W. R. (2004) The phenomenon of quantum change. *Journal of Clinical Psychology: In Session*, 60(5): 453–60.

Miller, W. R. and C'de Baca, J. (1994) Quantum change: Toward a psychology of transformation. In Heatherton, T. and Weinberger, J. (eds), *Can Personality Change?* Washington, DC: American Psychological Association, pp. 253–80.

Miller, S. D., Duncan, B. L., Brown, J., Sparks, J. A. and Claud, D. A. (2003) The outcome rating scale: A preliminary study of the reliability, validity, and feasibility of a brief visual analog measure. *Journal of Brief Therapy*, 2(2): 91–100.

Milner, B., Squire, L. R. and Kandel, E. R. (1998) Cognitive neuroscience and the study of memory. *Neuron*, 20(3): 445–68.

Mineka, S. and Oehlberg, K. (2008) The relevance of recent developments in classical conditioning to understanding the etiology and maintenance of anxiety disorders. *Acta Psychologica*, 127(3): 567–80.

Mischel, H. N. and Mischel, W. (1983) The development of children's knowledge of self-control strategies. *Child Development*, 54(3): 603–19.

Moines, D. (1981) A psycholinguistic study of the patterns of persuasion used by successful salespeople. *Dissertation Abstracts International*, 42 (5): 2135-B, University of Oregon, 271pp.

Morin, A. (2004) A neurocognitive and socioecological model of self-awareness. *Genetic, Social and General Psychology Monographs*, 130(3): 197–222.

Morin, A. (2005) Possible links between self-awareness and inner speech: Theoretical background, underlying mechanism, and empirical evidence. *Journal of Consciousness Studies*, 12(4–5): 115–34.

Morin, A. (2011) Self-recognition, theory-of-mind, and self-awareness: What side are you on? *Laterality*, 16(3): 367–83.

Morin, A. and Everett, J. (1990) Mediator of self-awareness, self-consciousness, and self-knowledge: An hypothesis. *New Ideas in Psychology*, 8(3): 337–56.

Morin, A. and Michaud, J. (2007) Self-awareness and the left inferior frontal gyrus: Inner speech use during self-related processing. *Detail Brain Research Bulletin*, 74(6): 387–96.

Morris, R. G. M. (2006) Elements of a neurobiological theory of hippocampal function: The role of synaptic plasticity, synaptic tagging and schemas. *European Journal of Neuroscience*, 23(11): 2829–46.

Morschitzky, H. (2006) *Psychotherapy Advisor: A Road Sign to Psychological Health*. New York: Springer Verlag.

Moynihan, R. (2011) A new deal on disease definition. How do we replace the old panels of conflicted experts? *British Medical Journal*, 342: 2548.

Muhlberger, A., Neumann, R., Wieser, M. J. and Pauli, P. (2008) The Impact of Changes in Spatial Distance on Emotional Responses. *Emotion*, 8(2): 192–8.

Muss, D. (1991) A new technique for treating post-traumatic stress disorder. *British Journal of Clinical Psychology*, 30(1): 91–2.

Muss, D. (2002) The Rewind Technique In the treatment of Post-Traumatic Stress Disorder: Methods and Application. In Figley, C. R. (ed.), *Brief Treatments for the Traumatized*. West Port, CT: Greenwood Press, pp. 306–14.

Nagel, T. (1986) *The View From Nowhere*. Oxford: Oxford University Press.

National Institutes of Drug Abuse (NIDA) (2002) *Stress and Substance Abuse: A Special Report*. National Institute on Drug Abuse. Available online: http://www.drugabuse.gov/stressanddrugabuse.html (accessed 26 February 2002).

Neumann, M., Bensing, J., Mercer, S., Ernstmann, N. and Oliver, P. H. (2009) Analyzing the 'nature' and 'specific effectiveness' of clinical empathy: A theoretical overview and contribution towards a theory-based research agenda. *Patient Education and Counseling*, 74(3): 339–46.

Norcross, J. C., Koocher, G. P. and Garofalo, A. (2006) Discredited psychological treatments and tests: A Delphi poll. *Professional Psychology: Research and Practice*, 37(5): 515–22.

Notz, W. (1975) Work motivation and the negative effects of extrinsic rewards. *American Psychologist*, September, pp. 884–91.

Nuechterlein, K. H. and Dawson, M. E. (1984) A heuristic vulnerability/stress model.of schizophrenic episodes. *Schizophrenia Bulletin*, 10: 300–12.

O'Brien, C. P. and Gardner, E. L. (2005) Critical assessment of how to study addiction and its treatment: Human and non-human animal models. *Pharmacology and Therapeutics*, 108: 18–58.

O'Connor, J. and Van der Horst, B. (1994) Neural Networks and NLP Strategies: Part 2. *Anchor Point*, 8(6): 30–8.

O'Connor, J. and Seymour, J. (1990) *Introducing NLP. Psychological Skills for Understanding and Influencing People*. London: Thorsons.

Öhman, A. and Mineka, S. (2001) Fears, phobias and preparedness: Toward an evolved module of fear and fear learning. *Psychological Review*, 108(3): 483–522.

Öhman, A., Eriksson, A. and Olofsson, C. (1975) One-trial learning and superior resistance to extinction of autonomic responses conditioned to potentially phobic stimuli. *Journal of Comparative and Physiological Psychology*, 88(2): 619–27.

Ohman, A., Fredrikson, M., Hugdahl, K. and Rimmo, P.-A. (1976) The premise of equipotentiality in human classical conditioning: Conditioned electrodermal responses to potentially phobic stimuli. *Journal of Experimental Psychology: General*, 105(4): 313–37.

Olson, J. A. (1985) Application of the neurolinguistic programming techniques of pacing and anchoring in pain management. Thesis (M.S.N.), Kent State University.

Ouellet, M., Santiago, J., Funes, M. J. and Lupiáñez, J. (2010) Thinking about the future moves attention to the right. *Journal of Experimental Psychology: Human Perception and Performance*, 36(1): 17–24.

Palubeckas, Aurelia J. (1981) Rapport in the therapeutic relationship and its relationship to pacing. Doctoral Dissertation, Boston University School of Education. *Dissertation Abstracts International.*

Pantin, H. M. (1982) The relationship between subjects' predominant sensory predicate use, their preferred representational system and self-reported attitudes towards similar versus different therapist-patient dyads. Doctoral Dissertation University of Miami, 1982) *Dissertation Abstracts International,* 43(7): 2350-B.

Paul, R. (1993) *Critical Thinking: How to Prepare Students for a Rapidly Changing World.* Tomales, CA: Foundation for Critical Thinking.

Pavlov, I. P. (1927) *Conditioned Reflexes.* London: Routledge.

Paxton, L. K. (1980) Representational systems and client perception of the counseling relationship. *Dissertation Abstracts International,* 41(9): 3888-A, Indiana University, 141pp.

Pedreira, M., Perez-Cuesta, L. and Maldonado, H. (2004) Mismatch between what is expected and what actually occurs triggers memory reconsolidation or extinction. *Learning and Memory,* 11(5): 579–85.

Peele, S. (1989) *Diseasing of America: Addiction Treatment Out of Control.* Lexington, MA: Lexington Books.

Peele, S. and Brodsky, A. (1991) *The Truth About Recovery and Addiction.* New York: Simon and Schuster.

Perls, F. S. (1969) *Gestalt Therapy Verbatim.* Gouldsboro, ME: Gestalt Journal Pres.

Pert, C. (1997) *Molecules of Emotion. Why You Feel the Way You Feel.* London: Pocket Books.

Pham, L. and Taylor, S. (1999) From Thought to Action: Effects of Process–Versus Outcome-Based Mental Simulations on Performance, *Personality and Social Psychology Bulletin,* 25(2): 250–60.

Podolsky, E. (1938) *The Doctor Prescribes Colours.* New York: National Library Press.

Poffel, S. A. and H. J. Cross (1985) Neurolinguistic programming: A test of the eye-movement hypothesis. *Perceptual and Motor Skills,* 61(3, Pt 2).

Popper, K. R. (1934) *The Logic of Scientific Discovery.* New York: Routledge Classics.

Popper, K. R. (1963) *Conjectures and Refutations: The Growth of Scientific Knowledge.* New York: Routledge Classics.

Prochaska, J., Norcross, J. and DiClemente, C. (1992) In search of How People Change: Application to Addictive Behaviors. *American Psychologist,* 5(9): 1102–14.

Prochaska, J., Norcross, J. and DiClemente, C. (1994) *Changing for Good.* New York: William Morrow.

Prochaska, J. O. (1994) Strong and weak principles for progressing from precontemplation to action on the basis of twelve problem behaviors. *Health Psychology,* 13(1): 47–51.

Quirk, G. J. and Mueller, D. (2007) Neural mechanisms of extinction learning and retrieval. *Neuropsychopharmacology,* 33(1), 56–72.

Rachman, S. (1967) Systematic desensitization. *Psychological Bulletin,* (67)2: 93–103.

Raguram, R. and Weiss, M. (2004) Stigma and somatisation. *British Journal of Psychiatry,* 185: 174.

Raichle, M. E. and Snyder, A. Z. (2007) A Default Mode of Brain Function: A Brief History of an Evolving Idea, *NeuroImage.*

Rainey, J. M., Aleem, A., Ortiz, A., Yaragani, V., Pohl, R. and Berchow, R. (1987) Laboratory procedure for the inducement of flashbacks. *American Journal of Psychiatry,* 144: 1317–19.

Ramachandran, V. S. (2003) Mirror neurons and imitation learning as the driving force behind 'the great leap forward' in human evolution. *Edge,* No. 69. Available online: http://edge.org/conversation/mirror-neurons-and-imitation-learning-as-the-driving-force-behind-the-great-leap-forward-in-human-evolution.

Ramachandran, V. and Hubbard E. (2006) Hearing Colors, Tasting Shapes. *Scientific American* (special edition: *Secrets of the Senses*).

Rapp, A. M., Leube, D. T., Erb, M., Grodd, W. and Kircher, T.T. (2006) *Laterality in Metaphor Processing: Lack of Evidence from Functional Magnetic Resonance Imaging for the Right Hemisphere Theory*. Dept of Psychiatry, University of Tuebingen, Germany.

Rebstock, M. E. (1980) The effects of training in matching techniques on the development of rapport between client and counselor during initial counseling interviews. *Dissertation Abstracts International*, 41(3), 946-A. University of Missouri, Kansas City, 89pp.

Redmond, M., Rooney, R. and Bishop, B. (2006) Unipolar depression across cultures: A Delphi analysis of the methodological and conceptual issues confronting the cross-cultural study of depression. *Australian e-Journal for the Advancement of Mental Health*, 5(2).

Renner, W. and Platz, T. (1999) Cognitive and symptom related effects of standardized behaviour therapy. Evaluation of an out-patient group program. *Zeitschrift fur Klinische Psychologie, Psychiatrie und Psychotherapie*, 47: 271–91.

Rescorla, R. A. (1988) Pavlovian conditioning: It's not what you think it is. *American Psychologist*, 43(3): 151–60.

Riccio, D., Millin, P. and Bogart, A. (2006) Reconsolidation: A brief history, a retrieval view and some recent issues. *Learning and Memory*, 13(5): 536–44.

Richardson, F. C. and Suinn, R. M. (1974) Effects of two short-term desensitization methods in the treatment of test anxiety. *Journal of Counseling Psychology*, (21)8: 457–8.

Rizzolatti, G. and Arbib, M.A. (1998) Language within our grasp. *Trends in Neuroscience*, 21: 188–94.

Rizzolatti, G. and Craighero L. (2004) The mirror-neuron system. *Annual Review of Neuroscience*, 27: 169–92.

Rizzolatti, G., Fadiga, L., Gallese, V. and Fogassi, L. (1996) Premotor cortex and the recognition of motor actions. *Cognitive Brain Research*, 3: 131–41.

Robbins, A. (1986) *Unlimited Power*. New York: Fawcett Columbine.

Robins, L. N., Davis, D. H. and Nurco, D. N. (1974) How Permanent Was Vietnam Drug Addiction? *American Journal of Public Health*, Supplement, 64, December.

Robinson, T. E. (2004) Addicted Rats. *Science*, 305: 951–3.

Robinson, T. E. and Berridge, K. C. (2001) Incentivesensitization and addiction. *Addiction*, 96(1): 103–14.

Robinson, T. E. and Berridge, K. C. (2003) Addiction. *Annual Review of Psychology*: 54: 25.

Rogers, C. (1967) *On becoming a Person. A Therapist's View of Psychotherapy*. London: Constable & Robinson.

Rossi, E. L. (1986) *The Psychobiology of Mind–Body Healing*. New York: W.W. Norton and Company.

Rossi, E. L. (2000) In search of a deep psychobiology of hypnosis: visionary hypotheses for a new millennium. *American Journal of Clinical Hypnosis*, 42(3)/42(4): 178–207.

Rossi, E. L. and Cheek, D. B. (1988) *Mind–Body Therapy*. New York: W.W. Norton and Company.

Roth, A., Fonagy, P., Parry, G., Target, M. and Woods, R. (2005) *What Works for Whom? A Critical Review of Psychotherapy Research* (2nd ed.). New York: Guilford Press.

Roth, R. M., Saykin, A. J., Flashman, I. A., Pixley, H. S., West, J. D. and Mamourian, A. C. (2006) Event-related functional magnetic resonance imaging of response inhibition in obsessive-compulsive disorder. *Biological Psychiatry*, 62(8): 901–9.

Rothbaum, B. O. and Davis, M. (2003) Applying learning principles to the treatment of post-trauma reactions. *Annals of the New York Academy of Sciences*, 1008(1): 112–21.

Rothbaum, B. O., Meadows, E. A., Resnick, R. and Foy, D. W. (2000) Cognitive Behavioral Therapy. In Foa, E.A., Keane, T. M. and Friedman, M. J. *Effective Treatments for PTSD*. New York: The Guilford Press, pp. 60–83.

Ruden, Ronald (1997) *The Craving Brain*. New York: Harper Collins.

Rushworth, C. (1994) *Making a Difference in Cancer Care: Practical Techniques in Palliative and Curative Treatment*. London: Souvenir Press.

Rygh, J. L. and Sanderson, W. C. (2004) *Treating Generalized Anxiety Disorder: Evidence-based Strategies, Tools and Techniques*. New York: The Guilford Press.

Sackett, D. L., Rosenberg, W. M. C., Muir Gray, J. A., Haynes, R. B. and Richardson, W. S. (1996) Evidence based medicine: What it is and what it isn't. *British Medical Journal*, 312: 71.

Sackett, D. L., Straus, S. E., Richardson, W. S. *et al.* (2000) *Evidence-based Medicine: How to Practice and Teach EBM*, 2nd edn. Edinburgh: Churchill Livingstone.

Sacks, O. (1995) Scotoma: Forgetting and neglect in science. In Silvers, R. (ed.), *Hidden Histories of Science*. London: Granta.

Salkovskis, P. M. (1995) Demonstrating specific effects in cognitive and behavioural therapy. In Aveline, M. and Shapiro, D. A. (eds), *Research Foundations for Psychotherapy Research*. Chichester: Wiley and Sons, pp. 191–228.

Sanchez-Burks, J., Bartel, C. A. and Blount, S. (2009) Performance in intercultural interactions at work: Cross-cultural differences in response to behavioral mirroring. *Journal of Applied Psychology*, 94(1): 216–23.

Sandhu, D. S. (1984) The effects of mirroring vs. non-mirroring of clients' nonverbal behavior on empathy, trustworthiness and positive interaction in cross-cultural counseling dyads. *Dissertation Abstracts International*, 45(4): 1042.

Sandhu, D. S., Reeves, T. G. and Portes, P. R. (1993) Cross-cultural counseling and neurolinguistic mirroring with native American adolescents. *Journal of Multicultural Counseling and Development*, 21(2): 106–18.

Santiago, J., Román, A., Ouellet, M., Rodríguez, N. and Pérez-Azor, P. (2010) In hindsight, life flows from left to right. *Psychological Research/Psychologische Forschung*, 74(1): 59–70.

Satir, V. (1972) *Peoplemaking*. Palo Alto: Science and Behaviour Books.

Satir, V. and Baldwin, M. (1983) *Satir. Step by Step*. Palo Alto, CA: Science and Behaviour Books.

Schachter, S. and Singer, J. E. (1962) Cognitive, social and psychological determinants of emotional states. *Psychological Review*, 69, 379–99.

Schaeffer, H. and Martin, P. (1969) *Behavioral Therapy*. New York: McGraw Hill.

Schiller, D. and Phelps, E. A. (2011) Does reconsolidation occur in humans? *Frontiers in Behavioral Neuroscience*, 5.

Schiller, D., Monfils, M., Raio, C., Johnson, D., LeDoux, J. and Phelps, E. (2010) Preventing the return of fear in humans using reconsolidation update mechanisms. *Nature*, 463(7277): 49–53.

Schmedlen, G. W. (1981) The impact of sensory modality matching on the establishment of rapport in psychotherapy. Doctoral Dissertation, Kent State University. *Dissertation Abstracts International*, 42(5): 2080-B.

Schneider, M. E. (1984) The relationship among primary representational systems and counselor empathy, trustworthiness, attractiveness, expertness and subject preference. *Dissertation Abstracts International*, 45(2).

Schooler, J. W., Smallwood, J., Christoff, K., Handy, T. C., Reichle, E. D. and Sayette, M. A. (2011) Meta-awareness, perceptual decoupling and the wandering mind. *Trends in Cognitive Sciences*, 15(7): 319–26.

Schore, A. N. (2003) *Affect Regulation and the Repair of the Self*. London: W.W. Norton.

Schreiber, R., Stern, P. N. and Wilson, C. (1998) The contexts for managing depression and its stigma among black West Indian Canadian women. *Journal of Advanced Nursing*, 27(3): 510–17.

Schultz, W., Dayan, P. and Montague, P. R. (1997) A neural substrate of prediction and reward. *Science*, 275: 1593–9.

Schweckendiek, J., Klucken, T., Merz, C. J., Tabbert, K., Walter, B., Ambach, W. *et al.* (2011) Weaving the (neuronal) web: Fear learning in spider phobia. *NeuroImage*, 54(1): 681–8.

Scott, E. K. (1987) The effects of the neurolinguistic programming model of reframing as therapy for bulimia. *Dissertation Abstracts International*, 48(7), 1713-A 1714-A, Northern Arizona University.

Searson, R., Mansell, W., et al. (2012) Think Effectively About Mood Swings (TEAMS): A case series of cognitive–behavioural therapy for bipolar disorders. *Journal of Behavior Therapy and Experimental Psychiatry*, 43(2): 770–9.

Segerstrom, S. C and Miller, G. E. (2004) Psychological Stress and the Human Immune System: A Meta-Analytic Study of 30 Years of Inquiry. *Psychological Bulletin*, July, 130(4): 601–30.

Seligman, M. E. P. (1971) Phobias and preparedness. *Behavior Therapy*, 2, 307–20.

Seligman, M. E. P. (1995) The effectiveness of psychotherapy. The consumer reports study. *American Psychologist*, 50(12): 965–74.

Seligman, M. E. P. (1997) *Learned Optimism*. Sydney: Random House.

Sexton, K. A. and Dugas, M. J (2009) Defining distinct negative beliefs about uncertainty: Validating the factor structure of the intolerance of uncertainty Scale. *Psychological Assessment*, 21(2): 176–86. American Psychological Association.

Shalev, A. Y., Bonne, O. and Eth, S. (1996) Treatment of posttraumatic stress disorder: A review. *Psychosomatic Medicine*, 58(2): 165–82.

Shapiro, F. (1985) Neurolinguistic programming: The new success technology. *Holistic Life Magazine*, pp. 41–3.

Sharot, T., Davidson, M. L., Carson, M. M. and Phelps, E. A. (2008) Eye movements predict recollective experience. *PLoS ONE*, 3(8): e2884.

Sharpley, C. (1984) Predicate matching in NLP: A review of research on the preferred representational system. *Journal of Counseling Psychology*, 31(2): 238–48.

Sharpley, C. F. (1987) Research findings on neurolinguistic programming: Nonsupportive data or an untestable theory? *Journal of Counseling Psychology*, 34(1): 103–7.

Shattuck, D. K. (1994) Mindfulness and metaphor in relapse prevention: an interview with G. Alan Marlatt. *Journal of the American Dietetic Association*, 94(8): 846–8.

Shelden, V. E. and Shelden, R. G. (1989) Sexual abuse of males by females: The problem, treatment modality and case example. *Family Therapy*, 16(3): 249–58.

Sherman, E. and Skinner, K. W. (1988) Client language and clinical process: A cognitive-semantic analysis. *Clinical Social Work Journal*, 16(4): 391–405.

Shobin, M. Z. (1980) *An investigation of the effects of verbal pacing on initial therapeutic rapport.* Doctoral Dissertation, Boston University School of Education. *Dissertation Abstracts International*, 41(5).

Simons, R. F., Detenber, B. H., Reiss, J. E. and Shults, C. W. (2000) Image motion and context: A between- and within-subjects comparison. *Psychophysiology*, 37: 706–10.

Simons, R. F., Detenber, B. H., Roedema, T. M. and Reiss, J. E. (1999) Emotion processing in three systems: The medium and the message. *Psychophysiology*, 36: 619–27.

Skinner, B. F. (1957) *Science and Human Behavior*. New York: Free Press.

Smallwood, J., Brown, K., Baird, B. and Schooler, J. W. (2012) Cooperation between the default mode network and the frontal–parietal network in the production of an internal train of thought. *Brain Research*, 1428: 60–70.

Smith-Hanen, S. (1977) Effects of nonverbal behaviors on judged levels of counselor warmth and empathy. *Journal of Counseling Psychology*, 24: 87–91.

Sonnby-Borgstrom, M., Jonsson, P. and Svensson, O. (2003) Emotional empathy as related to mimicry reactions at different levels of information processing. *Journal of Nonverbal Behavior*, 27(1): 3–23.

Soon, C. S., Brass, M., Heinze, H. and Haynes, J. (2008) Unconscious determinants of free decisions in the human brain. *Nature Neuroscience*, 11: 54–5.

Southwick, S. M., Krystal, J. H., Morgan, C. A., Johnson, D., Nagy, L. M., Nicolauuo, A. et al. (1993) Abnormal noradrenergic function in posttraumatic stress disorder. *Archives of General Psychiatry*, 50: 266–74.

Sparks, D. (1999) Conceptual issues related to the role of the superior colliculus in the control of gaze. *Current Opinion in Neurobiology*, 9: 698–707.

Spector, F. and Maurer, D. (2009) Synesthesia: A New Approach to Understanding the Development of Perception. *Developmental Psychology*, 45(1): 175–89.

Sperber, K. (1983) The language of empathy. *Dissertation Abstracts International*, 45(2): 688-B. University of Maine, 173 pp.

Spiegler, M. D., Cooley, E. J., Marshall, G. J., Price, H. T, II, Puckett, S. P. and Skenazy, J. A. (1976) A self-control versus a counterconditioning paradigm for systematic desensitization: An experimental comparison. *Journal of Counseling Psychology*, 23: 83–6.

Spielberger, C. D. (1983) *Manual for the State-Trail Anxiety Inventory Form Y: Self-Evaluation Questionnaire*. Palo Alto, CA: Consulting Psychologists Press.

Spreng, R. N. and Grady, C. L. (2010) Patterns of brain activity supporting autobiographical memory, prospection and theory of mind and their relationship to the default mode network. *Journal of Cognitive Neuroscience*, 22(6): 1112–23.

Spreng, R. N., Mar, R. A. and Kim, A. S. N. (2008) The common neural basis of autobiographical memory, prospection, navigation, theory of mind and the default mode: A quantitative meta-analysis. *Journal of Cognitive Neuroscience*, 21(3): 489–510.

Stanton, H. E. (1993) Submodalities: I. Adolescent happiness. *International Journal of Psychosomatics*, 40(1–4): 86–9.

Steketee, G. S. (1993) *Treatment of Obsessive-Compulsive Disorder*. New York: Guilford Press.

Sternman, C. (1990) *Neuro Linguistic Programming in Alcoholism Treatment*. New York: The Haworth Press.

Stewart, S. M., Kennard, B. D., Lee, P. W. H., Hughes, C. W., Mayes, T. L., Emslie, G. J. and Lewinsohn, P. M. (2004) A Cross-Cultural Investigation of Cognitions and Depressive Symptoms in Adolescents. *Journal of Abnormal Psychology*, 113(2): 248–57.

Stiles, W. B., Barkham, M., Twigg, E., Mellor-Clark, J. and Cooper, M. (2006) Effectiveness of Cognitive-Behavioural, Person-Centred and Psychodynamic Therapies as Practised in UK National Health Service Settings. *Psychological Medicine*, 36: 555–66.

Stipancic, M., Renner, W., Schütz, P. and Dond R (2010) Effects of Neuro-Linguistic Psychotherapy on psychological difficulties and perceived quality of life. *Counselling and Psychotherapy Research*, 10(1): 39–49.

Sumin, A. N., Khairedinova, O. P., Sumina, L., Variushkina, E. V., Doronin, D. V. and Galimzianov, D. (2000) Psychotherapy impact on effectiveness of in-hospital physical rehabilitation in patients with acute coronary syndrome. *Klin Med (Mosk)*, 78(6): 16–20.

Swets, J. A. and Bjork, R. A. (1990) Enhancing Human Performance: An Evaluation of 'New Age' Techniques considered by the U.S. Army. *Psychological Science*, 1(2): 85–6.

Taba, H. (1966) *Teaching strategies and cognitive functioning in elementary school children*. Cooperative Research Project No. 2404. San Francisco, CA: San Francisco State College.

Taylor, R. J. (2004) Therapeutic intervention of trauma and stress brought on by divorce. *Journal of Divorce and Remarriage*, 41(1–2): 129–35.

Thom, A., Sartory, G. and Johren, P. (2000) Comparison between one-session psychological treatment and benzodiazepine in dental phobia. *Journal of Consulting and Clinical Psychology*, 68(3): 378–87.

Thomason, D. D. (1984) Neurolinguistic Programming: an aid to increase counselor expertness. Doctoral Dissertation, Biola University. *Dissertation Abstracts International*, 44(9), 2909-B.

Thomason, T. C., Arbuckle, T. *et al*. (1980) Test of the eye-movement hypothesis of neurolinguistic programming. *Perceptual and Motor Skills*, 51(1): 230.

Titone, D. (1998) Hemispheric differences in context sensitivity during lexical ambiguity resolution. *Brain and Language*, 65: 361–94.

Tobler, P. N., Fiorillo, C. D. and Schultz, W. (2005) Adaptive Coding of Reward Value By Dopamine Neurons. *Science*, 307: 1642–5.

Tope, R., Thomas, E. and Jones, M.E. (2010) *The Waking Up and Moving On (WUMO). Programme for Young People with Anti-Social Behaviour: An Evaluation*. Cardiff: HERC Associates.

Tosey, P. and Mathison, J. (2009) *Neuro-Linguistic Programming: A Critical Appreciation for Managers and Developers*. Basingstoke: Palgrave Macmillan.

Tronel, S., Milekic, M. H. and Alberini, C. M. (2005) Linking New Information to a Reactivated Memory Requires Consolidation and Not Reconsolidation Mechanisms. *PLoS Biol*, 3(9): 293.

Tse, D., Langston, R. F., Bethus, I., Wood, E. R., Witter, M. P. and Morris, R. G. M. (2008) Does assimilation into schemas involve systems or cellular consolidation? It's not just time. *Neurobiology of Learning and Memory*, 89(4), 361–5.

Tversky, B., Kugelmass, S. and Winter, A. (1991) Cross-cultural and developmental trends in graphic productions. *Cognitive Psychology*, 23(4): 515–7.

Ursano, R. J., Bell, C. *et al.* (2004) *Practice Guideline for the Treatment of Patients with Acute Stress Disorder and Posttraumatic Stress Disorder*. Washington, DC: APA Practice Guidelines.

US Department of Health and Human Services (DHHS) (1999) *Mental Health: A Report of the Surgeon General*.

Utuza, A. J., Joseph, S. and Muss, D. C. (2012) Treating traumatic memories in rwanda with the rewind technique: Two-week follow-up after a single group session. *Traumatology*, 18(1): 75–8.

Van der Kolk, B. A., McFarlane, A. C. and Weisaeth, L. (eds) (1996) *Traumatic Stress*. New York: Guilford.

Vasey, M. W. and Borkovec, T. D. (1992) A catastrophising assessment of worrisome thoughts. *Cognitive Therapy and Research*, 16: 505–20.

Veronen, L. and Kilpatrick, D. (1983) *Stress Management for Rape Victims*. In D. Meichenbaum and Jaremko, M. E. (eds), *Stress Reduction and Prevention*. New York: Plenum, pp. 341–74.

Vervliet, B. (2008) Learning and memory in conditioned fear extinction: Effects of D-cycloserine. *Acta Psychologica*, 127(3): 601–13.

Vianna, L. A. C., Bomfim, G. F. T. and Chicone, G. (2006) Self-esteem of raped women. *Revista Latino-Americana de Enfermagem*, Sep–Oct, 14(5): 695–701.

Volkow, N. D. and Fowler, J. S. *et al.* (2002) Role of dopamine, the frontal cortex and memory circuits in drug addiction: Insight from imaging studies. *Neurobiology of Learning and Memory*, 78(3): 610–24.

Von Bertalanffy, L. (1968) *General Systems Theory, Foundations, Developments, Applications*. New York: Braziller.

Wachelka, D. and Katz, R. (1999) Reducing test anxiety and improving academic self-esteem in high school and college students with learning disabilities. *Journal of Behavior Therapy and Experimental Psychiatry*, 39(3): 191–8.

Waelti, P.; Dickenson, A. and Schults, W. (2001) Dopamine responses comply with basic assumptions of formal learning theory. *Nature*, July, 412: 43.

Wake, L. (2008) *Neurolinguistic Psychotherapy: A Postmodern Approach*. London: Routledge.

Wake, L. (2010) *NLP Principles in Practice*. St. Albans: Ecademy Press.

Wake, L. (2010b) *The Role of Brief Therapy in Attachment Disorder*. London: Karnac.

Wake, L. (2009) A study of the relationship between the core belief structures of neurolinguistic psychotherapy and object relations theory. Current Research in NLP. *NLP*, 1: 50–66.

Wake, L. (2011) Waking up and moving on: a programme evaluation of an intervention with adolescents identified as at risk of offending behaviour. Current research in NLP. *NLP*, pp 43–53.

Walker, W. (1996) *Abenteuer Kommunikation Bateson, Perls, Satir, Erickson und die Anfange des Neurolinguistischen Programmierens (NLP)* 4th edn. Stuttgart: KlettCott.

Watson, D., Clark, L.A. and Tellegen, A. (1988) Development and validation of brief measures of positive and negative affect: The PANAS scales. *Journal of Personality and Social Psychology*, 54(6): 1063–70.

Watzlawick, P. (1978) *The Language of Change*. New York: Norton and Norton.

Weathers, F., Litz, B., Herman, D. Huska, J. and Keane, T. (1993) *The PTSD Checklist (PCL): Reliability, validity and diagnostic utility*. Texas, The Annual Meeting of International Society for Traumatic Stress Studies. San Antonio. October. Available online: www.pdhealth.mil/library/downloads/PCL_sychometrics.doc.

Weathers, F., Litz, B., Huska, J. and Keane, T. (1994) *The PTSD Checklist—Civilian Version (PCL-C)*. Boston, MA: National Center for PTSD.

Weaver, M. (2009) An Exploration of a Research-Based Approach to the Evaluation of Clients' Experience of Neuro-Linguistic Psychotherapy within a Private Practice Making use of the CORE Model. Current Research in NLP: Proceedings of 2008 NLP Conference, 1: 67–83.

Webb, E. J., Campbell, D. T., Schwartz, R. D. and Sechrest, L. (2000) *Unobtrusive Measures*, revised edition. Thousand Oaks, CA: Sage.

Weger, U. W. and Pratt, J. (2008) Time flies like an arrow: Space-time compatibility effects suggest the use of a mental timeline. *Psychonomic Bulletin and Review*, 15(2): 426–30.

Wegner, D. M., Schneider, D. J., Carter, S. and White, T. (1987) Paradoxical effects of thought suppression. *Journal of Personality and Social Psychology*, 53: 5–13.

Wells, A. (1995) Meta-cognition and worry: A cognitive model of generalized anxiety disorder. *Behavioural and Cognitive Psychotherapy*, 23: 301–20.

Wessa, M. L. and Flor, H. (2007) Failure of extinction of fear responses in posttraumatic stress disorder: Evidence from second-order conditioning. *American Journal of Psychiatry*, 164(11): 1684–92.

Williams, L., Kemp, A., Felmingham, K., Barton, M., Olivieri, G., Peduto, A. *et al.* (2006) Trauma modulates amygdala and medial prefrontal responses to consciously attended fear. *NeuroImage*, 29(2): 347–57.

Wiers, R. W., Eberl, C., Rinck, M., Becker, E. S. and Lindenmeyer, J. (2011) Retraining automatic action tendencies changes alcoholic patients' approach bias for alcohol and improves treatment outcome. *Psychological Science*, 22(4): 490–97.

Wilhelm, F. H. and Roth, W. T. (1997) Acute and delayed effects of alprazolam on flight phobics during exposure. *Behavioural Research and Therapy*, 35(9): 831–41.

Williams, L. and Bargh, J. (2008) Experiencing physical warmth promotes interpersonal warmth. *Science*, 322: 606–7.

Williams, J. H. G., Whiten, A., Suddendorf, T. and Perrett, D. I. (2001) Imitation, mirror neurons and autism. *Neuroscience and Biobehavioural Review*, 25: 287–95.

Winner, E. and Gardner, H. (1977) The comprehension of metaphor in brain-damaged patients. *Brain*, 100, 717–29.

Witt, K. (2003) Psychological treatment can modulate the skin reaction to histamine in pollen allergic humans. *Psychosomatics*, 4: 33–7.

Witt, K. (2008) Neuro-linguistic psychotherapy (NLPt) treatment can modulate the reaction in pollen allergic humans and their state of health. *International Journal of Psychotherapy*, 12(1): 50–60.

Wittchen, H.-U., Zhao, S., Kessler, R. and Eaton, W. W. (1994) DSM-III-R generalized anxiety disorder in the National Comorbidity Survey. *Archives of General Psychiatry*, 51: 355–64.

Witkowski, T. (2010) Thirty-five years of research on Neuro-Linguistic Programming. NLP research data base. State of the art or pseudoscientific decoration? *Polish Psychological Bulletin*, 41(2): 58–66.

Wohldmann, E., Healy, A. and Bourne, L. (2007) Pushing the limits of imagination: Mental practice for learning sequences. *Journal of Experimental Psychology: Learning, Memory and Cognition*, 33(1): 254–61.

Wolitzky-Taylor, K. B., Horowitz, J. D., Powers, M. B. and Telch, M. J. (2008) Psychological approaches in the treatment of specific phobias: A meta-analysis. *Clinical Psychology Review*, 28(6), 1021–37.

Wolpe, J. (1958) *Psychotherapy by Reciprocal Inhibition*. Stanford, CA: Stanford University Press.

World Health Organization (2012) Available online: http://www.who.int/mental_health/management/depression/definition/en/ (accessed 31 October 2011).

Yang, Y. C., Newby. T. and Bill. R. L. (2005) Using Socratic questioning to promote critical thinking skills through asynchronous discussion forums in distance learning environments. *The American Journal of Distance Education*, 19(3):163–81.

Yeager, J. (1985) *Thinking About Thinking with NLP*. Cupertino, CA: Meta Publications.

Zigmond, A. S. and Snaith, R. P. (1983) The hospital anxiety and depression scale. *Acta Psychiatrica Scandinavica*, 67: 361–70.

Zika, B. (1985) Transformational hypnotherapy: Historical antecedents and a case example. *Australian Journal of Clinical Hypnotherapy and Hypnosis*, 6(2): 57–66.

Zinbarg, R. E., Uliaszek, A. A. and Adler, J. M. (2008) The role of personality in psychotherapy for anxiety and depression. *Journal of Personality*, 76(6): 1649–88.

Index

Note: Page numbers followed by 'f' refer to figures, 't' refer to tables.

Ad K loop 147
addictions 95–125; and default mode network (DMN) 102, 116–17, 123; as diseases 95–6; dissociation of behavioural networks 103–4; incentive salience and 99, 101, 102, 104, 107, 115; mid brain dopamine system 99, 100, 101, 102, 103, 121; nature of 102–3; neuroscience and 98–103; NLP approaches to 104–6; NLP perspective on 96–8; problems to target in overcoming 104, 115–19; study of opioid use for palliative care in pain treatment 98; in Vietnam GIs 96, 97
adolescents 56–7, 66t, 132–3
akinetopsia 166
alcoholism 95, 98, 105, 139–40
Allen, K.L. 12–13, 15t, 168
allergic responses, NLP interventions for 57–8, 62–3t
alphabetic task to evaluate PRS 204–6
anchoring 23–4, 29, 50, 107, 208; in Brooklyn Program 107, 109–10, 112–15, 122, 123, 124; and environmental triggers 79; research to support use in state management 180–1; and use of desensitizing protocol in treatment of phobias 27–8; utilisation in NLPt 49, 50; *see also* collapsing anchors
Andreas, S. 4, 16, 35, 36, 46, 105, 128, 129, 130, 133, 134, 142, 186, 196
Andreas, S. and C. Andreas 4, 12, 16, 27, 33, 35, 43, 80, 107, 108, 117, 128, 129, 130, 133, 135, 136, 137, 142, 143, 153, 154, 162, 165, 173, 184, 185, 188, 234
anger, NLP interventions for 48, 50, 64t, 180
anxiety disorders 69–94; case study 81–7; difference between anxiety and depression 69–70; DSM diagnostic categories for 69, 71; effects of NLPt on psychological difficulties and perceived quality of life 48–9, 64t, 88–9, 94, 149, 237; generalized anxiety disorder (GAD) 74–7; NLP theoretical orientations 77–81; NLPt to reduce claustrophobia in patients requiring an MRI scan 15t, 24–7, 60, 63t, 89–90, 94; obsessive compulsive disorder (OCD) 72–4, 176, 185; panic disorder 70–2, 81–7; public anxiety 91–3; research into NLP and 87–94
APET model 78, 78f, 80
Association for NLP (ANLP) 221
asthma, NLP interventions for 57–8, 62–3t
auditory digital system 158–9, 165
avoidance theory 76, 77

Baddeley, M. 49, 66t
Bandler, R. 11, 12, 22, 23, 33, 35, 36, 40, 42, 43, 53, 71, 78, 91, 93, 96, 97, 104, 105, 107, 115, 129, 130, 131, 134, 135, 136, 137, 139, 142, 143, 147, 153, 154, 156, 158, 160, 162, 164, 165, 173, 180, 181, 182, 183, 184, 185, 186, 187, 190, 195, 196, 197, 198, 199, 200, 201, 203
Bandura, A. 77, 109, 136, 183
Bargh, J.A. 167, 181
Bateson, G. 59, 77, 79, 129, 140; levels of learning 214, 215, 216t, 222
Beck, A.T. 69, 70, 81, 87, 131
behavioural change, well-formedness conditions for 189–91, 191t
behavioural networks, dissociation of 103–4, 175
belief change techniques 142, 147
Bentall, R.P. 35, 36, 38, 39t, 42
bereavement 128–9
Bertoli, J.M. 49, 67t
Bigley, J. 15t, 24, 60, 63t, 89–90, 94
bipolar disorder 140–2
Bokuro-Shafé, K. 61

Borkovec, T.D. 75–6, 77, 80, 86
Bourke, F. 35, 156
Bowers, L.A. 59, 63t, 170
brain: anterior cingulate cortex 74, 102, 103, 104, 116, 148; dorsolateral prefrontal cortex 103, 104; mid brain dopamine system 99, 100, 101, 102, 103, 121; neural systems 103, 169, 175, 176, 179, 192; orbito-frontal cortex 99, 102, 103, 104, 118, 168; pre-frontal cortex (PFC) 177; scans 116, 155, 156, 175, 213; summary of NLP and 191–3; ventromedial prefrontal cortex 103, 104, 116; *see also* neuroscience
Brandis, A.D. 50, 64t, 180
Broca's aphasia 165
Brooklyn Program 106–25, 169; applying mechanism 119–22; evaluating hypotheses of 122–4; NLP tools used in 107–8; process 110–15; proposed mechanism 115–19
Buckner, M. 160, 164
bulimia, NLP interventions for 59, 67t
Bull, L. 180–1, 183

Cade, B. 108, 117, 174, 188
cancer 60, 61, 139
cardiovascular rehabilitation 60, 65t
Carroll, R.T. 212–13
certification, NLP 219–20, 221–2, 230, 233, 236, 237, 238
Chambers, R.A. 101, 103, 104, 121, 175
Cheek, D.B. 104, 174, 175, 176
Chomsky, N. 77, 129, 134, 137, 184, 185
Clark, D.A. 70, 71
classical conditioning 40, 79, 103, 107, 175
claustrophobia in patients requiring an MRI scan, using NLP to reduce 15t, 24–7, 60, 63t, 89–90, 94
Codispoti, M. 168
cognitive behavioural therapy (CBT) 87, 155, 187; comparison of linguistic patterns from NLP and 137–8, 138t, 187; imagery and parallels with submodalities in NLP 138–9; meta-study of techniques in 136–7; for OCD 74; paucity of NLP studies compared to CBT studies 87, 94; and pharmacotherapy compared in a randomized trial 136; role playing and parallels in NLP 135–7; and similarities with NLP 134–40; Socratic questioning and cognitive distortion and parallels in NLP 137–8, 138t
cognitive bias 240
cognitive bias modification (CBM) 139–40
cognitive linguistics 157, 219, 239, 240, xiv
cognitive psychology 185, 240

collapsing anchors 22–4, 29, 189–90; use of technique to reduce claustrophobia in MRI scan patients 15t, 24–7, 60, 63t, 89–90, 94
Colleau, S.M. 98
contextual renewal 9, 40
CORE Systems Research Tool 49, 56, 66t, 237
core transformation 80–1, 80f, 105–6
Craig, A.D. 102, 103, 104, 116, 120

Daniell, J. 204
Davis, S.L. and D.I. Davis 49, 67t
De Cesarei, A. 168
deep-brain stimulation (DBS) 74
default mode network (DMN) 102, 116–17, 123
DeLozier, J. 12, 22, 23, 33, 35, 43, 101, 107, 108, 117, 119, 135, 137, 154, 156, 158, 187, 188, 190, 212
Depression Report 126
depressive disorders 126–50; belief change techniques and 142, 147; current context of 126–7; developing positive self-identity in an elderly patient 131–2, 170; difference between anxiety and 69–70; DSM diagnostic categories for 126–7; and energy levels 149; and future research 56, 149–50; imagery in CBT and submodalities in NLP 138–9; joystick treatment in CBM and relation to submodalities and future pacing in NLP 139–40; mechanism of submodality manipulation 134; multi-level NLP intervention for 145–9; NLP and studies in treatment of 129–34; NLP model of change for 143–5; NLP perspective on 127–9; and physical activity levels 149; prevalence of 126; role playing in CBT and relation to future pacing and New Behavior Generator in NLP 135–7; similarities in methods used in CBT and NLP 134–40; Socratic questioning and cognitive distortion and parallels in NLP 137–8, 138t; strategies and patterns resulting in 147, 172; swish technique in treatment of 142; symptoms of 144; TEAMS model and treatment of bipolar disorders 140–2
desensitization protocol 27–8
Dilts, R.B. 4, 12, 22, 23, 33, 35, 43, 53, 101, 107, 108, 117, 119, 129, 130, 134, 135, 137, 142, 145, 147, 154, 156, 158, 159, 161, 162, 171, 172, 173, 178, 187, 188, 189, 190, 199, 212
discredited psychological treatments, study of 209, 231

domestic violence project 49–50
DSM diagnostic categories: for anxiety disorders 69, 71; for bulimia 59; conflicts of interests on panel of 231; for depressive disorders 126–7; for phobias 7; for PTSD 32–3
Duncan, R.C. 50, 65t
dyslexia, management of 180–1

EAP 226–9t
eating disorders 59, 67t
Einspruch, E.L. 12, 15t, 168, 199–201, 203, 207, 208, 212
Elich, M. 204, 206
empathy 117, 158, 160, 183; in therapeutic relationships 183–4, 196, 198, 199, 208
Erickson, M. 42, 77, 78, 108, 173, 174, 183
ethics, code of 88, 94, 221, 222, 223, 227t
European Association for Neurolinguistic Psychotherapy (EANLPt) 221, 226–9t
evidence-based medicine 2, 47, 210, 210t, 211t, 219, 230–2, 236
Evidence Pyramid 210, 211t
exposure treatments 8–9, 40, 73, 74
extinction 9–10, 16, 32, 40, 44, 45, 46
eye accessing cues (EACs) 158, 159–62, 184, 197, 203, 206, 207; directions for further research 164; NLP specific research on 162–4, 196, 201, 204; Sharpley's review of research on 196; Witkowski's review of research on 204, 206
eye movement desensitization and reprocessing (EMDR) 51, 209, 231

family therapy 50, 67t
Fast Phobia Cure 8, 24, 33, 60, 208; see also visual kinesthetic dissociation (V/KD)
Faulkner, C. 154, 238–9
feed-forward and feedback loops 129, 133, 134
Field, E.S. 49, 65t, 168
Foa, E.B. 10, 32, 33, 40, 42, 43, 46, 214, 236
Forman, B.D. 12, 15t, 160, 168, 199–201, 203, 208, 212
Freud, S. 173, 175
Fromme, D.K. 204
future pacing 108, 109–10, 135–7, 139–40

Gallese, V. 181
generalized anxiety disorder (GAD) 74–7
genocide survivors study 36–7, 38, 39t
Genser-Medlitsch, M. 47, 56, 64t, 237
Glezer, L.S. 134, 185
goal setting 135–6, 169
Goodrich, W.E. 14, 15t
Gordon, D. 157, 165, 239
Graunke, B. 160, 204, 207

Gray, R.M. 4, 12, 23, 27, 29, 30, 40, 41, 97, 105, 106, 107, 108, 109, 110, 113, 114, 115, 117, 119, 120, 121, 122, 165, 168, 169, 178, 180, 190, 235
Griffin, J. 78, 78f
Grinder, J. 22, 23, 42, 53, 78, 91, 93, 96, 97, 104, 105, 107, 115, 129, 130, 131, 134, 135, 136, 137, 143, 147, 153, 154, 156, 158, 160, 162, 173, 181, 182, 183, 184, 185, 186, 187, 190, 195, 196, 197, 198, 199, 200, 201, 203
grounded theory study 49, 68t
Guy, K. and N. Guy 12, 33, 35, 36

Hale, R.L. 14, 168
Hall, L.M. 84, 97, 108, 115, 117, 154, 165, 179, 213, 214
Harris, B. 194, 195
Heap, M. 202
Hossack, A. 35, 36, 38, 39t, 42, 130, 131, 170
hypnosis 168–9; allergic responses and 57; anxiety disorders and 93; double hypnotic induction 93; Eriksonian 49, 60, 65t, 93, 173–4; phobias and 12, 13; post-cardiac rehabilitation and 60, 65t; psychotherapy and 49, 65t; PTSD and treatment with 36, 37, 38, 39t, 168–9; relationship counselling and 49, 66t, 68t; research into 170; transformational hypnotherapy 49, 68t

identity in NLPt 146
imagery in CBT and submodalities in NLP 138–9
imaginal practice 108, 135, 136, 181, 189
incentive salience of addictive behaviours 99, 101, 102, 104, 107, 115
individual client outcome scales 237
information processing 78–9
interoceptive exposure 72
intrinsic motivations, psychology of 118, 188–9

James, W. 157–8, 166
Jiang, X. 185
joystick treatment in CBM and relation to submodalities and future pacing in NLP 139–40
Juhnke, G.A. 50, 67t
Jung, C.G. 105, 106, 109, 114, 115, 119, 120, 124, 216t

Kahneman, D. xiii
Kono, M. 61
Korzybsky, A. 77, 129, 140
Koziey, W. 35, 36, 37, 38, 39t, 42, 168
Krugman, M. 91–3

Ladouceur, R. 73, 75, 76, 86
language and syntax 184–6
LeDoux, J. 79, 103, 104, 157, 175
Lee, J.L.C. 14, 28, 30, 42, 121, 190
levels of learning, Bateson's 215, 216t, 222; NLP levels of learning consistent with 79, 80f, 81
levels of research studies 1–2, 62–8t, 237
Liberman, M.B. 13, 15t, 168
linguistic patterns: comparison of patterns from CBT and NLP 137, 138t, 187; mirroring of 183; NLP direct evidence 187–8; syntax and language 184–6
Liotta, R. 4, 12, 29, 40, 41, 190, 236
Little Albert 194–5

Malloy, T.E. 161, 235
Maslow, A. 115, 119, 120, 124
McLeod, G. 35, 36, 37, 38, 39t, 42, 168, 232
McLeod, J. 209, 210, 232
Meadows, E.A. 10, 32, 33, 40, 42
measurement tools: ANOVA 50, 58, 62t, 64t, 93; Barrett-Lennard Relationship Inventory 160; Bartlett Test 58, 62t; Beck Anxiety Inventory 81; CORE Systems Research Tool 49, 56, 66t, 237; Croatian Scale of Quality of Life 48, 64t, 88; Individual Discomfort List 47, 64t; IPC questionnaire on locus of control 47, 64t; Parental Provocation Inventory 50, 64t; Parents' Report 50, 64t; Personal Orientation Inventory 50, 65t; in phobia studies 15t; psychological tests 58, 62t; in PTSD studies 39t; SCID II 48, 64t, 88; State Anxiety Inventory 24, 37, 39t, 60, 63t, 89; stress management questionnaire 47, 64t; Visual Analogue Scale 59, 63t, 170; in VK/D treatment studies 37, 39t
memories: behaviour triggering negative 148; Brooklyn Program exercises 110–12; creation and consolidation of 29, 119, 190, 191; depression strategy based on past positive 147–8; extinction and creating of new 9, 16, 40; flashbulb 23, 177; left–right distinctions in 162–3; long-term memory schema 30, 119, 121; protein synthesis and recall of 14, 28, 30, 41, 190; reconsolidation mechanism 14–15, 28, 29–30, 33–5, 40–4, 45, 190, 191; rewriting of 40–1; state-dependent 104, 173–7; study of submodality manipulations of unpleasant 130–1; submodality manipulations to enhance access to positive memory scenarios 131–2; syntax for behavioural change in emotional 190, 191t; *see also*

Reconsolidation of Traumatic Memories Protocol (RTM)
meta-model 129, 137–8, 138t, 142, 187–8
meta-programmes, NLP 83, 234
meta-states 84, 179, 213
metacognitive theory 75, 76
metaphors 157, 169–70, 239
methodological flaws, summary of 207–8
mid brain dopamine system 99, 100, 101, 102, 103, 121
Miller, G. 43, 111, 129, 140, 157, 171, 172
mind–body system 79
mirror neurons 181–2, 183, 186, 192, 235
Mischel, H.N. and W.Mischel 166
modalities 157–8, 191, 192, 196, 207
modelling 77, 78, 136, 143, 202, 215, 216t
Morin, A. 51
Morris, R.G.M. 23, 30, 119, 121
Motivational Enhancement Therapy 235
motivational interviewing 235
Moynihan, R. 231
Muss, D. 12, 33, 35, 36, 37, 38, 39t, 42, 43, 46

National Research Council (NRC) 154, 199
neural systems 103, 169, 175, 176, 179, 192
Neurolinguistic Programming Research Data Base 203–4
Neurolinguistic Psychotherapy and Counselling Association (NLPtCA) 221
Neurological Levels model 145–9
neuroscience: and addictions 98–103; dissociation of behavioural networks 103–4, 175; processing of metaphors and symbolic language 169–70; reactions to experiences of extreme stress 176–7; research to support NLP techniques 156–7, 208, 214, 234, 239; sensory systems areas in the brain 158
New Behavior Generator, future pacing and parallels in CBT 135–7
NLP Research and Recognition Project (NLP R&R) 33, 35, 155–6, 221, 233, 234

object relations theory 49, 68t
obsessive compulsive disorder (OCD) 72–4, 176, 185; Primarily Obsessional OCD 73
obsessive compulsive personality disorder (OCPD) 72
O'Hanlon, W.H. 78, 108, 174, 188
Ouellet, M. 162, 163

pain management 59–60, 63t, 98, 170
panic disorder 70–2, 75, 81–7
parental anger responses study 48, 50, 64t, 180
Pavlov, I.P. 134, 171, 172
Pedreira, M.E. 42, 43, 44, 121

Peele, S. 96, 97
Perls, F.S. 77, 137
pharmacotherapy 8, 73, 127, 136
phobias 7–31; classical models and approaches 8–11; collapsing anchors treatment for claustrophobia in MRI scan patients 15t, 24–7, 60, 63t, 89–90, 94; desensitization protocol 27–8; DSM diagnostic criteria for 7; exposure 8–9; extinction of 9–10, 16; future research 28–9, 208, 236; measurement tools in studies 15t; NLP procedures for treatment of 8; observing behavioural changes to test effectiveness of treatments for xiii; outcome measures 15t; pharmacotherapy in treatment of 8; prevalence of 7–8; RTM in 29–30; systematic desensitization 8, 10–11, 12–13, 14, 28, 30; V/KD procedure 11–15, 33–5; V/KD protocol case study 16–22; V/KD protocol efficacy, published reports on 12–14, 15t, 168–9
post-traumatic stress disorder (PTSD) 32–46; case studies 44–5; DSM-IV definition 32–3; EMDR treatment for 231; extinction treatment for 40, 44, 45, 46; future research 45–6, 236; mechanisms underlying changes in behaviour 40–4, 45; outcome measures 39t; police officers study 36, 37–8, 39t; published reports on V/KD protocol efficacy 35–40, 39t; studies on state-dependent nature of symptoms 176–7; treating war veterans 32, 44–5, 46, 51–6; V/KD procedure 11–12, 33–5
postural mirroring 182, 183
predicate matching 182–4
preferred representational systems (PRS): Bandler and Grinder's references to 153, 162, 196–7; and claims for in right-handed people 201; clinical depression treatment and use of 131–3; Einspruch and Forman's review of Sharpley's critique 199–201, 203; empathy and 184; errors in early research on 153–4; Fromme and Daniell's alphabetic imagery task 204–6; further research on representational systems 164; Heap's review of 202; misunderstandings over position in NLP 153–4, 195, 196–7, 202–3, 208, 235; Sharpley responds to Einspruch and Forman 201–2; Sharpley's review of studies on 195–9; as a teaching tool 153; Witkowski's review of 202–4; Witkowski's review of Elich's study of 206; Witkowski's review of Graunke and Roberts' study of 207

presuppositions, NLP 77–8
private practice study 49, 66t, 237
Prochaska, J. 107, 110, 115, 117, 118, 120, 122, 124, 189, 226t, 239
progressive muscular relaxation technique 10–11, 36, 38, 60, 65t, 83, 84, 87
protein synthesis 14, 28, 30, 41, 190
psychological difficulties and perceived quality of life, effects of NLPt on 48–9, 64t, 88–9, 94, 149, 237
psychological treatments, study of discredited 209, 231
psychotherapy, NLP as 47–51; case examples of therapeutic interventions 49; controlled trial with people with a range of DSM diagnoses 47–8; criteria for therapeutic outcomes in 144; and effectiveness with eating disorders 59; effects on psychological difficulties and perceived quality of life study 48–9, 64t, 88–9, 94, 149, 237; future research 56, 149–50, 237; grounded theory study 49, 68t; in improving quality of life and self-actualisation 50–1, 65t; as an intervention in depression 143–4; multi-level intervention for depressive disorders 145–9; parental anger responses study 48, 50, 64t, 180; relationship challenges and use of 49–50, 67t; research into 47–51; supporting suicide survivors 51, 67t; training and accreditation umbrella bodies 221; use of CORE tool in private practice 49, 66t, 237; using an adapted version to measure effect on allergic responses 57–8, 62t; verification 209
public anxiety, NLP treatment for 91–3

quality of life: effects of NLPt on psychological difficulties and perceived 48–9, 64t, 88–9, 94, 149, 237; and self-actualisation, use of technology in improving 50–1, 65t

Rachman, S. 10, 11, 28
randomized controlled trials (RCT) 58, 60, 136, 231; developing protocols to be researched in format of 214, 215, 235, 236; NLP studies using 130, 170, 180–1, 237
rape victims: phenomenological study for self-esteem in 49–50, 68t; using unobtrusive measures to treat male 52–3; V/KD and hypnosis study with 36, 37, 38, 39t, 168–9
rapid re-acquisition 10, 40
rapport: definitions of 197, 207, 208; and mirror neurons 181–2; NLP specific

research on 182–4; predicate matching 182–4; skills in therapists 145, 157, 182–3; testing of 160, 201
reconsolidation mechanism 14–15, 28, 29–30, 33–5, 40–4, 45, 190, 191
Reconsolidation of Traumatic Memories Protocol (RTM) 12, 33, 35, 39t, 190–1, 208, 233, 236
reframing 59, 67t, 104–5, 143
reinstatement 10, 40
Reisenhuber, M. 185
relationship counselling 49–50, 66t, 67t, 68t
research, academic critiques of NLP: Einspruch and Forman's reply to Sharpley 199–201, 203; false understandings of NLP in 195, 196–7, 202–3, 208; lack of "hard science" in early 153–5; misrepresentation of NLP 194–5; National Research Council negative conclusions 199; NLP Research and Recognition Project 155–6; NLP reviewed in a study of discredited psychological treatments 209, 231; Sharpley's response to Einspruch and Forman 201–2; Sharpley's review 195–9; summary of researchers' methodological flaws 207–8; Witkowski's review 202–7
research development: A level studies 1, 237; B to D level studies of practice and techniques 1–2, 62–8t, 237; Bateson's levels and relationship to NLP theory and practice 215, 216t; evidence-based clinical practice 2, 47, 210, 210t, 211t, 219, 230–2, 236; evidence-based model for 210, 210t, 211t; and further challenges for researchers 213–15; future recommendations for 4, 235–6; legitimate studies for future 208–9; need for more qualitative research 209; networking NLP expertise with universities 239–40; neuroscience research to support NLP techniques 156–7, 208, 214, 234, 239; paucity of NLP studies compared to CBT studies 87, 94; science and scientific methods and applicability to 210, 212–13; and use of individual client outcome scales 237
research into applications of NLP, indirect: brain and NLP in research summary 191–3; further research on representational systems 164; language patterns in NLP, direct evidence of 187–8; rapport and mirror neurons 181–2; rapport and predicate matching 182–4; resources and state-dependent memory 173–7; sensory accessing and representational cues 157–64; sensory accessing and representational cues, NLP specific research on 162–4; states and strategies 177–8; states, NLP specific research on 180–1; states that regulate states 179; strategies 170–3; submodalities 165–8; submodalities, direct research on 168–9, 240; support for NLP techniques in mainline research 156–7; syntax and language 184–6; visualization and imagery 169–70; visualization and imagery, NLP specific research on 170; well-formedness conditions for behavioural change 189–91, 191t; well-formedness conditions for language in therapy 186–8; well-formedness conditions for outcomes 188–9
researchers, training of 94, 200–1, 208
resources and state-dependent memory 173–7
rewind technique 33, 36, 39t
Roberts, T.K. 160, 204, 207
Rogers, C. 77
role playing in CBT and parallels in NLP 135–7
Rossi, E.L. 42, 104, 108, 112, 174, 175, 176
Rygh, J.L. 75, 76, 77, 86

Sackett, D.L. 210, 230
Sanderson, W.C. 75, 76, 77, 86
Satir, V. 77, 137, 146, 179
Schutz, P. 47, 56, 64t, 237
scientific methods 210, 212; NLP and use of 212–13
Scott, E.K. 59, 67t
self-actualisation study in NLP trainees 50–1, 65t
sensory accessing and representational cues 157–62; directions for further research 164; NLP specific research on 162–4; see also eye accessing cues (EACs)
sensory acuity, standards of 238
sexual abuse of males by females 50, 68t
Sharpley, C.: Einspruch and Forman's reply to 199–201, 203; literature review 195–9; response to Einspruch and Forman 201–2
Shelden, V.E. and R.G. Shelden 50, 68t
six-step reframe 8, 83–4, 105, 106
Sleight of Mouth and meta-model and parallels in CBT 137–8, 138t
Socratic questioning and cognitive distortion and parallels in NLP 137–8, 138t
speech anxiety 14, 91–2
spontaneous recovery 9, 40
Standidge, K. 130, 131, 170

Stanton, H. E. 132–3
state-dependent memory 104, 173–7
states: defining 177; lack of distinction between primary and meta 213–14; NLP specific research in management of 180–1; and strategies 177–8; that regulate states 179
Sternman, C. 105, 106
Stipancic, M. 1, 48, 64t, 88–9, 94, 149, 216t, 237
strategies 192, 208; indirect research into 170–3; and states 177–8; that result in depressive symptoms 147, 172
strong principle of change 110, 115, 118, 120, 122, 124, 189, 239
submodalities 128, 191, 213; direct research on 168–9, 240; indirect research into 165–8; visual 165–8
submodality manipulations 122, 132, 134; adolescent subjects study 132–3; in Brooklyn Program 107, 108–9, 110–12; children's self-control and 166–7; in depression 135, 148; enhancing access to positive memories study 131–2; and future pacing and parallels in CBM 139–40; imagery in CBT and parallels with NLP 138–9; mechanism 134; unpleasant memories study 130–1
suicide survivors 50, 67t
Sumin, A.N. 60, 65t
swish pattern 50, 67t, 139–40, 142, 169
synaesthesia 165
syntax: for behavioural change in emotional memory 190, 191t; and language 184–6
systematic desensitization 8, 10–11, 12–13, 14, 28, 30; *see also* desensitization protocol

TEAMS 80, 140–2, 240
theory, NLP 77–81, 94, 214; Bateson's levels and relationship to 215, 216t, 222
therapeutic relationships 143, 145, 182–3; first person report on treating a war veteran 51–7; rapport skills in 145, 157, 182–3
Think Effectively About Mood Swings (TEAMS) 80, 140–2, 240
TOTE 129, 130, 140, 157, 171, 172, 173, 192
training 219–33; certification and 219–20, 221–2, 230, 233, 236, 237, 238; correspondence courses 224; current standards 225, 226–9t; evidence-based clinical practice requirement 230–2; length of courses 222–3; and manualized clinical certification programmes of treatment protocols 238; recommendations for 4, 232–3; of researchers 94, 200–1, 208; status of NLP 220–3; training standards typologies 224–5; typology on NLP institutes 223–4; and university accredited Masters Degree 220, 233, 238–9
transcranial magnetic stimulation (TMS) 182
trauma, unobtrusive measures to treat 51–6
Tse, D. 30, 119
Tyrrell, I. 78, 78f

UK Council for Psychotherapy 221, 226–9t
uncertainty, dealing with 75–6, 86
universities: networking NLP expertise within 239–40; university accredited Masters Degrees 220, 233, 238–9
US Army review of "new-age" techniques 180
Utuza, A.J. 12, 33, 35, 36–7, 39t

Vasey, M.W. 76, 80, 86
vertical descent technique 76, 86
Vianna, L.A.C. 49–50, 68t
visual digital thinking 159
visual kinesthetic dissociation (V/KD): case studies 16–22, 44–5; future research 45–6; and hypnosis in treatment of rape victims 36, 37, 38, 39t, 168–9; measurement tools in studies 37, 39t; mechanisms 14, 16, 40–4; procedure 11–12, 33–5; published reports on phobias and 12–14, 15t, 168–9; published reports on PTSD and 35–40, 39t
visual stimuli, movement of 167–8
visual submodalities 165–8
visualization and imagery 36, 38, 131–2, 169–70

Wake, L. 4, 49, 56, 57, 66t, 68t, 145, 165, 166, 169, 181, 185, 214
war veterans 32, 44–5, 46, 51–6, 96, 97
Weaver, M. 49, 56, 66t, 237
well-formedness conditions for language in therapy 186–8
well-formedness conditions for outcomes 157, 186, 188–91, 191t; in Brooklyn Program 108, 110, 115, 117–18, 120, 124
Wells, A. 75, 76
Williams, L. 43, 167
Witkowski, T. 202–7
Witt, K. 57, 58, 62–3t
Wolpe, J. 10–11, 28, 74, 103, 104, 120, 175, 189

Zika, B. 49, 68t